Redeeming a Nation

Biblical Reflections on English History

Philip Quenby

ONWARDS AND UPWARDS PUBLISHERS
Copyright 2011 © Philip Quenby

Onwards and Upwards Publications
Berkeley House
11 Nightingale Crescent
West Horsley
Surrey
KT24 6PD
England

www.onwardsandupwards.org

ISBN: 978-1-907509-40-7

First edition published in 2011 by Onwards and Upwards Publishers.
Second edition published in 2012.

Cover design: Leah-Maarit

Printed in the UK

Dedication

Thine be the glory.

Acknowledgements

We are bound so close in the bundle of life that it is difficult to thank one without expressing gratitude to all. There is nevertheless a person whom it is right to single out: my mother, who taught me to know and love the Lord, whose passion for history fired my own and whose example is ever before me. No greater gifts can a parent give their child.

Contents

Preface

"But I have raised you up for this very purpose, that I might show you my power,
and that my name might be proclaimed in all the earth." Exodus 9:16.

There was a time when it did not seem too fanciful to think that, if God were not exactly an Englishman, then he did at least seem particularly well-disposed to this island race. In British India, the sons and daughters of the Raj were even called "heaven's breed."

Gone are the days when England stood head and shoulders above the rest of the world in almost all fields of endeavour. A lead that had been substantially eroded by the start of the First World War was obliterated by the Second. Amidst the exhaustion and bankruptcy that attended the end of that subsequent conflict, the country famously lost an Empire and failed to find a role.[1] One statistic will suffice to illustrate the straitened circumstances of those times. Before the titanic struggle with Germany, some 40% of *all* cargoes were carried in British ships. By 1945, the great majority of those vessels had been sunk. The nation's depleted resources were cruelly exposed by the Suez crisis.

Since then, mass immigration and social change have transformed the land. There is a sense that the nation is in danger of forgetting its history, of losing its moral and cultural bearings: hence this book. It is not exactly a history, and certainly it contains nothing that is new in terms of historical research. Its purpose is not to break new ground but rather to apply old knowledge. Each chapter is designed to be read in conjunction with the Bible passage that is highlighted at its start.

The selection of characters and events for this book is unashamedly subjective. With some exceptions, I have generally steered clear of those who tend to be thought of as being great men of faith. What I have sought to show is that God has worked in the secular history of this land just as he has guided its religious life.

One last point: England has been greatly used and blessed by God, but she has not been always and everywhere on the side of right. Where she has been the oppressor, God has raised up men and women against her – William Wallace, Robert the Bruce, Joan of Arc, Erskine Childers, Roger Casement and Mohandas Gandhi, to name just those who figure in these pages. Americans will no doubt bemoan the absence of their founding fathers and other nations their own heroes

---

1 *Pace* Dean Acheson, former US Secretary of State (from a speech given at West Point on 5 December 1962).

of resistance and independence, but there simply is not space to cover every injustice of fifteen-and-a-half centuries.

For all that, this is a history of which we can be proud. My prayer is that understanding what God has done for us, with us and through us in the past will spur us once again to seek the face of our Lord, that we might truly be "a royal priesthood, a holy nation, a people belonging to God." (1 Peter 2:9).

London 2009.

1. Legacy

Matthew 5:1-12.

Key word: compassion.

"Compassion is a moral defect." That is not the statement of a sadist or a psychopath or a mass murderer. It was not made by the apologists of Nazism, neither by Chairman Mao's Red Guards, nor by the wild-eyed fanatics of any modern political or religious movement. It was instead the sober reflection of a man honoured in his age and in ours. This was the world view of Seneca, who lived from 4 BC to AD 65. He was a man of learning and sophistication – lawyer, philosopher, author and playwright, companion to the wealthy and advisor to the powerful. His tragedies such as *Phaedra*, *Medea* and *Oedipus* have had a lasting impact on European literature. Yet he also had the dubious distinction of being tutor to the infamous Emperor Nero, the man who fiddled while Rome burned and had Christians thrown to the lions, whose crimes Seneca tried to check but ultimately condoned.

It is almost impossible for us now to recapture the spirit of the pre-Christian pagan world. We perhaps know something of their monuments and histories, their poetry and legends, but we cannot readily put ourselves back into their way of looking at nature and their fellow man. If we think about it at all, we tend to regard the ancients as people pretty much akin to ourselves. True enough, they did not have our technologies, but in all essentials they seem men and women just like us. Not only that, but they created empires of astonishing culture, complexity and achievement. It is precisely for this reason that we can be so profoundly shocked when we are confronted by the reality of what the world was like before the Christian era. For the Roman Empire, like those it replaced or existed alongside, was first and foremost a creation of power. As far as the Romans were concerned, might most assuredly was right. Year after bloody year, internal dissent was brutally crushed, rebellious provinces brought to heel and barbarian nations treated merely as sources of slaves and tribute.

The brutality of Rome was casual and expressed in the commonplace, but also calculated. In the hands of the state it was the studied projection of power over every man, woman and child in Republic or Empire. In 71 BC, for example, the Roman general Crassus finally crushed the slave revolt that for years had laid waste the south of Italy and struck fear into the people of Rome. The slave leader Spartacus was killed and he and his fellow slaves were crucified to show the world how this mighty nation treated those who dared defy her. Some 5,000 spread-eagled captives lined 300 miles of road leading to the outskirts of the Eternal City herself, carefully spaced out over intervals of 165 paces, a monument to the Roman genius: order alongside the most exquisite cruelty.

Indeed, crucifixion was so common in this "kingdom, strong as iron" (Daniel 2:40) that the killing of an obscure carpenter from Nazareth could easily have passed without notice.[2] Rome brutalised the powerful just as she brutalised outcasts: like the poet Petronius, Seneca at length took his own life when he lost the favour of Nero. Such was the old paganism.

The Beatitudes.

On a hill in this self-same Roman Empire, Jesus taught us a new way. Even today, after two thousand years of Christianity, the Sermon on the Mount can still astound and discomfort with the radicalism of its message. At the time it was spoken, it amounted to nothing less than standing the world on its head. If you seriously believe that compassion is a moral defect, how do you begin to grapple with the idea that the merciful and the persecuted are blessed? (Matthew 5:7 and 10). If your world is built on military might, how do you respond when told to love your enemies? (Matthew 5:43-44). If you value wealth and display, how do you react to the idea that the poor are blessed (Matthew 5:3, Luke 6:20) and that giving to the needy should be done in secret? (Matthew 6:1-4).

The Beatitudes form only a small part of the Sermon on the Mount, yet so profound are they that they have inspired men to the heights of Christian endeavour. This chapter examines just three aspects of them: place, people and God's standards. Or, to put it another way, where Jesus taught, whom he taught and what he taught.

Place.

In Matthew 5:1 we are told that when Jesus saw the crowds "he went up on a mountainside and sat down." The location invites a parallel between these events and those of the time of Moses, who also received divine instruction when "the LORD called to him from the mountain and said, 'This is what you are to say to the house of Jacob and what you are to tell the people of Israel'" (Exodus 19:3). Moses was the great prophet and teacher of the Old Covenant and in the Sermon on the Mount Jesus expounded the central teachings of the New Covenant, proclaiming the manifesto of the Kingdom of God. In each case, the choice of a mountain symbolises a halfway place between heaven and earth, where we see the celestial interacting with the human in a particularly immediate way.

---

[2] Crucifixion was finally abolished by Emperor Constantine in AD 337. As Christian influence grew increasingly pronounced, it became widely considered an unduly cruel form of execution.

The location, therefore, leaves no doubt that the words which Jesus spoke are of the most immense significance.

People.

We know from Matthew 4:23-25 that Jesus had already been throughout Galilee teaching, preaching and healing and that "large crowds ... followed him." Yet we are told in Matthew 5:1-2 that when the Lord sat down on the hillside it was his disciples who gathered near to him "and he began to teach them." Indeed, the word that is translated "disciples" literally means "learners." It is significant that Jesus taught close followers, not the crowd as a whole. This pattern is repeated throughout Christ's earthly ministry: often, though by no means always, a chosen few receive the message and are sent out to share this with others. Jesus had done the groundwork. His audience was waiting expectantly. The time had come for the disciples to learn in greater detail what they needed to know and do and say. Jesus taught and empowered these faithful ones, just as he teaches and empowers those who listen to his voice today. Hence, the Great Commission given by him to his followers is to: "go and make disciples of all nations, baptising them in the name of the Father and of the Son and of the Holy Spirit, and teaching them to obey everything I have commanded you." (Matthew 28:19-20).

The discourse that comprises the Sermon on the Mount ends with the parable of the wise and foolish builders (Matthew 7:24-27), which emphasises the importance of practising what has been preached. This should cause all those who count themselves followers of Christ to reflect on what we should be doing to share what he said. Not just to share it, but to sense the profound challenge to all our assumptions about the way in which human beings should relate to each other and to God.

God's standards.

In the Beatitudes we see some of the things that God particularly identifies as blessed. To be blessed means more than just to be happy, because happiness is an emotion often dependent on outward circumstances. The blessings that Jesus describes mean the ultimate well-being and the distinctive spiritual joy of those who share in the salvation of the Kingdom of God. We see that there is no easy identification of divine blessing with worldly success, since the values of the Kingdom of Heaven are not those of the world: "'For my thoughts are not your thoughts, neither are your ways my ways,' declares the LORD. 'As the heavens are higher than the earth, so are my ways higher than your ways and my thoughts higher than your thoughts.'" (Isaiah 55:8-9).

This distinction between God's standards and those of the world appears very powerfully in the blessing that is pronounced on "the poor in spirit". The phrase might at first sight seem perplexing, but other parts of Scripture help throw light on it. The version of the Beatitudes that is contained in Luke's Gospel (the so-called Sermon on the Plain) says "Blessed are you who are poor" (Luke 6:20), whereas Matthew's Gospel makes it clear that Jesus is talking about something more than material poverty by including the words "poor *in spirit*" (Matthew 5:3). In his letter to the early church James, the brother of Jesus, asked the rhetorical question: "Has not God chosen those who are poor in the eyes of the world to be rich in faith and to inherit the kingdom he promised to those who love him?" (James 2:5).

To be poor in spirit, then, means to be poor in the eyes of the world, since it involves living according to God's values, not those of fallen humankind. Yet perhaps for precisely that reason it also denotes being rich in faith. It necessitates being humble in our relationship with God, recognising that we owe everything to him. It entails complete dependence on God and it signifies regarding everything we possess – spiritually, intellectually and materially – as God's. It is no accident that the Beatitudes begin and end by talking about those to whom the kingdom of heaven belongs – the poor in spirit and those who are persecuted because of righteousness. Again, we need to reflect on whether we have such poverty of spirit, whether we are applying God's standards in the way that we live our lives and whether we are standing up for what is right.

The teachings of the Beatitudes (and indeed of the Sermon on the Mount as a whole) help deepen our understanding of the earlier teachings given through Moses, including the Ten Commandments. What Jesus says makes it clear that it is not enough to live within the letter of laws relating to killing, adultery, divorce, oaths or retribution: the spirit of the Beatitudes demands a root and branch approach, with no place for inner dispositions that breed violence or injustice. Such things are entirely at odds with the generosity and compassion of God, whose perfection is the model for the righteousness that Jesus demands. Later in the Sermon on the Mount he says: "Be perfect therefore, even as your heavenly father is perfect." (Matthew 5:48 and 6:1-8. See also Matthew 5:27-28).

What Jesus was driving at in the Beatitudes is that there should be consistency between our attitudes and actions, our beliefs and behaviour. What he said was equally upsetting to the rule- and law-obsessed Jewish establishment of his day as it was to the pagan Romans. The Beatitudes reminded them, as they remind us, that applying God's standards in our lives and in our nation is not a box-ticking or form-filling exercise. It is not about the nature of the food we eat or the kind of clothes we wear. It is not about having laws against discrimination or anti-social behaviour. It is about our innermost being. It is about the attitudes that we have towards both God and man, and the way in which we act these out in our lives. The Sermon on the Mount as a whole sets an ethical standard so high that some have dismissed it as completely unrealistic or have projected its fulfilment to the future Kingdom of God. Yet it contains the values that

Christians for centuries have striven to make real in the world in which they live. Above all, it reminds us of what God's standards look like.

Conclusion.

The growth of Christian influence in the Roman Empire is one of the most remarkable stories in all of human history. It is almost literally incredible that a small and persecuted group could have overcome the might of Rome, not by force of arms but by the power of an idea. That this was achieved by an idea that flew in the face of all that the pagan world stood for makes the story more extraordinary still. Yet such was the extent of Christian influence that in AD 313 Emperor Constantine signed the Edict of Milan, which extended tolerance to Christians throughout the Empire and began the Christianising of the Roman state itself.

There are many reasons for the decline and fall of the Roman Empire, but one thing is clear: a Christian Rome was bound ultimately to collapse under the weight of its own contradictions or become something fundamentally different from the Rome of old, for the contrast between the attitude of Seneca and the things that Jesus said and did could not be starker. Time and again we read of Jesus having compassion on the people who came to him: Matthew 9:36, 14:14, 15:32 and 20:34; Mark 1:41, 6:34 and 8:2; Luke 15:20. His teachings are full of compassion – there are blessings in the Beatitudes for those in mourning, those who hunger and thirst and for the merciful – and his actions were full of compassion, both in his healing ministry and ultimately through his death on the cross. Thus were fulfilled words spoken by and through the prophet Isaiah: "He who has compassion on them will guide them and lead them beside springs of water" (Isaiah 49:10); "'with deep compassion I will bring you back ... I will have compassion on you,' says the LORD your Redeemer." (Isaiah 54:7-8).

The gulf between the values of our society and those of the pagan world is a measure of how our sensibilities have been shaped by Christianity. It affirms the central role that this faith has played in the formation of England. It is fundamental to understanding the wellsprings of our nation, because ideas shape societies and societies shape those who live in them. From William Wilberforce seeking the abolition of slavery to Elizabeth Fry championing prison reform, the history of England is full of Christian compassion in action transforming individuals, the nation and even the world. Of course, those whose names have come down to us through history were generally exceptional people and most of us feel anything but exceptional. Yet we should never underestimate the difference that the smallest of contributions can make.

Compassion is one of the centrepieces of God's standards. That is why we are called to offer it to others. Christian compassion has been behind much of what is greatest and most truly memorable in the life of this land. It is up to us to make sure that we continue to make it so. Never again must we live in a country or in a world where educated men and women treat compassion as a moral defect.

2. Beginnings

Isaiah 9:1-7.

Key word: truth.

The last legions were withdrawn from the province of Britannia in AD 410 to defend Rome from the Goths. They left behind the infrastructure of some three and a half centuries of occupation and a highly Romanised elite. For all its outward sophistication, however, this Romano-British world was fragile within and without. Soon, the rich pickings it offered were attracting barbarian adventurers from across the seas. Amongst those who terrorised the coasts were tribes from northern Germany and southern Denmark: Angles, Saxons and Jutes. Their names are preserved in English regions and counties such as East Anglia, Sussex (land of the south Saxons) and Essex (land of the east Saxons). England herself is Engla-lond, land of the Angles.

In common with their former masters, Britons sought to divide and rule by paying one group of enemies to fight another. Thus was a Jute war-band led by Hengist and his brother Horsa invited to settle in Kent, to serve as mercenaries in defending Britannia against incursions by the Picts.[3] In AD 449 these Jutes landed at Ebbsfleet on the Isle of Thanet and in due course helped their masters to a great victory over the raiders from the north. Yet within a short while employer and employee came to blows. In the ensuing conflict Horsa was killed,[4] but in AD 455 his people were victorious at the battle of Aylesford. So tradition has it that the English conquest began. It was bloody and bitter. In contrast to barbarian conquerors in continental Europe, the newcomers seem to have conducted a campaign of what we would now call ethnic cleansing, dispossessing and driving back the people they overcame. The invaders were pagans. They were pitiless.

They remained so until the coming of St Augustine in AD 589 and their subsequent conversion to Christianity. The arrival of the missionary from Rome was attended by strange correspondences and coincidences. He landed at the

---

[3] The Picts lived in what is now Scotland. The invitation to Hengist and Horsa was extended by the British leader Vitalinus, also known as Vortigern (meaning "supreme leader"). The last Roman commander had departed some time before. He was called Coel Hen by the British, a name which survives in the nursery rhyme *Old King Cole*.

[4] Horsa's memory is still faintly traceable in place-names such as Horsted and Horsham. Following his death, Hengist and his son Aesc ruled in what became the kingdom of Kent.

very spot at Ebbsfleet where Hengist and Horsa had disembarked one hundred and forty years earlier. Augustine was sent by Pope Gregory the Great, who some time before had seen fair-haired slaves for sale in Rome and had asked where they came from. On being told that they were Angles from Deira, he replied: "Not Angles, but angels," and "plucked from God's ire, and called to Christ's mercy!"[5] When informed that the name of their king was Aella, Gregory seized on this as a good omen: "Alleluia shall be sung in Aella's land!" he cried. So it was.

Walking in darkness.

Our earliest forefathers worshipped gods common to German and Scandinavian tribes: Odin (Wotan), Thor, Frey and a dozen more. The names of some were given to the days of the week: hence Thursday (Thor's day) and Friday (Frey's day). Like all pagan gods, these were made in the image of man, with human foibles and weaknesses. They were idols: capricious, calculating and cruel.

The tribes which began the English conquest walked in darkness. The prophet Isaiah describes what this means: there is gloom and distress (Isaiah 9:1), darkness and the shadow of death (Isaiah 9:2), the people are burdened, like an animal under the yoke (Isaiah 9:4) and oppressed (Isaiah 9:4). The hand of God is against the people, whom he humbles (Isaiah 9:1).This is not ancient history. It is with us now, for this is the experience of all too many in our land today. Idols are not just for yesteryear. They exist at all times and in all places and they take many forms. They need not bear the name of gods: anything that usurps the place in the human heart that should be occupied by the one true God is an idol.

In Isaiah 9 these things are together characterised as "Midian" (Isaiah 9:4), the great enemy and oppressor of Israel in the days of the judges, overcome after seven years by Deborah and Gideon (Judges 6-7).

Breaking free.

Isaiah tells what happens when we break free of the things that enslave us and turn in true worship to God. The contrast could not be starker: there is honour (Isaiah 9:1) instead of degradation, light and dawn (Isaiah 9:2) instead of darkness and death, a shattering of the yoke (Isaiah 9:4) instead of enslavement, enlarging, rejoicing and victory (Isaiah 9:3) instead of oppression, gloom and

---

[5] Gregory's remark is a pun on Deira, *de ira* meaning 'from anger' or 'out of wrath' in Latin. The Anglo-Saxon kingdom of Deira was later absorbed into the kingdom of Northumbria.

distress. A great harvest is brought in (Isaiah 9:3) and the enemy is plundered (Isaiah 9:3).

The wording makes it clear that transformation of people and societies comes about at the initiative of God, not through any act on our part. Thus "a great light ... has dawned" (Isaiah 9:2), "you [God] have enlarged the nation and increased their joy" (Isaiah 9:3) and "you [God] have shattered the yoke that burdens them, the bar across their shoulders, the rod of their oppressor." (Isaiah 9:4). More than that, redemption comes in spite of what we have done, not because of it: the very first word of the first verse of Isaiah 9 is 'nevertheless' – that is, despite all that has gone before. The High King of Heaven is not petty, mean and vindictive like the deities of the pagan world: "The LORD is compassionate and gracious, slow to anger, abounding in love ... as a father has compassion on his children, so the LORD has compassion" (Psalm 103:8 and 13).

Peace and new government.

Above all, there is peace. In fact, the English word 'peace' does not do justice to the wealth of meaning contained in the Hebrew word '*shalom.*' It encompasses wholeness, health, wellbeing both spiritual and material. So great is the peace that God ushers in that "Every warrior's boot used in battle and every garment rolled in blood will be destined for burning, will be fuel for the fire." (Isaiah 9:5).

With peace comes new government (Isaiah 9:6), reflecting the character of God himself. There will be "justice and righteousness" (Isaiah 9:7). Since this new government will be the opposite of what has gone before, we may surmise that there will also be freedom, life and health, light and joy. There will be order instead of chaos and growth instead of decay: "Of the increase of his government and peace there will be no end." (Isaiah 9:7).

The zeal of the Lord.

These are astonishing promises. They are not made lightly. We are told that "the zeal of the LORD Almighty will accomplish this." (Isaiah 9:7).[6] The dictionary definition of 'zeal' includes "ardour, earnestness, enthusiasm, intense and eager pursuit or endeavour to attain or accomplish some object."

---

[6] The same phrase appears in identical verses in Isaiah 37:32 and 2 Kings 19:31: "For out of Jerusalem will come a remnant, and out of Mount Zion a band of survivors. The zeal of the Lord Almighty will accomplish this."

Reference elsewhere in Isaiah to the 'zeal of the Lord' emphasises the fact that God takes the first step in rescuing humanity from the consequences of its own sinfulness: "The LORD looked and was displeased that there was no justice. He saw that there was no-one, he was appalled that there was no-one to intervene. He put on righteousness as his breastplate, and the helmet of salvation on his head; he put on the garments of vengeance and wrapped himself in zeal as in a cloak ... The Redeemer will come to Zion, to those in Jacob who repent of their sins" (Isaiah 59:15-17 and 20). We see in these verses what is required for mankind to take hold of God's free gift of salvation: to "repent of [our] sins" (Isaiah 59:20), to turn decisively from what is wrong and to the loving God who longs for our return.

The Messiah.

The means by which God brings his promises about is through the Messiah (the Christ, the anointed one). Again, the language brooks no doubt. The transformation from bad to good hinges on the word 'for', which introduces the coming Messiah: "for to us a child is born, to us a son is given" (Isaiah 9:6). We are told that the Messiah will be a king: "He will reign over David's throne and over his kingdom" (Isaiah 9:7) and this king will bear four throne names: "he will be called Wonderful Counsellor, Mighty God, Everlasting Father, Prince of Peace." (Isaiah 9:6). His reign will be eternal: "He will reign ... from that time on and for ever." (Isaiah 9:7).

The throne names given to the Messiah and the description of his reign are truly extraordinary. "Wonderful Counsellor" and "Prince of Peace" might perhaps have passed in Isaiah's day for the hyperbole expected in describing royalty. "Mighty God" and "Everlasting Father", however, are of quite a different order altogether. Pagan nations might claim that their kings were gods or the descendants of gods, but such a thing would have been the vilest blasphemy in Israel. The specific identification of the Messiah with the divine was still an issue of contention in the time of Jesus, more than six and a half centuries after Isaiah's death. In the prophet's day it would have been a cause for astonishment amongst those who heard it.

To God alone belongs that which is eternal and everlasting. There can be no mistaking the meaning of this passage: God will himself come to rule and reign amongst us and over us. For "The virgin will be with child and will give birth to a son, and will call him Immanuel." (Isaiah 7:14).[7]

---

[7] Immanuel means "God with us."

Harvest and plunder.

The images of harvest and plunder that appear in Isaiah 9:3 are later used by Jesus. Harvest describes the great crop of souls that God will bring to salvation: "The harvest is plentiful, but the workers are few. Ask the Lord of the harvest, therefore, to send out workers into his harvest field." (Matthew 9:37-38). Any soul harvested for God is a soul lost to Satan, whose house is thereby plundered: "no-one can enter a strong man's house and carry off his possessions unless he first ties up the strong man. Then he can rob his house." (Mark 3:27). Again, the work of God is clear: without his binding of Satan through the redemptive work of Christ on the cross, salvation for mankind would not be possible.

When the Lord "enlarge[s] the nation" (Isaiah 9:3) he extends his own kingdom at the expense of Satan's. We are put in mind of the physical and spiritual enlargement that is envisaged by Jabez when he prays to the Almighty: "O, that you would bless me and enlarge my territory! Let your hand be with me, and keep me from harm so that I will be free from pain." (1 Chronicles 4:10). God holds out the prospect of growth in all that is good and worthy: growth as individuals, growth as a church and growth as a nation, but most of all growth of the Kingdom of God itself.

Conclusion.

As England became Christianised, so the nature of the English conquest began to change. Campaigns of extermination and dispossession seem gradually to have given way to increased readiness to live alongside the conquered British. Christianity during this period was not yet so deeply rooted that it stopped conquest altogether, but already there appears a greater gentleness about the English than before. Seeds of growth were planted amongst this people by God, working through St Augustine and those who came after him. Through the lives of generations of godly English men and women, huge transformations have been wrought in our land and in the world. No-one could seriously claim that England has ever been a place of Christian perfection, yet our direction of travel has been clear to the present day: with much stumbling and backsliding, we have moved from darkness towards the light.

Something has changed in the recent past. Our direction of travel has altered. Many changes have been subtle, almost imperceptible. The cumulative effect is undeniable. Our response as a nation has largely been concerned with symptoms, not the underlying cause. It is time that we looked ourselves full in the face and recognised honestly that we have taken a wrong turning.

There is a great lie stalking our land. It says that one set of ideas is just as valid as another. It whispers that there is no objective truth and that morality is in effect merely a matter of opinion. If that were really true, there would be no basis on which to condemn murder, rape, child abuse or any other crime. Such foolishness has already cast a shadow over England. If we persist in acting as though it were true, we will once again find ourselves walking in darkness. Here is our challenge, for we risk slipping back towards paganism and idolatry. Isaiah tells us where that road leads. He tells us also how to turn from it: through Jesus Christ, Son of the living God, who "is the radiance of God's glory and the exact representation of his being, sustaining all things by his powerful word." (Hebrews 1:3).[8]

---

[8] Einstein posited the existence of what he called the Cosmological Constant, a theory that he initially discarded but to which he later returned. He believed this was mathematically necessary to explain why the universe neither expands to infinity nor collapses upon itself. In that context, it is intriguing that the Bible describes Jesus as "upholding all things by the word of his power" (Hebrews 1:3, KJV) and says that: "in him all things hold together" (Colossians 1:17).

3. Survival

1 Samuel 22:1-5.

Key word: action.

Alfred, king of Wessex from 849 to 899, is the only English monarch to bear the epithet "Great." It is a title he amply deserves, for without him there would quite simply be no England.

In 793 Danish raiders attacked the monastery at Lindisfarne on the east coast of Northumbria, putting the defenceless monks to the sword before looting priceless manuscripts and works of art. Thereafter, Danish raids became more frequent and daring year by year. In 865 pillage turned to conquest as a large Danish army landed in Kent.[9] By 876 the Anglo-Saxon kingdoms of Northumbria, Mercia and East Anglia had been destroyed in battle and their lands settled by the rank and file of the Danish armies. Only Wessex remained outside their control. Alone of the English kingdoms, she had offered resistance stiff enough to turn the invaders' attention elsewhere, but the respite was short. A renewed Danish assault came in 878. The Viking leader Guthrum launched a surprise attack in the depths of winter, striking deep into West Saxon territory. Alfred was caught off balance and driven with a small band of followers to seek refuge in the marshes of Athelney in Somerset.

The king was on the run for several months, launching hit and run raids against the Danes. Then, seven weeks after Easter, he emerged from the marshes and called his people to join him. The Anglo-Saxon Chronicle (the great early history of the English) records that when he did so: "there came to meet him all the people of Somerset and Wiltshire and ... Hampshire, and they rejoiced to see him." In this sparse account we see the strength of Wessex and the regard in which the people held their king. In the depths of defeat and despair, they rallied to him.

Soon afterwards, Alfred led his nation to a resounding victory at Edington, where a white horse was carved into the chalk hillside on the king's orders after the battle.[10] In the course of the fighting, the English captured the Danes' standard, a banner depicting a raven (representing the ravens said to attend on their war god, Odin). The spiritual symbolism was powerful. It was underlined a

---

[9] The kingdom of Kent had by this time been subsumed within Wessex.

[10] The white horse now visible on Westbury hill just outside Edington was carved in 1788, obliterating the original carved following Alfred's victory.

fortnight later when Guthrum sued for peace and agreed to be baptised. The Danes were expelled from Wessex.

For the next eighteen years Alfred was engaged in continual warfare against the Danes, yet never again was the survival of his kingdom seriously threatened. Gradually, he began to take the offensive and to expand the areas under his control. England was kept alive and, in old age, Alfred at last enjoyed a measure of rest and security he had rarely known: the final three years of his reign were ones of peace.

Taking refuge.

In the marshes of Athelney, Alfred found the strength of mind and will to sustain him through a truly bleak midwinter. We have no record of what passed through the king's mind at this time, but his suffering would have been familiar to another king from long ago and far away, a king whose words perhaps comforted and inspired Alfred as he pondered.

Like Alfred, David had to flee for his life and seek refuge in wild places. Threatened by the jealous and unhinged king Saul, he too kept on the move lest his enemies learn of his whereabouts and seek him out. For a while, David even lived amongst the Philistines, arch enemies of the Israelites whom he had many times encountered in battle, until his position became too precarious and he again had to move on. So we are told that: "David left Gath [one of the five main Philistine cities] and escaped to the cave of Adullam." (1 Samuel 22:1).

There are times when we have to come out and fight, but there are also seasons when we need to take refuge. This should not be an excuse to flee responsibility or shirk the tasks that God has in mind for us, but should instead be a time to gather ourselves, to reflect and to pray so that we emerge stronger. This is precisely how David and Alfred used this phase of their lives.

Taking stock.

In the cave of Adullam, David took stock of his predicament. Adullam lies about twenty miles south-west of Jerusalem, which in years to come David would capture from the Jebusites and make his capital. In the same way, in the years following victory at Edington Alfred would capture London (the future capital of England)[11] from the Danes. At the time, however, these events must have seemed impossible dreams to men who were fugitives in their own lands.

The memory of David's time in the cave is preserved in Psalm 142. It would have been easy for him to have been bitter against God or to doubt his

---

[11] The capital of Wessex was Winchester.

promises. Whilst yet a mere stripling he had been anointed by the prophet Samuel as future king of Israel (1 Samuel 16:1-13), but there had been no coronation and indeed ever since this time he had experienced little but toil and trouble. Any indication of divine favour must have seemed at times like a sick joke and the promise of the future so much hot air. Bitterness and doubt do not figure in David's response, however. Quite the opposite – it is God to whom he looks to and in whom he places his trust: "When my spirit grows faint within me, it is you who know my way ... you are my refuge" (Psalm 142:3 and 5).

We have reason to take heart from the experience of David and Alfred and remind ourselves that we should not necessarily judge the future by the present. Above all, we should not doubt God but rather redouble our faith in him and our efforts to walk in the way that he has set for us.

Taking leave.

We need to do this with our eyes open. The fact that God is faithful and his promises are sure is no guarantee that all will be plain sailing for us any more than it was for David or Alfred. There will assuredly be periods of anguish and heartache, for that is our lot on earth. There will be times when we have to take our leave of things and of people that are dear to us in order that we can move on in the way that God wishes.

David's meeting with his family at Adullam was just such a moment. It must have witnessed extremes of joy and pain. His relatives were understandably anxious to see someone dearly beloved who had been away a long time, whom they knew to be in grave danger: "When his brothers and his father's household heard [that David was at Adullam], they went down to him there." (1Samuel 22:1). We are told no more about what was done and said, but it takes little imagination to picture the concern of David's parents for their youngest son and of his siblings for their little brother. Yet after a brief time together, the fugitive had to say goodbye to his family again, both for their safety and in order to allow him complete freedom of action: "So he left them with the king of Moab, and they stayed with him as long as David was in the stronghold." (1 Samuel 22:4). None were then to know that, in the fullness of God's timing, they would be reunited in circumstances of rejoicing when David at last became king.

It is difficult for us to keep a godly perspective on what happens in our lives. Like little children, we cry out in pain with no understanding that what we experience today will not last forever. When difficulties come, we should reflect on the lives of people like David and Alfred and know that, whatever we are going through, it will run its course.

Taking opportunities.

At such moments above all others, we need to be alert to the opportunities that God gives. Whatever our position and however grim the outlook, God can and will provide for us. When David first arrived at Adullam, he was either entirely alone or accompanied by a mere handful of companions. Yet in this wild place: "All those who were in distress or in debt or discontented gathered round him, and he became their leader. About four hundred men were with him." (1 Samuel 22:2).

God used the enmity of Saul and difficult circumstances in the lives of others to equip David with "brave warriors, ready for battle" (1 Chronicles 12:8). In the same way, he also ensured David of a safe refuge for his family: the king of Moab was a natural ally for David since Saul had recently fought against him (1 Samuel 14:47) and David's great-grandmother Ruth was a Moabitess (Ruth 4:13 and 22). So David "went to Mizpah in Moab and said to the king of Moab, 'Would you let my father and mother come and stay with you until I learn what God will do for me?'" (1 Samuel 22:3).

We need to look beyond our immediate fears and worries. Instead of concentrating only on the magnitude of the tasks we face or the resources of those who oppose us, we should instead reflect on the might of the great God who is our "strength and [our] shield." (Psalm 28:7). We should be ready at all times and in all places to seize the opportunities that he puts our way.

Taking risks.

Seizing opportunities involves risk. To take hold of what is possible, there comes a point at which we need to come out of our place of refuge and take a step of faith. We need to put our money where our mouth is. This does not mean that we should be foolhardy or precipitate in our actions. Like David, we need first to "learn what God will do for me" (1 Samuel 22:3). Having learnt, however, we need to act.

The moment for action came to David when "the prophet Gad said to David, 'Do not stay in the stronghold. Go into the land of Judah.'" (1 Samuel 22:5). The moment for action came to Alfred when he left the marshes of Athelney. Each of these men seized opportunity without flinching. They did so even though they had to leave a safe place and confront an enemy who was powerful, even though, humanly speaking, the odds must have seemed stacked against them. In David's case, he had a mere four hundred men against the resources of a whole country. In Alfred's case, he could not be sure that his people would join him and, even if they did, they would face in battle a mighty army that had already shattered three English kingdoms. David and Alfred dared and prevailed because they had faith.

We do not know if the word of the Lord came to Alfred before he left Athelney, but we know that it came to David through one of God's prophets. In response to this word, "David left and went to the forest of Hereth." (1 Samuel 22:5). On one level, he was going into the lion's den, into territory where Saul might more readily track him down and kill him, away from his stronghold. David was far from foolhardy, though. He did not treat God's instruction as a reason to be negligent in his own preparations or incautious in his behaviour. For this reason, he did not go into open country, where his small force would have been vulnerable, but "to the forest of Hereth." (1 Samuel 22:5). David used his own intellect to give the best possible human effect to what God was telling him to do.

Both David and Alfred took a risk. It was a calculated risk, but a risk nevertheless. Only through taking the risk was all that came afterwards possible.

Conclusion.

Alfred ensured the survival of the Wessex, yet his achievement goes beyond this. He was a great military leader, but much more besides. Through wise policy he ensured that the West Saxon kings became the acknowledged leaders of all Englishmen who were not under Danish rule.[12] Through generosity in victory and friendship in peace, he laid the foundations for integrating Viking settlers into a new polity. Through promotion of learning, sponsorship of Christianity and promulgation of sound laws he helped create a state more solidly based and a system of government more sophisticated than any other in west Europe. His originality of mind and breadth of outlook gave a new dimension to English kingship.

Above all, Alfred was a godly man. He strained every nerve to live as a Christian and to rule as a Christian king. Amongst many works that he selected for translation into English were the *Soliloquies* of St Augustine. In his preface to this book, Alfred wrote: "It is for every man to live and work on earth in such a way that he may pass on with sure and certain hope to the eternal dwelling, to the work which has no end, the infinite increasing of knowledge in the nearer Presence of God ... He who created both [heaven and earth], may He grant that I fail not in either, but give it to me to fulfil my service here and, above all, to reach that house beyond."

The experiences of Alfred and of David remind us that there are seasons in life: times to take refuge, to take stock, to take our leave, to take opportunities and to take risks. Like these great kings of old, we need to assess the times and

---

[12] After centuries of rivalry, Mercia accepted West Saxon overlordship in 879 or thereabouts.

behave according to the season. In our land at present we are in danger of spending more time than we need taking refuge and taking stock. If we delay too long, we will allow the forces that are ranged in opposition to God to rage unchecked. Now is the time to act: to take our leave of the things that inhibit service of God, to take hold of the opportunities that he gives and to take risks for him. If we do, we have the prospect of setting our people free as did Alfred by his victory at Edington. If we do not, our land will be forever burdened. The choice is ours.

4. Onslaught

Joel 2:10-27.

Key word: leadership.

The reign of Aethelred the Unready (the un-redd, or badly advised) groans under a weight of adverse circumstance, made worse by the character of the king himself. There is no doubt that he succeeded to a difficult inheritance. He was only eleven years old, and his elder brother Edward fourteen, when their father King Edgar died in 975. There was a disputed succession, with some taking the side of one boy and some of the other. Edward was crowned, but there was civil war and in 978 the young ruler was murdered. The taint of a foul deed clung to Aethelred for many years, though there is no suggestion that he was in any way personally involved in his brother's killing.

Barely had Aethelred ascended the throne than the Danes resumed their raids on England for the first time in decades. No blame attaches to the monarch for this – the renewed assault was the result of developments within Scandinavia – but his reaction to the attacks was disastrous. Starting in 980, raiding continued with unabated ferocity so that almost every year for thirty years some part of England was harried. Aethelred lacked the steadfastness needed to bring good plans to fruition and he proved a terrible judge of character. Time and again he promoted the lazy, incompetent, corrupt or traitorous. He seemed incapable of choosing good subordinates or of placing confidence even in those few decent men who occupied positions of power and influence. Property was expropriated on the flimsiest excuse. Several times those in high office or their relatives were blinded on the king's orders for faults real or imaginary. His own arbitrary and inconstant behaviour fed distrust of the crown and ultimately disloyalty.

The result was that, although there were honourable exceptions at local level, all too often the armies that England put in the field against the invaders were betrayed by their own leaders. When properly led, English troops showed repeatedly that they were still able to give a good account of themselves, but as time passed the creeping rot of demoralisation spread wider. Year by year the payments required to buy off the Danes (the so-called Danegeld) became larger.[13] The burden on the country, which was required to support the armies of friend and foe alike, was enormous. In 1005 the Anglo-Saxon Chronicle speaks of a famine "more severe than any that could be remembered."

---

[13] Between 991 and 1014 official payments of Danegeld totalled more than 150,000lbs of silver, equivalent to 36 million coins of the day.

In 1002 Aethelred's poor judgment broke out in infamy. The Anglo-Saxon Chronicle records his hearing that the Danes in England "intended to kill him and all his counsellors, and afterwards to possess his kingdom," so he ordered their massacre. The order was never fully carried out and in any event was impractical of execution in areas of heavy Danish settlement, but amongst those killed was Gunnhild, sister of king Svein Forkbeard of Denmark. Aethelred could scarce have conceived a better way to ensure the undying enmity of a dangerous adversary. So the onslaught continued, without let-up or relief, as long as Aethelred lived. His miserable reign came to an end in 1016.

Thereafter, his son Edmund Ironside led a brief English revival, showing what could be done with proper leadership, but died in the very year of his accession a few weeks after defeat at Assandun by King Cnut of Denmark. On his passing, the exhausted and ravaged country meekly acquiesced in the claim to the throne advanced by Cnut, comforted perhaps by the fact that this Viking ruler was no longer pagan, but baptised a Christian.[14] Not until 1042 was the house of Wessex, Europe's oldest royal line, restored by Edward the Confessor, another son of Aethelred.

A call to arms.

To the English, the Danes who ravaged their land in the reign of Aethelred might well have seemed an army of locusts, like that described by the prophet Joel: "Before them the earth shakes, the sky trembles, the sun and moon are darkened, and the stars no longer shine." (Joel 2:10). The adversary described by the prophet is sent by God: "The LORD thunders at the head of his army; his forces are beyond number, and mighty are those who obey his command." (Joel 2:11). God describes them as "my great army that I sent among you." (Joel 2:25). Faced with this, Joel not surprisingly asks: "Who can endure it?" (Joel 2:11).

In response, there is a call to arms: "Blow the trumpet in Zion" (Joel 2:15). The war that it calls the people to wage is a spiritual one. Hence their response should be to "declare a holy fast, call a sacred assembly" (Joel 2:15).

A call to repentance.

As a first step in its spiritual war, the nation is called to a corporate act of repentance: "Return to the LORD your God, for he is gracious and compassionate, slow to anger and abounding in love ... Gather the people, consecrate the assembly" (Joel 2:13 and 16). The assembly is to encompass:

---

[14] Cnut had already been awarded half the kingdom as the fruit of his victory at Assandun.

"elders ... children ... those nursing at the breast ... the bridegroom ... and the bride" (Joel 2:16). The situation is so urgent and the extent of the problem so widespread that there can be no delay, no excuse for not becoming involved and no exemption from duty.

The issues that the Israelites face are spiritual first and foremost. For sure, these have earthly manifestations, but the prime cause lies elsewhere: in a nation that has forsaken God, trampled his laws and derided his prophets. The priests are called upon to intercede: "Let the priests, who minister before the Lord, weep ... [and] say, 'Spare your people, O LORD'" (Joel 2:17). The things that the Israelites are instructed to do apply equally to the present day. In worship, prayer and repentance, an example should be set by those whose lives ought most to be characterised by devotion to God, but this is not just a task for professional clergy. Unless the people as a whole take part and follow the lead that is given, there will be a spiritual shortfall and the blessing that we receive will be incomplete. Neither can we put the cart before the horse. If we try to do things on our own and to better our material circumstances without turning to God, we will fail: "But seek first [God's] kingdom and his righteousness, and all these things will be given to you as well." (Matthew 6:33).

The people are reminded that repentance must be sincere, not just a form of words or an outward display: "Rend your heart and not your garments." (Joel 2:13). They are reminded, too, that with God it is never too late to say that we are sorry and to turn to him again: "Even now ... return to me with all your heart, with fasting, weeping and mourning." (Joel 2:12). If we will do this, "he relents from sending calamity." (Joel 2:13).

A call to joy.

When the nation genuinely repents and turns again to him, "the LORD will ... take pity on his people" (Joel 2:18). In words that Englishmen of Aethelred's day must have longed to hear, the Lord says: "I will drive the northern army far from you" (Joel 2:20). The instrument of God's wrath will be turned aside.

With that comes a threefold call to joy as land, animals and people are called to rejoice in the Lord's bounty: "Be not afraid, O land; be glad and rejoice. Surely the Lord has done great things. Be not afraid, O wild animals, for the open pastures are becoming green, the trees are bearing their fruit; the fig-tree and the vine yield their riches. Be glad, O people of Zion, rejoice in the LORD your God, for he has given you the autumn rains in righteousness." (Joel 2:21-23). The first signs of renewed and imminent blessing start to show themselves straight away.

A call to the future.

The call to joy deliberately echoes the threefold call to grief in Joel 1:5, 8 and 13. Indeed, the Lord does not merely counterbalance the misfortune that was visited on the people earlier. He far outweighs it with the good things that he showers on them.

If we will turn to God, we can look to the future with confidence, for he promises an abundance of good things: "I am sending you grain, new wine and oil, enough to satisfy you fully ... The threshing-floors will be filled with grain; the vats will overflow with new wine and oil ... You will have plenty to eat, until you are full" (Joel 2:19, 24 and 26). Most extraordinary of all, God is able to take things that have been wasted, destroyed, damaged, disfigured and perverted and turn them to good account: "I will repay you for the years the locusts have eaten ... and you will praise the name of the LORD your God, who has worked wonders for you; never again will my people be shamed" (Joel 2:25-26).

When we are going through times of testing and trial, it is difficult for us to focus on anything other than our present misery. We lack perspective, both as regards our own personal situation and as regards that of our nation. We have trouble accepting God's promises because we expect instant results rather than recognising that God's timing is not the same as ours. Our viewpoint needs to change. The facts are these: whatever difficulties we face, even when we are confronted by "forces ... beyond number ... and mighty" (Joel 2:11), if we turn to him, God "will drive [them] far from [us], pushing [them] into a barren and parched land" (Joel 2:20). The power that these things had over us will be broken once and for all.

A call to see clearly.

With this in mind, we are called to see clearly. We need to adopt the proper way of looking at things:

To distinguish what is true ("rend your heart") (Joel 2:13) from what is false ("rend ... your garments") (Joel 2:13).

To differentiate between spiritual reality ("the LORD thunders at the head of his army") (Joel 2:11) and earthly manifestation ("an object of scorn, a byword among the nations") (Joel 2:17).

To recognise our own fault and repent ("return ... with fasting, weeping and mourning") (Joel 2:12), not pretend that we are mere victims of a malign fate.

To make a deliberate and settled decision to turn again to God ("Return to the LORD your God") (Joel 2:13).

To recognise God for who he is and give him the proper place in our lives ("Then you will know that I am in Israel, that I am the LORD your God, and that there is no other") (Joel 2:27).

These things are true for us as a nation, just as they are true for us as individuals.

Conclusion.

Leadership matters. Aethelred came to the throne of a unified England[15] exactly one hundred years after Alfred the Great won the battle of Edington with the resources of Wessex alone. The hand dealt to the former was no worse than that dealt to the latter. Indeed, in many ways Alfred's position would have seemed the more precarious at the outset of his reign. Yet Alfred survived and laid the foundations for comprehensive victory, whilst Aethelred presided over the despoiling of his kingdom and the steadily increasing misery of his people. There is more to this than mere happenstance. Aethelred's character faults were above all a spiritual issue. Alfred's ability to stand firm was grounded in his Christian faith. This faith sustained him, strengthened him and brought him victory. It meant, too, that during his reign there was a deepening and quickening of the spiritual life of the whole nation. The chronicler Asser describes Alfred as "enthusiastic and generous in alms-giving to fellow-countrymen and foreigners, extremely affable and pleasant to all men, and a skilful enquirer into the unknown. Many ... submitted voluntarily to his dominion, all of whom he ruled, loved, honoured and enriched as if they were his own people." Aethelred could hardly have been more different. Under him the spiritual health of the nation declined precipitately.

In the Old Testament we see time and again such a strong identification of the country with its king that the character of the monarch determines the fate of the nation. When the ruler is godly, the Lord bestows blessing. When the ruler goes against God's laws, blessing is withheld. In a democratic state, we share a responsibility for the spiritual condition of the nation that was previously the king's alone. We can therefore expect God to bless or withhold blessing according to the way in which we each live our own lives. There are two aspects to this, a public and a private. It is not enough for us to be godly in our personal lives but to treat the Lord as though he had no part in the political or working life of the land. That being so, we have to ask ourselves: what leadership are we

---

[15] The kingdom of Athelstan (grandson of Alfred the Great) covered most of modern England by 927. Succeeding kings cemented this achievement. In 973 Aethelred's father King Edgar was the first ruler to be crowned king of all England.

giving to England today? What are we doing to call the people to arms, to call them to repentance, to call them to recognise the joy and the future that the Almighty will bring if we turn again to him? What are we doing to call the people to see clearly, to "know that I am in Israel, that I am the LORD your God, and that there is no other" (Joel 2:27)?

Good leadership is not just for those at the very top of the tree. It must exist at all levels of society if a nation is to be whole and healthy. We must take up the baton handed over by earlier generations. We must lead, and lead well, if God is to bless us again.

5. Defeat

Lamentations 3:19-48.

Key word: prayer.

Harold Godwinson is one of the nearly men of English history. He came to the throne on the death of Edward the Confessor in January 1066, having been nominated by the dying king on his deathbed and unanimously elected by the Witan (the high council). In the course of less than 10 months he showed talent, energy and courage worthy of the greatest monarchs. If an air of inevitable doom now hangs over his reign, it is largely the product of hindsight and Norman propaganda. Bad luck dogged his attempts to defend the realm, however. Alert to possible Norman attack, he mobilised a fleet to guard the Channel, but bad weather delayed William's crossing. By the time the Duke of Normandy was able to move, the English ships had run out of supplies and been dispersed, whilst Harold had been called north to face a second invading army under Harald Hardrada ("hard ruler") of Norway.

To cap it all, there was treachery: Harold's disaffected brother Tostig, who had been exiled in 1065, raided the English coast with a fleet of sixty ships from May 1066. Although defeated by earl Edwin of Mercia at the battle of Lindsey, he escaped to Scotland and subsequently returned to make common cause with Hardrada. Together they were a fearsome army – the joint force numbered some five hundred ships – and after a bloody fight which cost both sides dear, they beat Earl Edwin and his brother Morcar, earl of Northumbria, at the battle of Fulford Gate on 20 September. Meanwhile, however, the king was hurrying to meet the threat.

The campaign that Harold fought in September and October 1066 deserves to rank alongside the finest feats of arms. He surprised the enemy at Stamford Bridge a few miles east of York on 25 September, winning a tremendous victory in which both Tostig and the Norwegian king were killed. So great was the slaughter that the survivors needed just twenty ships to make their escape. Scarce was the battle over before news came that William had landed at Pevensey Bay in Sussex. Straight away Harold led his best troops south by forced marches. They covered 400 miles in just over a fortnight, having destroyed the Norwegian army on the way. The king allowed them a week's respite in London whilst he gathered men from the southern counties to face William, though most of the new recruits were village levies, many armed with little more than clubs or billhooks. Yet still the battle of Hastings was so hard-fought that its outcome was in the balance almost to the end.

Harold fell on Saturday 16 October 1066 on Caldbeck Hill, which the Normans called Senlac (lake of blood). His brothers Gyrth and Leofwin, together with almost all the nobility and gentry of the southern shires, fell with him. In a single afternoon, England lost her finest soldiers and practically her whole leadership. She was at the mercy of the Conqueror.

Ruin and captivity.

The book of Lamentations is written in the context of the conquest of the southern Israelite kingdom of Judah by the Babylonians in 586 BC. Jewish and early Christian tradition ascribes authorship to Jeremiah, the prophet who had warned for years beforehand that God's judgment was coming. Like the Anglo-Saxons in 1066, the people of Judah suffered not just defeat but also the effective decapitation of their state: those of the leading citizens who survived were marched to captivity in Babylon, where they and their descendants were held for seventy years. Terrible privations were suffered during Nebuchadnezzar's siege of Jerusalem, but even when this ended there was no respite.

Lamentations records the litany of suffering: there is affliction, bitterness and gall (Lamentations 3:19); many have become refugees, "wandering" (Lamentations 3:19); the people "have suffered terror and pitfalls, ruin and destruction." (Lamentations 3:47). Worse still, they are now under Babylonian rule. The author says that: "It is good for a man to bear the yoke when he is young" (Lamentations 3:27), but it is a harsh yoke indeed. The Babylonians were noted for their cruelty. They "crush underfoot all prisoners in the land, to deny a man his rights before the Most High" (Lamentations 3:34).

There is a terrible irony in the Israelites now finding themselves under the brutal yoke of man for consistently rejecting the gentle yoke of God. Jesus says: "Take my yoke upon you and learn from me, for I am gentle and humble in heart, and you will find rest for your souls. For my yoke is easy and my burden is light." (Matthew 11:29-30). The conquerors, Babylonian and Norman, could not have been more different.

Grounds for hope.

Incredibly, amidst the awfulness that surrounds him, the author finds reason to hope. On the face of it, his hope is against all human reason. He writes that "Streams of tears flow from my eyes because my people are destroyed" (Lamentations 3:48), yet at the same time: "Because of the LORD's great love we are not consumed" (Lamentations 3:22). That this should be so is the more remarkable given that "All our enemies have opened their mouths wide against us." (Lamentations 3:46).

Hope is grounded in God: "Yet this I call to mind and therefore I have hope ... for [The LORD's] compassions never fail. They are new every morning; great is your faithfulness ... The LORD is good to those whose hope is in him, to the one who seeks him ... Let him bury his face in the dust – there may yet be hope." (Lamentations 3:21, 22, 25 and 29). The picture of burying one's face in the dust is of heartfelt and sincere prostration before God in prayer and submission to his will, just as did the prophet Daniel when he "three times a day got down on his knees and prayed" (Daniel 6:10) and "turned to the Lord God and pleaded with him in prayer and petition, in fasting, and in sackcloth and ashes." (Daniel 9:3).

The result of well-founded hope is that, although the outward circumstances are dire and "my soul is downcast within me" (Lamentations 3:20), the author still looks for good things from the Almighty. This is the most astonishing expression of trust in the mercy of God, for the author recognises that what his nation has suffered has come about because God has allowed it: "Let him sit alone in silence, for the LORD has laid it on him." (Lamentations 3:28). Indeed, "You [God] have covered yourself with anger and have pursued; you have slain without pity. You have covered yourself with a cloud so that no prayer can get through. You have made us scum and refuse among the nations." (Lamentations 3:43-45). The Babylonians have been the mere instruments of God's judgment against the Israelites.

To us, this might sound harsh, but the author is in no doubt that God's actions are completely justified: "Let us lift up our hearts and our hands to God in heaven, and say: 'We have sinned and rebelled'" (Lamentations 3:41-42). He states quite explicitly that there is no cause to question the rightness of what God has done: "Is it not from the mouth of the Most High that both calamities and good things come? Why should any living man complain when punished for his sins?" (Lamentations 3:38-39). The reality is that prophets had been warning of impending disaster for decades and urging the people to turn back to God, but to no avail. At last, the Lord will delay punishment no longer, but we are reminded that "he does not willingly bring affliction or grief to the children of men." (Lamentations 3:33). The prophet Ezekiel records the same sentiment: "'Do I take pleasure in the death of the wicked?' declares the Sovereign LORD. 'Rather, am I not pleased when they turn from their ways and live?'" (Ezekiel 18:23). Likewise, St Paul writes that "God our Saviour ... wants all men to be saved and to come to a knowledge of the truth." (1 Timothy 2:3-4).

The author recognises that God has punished their Israelites for their sinfulness, since he is a god of righteousness and justice. Yet he expects God to show compassion (Lamentations 3:22 and 32) and bring salvation to his people (Lamentations 3:26) because he is also a god of "unfailing love" (Lamentations 3:32) and mercy. "Men are not cast off by the Lord for ever." (Lamentations 3:31).

Waiting.

This expectation is not the product of mere daydreaming. It is realistic. The author knows that we often have to wait for deliverance from hardship and for the blessings that God wishes to give us: "The LORD is my portion; therefore I will wait for him." (Lamentations 3:24) and "It is good to wait quietly for the salvation of the LORD." (Lamentations 3:26). He knows that we have to be patient and make sure that we use the time of waiting wisely: to learn from our mistakes ("let us examine our ways and test them") and to confess to God the things that we have done wrong ("Let us say... we have sinned and rebelled").

Whilst waiting, we need to have the right attitude: "Let him offer his cheek to the one who would strike him, and let him be filled with disgrace." (Lamentations 3:30). The words directly mirror the teaching of Jesus during the Sermon on the Mount: "But I tell you, do not resist an evil person. If someone strikes you on the right cheek, turn to him the other also."(Matthew 5:39). This is difficult. It does not come easily or naturally to us, but it is the way to ensure that we come as close as we can to a holy God. So often, it is in times of waiting and of trial that God takes his people and refines them, teaches them and makes them ready for the tasks ahead.

Coming back to God.

All is within the power and timing of God: "Who can speak and have it happen if the Lord has not decreed it?" (Lamentations 3:37). That, however, does not mean that we have no part to play or that we can lapse into fatalism or apathy. We need to turn to God in order to receive the good that he wishes to bestow on us.

Moreover, we need to recognise that our actions have consequences. Our sinfulness creates a barrier between ourselves and God: "You [God] have covered yourself with a cloud so that no prayer can get through." (Lamentations 3:44). This is not because God wishes there to be separation between him and man. It is merely that separation is an inevitable result of his holiness and justice, for "[God's] eyes are too pure to look on evil." (Habbakuk 1:13). If we wish our prayers to be effective, we must do what we can to remove the barrier between us and God. This involves repentance, turning from what is wrong and resolving henceforth to follow what is right. What is needed is an honest appraisal of what we have done and failed to do: "Let us examine our ways and test them, and let us return to the LORD ... We have sinned and rebelled" (Lamentations 3:40-42). Turning from what is wrong, however, is only part. We need also to lay hold of the salvation that God offers. We do this by placing our faith (trust) in Jesus Christ.

Conclusion.

In 1066 it must indeed have seemed to the English that "all our enemies have opened their mouths wide against us" (Lamentations 3:46). Worse was to come. In the aftermath of defeat at Hastings, they might have been forgiven for thinking that "you have covered yourself with anger and pursued us; you have slain without pity." (Lamentations 3:43). Many fled overseas, "wandering" (Lamentations 3:19) just like the author of Lamentations. A large contingent of exiled Englishmen joined the Varangian Guard, crack household troops of the Byzantine Emperor. Others sought refuge elsewhere. No doubt in foreign lands they would oft "remember [their] affliction ... the bitterness and the gall" (Lamentations 3:19).They would not have been human had they not thought, too, about why such things should have happened to England.

We need to go through the same process of examination today. We need to do it both personally and as a nation. We have first of all to "examine our ways and test them" (Lamentations 3:40). We must shine the light of truth on the dark corners of our own attitudes and behaviour, on the things that are rotten and unjust in our society. Truth can be painful. It means having to lay aside prejudices and preconceptions, taboos and shibboleths. Unless we correctly appraise what is wrong, however, the chances of our ever being able to put it right are slim.

We need not just to analyse the facts correctly, but to draw the proper conclusions from them. The author of Lamentations was in no doubt: "We have sinned and rebelled" (Lamentations 3:42). At present, we still give the impression of denying what the root cause of our malaise is. One thing is sure. It has nothing to do with a lack of resources. It is not even a matter of how we choose to employ our resources. It is instead a question of the spiritual health of the nation. Our problems would be over in an instant if we truly put into practice two of the central teachings of Jesus: "Do to others as you would have them do to you" (Luke 6:31) and "Love your neighbour as yourself" (Matthew 22:39).

Analysing and drawing conclusions is the start, but then we need to act. We need to resolve to put things right: "let us return to the LORD" (Lamentations 3:40). We act upon our resolve by confessing what we have done wrong, by putting our faith in God, by doing our utmost to live pure and holy lives. From where we stand at the moment, this is a tall order. Like Shakespeare's Macbeth, we might imagine ourselves "in blood stepp'd in so far that, should I wade no more, returning were as tedious as go o'er." The amazing thing about God, however, is that whatever we have done or failed to do, there is always a way back to him.

We need only to ask for his help. We have gone so far astray and the task is so great that it is not something that we can do alone. Like Daniel, like the author of Lamentations, we need to turn to God in prayer, to "bury [our] face in the dust" (Lamentations 3:29). This is the urgent task that each of us needs to undertake. There is no time for delay.

6. Resistance

James 4:1-12.

Key word: combat.

Defeat at Hastings dealt a grievous blow to England, but her spirit was not altogether broken. For two hundred years and more she had borne the assaults of Vikings from Denmark and Norway. She roused herself for a further effort against the Northmen from Normandy. On news of Harold's death, the youngster Edgar the Atheling,[16] the only surviving prince of the house of Wessex, was elected king. Yet as William slowly advanced through Kent and Surrey to encircle London, one by one the remaining English leaders (most prominent amongst them Edwin and Morcar, respectively earls of Mercia and Northumbria) began to submit to him. They were influenced no doubt by William's claim that the throne was his by right, by his promise to uphold English laws and by the fact that the boy-king Edgar was of no age to exercise real leadership. They could not then have envisaged what the reality of Norman rule would be.

Despite this initial submission to William, hardly a year passed between 1066 and his death in 1087 when the Conqueror was not in the saddle directing the suppression of rebellion somewhere in his new kingdom. In truth, many of these outbreaks were minor local affairs that posed no real threat to Norman rule. Some were more in the nature of feudal quarrels amongst the Normans themselves. The exception, however, which clearly shook William and lead to far harsher rule on his part, was the great national revolt of 1068-71.

The catalyst for widespread uprising was the killing of the Norman Robert of Comines, whom William had made earl of Northumbria beyond Tees, in 1069. Thereupon, the men of Yorkshire joined with a Danish force to take the newly built castle at York and at this the West Saxons and Mercians, too, took up arms. William's response was typically vigorous. He bought off the Danes, leaving him free to engage and defeat the English rebels. Thereafter, he showed no mercy. In the winter of 1069-70, the king set about the deliberate devastation of the most fertile and populous parts of Yorkshire. Not only was livestock slaughtered and stores of grain and other foodstuffs burnt, but the implements which the

---

[16] The term Atheling literally means a member of the nobility but was often restricted to a prince of the royal blood or the heir apparent.

survivors needed to recover from the disaster by planting and harvesting were systematically destroyed. The destruction was appalling, the suffering agonising.[17]

At length, such resistance as remained centred on the fenland of Cambridgeshire. At Ely lay an island of firm ground amidst the swamp, then so wide and deep that the only practicable means of transport was by boat. Here gathered a desperate group, led by an English thane called Hereward, known to posterity as the Wake, meaning "the Watchful" or "the Wary." The battle was noble but forlorn, and utterly hopeless once William had ensured that there was no chance of Danish support. The Normans blocked escape routes from Ely with ships and built a causeway across the marsh, whereupon all surrendered save Hereward, who escaped with a handful of followers. What became of him thereafter is unknown. So ended the last serious English challenge to the Conquest.

The battle within.

The English struggled manfully against their foes. There was no shortage of "fights and quarrels" (James 4:1). Yet, try as they might, after Hastings they were unable to throw off the Norman yoke. As one Norman king succeeded another, Englishmen came to accept the fact of foreign rule, even if they were not entirely reconciled to it. Love between the people and their overlords there was little or none, but the Conqueror's sons William Rufus and Henry I reigned secure in England. Further revolt and restoration of the West Saxon monarchy gradually became the stuff of fantasy. For ordinary people, the most important struggle increasingly became, as at most times and in most places in human history, the "battle within" (James 4:1).

In his letter to the early church James, the brother of Jesus, tells his readers how to wage this battle and to emerge victorious, whatever the outward circumstances may be. The starting point is to identify the root of the problem correctly: "What causes fights and quarrels among you?" (James 4:1). James' answer is clear and uncompromising. The cause lies in "desires that battle within." (James 4:1). The result is failure to obtain God's blessing: "You do not have, because you do not ask God. When you ask, you do not receive, because you ask with wrong motives, that you may spend what you get on your pleasures." (James 4:2-3). The indictment rings just as true today as when it was written.

---

[17] So widespread and devastating was this "harrowing of the north" that in 1086 the Domesday Book described hundreds of villages as still being waste or wilderness (In Latin, *vasta est*).

What we need to look to first and foremost are our own attitudes and behaviour: "don't you know that friendship with the world is hatred towards God? Anyone who chooses to be a friend of the world becomes an enemy of God." (James 4:4). There is a constant temptation to conform to the values and standards of the world around us at the expense of doing and saying what is right. This we must do our utmost to resist. Instead, we need to keep a proper perspective on the passing fads and fancies of the human world and fix our eyes on the unchanging truths and values of God: "For here we do not have an enduring city, but we are looking for the city that is to come." (Hebrews 13:14).

Resistance and submission.

Thoughtless strife and striving are not the answer. Instead, we need a balance between resistance and submission. There is a time to resist and a time to submit. There are circumstances which we should resist and ones to which we should submit. Above all, there is a person whom we should resist and a person to whom we should submit: "Submit yourselves, then, to God. Resist the devil, and he will flee from you. Come near to God and he will come near to you." (James 4:7-8).

There is a strand running through both Old and New Testaments that brings into sharp relief the difference between human ways and the values of the kingdom of God. "If your enemy is hungry, give him food to eat; if he is thirsty, give him water to drink. In doing this, you will heap coals on his head, and the LORD will reward you." (Proverbs 25:21-22). Or, as St Paul puts it in his letter to the Christians in Rome: "Bless those who persecute you ... Do not repay anyone evil for evil ... Do not take revenge ... Do not be overcome by evil, but overcome evil with good." (Romans 12:14, 17, 19 and 21).

This is counter-intuitive and can lead to confusion about whether our resistance to evil must always be passive. Richard Wormbrand, a Romanian pastor who suffered terrible persecution under that country's fascist and communist regimes from the nineteen thirties onwards, neatly summed up one way of striking the balance between resistance and submission: "The enemy we have conquered must also have our help. But any help given to an enemy when he is in power is wrong, because it makes us his accomplices." Sometimes Christian resistance to evil in our land has seemed passive almost to the point of invisibility. As a nation, our recent past has too often been characterised by capitulation to the devil and resistance to God. These things need to change before there can be any hope of improvement. There is a war to be fought and we must not flinch from fighting it.

Fighting the good fight.

When James talks about the battle within he is referring to the war between good and evil within our own souls, but there is also a battle for the soul of society. We need to take great care in how we go about waging this battle. It must not become a witch hunt or an excuse for pointing fingers at those who happen to be different: "Who are you to judge your neighbour?" (James 4:12). We should remember that: "When [we] judge the law, [we] are not keeping it but sitting in judgement on it. There is only one Lawgiver and Judge, the one who is able to save and destroy." (James 4:12).

That, however, does not allow us to sit back or wash our hands of responsibility for what is going on around us. The prescription that James gives his readers applies equally to the battle within and without. Like any army, we must:

Mobilise: we must clear the decks of things that will impede our ability to fight. In a spiritual context, what hampers us is sin. James makes the point three times for emphasis: "Wash your hands, you sinners ... Grieve, mourn and wail ... Change your laughter to mourning and your joy to gloom" (James 4:8-9). This does not mean that we are to go around with long faces all the time, for joy is one of the fruits of the Holy Spirit (Galatians 5:22). It does mean, however, that before we can fight properly we need to confess our faults to God and bring ourselves under the umbrella of his forgiveness.

Train: having dealt with the negative by getting rid of the things that form a barrier between ourselves and God, we then need to acquire the positive things that will aid us in the fight. This takes effort and training. We are told to: "Purify your hearts" (James 4:8). The more we are able to "call on the Lord out of a pure heart" (2 Timothy 2:22), the more we are likely to find power in prayer. Jesus taught: "blessed are the pure in heart" (Matthew 5:8).

Equip: if we want God to equip us, we need to humble ourselves before him. Humility is a precursor to blessing (2 Chronicles 7:14), wisdom (Proverbs 11:2), guidance (Psalm 25:9), honour (Proverbs 22:4) and salvation (Psalm 18:27 and 149:4). Humility is not just desirable. It is one of the characteristics of God himself: Jesus says, "I am gentle and humble in heart." (Matthew 11:29). Thus James emphasises the need for us to: "Humble yourselves before the Lord" (James 4:10). We do so by recognising that there is nothing we are able to do in our own strength, nothing we possess that is our own, nothing for which we are not dependent on God.

Work as a unit: a united front is vital in any conflict. Unity amongst his people is dear to the heart of God. That is why one of Jesus' last prayers was that "they may be one, as we are one" (John 17:11). When James tells us, "do not slander one another" (James 4:11), he is likewise making a plea for unity. Too often, Christians have concentrated on the things that divide them. Now above all times we need to concentrate on the things that unite us.

As St Paul advises, we must don the full armour of God (Ephesians 6:10-18). Not merely put it on, but use it, remembering that along with things for our defence we are also given the most powerful offensive weapon of all: "the sword of the Spirit, which is the Word of God." (Ephesians 6:17).

Conclusion.

Hereward the Wake makes an unlikely freedom fighter. His identity is obscured by lack or contradiction of details, but such fragmentary records as exist suggest that he was a native of Lincolnshire and that he was of turbulent and lawless character, one who would forever be picking "fights and quarrels" (James 4:1).[18] It seems that he was already an outlaw before ever he was in revolt against Norman rule. Worse yet for those seeking a hero, at least some aspects of his career seem rather less glorious than the afterglow of the centuries has painted them. The Anglo-Saxon Chronicle recounts that, upon the appointment of the Norman Turold as abbot of the monastery of Peterborough, Hereward and a group of Danes attacked and destroyed not just the monastery but the town as well. Only one house and one sick man are said to have remained untouched. That looks less like spirited resistance to foreign rule than out and out brigandage. At the very least, it shows a woeful inability to distinguish friend from foe, since the dwellings laid waste in Peterborough presumably belonged mostly or even entirely to Anglo-Saxons.

After the Peterborough raid, the Danes headed home (they are said to have been lost in a shipwreck on the way back), whilst Hereward and his men repaired to the fastness of Ely. It is on the fight there that his reputation is built. Doubtless he was brave and strong. He must have been an inspirational leader, since he remained head of this band even when they were joined by men of greater position and wealth, but he was not to be England's saviour.

We are presently fighting a battle for the life and soul of our country. It is above all a spiritual battle, a "battle within" (James 4:1). Our situation is grave precisely since so many have scarcely noticed that a battle is under way. Amongst those who have, there is too often a reluctance to recognise the true nature of the fight.

---

[18] Recent research suggests that Hereward was of Danish ancestry and that he was employed as a mercenary by the Count of Flanders before returning to England to confront the Norman invaders.

There is reluctance, too, to identify and take hold of the means of victory. We already have a Saviour. The issue is whether we will give Him pride of place in the life of our nation and thereby allow Him to cleanse and renew us. The prescription is simple. We need to mobilise, train, equip and work together. We need to: "Wash [our] hands ... purify [our] hearts ... Humble [ourselves] before the Lord and he will lift [us] up." (James 4:8 and 10). When we free ourselves of "wrong motives" (James 4:3), we will be able to ask God and then to receive from him. Each of us must take a lead in showing our people the way, for: "How, then, can they call on the one they have not believed in? And how can they believe in the one of whom they have not heard? And how can they hear without someone preaching to them?" (Romans 10:14). We must not flinch and we must not fail in this great task.

7. A nation divided

Habbakuk 1:1 -2:4.

Key word: faith.

There are around 600 loan words thought to be of Scandinavian origin in modern English. Most are seafaring or everyday words, such as cast (kasta), knife (knifr), take (taka), window (vind-auga), egg (egg), ill (illr) and die (deyja). The Vikings also introduced the plurals 'they', 'them' and 'their.' English dialects contain even more Norse words, many relating to agriculture. The strong linguistic influence resulted from the similarity between Anglo-Saxon and Old Norse, so that words were readily imported from one to the other. The nature of the terms that have come into English reflects the fact that Scandinavian settlers cultivated their own land and tended their own animals. It is true that for decades Viking and Englishman may have lived parallel lives, but at no point did one form a caste of masters and the other of servants. Assimilation of the newcomers was thus based on relations of equality.

Words that have come into English from French paint a very different picture of the Normans. It is no great exaggeration to say that, to this day, English can be seen almost as a French dialect or as a German dialect, depending on how it is spoken and what words are used. The Normans lived apart from the conquered people, whom they treated as labourers and servants, with whom they spoke only as these roles demanded: thus the remarkable linguistic apartheid that attends the English tongue. When a domestic animal is alive, we use a Germanic word for it, since the Anglo-Saxons were the ones who continued to tend the land: hence cow (*Kuh*), pig or swine (*Schwein, Pigge*), dog or hound (*Hund, Dogge*), sheep (*Schaf*) and roe deer (*Reh*). Once dead, however, the meat of the animal bears a French name, for it was served at table to Normans who would have described it in their vernacular. So we eat beef (*boeuf*), pork and ham (*porc, jambon*), mutton (*mouton*) and venison (*venaison*). To control the subject population, the Normans imposed curfews (a word derived from the French *couvre-feu*).

The very language preserves a memory of the oppression of our forefathers.[19] This was no short-lived phase. English did not supplant French in the law courts until the reign of Edward III (1327-77): in 1362 to be precise, almost exactly three hundred years after the Conquest.

---

[19] By the end of the Conqueror's reign most of England was owned by the king himself and two hundred of his followers. Only two Englishmen remained great landowners and all the English together held only one twelfth of England's farmland.

Oppression.

Habbakuk describes a time of coming oppression. He speaks in the form of an "oracle" (Habbakuk 1:1), a word specifically used for a declaration by God. He is amongst the several prophets sent to warn the Israelite kingdom of Judah that God is "raising up the Babylonians, that ruthless and impetuous people, who sweep across the whole earth to seize dwelling places not their own" (Habbakuk 1:6) and that Judah will fall to them. These are fearsome foes indeed: "They are a feared and dreaded people ... a law to themselves ... they fly like a vulture swooping to devour; they all come bent on violence." (Habbakuk 1:7-9). The Babylonians will be the instruments of God's justice: "O LORD, you have appointed them to execute judgment; O Rock, you have ordained them to punish" (Habbakuk 1:12).

God has been patient beyond measure with the Israelites, yet still they persist in their wrongdoing and their rejection of him. There is corruption and apostasy. Israelite society is awash with "Violence ... injustice ... wrong ... destruction ... strife ... [and] conflict" (Habbakuk 1:2-3) – so pervasive is the rot that "the law is paralysed, and justice never prevails. The wicked hem in the righteous, so that justice is perverted." (Habbakuk 1:4).

The Israelites were intended by God to be a light to the Gentiles, to be "a kingdom of priests and a holy nation." (Exodus 19:6). They were supposed to show the world how to worship God in holiness and truth. Instead, there is little to choose between them and the surrounding nations. Whilst the Babylonians "promote their own honour" and are "guilty men, whose strength is their god" (Habbakuk 1:11), sadly the Israelites, too, have relied on their own resources rather than on the Lord. They have sought their own glory rather than God's. Now they will learn that human strength alone cannot avail and that "pride goes before destruction, a haughty spirit before a fall." (Proverbs 16:18).

Questioning.

Against this background, Habbakuk asks three of the most fundamental questions of human existence: why does evil go unpunished? (Habbakuk 1:13); why does God not respond to prayer? (Habbakuk 1:2 and 13); and why must we wait so long? (Habbakuk 1:2). Within these is a subsidiary question: why does God use "the wicked [to] swallow up those more righteous than themselves?"

(Habbakuk 1:13).[20] The process of questioning and listening to God leads Habbakuk to a new way of looking at the world. It leads him beyond logic to faith, beyond form to truth and beyond acceptance to trust.

The questions were not just private musings and the prophet did not keep the answers to himself. They were designed for use by the nation as a whole. The book ends, for example, with the words: "For the director of music. On my stringed instruments" (Habbakuk 3:19), showing that it was intended to be sung and used in worship.

Logic and faith.

God is almighty and eternal, the creator of the universe and all that is in it: "O LORD, are you not from everlasting? ... You have made men" (Habbakuk 1:12 and 14). Despite this, he is accessible to humankind. He does not hide himself from his creatures, but invites us to speak to him, saying: "Come, let us reason together" (Isaiah 1:18). God does not censure Habbakuk for questioning, even though the prophet himself describes his questions as a "complaint" (Habbakuk 2:1).

This is worth emphasising: God asks us to have faith, but this does not mean that we are forbidden to question. Faith is not blind, unreasoning or irrational, but it does involve something more than the mere application of logic. In our present-day culture we elevate logic above all other forms of knowing. Undoubtedly, logic is good. Our reasoning ability is given to us by God precisely so that we should use it, not so that we should leave our brains behind when we come before him. However, we need to recognise that there are some things that are beyond our logic. Paradoxes arise precisely because we are not God: we do not know all things, we were not present at the creation of the world and we do not think like God: "'For my thoughts are not your thoughts, neither are your ways my ways,' declares the LORD. 'As the heavens are higher than the earth, so are my ways higher than your ways and my thoughts higher than your thoughts.'" (Isaiah 55:8-9). Unless we have faith, therefore, our understanding of the world will always be incomplete and our ability to serve God will be constrained.

---

[20] These are perennial questions. The prophet Jeremiah asked: "Why does the way of the wicked prosper? Why do all the faithless live at ease?" (Jeremiah 12:1). Job demanded: "Why do the wicked live on, growing old and increasing in power?" (Job 21:7). David gives God's perspective: "Do not fret because of evil men or be envious of those who do wrong; for like the grass they will soon wither, like green plants they will soon die away." (Psalm 37:1-2). Asaph provides the same insight: "When I tried to understand all this, it was oppressive to me till I entered the sanctuary of God; then I understood their final destiny. Surely you place them on slippery ground; you cast them down to ruin. How suddenly are they destroyed, completely swept away by terrors!" (Psalm 73:16-19).

God makes clear that man cannot fully grasp the way in which he works: "Look at the nations and watch – and be utterly amazed. For I am going to do something in your days that you would not believe even if you were told." (Habbakuk 1:5). The fact that the Almighty is beyond our complete understanding is emphasised by St Paul: "Oh, the depths of the riches of the wisdom and knowledge of God! How unsearchable his judgments, and his paths beyond tracing out! 'Who has known the mind of the Lord? Or who has been his counsellor?'" (Romans 11:33-34, quoting Isaiah 40:13).

Form and truth.

The Israelites believed that they had been faithful to God. They believed that they were "more righteous than [the Babylonians]" (Habbakuk 1:13). They had used all the correct forms for their worship and sacrifices, without realising that these had been little more than empty show, a farce and a travesty. They had obeyed the letter of the law whilst ignoring its spirit. Now they are confronted by the fact that form without truth is worthless in the sight of God. For God has seen the "injustice ... wrong ... destruction and violence ... strife and conflict" (Habbakuk 1:3) of which Habbakuk complained and is bringing judgment on those responsible for it. The message for us is that, unless we move beyond form to truth, we will always be less than we should be. We need to grasp hold of truth, for "the truth will set [us] free." (John 8:32).

Acceptance and trust.

From the start, Habbakuk accepts the will of God. He acknowledges that God has "appointed [the Babylonians] to execute judgment" (Habbakuk 1:12) and he does not question God's justice in doing so. Yet it is a grudging acceptance. Still he asks: "Your eyes are too pure to look on evil; you cannot tolerate wrong. Why then do you tolerate the treacherous? Why are you silent while the wicked swallow up those more righteous than themselves?" (Habbakuk 1:13).

God's answers do not entirely do away with Habbakuk's perplexity. Indeed, to some extent they even increase it, since it is difficult for a human being to comprehend how God might bring good through an event like the Babylonian conquest and the Israelites' subsequent captivity. Even though he is told that the corrupt destroyer (Babylon) will eventually be destroyed, that must have seemed cold comfort. In short, Habbakuk had to learn trust, and so do we. Our task is to rest in God's appointments and await his activity in a spirit of worship.

Living by faith.

The complaints that Habbakuk makes to God are remarkable in several ways: they assume the possibility of dialogue; they assume that God cares; and they assume that God intervenes in his world. These assumptions and the way in which God responds show some of the essential differences between the God of the Bible and the deities of other religions. He is not an impersonal force, but a person. He is not so far above and beyond man that there is no way for us to interact with him, but he is instead a God who yearns for relationship with us. He is not remote from his creation, but intimately concerned with every aspect of it.

The fundamental questions that Habbakuk puts to God are: "Why do you tolerate wrong?" (Habbakuk 1:3); "Why are you silent ...?" (Habbakuk 1:13); and "How long ...?" (Habbakuk 1:2). The answers are surprising. It is not the case that God tolerates wrong: "I am going to do something in your days" (Habbakuk 1:5), just that his timing and his way of working are different from ours. Far from being silent, God engages in debate with Habbakuk , but he does not work according to human agendas. God "is not slow in keeping his promise, as some understand slowness. He is patient with you, not wanting anyone to perish, but everyone to come to repentance." (2 Peter 3:9).

God's replies take Habbakuk beyond logic to faith, beyond form to truth and beyond acceptance to trust. The prophet comes to see that the proper response is to "stand at my watch ... to see what [God] will say to me" (Habbakuk 2:1). In the light of God's revelation about how and when he is working, his people are to live patiently and to live by faith, trusting in their sovereign Lord. These same principles that apply in the realm of our personal spiritual deliverance apply equally to our national salvation.

Conclusion.

For centuries, Norman oppression created a divided society in England. The breach is writ not just in language, but in the physical environment. In Nottingham, for example, there were long two separate boroughs: a Norman clustered around the castle and an Anglo-Saxon centred on St Mary's church, about a mile away. Only gradually did a unified city emerge, just as a new nation was knit painfully from the long years of Norman rule.

Currently our society is more divided than it has been for many years. Beneath a pleasing surface and the illusion of harmony lie divisions of wealth, race, religion, culture and language. Some who are citizens of this land inhabit a country of the mind that is not England. Some are excluded from the opportunities that most of us take for granted. Some have lives that are blighted by hardship and pain. In responding to these situations, too often we trust to our own strength rather than turning to God. Too often we hide behind correct forms rather than risk telling the truth. Too often we accept our fellows grudgingly rather than placing genuine trust in them. We should ask ourselves how God reacts to these things and what He wants us to do about it. Like Habbakuk, we need to "stand at [our] watch and station [ourselves] on the ramparts ... to see what he will say to [us]" (Habbakuk 2:1). Like the Israelites of old, we need to "write down the revelation and make it plain" (Habbakuk 2:2) by speaking God's truth into our workplaces, homes and politics. Like our spiritual forebears, we need to "wait for [God's revelation]" (Habbakuk 2:3) and learn that "the righteous will live by his faith" (Habbakuk 2:4).

Above all, we need to move beyond logic to faith, beyond form to truth and beyond acceptance to trust. This is the way to build a restored England, harmonious and in right relationship with her God. This is the way to integrate the stranger, the outcast and the lost. This is the way to salve the hurts of the despised and downtrodden.

8. Stirrings

Mark 4:30-34.

Key word: freedom.

In a muddy field by the banks of the Thames gathered the signatories to a momentous document: on one side a disgruntled King John, on the other a knot of rebellious barons and the Archbishop of Canterbury, Stephen Langton. Magna Carta (the Great Charter) was signed at Runnymede in Surrey on 15 June 1215. It is widely regarded as the foundation stone of English liberties and a key text of the English constitution. Such was its totemic power that it was repeatedly re-issued by subsequent kings: by Henry III and Edward I. An amendment during the latter's reign established the principle of 'no taxation without representation.'

On its face, the document is hardly a democrats' manifesto. Its sixty three clauses focus largely on matters of concern only to a privileged few, with two primary aims: to define (and thereby limit) the feudal rights of the Crown and to protect the privileges of the Church. Yet by placing a brake on the unfettered exercise of royal authority, it became a bulwark against all oppression. Combined with the writ of habeas corpus (a requirement for the authorities to produce in court those being held in custody), the result was to secure for Englishmen an unprecedented degree of freedom from arbitrary rule.[21] Thus reaction to the rapacity of grasping John Lackland redounded to the ultimate benefit of his subjects.

The aggressive expansionism of Plantagenet kings produced a similar defining moment in Scotland: the signing of the Declaration of Arbroath in 1320. The signatories declared, "We are resolved never to submit to English domination. We are fighting for freedom and freedom only." It was a long struggle. William Wallace (1270-1305) first roused Scottish resistance, but success at the battle of Stirling Bridge in 1297 was followed by defeat at Falkirk the very next year. Wallace went into hiding, was betrayed and at length was hanged in London as a common bandit, becoming both martyr and hero of Scotland's cause. After his death Robert the Bruce took up the baton. He, too, was hounded and defeated, until inspired by a spider in a cave to try, try and try again. His perseverance was rewarded. Though it was not fully apparent for generations, victory over the forces of Edward II at Bannockburn in 1314 effectively set the

---

[21] The Habeas Corpus Act was passed in 1679 during the reign of Charles II.

seal on Scottish independence. Thus were seeds of freedom nurtured in England and her northern neighbour. From them in time grew great oaks.

Seed.

The parable of the mustard seed appears in the gospels of Matthew (Matthew 13:31-32), Mark (Mark 4:30-32) and Luke (Luke 13:18-19). In it, Jesus tells one of many stories in which he describes what the kingdom of heaven is like. The similes in other parables range from growing seed (Mark 4:26-29) to yeast (Matthew 13:33), hidden treasure (Matthew 13:44), a valuable pearl (Matthew 13:45-46) and a net (Matthew 13:47-50).

From amongst all these, Mark chooses to concentrate on the two that use seeds to illustrate the point, and places these hard on the heels of a parable about a farmer sowing (Mark 4:1-20). In doing this, he emphasises that the images of seed are redolent with meaning, both explicit and implicit. They tell of extraordinary results coming from what might look like unpromising material, results that come about with some element of human involvement, but the real source of which is God. They tell of activity that is hidden from the eyes of man, but which is of tremendous significance nevertheless. They give an inkling of great things to come.

Planting and nurturing.

There is hidden potential in seed. Whether this potential is realised depends on what is done with and to it. In deserts, seeds can lie dormant for years, yet burst suddenly to life at the first drop of rain. The key word is 'when': "Yet when it is planted, it grows" (Mark 4:32). This points to the part that human beings have to play in furthering the kingdom of God, for the seed is one that "you [that is, we] plant in the ground." (Mark 4:31). We need to undertake the actions of planting and nurturing, and then God will do the rest. He has created the seed and all its potential. He will cause it to germinate, bud and flower. In the tremendous work of bringing about the kingdom of God on earth, however, he has made us his co-workers.

Our role is important, but needs to be kept in perspective. Speaking about the growth of the Christian community in Corinth, St Paul said: "I planted the seed, Apollos watered it, but God made it grow. So neither he who plants nor he who waters is anything, but only God, who makes things grow. The man who plants and the man who waters have one purpose, and each will be rewarded according to his own labour. For we are God's fellow-workers; you are God's field, God's building." (1 Corinthians 3:6-9).

Human involvement in the process of helping bring about God's kingdom does not end with the act of planting. Seeds need nurturing. They need to be watered, protected from frost and kept free of weeds. Of course, God is capable of bringing about astonishing things without help from anyone, but if we wish to see the fullness of his kingdom on earth, we need to be involved and to remain so. Unless the church, which is the community of all believers, really acts as the body of Christ and is unified, being "a unit, though it is made up of many parts" (1 Corinthians 12:12), potential will remain unfulfilled.

Growth.

The results that we can expect God to bring from our activity are out of all proportion to what we do. We start with "the smallest seed you plant in the ground" (Mark 4:31) and end up with "the largest of all garden plants, with such big branches that the birds of the air can perch in its shade." (Mark 4:32). In the wondrous process of growth, we are reminded of the cycle of life and its seasonality. We are reminded of God's bounty, of his comfort and of his protection. We see, too, the economy of his activity: that there will be from one and the same plant food, shelter and the source of future growth as more seeds are generated.

The goodness of God is shown by the fact that the blessings that come through growth in his kingdom work to the benefit of all, not merely the righteous. Thus "the birds of the air can perch in [the] shade [of the plant]." (Mark 4:32). There is no restriction on who has access to these benefits, for God "causes his sun to rise on the evil and the good, and sends rain on the righteous and the unrighteous." (Matthew 5:45). Blessing is there for all who care to take advantage of it, though the element of choice is always present: birds may seek shade by perching in the branches and men by sheltering under them, but they do not have to. We have to opt in to the Kingdom of God.

Jesus twice came back to the image of seeds to illustrate essential elements in the process of our opting in to the kingdom of God and of being catalysts for its growth. He emphasised that our effectiveness is related to our faith: "if you have faith as small as a mustard seed ... nothing will be impossible for you." (Matthew 17:20-21). Time and again, we see people bringing what seem like inadequate resources to a task, and God giving the increase to make them more than equal to what is needed. We see this in history and we see it in Scripture: thus the feeding of the five thousand, for example (Matthew 14:15-21; Mark 6:35-44; Luke 9:12-17 and John 6:4-13). Faith works as a multiplier, sparking and turbo-charging growth.

Jesus also used seeds to remind us of life cycles and seasonality: "Unless a grain of wheat falls to the ground and dies, it remains only a single seed. But if it dies, it produces many seeds." (John 12:24). One of the paradoxes of God's kingdom is that prodigious growth involves death. The death that is spoken of is both literal and metaphorical. There are Christians in each generation who are called to die a literal death for their faith. All Christians, however, are called to die a metaphorical death: we must die to our former selves and we must "die to sins and live for righteousness." (1 Peter 2:24). The ultimate paradox is that, "He who believes in [Jesus] will live, even though he dies, and whoever lives and believes in [Jesus] will never die." (John 11:26). This paradox would be difficult indeed to grasp, were it not for the fact that we see its truth played out in the natural world around us, year by year and season by season.

Speaking in parables.

Jesus made great use of stories as an aid to teaching. Mark tells us that: "With many similar parables Jesus spoke the word to them, as much as they could understand. He did not say anything to them without using a parable. But when he was alone with his own disciples, he explained everything." (Mark 4:33-34) This underlines the fact that Jesus' message was carefully tailored. Parables were used to illustrate truths, stimulate thinking and awaken spiritual perception. Their images and language were accessible to all – everyday folk in a largely agricultural society would have identified easily with stories about seeds – but people in general were not ready for the full truth of the gospel. Jesus did not burden them with concepts that would have gone over their heads, but instead gave them "as much as they could understand." (Mark 4:33).

When alone with his disciples, Jesus taught more specifically, for even those closest to him usually had to have things explained. He was continually equipping and training his disciples. They needed to understand the message fully because in a short time it was they who would be preaching it to the nations. Yet something else is at work here. Jesus told his disciples that: "… The secret of the kingdom of God has been given to you. But to those on the outside everything is said in parables ..." (Mark 4:11). The underlying message of the parables was explosive. It was not what people wanted or expected to hear, though it was the truth. Many therefore found it difficult to accept, remaining "ever seeing but never perceiving, and ever hearing but never understanding" (Isaiah 6:9-10, Matthew 13:14, Mark 4:12 and Luke 8:10). On hearing the discourse in which Jesus called himself "the bread of life" (John 6:48), for example, "many of his disciples said, 'This is a hard teaching. Who can accept it?'" (John 6:60) and "From this time many of his disciples turned back and no longer followed him." (John 6:66).

Time and again, Jesus presaged what he said with the phrase "I tell you the truth." He said that he is "the way, the truth and the life" (John 14:6). He reminded us that with truth comes freedom, for "the truth will set you free." (John 8:32). The kind of truth that Jesus spoke about, a truth that permits no lame excuses or shifting of blame, a truth that cuts through dross and illuminates what is really worthwhile, a truth that can sometimes be uncomfortable or run counter to all that we want to hear seems in short supply in present-day England. We need to rediscover this truth, and with it our freedom.

Conclusion.

The Germanic tribes that settled England were noted for their love of freedom: the Roman historian Tacitus remarks on their independent spirit. Freedom is one of the essentials of what it is to be an Englishman: freedom from arbitrary rule, from government caprice and from the prying eyes of those who (to quote Elizabeth I) would "make windows into men's souls." Three hundred and sixty years ago the Parliamentary soldiers who reflected on why the Civil War was fought characterised it as having been for "the good old cause". By this they meant the cause of English liberty, which they traced back beyond Magna Carta to the days when our forebears first reached these shores.

Freedom is also one of the essentials of what it is to be a Christian. The prophet Isaiah proclaimed "freedom to the captives and release from darkness for the prisoners" (Isaiah 61:1). Jesus set people free: from sickness, from enslavement to dark forces and from the bonds of sin. He announced that he came to purchase our liberty: "the Son of Man did not come to be served, but ... to give his life as a ransom for many." (Mark 10:45).

The freedom that we enjoy has found fertile soil in England precisely because this has for generation upon generation been a Christian land. Sometimes in our history the flame of freedom has burned low, but it has never been wholly put out. Now we need to rouse ourselves afresh for the good old cause, since the flame gutters dangerously. If we are to preserve our freedom, we need first to disentangle cause and effect. Freedom of speech, freedom of association, freedom of the press and all the other freedoms we cherish are but effects. Their source is a much more fundamental freedom: the truth that sets us free to enjoy and use wisely all other liberties. Thus our starting point must be to nurture this truth, to sow it widely and cause it to grow.

The seeds that we plant and tend may seem tiny and insignificant to us, but they have eternal effects: for good or ill, through act or omission. Each time we forgo the chance to do the smallest thing to advance the Kingdom of God, there is a vast potential unfulfilled. Each time we fail to raise our voices against what is wrong, we permit the enemy to advance. Correspondingly, we have no way of knowing the full extent of the harvest that will come from our lives. Forgotten words of kindness, acts of love and moments of self-denial will all bear fruit in ways more wonderful than we can imagine. We too readily forget that "each man has his own gift from God" (1 Corinthians 7:7) and that for each there is a "field that God has assigned to us" (2 Corinthians 10:13).

We need to develop the perspective of the Kingdom of God and allow this to inform every aspect of our thoughts and conduct. We have been made co-workers with God. We are planting and nurturing for the sake of the present generation, but also for the seed that springs from us, our offspring and descendants, our physical and spiritual progeny. We must not let them down.

9. Apocalypse

Revelation 16:1-14.

Key word: direction.

In 1348 England caught the full force of a pandemic that had already ravaged Asia and other areas of Europe. It was fuelled by three related types of plague, two carried by rats and one on the air. The symptoms were horrific: the most common, bubonic form caused painful swellings in groin and armpit, with dark blotches on the skin from internal bleeding. Three or four days of unbearable pain were followed by certain death if the bubo did not burst beforehand. The affliction was called the Pestilence or the Great Pestilence, otherwise known as the Black Death.

It is commonly reckoned that something like one third of the population of Europe died between 1346 and 1353, though some hazard yet higher mortality. Contemporaries often speak of half or even three quarters of the people around them dying, though it is difficult to substantiate death on such an extravagant scale across entire countries. At all events, it is not fanciful to think of some one and a half millions dead in England, eight millions in France and perhaps some thirty millions for Europe as a whole. Those figures are horrific in themselves, the more so when we remember the population of the entire British Isles in 1346 probably did not exceed five millions.

Reactions to the horror varied from panic and wild debauchery to dutiful fortitude. Many clergy suffered disproportionately through bravely ministering to the sick and dying, whilst others fled for their lives.[22] The authorities were helpless, doctors useless. There was nothing for it but to let the disease run its course. At length, it burnt itself out in Russia in 1353, leaving behind a ravaged continent.

The psychological trauma ran deep, heightened by the fact that plague had been absent from Europe for six hundred years. No longer: there were further outbreaks from 1357 to 1365 and thereafter every ten years or so until the end of the century. The macabre Dance of Death made its appearance[23] and a new breed of mendicants, the so-called Flagellants, whipped themselves bloodily from

---

[22] The courageous and dutiful seem to have been the majority: the disease is estimated to have killed 45% of English parish priests.

[23] The earliest known painting of the Dance of Death dates from 1424. It is in the Cemetery of the Innocents in Paris.

town to town in a bizarre enactment of repentance. The conviction reigned that God was punishing mankind for its sins. Many claimed that the end of the world was nigh.

The wrath of God.

The book of Revelation speaks clearly of "God's wrath." (Revelation 16:1). It tells of seven plagues that are "poured out" (Revelation 16:2, 3, 4, 8, 10, 12 and 17). These are sent at God's instruction: "I heard a loud voice from the temple saying to the seven angels, 'Go, pour out the seven bowls of God's wrath on the earth.'" (Revelation 16:1). God is explicitly said to be the one who "had control over these plagues" (Revelation 16:9). They mirror many of those that came upon Egypt when Pharoah refused to free the Israelites: blood (Exodus 7:14-21), frogs (Exodus 8:5-14), boils (Exodus 9:8-11) and darkness (Exodus 10:21-26).

The whole concept of a God who can be angry and who can visit plagues upon the earth is one with which we tend to be deeply uncomfortable. We are uncomfortable since we imagine that this sits uneasily with the idea that "God is love" (1 John 4:8). We are uncomfortable because our society values tolerance so highly and to be angry seems so very intolerant. We are uncomfortable because of the implications that God's wrath has for ourselves and for the lives that we lead.

We need to grow up. We have to recognise that God cannot be consistent in his character without also having the capacity for anger. A God who loves and cares deeply for his Creation, who esteems all that is good, who is the personification of all that is just and true and holy cannot but be angry at evil, sin, injustice and vice. The consequence is this: the Lord has provided and holds out the means for our salvation, but if we reject it, judgment will come. It will come unwillingly on God's part, for he takes "no pleasure in the death of the wicked, but [desires] rather that they turn from their ways and live." (Ezekiel 33:11). It will come for no other reasons than our rebellion and rejection of the Almighty. It will come as an inevitable result of the application of the Lord's justice in circumstances where we have failed to seize his free offer of forgiveness. It will come after we have had every opportunity and all the evidence we need to see the right path and to take it.

Things could be different if only we would turn to God, but the awful truth is that many will not. In view of this, what is described is "what must take place." (Revelation 4:1).

Discipline and judgment.

God does not punish because he is a sadist. He acts with purpose and he acts proportionately.

The Lord's aim is first and foremost is to discipline us: to teach, train, prune, equip and turn from wrongdoing. This is not pleasant, with the result that we tend too often to confuse the positive of discipline with something negative. Scripture encourages us instead to: "Endure hardship as discipline; for God is treating you as sons. For what son is not disciplined by his father? If you are not disciplined (and everyone undergoes discipline), then you are illegitimate children and not true sons. Moreover, we have all had human fathers who disciplined us and we respected them for it. How much more should we submit to the Father of our spirits and live? Our fathers disciplined us for a little while as they thought best; but God disciplines us for our good, that we may share in his holiness. No discipline seems pleasant at the time, but painful. Later on, however, it produces a harvest of righteousness and peace for those who have been trained by it." (Hebrews 12:7-11)

Only as a last resort does God carry out judgment on those who will not turn from wrongdoing. This judgment is always just: "You are just in these judgments ... and you have given ... as they deserve ... Yes, Lord God Almighty, true and just are your judgments." (Revelation 16:5-7). Hence it is related in nature and extent to what is being punished. As Jesus warns, "with the measure you use, it will be measured to you." (Matthew 7:2). The proportionate nature of God's judgment means that the punishment fits the crime: "they have shed the blood of your saints and prophets, and you have given them blood to drink as they deserve." (Revelation 16:6).

The plague brought by the first angel is apparently world-wide in its effect, but aimed at a specific group. Although it is fashionable in some quarters to explain away and excuse wrong behaviour, we know from our own experience that in the long run individuals, communities and even whole nations tend to suffer for their crimes. When such suffering comes, often there is a grim and obvious correlation between cause and effect. "The first angel went and poured out his bowl on the land, and ugly and painful sores broke out on the people who had the mark of the beast and worshipped his image." (Revelation 16:2). We are given to understand that the followers of evil have things that specially characterise them and mark them off from others, and these are the ones who fall victim to the first plague. As in the present day, there are some evils that afflict those who give themselves over to wickedness but do not affect others.

The beast and his kingdom.

Just as those who follow "the beast and worshipped his image" (Revelation 16:2) are set apart, so the people of God should be set apart, too. The Bible often uses "the world" as contrast and counterpoint to the kingdom of heaven. Jesus reminds the people of God that they "do not belong to the world, but I have chosen you out of the world. That is why the world hates you." (John 15:19). Similarly, "they are not of the world any more than I am." (John 17:14). People who follow Christ are called upon to shun the world and its works: "Do not love the world or anything in the world ... the cravings of sinful man, the lust of his eyes and the boasting of what he has and does ..." (1 John 2:15). Indeed, "friendship with the world is hatred towards God." (James 4:4) and "the wisdom of this world is foolishness" (1 Corinthians 3:19).

The world, used in this sense, belongs to "the beast and his kingdom." (Revelation 16:10). In other words, it is under the control of Satan and the forces of darkness. Their aim is to deceive and destroy, to kill, scatter and frustrate the coming of the Kingdom of God. So, as the "water [of the great river Euphrates] was dried up to prepare the way for the kings of the east ... I saw three evil spirits that looked like frogs; they came out of the mouth of the dragon, out of the mouth of the beast and out of the mouth of the false prophet. They are spirits of demons performing miraculous signs, and they go out to the kings of the whole world, to gather them for the battle on the great day of God Almighty." (Revelation 16:12-14).

The picture is of insidious propaganda that will lead people to accept and support the cause of evil. The result is that right to the last there remain "people who had the mark of the beast and worshipped his image." (Revelation 16:2). This is so notwithstanding the fact that "The fifth angel poured out his bowl on the throne of the beast, and his kingdom was plunged into darkness." (Revelation 16:10). Incredible as it might seem, some will persist in stubborn denial of and hatred towards God despite all evidence.

Reaction and repentance.

Failure to accept the evidence is shown in the reaction to the plagues that God sends. It is wilful, muddled and misguided. People:

Confuse the problem and the solution: "Men gnawed their tongues in agony and cursed the God of heaven because of their pains and sores" (Revelation 16:10-11).

Set themselves in opposition to God: "they cursed the name of God ... and cursed the God of heaven" (Revelation 16:9 and 11).

Fail to learn from their mistakes: "they refused to repent and glorify him ... they refused to repent of what they had done." (Revelation 16:9 and 11).

There is a complete absence of the only proper response, which is repentance and turning to he who made us. It is through admitting what we have done wrong, saying sorry for it and making a decision to forswear ungodliness that we take the necessary first step towards salvation and God's blessing. If we fail to do this, we remain enemies of God and hence under his judgment.

Conclusion.

Nobody would seriously argue that only wicked people died in the Black Death. The disease was no respecter of age, status or personal sanctity. It was not the plague described in Revelation 16:2. We simply are not in a position to know whether it was a just judgment from God or merely a result of living in a fallen world. What we can know, however, is how to react to adversity and how to adopt a proper spiritual perspective on it, using it for our discipline and growth rather than as something that drives us further from our heavenly Father.

Our land is undergoing affliction. This is not primarily physical in its nature, though it has physical manifestations. It is not the passing hardship of an economic cycle but a more fundamental malaise that goes to the root of our society, a deep spiritual sickness. It will result in a miserable existence and everlasting death for large numbers of our countrymen unless we act vigorously to combat it. We have brought it on ourselves through our pride, our rejection of God and our disregard for his laws. Year by year and generation upon generation we see the spiral of decline grow steeper as minor delinquencies and relatively harmless failings turn to something altogether uglier and more intractable. With each turn of the screw, we ratchet up the pressure by applying force in the same direction instead of recognising that the direction itself needs to change. We face a choice: either to treat this as an occasion to learn discipline and turn back to what is right, or to carry on as we have in years gone by. If we choose the former, we can expect God's blessing. If we choose the latter, we will continue to experience "pains and sores" (Revelation 16: 11). We will then stand amongst those who "refused to repent and glorify [the Lord]" (Revelation 16:9) and those who "refused to repent of what they had done." (Revelation 16:11).

When we come to a fork in the road and do not know the way, it is usually a good idea to read the road signs. In the same fashion, we need to read the spiritual signs. For the best part of half a century, our society has followed a path that promised freedom. The underlying thrust of thought was this: that our troubles arose out of guilt and repression, which came from being in thrall to the outdated and unscientific concept of God. Far from our being in the grip of Original Sin, all that was needed to perfect man was to create the right environment for him. It was therefore necessary to change society. The major element of this change was to do away with God, for this would enable liberation – political, sexual and cultural. So we were to reach the sunlit uplands of a Brave New World. This promise has turned out to be utterly false. It has delivered the very opposite of what it claimed, yet is still peddled as a credible blueprint. It is deceptive and beguiling propaganda, but no less propaganda for all that.

We must be the ones to read the signs and give direction. We need to retrace our steps to where we left the true path and start anew on the right track. Such is the only hope of health and wellbeing for our nation.

10. Pilgrims and ploughmen

Micah 4:1-13.

Key word: praise.

Geoffrey Chaucer, who lived between about 1340 and 1400, is widely reckoned the poetic genius of Middle English. His life was full of incident, and he became an active participant in many of the major events of the day. He was almost certainly of an age to remember the horror of the Black Death. He fought in France during the Hundred Years' War, being captured and later ransomed, was employed on diplomatic missions to France and Italy and most likely on secret service in Flanders. He was probably present at Smithfield in 1381 when the young king Richard II confronted Wat Tyler and the rebels of the Great (or Peasants') Revolt.

Chaucer's *Canterbury Tales* are rightly famous, painting a picture of a whole society in the shape of thirty two pilgrims riding together from tavern to cathedral, entertaining each other and revealing themselves as they do so. His keen eye and sharp pen describe many of the issues of his day, being particularly scathing of corruption, greed and hypocrisy amongst the clergy.

More or less contemporary and almost equally esteemed is *The Vision concerning Piers Ploughman*, usually attributed to William Langland. Here Conscience preaches to the people, Repentance moves their hearts and many are prompted to seek the way of Truth with the guidance of the trusty ploughman.

The world that these poems describe was one of almost bewildering social change. Formerly immutable hierarchies were starting to crumble. Widespread death from plague loosened the bonds of feudalism and the survivors of a decimated peasantry found their bargaining position much improved. Pressure on the land was reduced, workers were in short supply and wages began to creep upwards. Increasingly, obligations of service were commuted to cash payments. All over Europe, attempts were made to preserve the old economic order. In England, the Statute of Labourers was passed in 1351 to hold down wages. Resentment against such measures was widespread and consequently popular risings were commonplace in France, Germany and elsewhere. Revolt usually fizzled quickly with the killing of rebel leaders and dispersal of their followers, but the medieval world was passing.

There was a ferment of ideas: John Wycliffe made the first translation of the Bible into English and the rebel priest John Ball spread egalitarian views. In the popular ditty of the day: "When Adam delved and Eve span, who was then the gentleman?" This caught the spirit of the time. Following Wycliffe's lead, the Lollards,[24] objected to prayers for the dead, priestly celibacy and other church ordinances. They attacked the wealth and intolerance of the clergy, proclaimed the right of every man to examine the Bible for himself and held that all authority was founded on God's grace. This was revolutionary indeed, for it led all too easily to the conclusion that wicked kings, popes and priests should have no power. The authorities could not let this pass. Wycliffe was silenced and those who espoused his teaching were persecuted to extinction. Their thoughts, however, were not so easily expunged and budded afresh in the Protestant Reformation some hundred and fifty years later.[25]

Pilgrims.

We, too, live in a world of ferment. The demise of deference, the end of old certainties and the undermining of formerly respected institutions all mark the passing of an era. With the way ahead uncertain, now more than ever we need to "walk in [the Lord's] paths" (Micah 4:2), to be a pilgrim people. This means that we need to:

Honour and worship God: to treat "the mountain of the LORDs temple ... as chief among the mountains" and to raise it "above the hills" (Micah 4:1).

Move in God's direction, not away from him: "let us go up to the mountain of the LORD, to the house of the God of Jacob." (Micah 4:2)

Learn from God: "He will teach us his ways, so that we may walk in his paths." (Micah 4:2).

Accept God's laws and judgments: "The law will go out from Zion, the word of the LORD from Jerusalem. He will judge between many peoples and will settle disputes for strong nations far and wide." (Micah 4:2-3)

In effect, this comes down to giving proper weight to the first four of the Ten Commandments, those which deal with the relationship between God and man. First and foremost: "You shall have no other gods before me." (Exodus 20:3). We should put God first, regardless of what others say or think: "All the

---

[24] Derived from the Dutch *lollen*, meaning to sing in a low voice. The same root gives us the word lullaby.

[25] Wycliffe's teachings influenced Bohemian religious reformer Jan Hus (1369-1415) and, through him, Martin Luther (1483-1546). Tradition dates the start of the Protestant Reformation to 1517, when Luther nailed his *Ninety-five Theses* to the door of the *Schlosskirche* (castle church) in Wittenberg.

nations may walk in the name of their gods; we will walk in the name of the LORD our God for ever and ever." (Micah 4:5).

Like Chaucer, we should have no time for corruption, greed or hypocrisy, wherever these may appear.

Ploughmen.

As well as being pilgrims, we need to be ploughmen, to prepare ground for planting. In painting a picture of the coming of the kingdom of God, Micah uses farming images: of ploughshares (Micah 4:3), of the gathering of "sheaves to the threshing-floor" (Micah 4:12) and of threshing (Micah 4:13). We are called to husbandry of the land, in both literal and metaphorical senses. Above all, we are called to husbandry of its people, so that a great crop may be harvested for God.

Micah shows how to go about this process of husbandry. We need so to order our affairs that the pursuit of peace, justice and goodwill will characterise our dealings amongst ourselves and with others, so that all obtain a decent stake in society. Then: "They will beat their swords into ploughshares and their spears into pruning hooks. Nation will not take up sword against nation, nor will they train for war any more. Every man will sit under his own vine and under his own fig tree, and no-one will make them afraid, for the LORD Almighty has spoken." (Micah 4:3-4).

So important is this message that the Lord sent two separate men to preach it. The words of Micah 4:1-3 repeat almost exactly those spoken by his near contemporary, the prophet Isaiah: see Isaiah 2:2-4. They also echo the last six of the Ten Commandments, those which deal with the relationships between men, which tell us to honour our parents and forbid us to murder, commit adultery, steal, lie and covet (Exodus 20:12-17). Or, as Jesus put it: "Love your neighbour as yourself" (Matthew 22:39) and "Do to others as you would have them do to you." (Luke 6:31).

Like the protagonists of *Piers Ploughman*, we must open ourselves to the workings of conscience, repentance and truth. When this genuinely happens in our lives, there will be an overflow to our fellow men and a transformation of society.

Ransomed, healed.

In present-day England relationships with both God and our fellow men have gone awry. We put man before God and ourselves before anyone else. We have become enslaved by the very things that promised to set us free and bring us fulfilment: by the mindless pursuit of material wellbeing, by treating things of no account as though they had moral and spiritual worth, by our own sin. Land that should be put to the plough has been lying fallow so long that it is choked with weeds. Too few pilgrims now tread the Lord's paths and they, too, are in danger of becoming overgrown.

The southern Israelite kingdom of Judah in Micah's day was in a similar state of moral and spiritual decline. Things had gone so far that God's judgment was about to be played out: "Writhe in agony, O Daughter of Zion, like a woman in labour, for now you must leave the city to camp in the open field. You will go to Babylon" (Micah 4:10). The coming Babylonian attack and the resulting exile were just around the corner.

Such is God's love for his people, however, that he is not prepared to let matters rest there. Micah describes a folk redeemed from slavery, bought back by the God who loves them: "you will be rescued ... the LORD will redeem you out of the hand of your enemies." (Micah 4:10). Where previously things were scattered, broken apart and estranged, there is gathering, mending and putting back together: "I will gather the lame, I will assemble the exiles and those I have brought to grief." (Micah 4:6).

The image of paying a ransom to redeem a captive or a slave appears again and again throughout the Bible.[26] The price of our freedom, of course, was beyond reckoning. It was paid by Jesus on the cross.

Restored, forgiven.

The people bought at such a cost have been redeemed for a purpose. They are to be the kernel of new growth. For this, God chooses the small, weak, crippled and outcast: "I will make the lame a remnant, those driven away a strong nation" (Micah 4:7). This ragtag group, so unpromising to human eyes, is to be the recipient of God's favour to an extraordinary degree. They are the ones who will become what God had always intended his people to be. For this coming "royal priesthood" (1 Peter 2:9), the spearhead and vanguard of God's kingdom come to earth, the language of sovereignty is used: "the former dominion will be restored to you; kingship will come to the Daughter of Jerusalem" (Micah 4:8).

As the remnant is restored, so will be the practice of true religion, alongside the kingdom of peace. Energy and resources will be turned from destruction to construction, as "swords [are beaten] into ploughshares and ... spears into pruning hooks." (Micah 4:3). The result is that there will be ease and plenty: "Every man will sit under his own vine and his own fig tree." (Micah 4:4).

With all this in view, God reminds his people that they have no need to fear and no need to be downcast, for he is their guide and ruler and he is

---

[26] The thirty pieces of silver that were paid to Judas Iscariot for his betrayal of Jesus was the price of a slave among the Israelites in ancient times: see Exodus 21:32.

sovereign over all the earth: "Why do you now cry aloud – have you no king? Has your counsellor perished, that pain seizes you like a woman in labour?" (Micah 4:9).

Conclusion.

Spiritually, the current state of England is dire. We might be tempted to agree that overwhelming forces "are gathered against [us, saying] 'Let her be defiled, let our eyes gloat over [them]'" (Micah 4:11).

The Lord has a part for us to play in helping to change this state of affairs and to assist in bringing about his kingdom. We are to act as the "watchtower of the flock [and the]... stronghold of the Daughter of Zion" (Micah 4:8). In the recent past, we have signally failed in these roles. Our failure should cause us shame and repentance, but should not lead to our becoming downhearted or inactive. We should remind ourselves that we have indeed a King and that our Counsellor has not perished. If we turn again to our Lord, there is the certainty that we and our land will be ransomed, healed, restored and forgiven.

Instead of leading us to give way to gloom, Micah's prophecy should inspire hope. For those who plot evil: "do not know the thoughts of the LORD; they do not understand his plan, he who gathers them like sheaves to the threshing floor." (Micah 4:12) Amidst all that is wrong in our society, amidst all that is broken and corrupted, there is the promise of redemption and renewal. To ensure that we make these promises our own, we need to be pilgrims and ploughmen. If we are faithful, God will say to us: "Rise and thresh, O Daughter of Zion, for I will give you horns of iron; I will give you hooves of bronze and you will break to pieces many nations." (Micah 4:13). A nation can be defined as a people under the same government and inhabiting the same country, and here the nations of which the prophet speaks are spiritual as much as physical – groups which stand in opposition to God and instead are denizens of the powers of darkness. These take many forms. Being evil, they do not form a homogeneous whole but are often characterised by hatred, division, strife, enmity and jealousy amongst themselves. Thus the nations whose power we must break are not so much external as internal. Our ability to confront and defeat them will come about not for our aggrandisement, but so that we may "devote their ill-gotten gains to the Lord, their wealth to the Lord of all the earth." (Micah 4:13).

Micah's prophecy reminds us that we should be full of praise for God, for his mercy and goodness. He is waiting to pour these out on us. Our nation needs only to turn to him with heartfelt sorrow for its wrongdoing, to ask in faith and trust for his blessing and the treasures of God's kingdom will be opened to us. The ball is in our court.

11. Side of the angels?

Proverbs 2:1-15.

Key word: vision.

For those who bemoan the moral decline of modern Englishmen, history can be a good antidote. Such was the profanity of the English soldiery during the Hundred Years' War that the French named them *"les goddams."* We are accustomed to look with pride and some degree of astonishment at the roll call of victory after victory against seemingly impossible odds during this conflict: on sea at Sluys (1340), on land at Crécy (1346), Poitiers (1356), Agincourt (1415), Rouvrai (1429) and a dozen more besides. We choose to avert our eyes from the widespread practice of the chevauchée, an armed raid through French-held territory characterised more often by pillage, rape and murder than any real military objective. We prefer not to consider the activities of the so-called Free Companies, mercenaries who treated France as their playground, where fortunes could be made on the back of plunder. In truth, beneath the gloss of victory lay little glory.

By 1429 France was in a pitiable state. Large swathes of the country were under the control of England or her ally, Burgundy. French armies had been defeated time and again by a foe whose weaponry, tactics and soldiering ability seemed in every way superior. Her capital was in the hands of the enemy and the royal court had been driven to a provincial backwater at Chinon. She had indeed no king, the dauphin being as yet uncrowned, his paternity in question and the legitimacy of his claim to the crown challenged by the English. Dissolution and dithering marked his conduct.

Worse yet, a new English offensive was under way. The fearsome warrior king Henry V had died in 1422 leaving an infant son, but the prosecution of the war scarce faltered. The Duke of Bedford, regent for the young Henry VI, urged his commanders forward. Orleans, key to control of the Loire valley and the French-held lands beyond, was invested. Its capture would almost certainly mark the final phase of the war and lead to all France coming under English rule.

Far from the fighting lay a little village called Domrémy. In its fields a peasant girl had since the age of thirteen heard voices and seen visions. She was known to her family and neighbours for her piety and prayerfulness, for her purity, compassion and gentleness. She is known to us as Joan of Arc (Jeanne d'Arc), the Maid of Orleans. Around eighteen years old in 1429, at this time of great peril her voices told her that now was the moment for her to save France. What she saw and heard changed the course of history. Within three years she was dead, yet in that short space the siege of Orleans was broken, the dauphin crowned king at Rheims and the English embarked on the long retreat that at length saw them expelled from France: by 1453, only the enclave of Calais remained in English hands.

Visions of victory.

By every human measure, France was without hope in the early months of 1429. By every human measure, it was ridiculous to suppose that an untutored shepherdess could win an audience with the future king of France, let alone persuade him to allow her a leading role in his armies. By every human measure, an innocent girl should have been the prey of mocking soldiers, not their revered heroine. That something more than human was at work in Joan's story is hard to deny: even her enemies conceded that, though they claimed her power was demonic. Accustomed to defeat and anticipating annihilation, the dauphin himself at first was sceptical. When Joan arrived at Chinon, he dressed as one of his courtiers and mingled with them – this in an age when few of the peasantry would have seen their ruler, or even a picture of his likeness. Yet unerringly she sought him out and fell on bended knee before him. "Most noble dauphin," she said, "the King of Heaven announces to you by me that you shall be anointed and crowned king in the city of Rheims, and that you shall be his vice-regent in France."

The dauphin nevertheless remained alert to the charge of having leagued himself with a sorceress. He thus ensured that every conceivable test was made of Joan's purity and orthodoxy, until at length he and his advisers were satisfied and she was sent with the army to relieve Orleans.

Joan's bursting on the national stage was accompanied by religious revival. Clergy travelled the country preaching and calling on the people to repent. Soldiers, mindful of the presence of the Maid in their midst, laid aside swearing and vice. Thus the French marched forth, with a girl at their head, clad in armour and bearing a banner of her own devising. The enemy against whom they turned were "wicked men ... men whose words are perverse, who leave the straight paths to walk in dark ways, who delight in doing wrong and rejoice in the perverseness of evil, whose paths are crooked and who are devious in their ways." (Proverbs 2:12-15). Generations had passed since last France claimed the field of battle against England, yet now her sons marched with new confidence. "For the LORD ... holds victory in store for the upright, he is a shield to those whose walk is blameless, for he guards the course of the just and protects the way of his faithful ones." (Proverbs 2:6-7).

Like Joan of Arc, we need to catch God's vision of the future, a vision of victory over the forces of darkness: to believe in it and work for it. Like the Maid of Orleans, we need to hear God's voice and act upon it, without quibble or delay.

Victory in store.

Since the Lord "holds victory in store for the upright" (Proverbs 2:7) we need to consider how we can claim this victory today against evil in our lives and in our land. To do so, we need the things that Solomon lists in the second chapter of Proverbs:

Wisdom: "Wisdom will save you from the ways of wicked men ..." (Proverbs 2:12).

Discretion: "Discretion will protect you ..." (Proverbs 2:11).

Understanding: "... understanding will guard you." (Proverbs 2:11).

Justice: "[the LORD] guards the course of the just ..." (Proverbs 2:8).

Faith: "[the LORD] protects the way of his faithful ones." (Proverbs 2:8).

With these will also come insight (Proverbs 2:3), knowledge (Proverbs 2:5) and the understanding of "what is right and just and fair – every good path." (Proverbs 2:9).

The source of these things is God: "For the LORD gives wisdom, and from his mouth come knowledge and understanding." (Proverbs 2:6). Indeed, "The fear of the LORD is the beginning of wisdom." (Psalm 111:10 and Proverbs 9:10). So also is it "the beginning of knowledge" (Proverbs 1:7). By speaking of "the fear of the LORD", the Bible does not mean that we are forever to live in terror of a wrathful and vengeful God. It means rather that we should bear a loving reverence for the Almighty that includes submission to his lordship and to the commands of his Word.

Laying hold of victory.

God will make wisdom, knowledge and understanding available to us in such a way that "wisdom will enter [our] heart, and knowledge will be pleasant to [our] soul." (Proverbs 2:10). However, in order for this to be so an effort on our part is called for. We need to:

Accept: "... accept [his] words and store up [his] commands within [us]" (Proverbs 2:1).

Turn: "... turn [our] ear to wisdom and apply [our] heart to understanding" (Proverbs 2:2).

Call out: "... call out for insight and cry aloud for understanding" (Proverbs 2:3).

Look: "... look for it as for silver and search for it as for hidden treasure" (Proverbs 2:4).

If we do these things, "then [we] will understand the fear of the Lord and find the knowledge of God." (Proverbs 2:5). That is to say, we will comprehend in the fullest way possible for human beings, since we will have a perspective that takes account of the spiritual as well as the earthly. Likewise, we will have the key to every kind of right conduct.

Applied on a national scale, understanding and knowledge of this kind would transform our land. Our recent history shows beyond a shadow of a doubt what wise men have always known: that technical progress avails naught unless there is wisdom in its application, that material advancement is empty unless it is regulated by "what is right and just and fair" (Proverbs 2:9) and that cleverness is of no use unless it is accompanied by insight and understanding. It shows, moreover, that action without discretion leads to excess and a society without faith crumbles from within.

Such is our current situation. We must change it by laying hold of the victory that Jesus made possible for us. This is our solemn charge: to be soldiers of Christ in the fight for the lifeblood of our land.

Victory assured.

There is an air of defeatism in present-day England that should have no place in our thinking. We, of all people, should know with firm assurance that victory is certain, not by virtue of our own strength or cleverness, but by virtue of the God who "will never leave you or forsake you." (Deuteronomy 31:6 and Joshua 1:5).Truly, "If God is for us, who can be against us?" (Romans 8:31).

We must look to the signs of God at work, be alert to his voice and be prepared to catch his vision. For this we need wisdom, understanding and insight, so that we do not just see surface effects but look behind them to spiritual reality. The people of God are reminded time and again that they should not "be ever hearing, but never understanding; be ever seeing, but never perceiving." (Isaiah 6:9, Matthew 13:14, Mark 4:12 and Acts 28:26). We need discretion so that our words and deeds will be characterised by "what is right and just and fair" (Proverbs 2:9), so that God will thereby be glorified and people will know Jesus through us. We need knowledge to help us tread "the course of the just" (Proverbs 2:8). Above all, we need faith, for it is through God that all this will come.

With eyes of faith we need to see the reality of both present and past, together with the possibilities of the future. We need to remind ourselves that:

Neither present nor past should constrain our view of what is possible.

God often chooses surprising people to be his agents – he delights in raising up the lowly to do mighty things in his name, from King David to Joan of Arc and multitudes before and since.

The decisions we make have influence – Joan could have ignored her voices and those to whom she was sent could have spurned her. When God is at work, we need to join in.

The Lord operates according to his timing, not ours. God is sovereign, but in the interval between Jesus' death on the cross and his coming again a defeated foe can still wreak havoc. We should thus be neither surprised nor discouraged by evidence of the enemy's work. Instead of disheartening us, this should fire us with God's passion for the suffering and the lost. It should encourage us to redouble our efforts.

Conclusion.

The story of Joan of Arc is a salutary one: salutary because our country was not then on the side of the angels, salutary because France endured decades of defeat before the Lord brought deliverance and salutary because Joan did not live to enjoy the earthly fruits of her success. Instead, she was captured by the Burgundians and sold to the English, who put her on trial for witchcraft. Under great pressure she at first disclaimed having received any divine commission, but when this did not set her free, she spoke with renewed courage: "If I said that God did not send me, I should condemn myself; truly, God did send me ... I have [abjured] for fear of the fire and my retraction was against the truth." She was burnt at the stake in Rouen on 30 May 1431.

All around us, at home and abroad, we see evil on the march. We see the innocent suffer and the wicked prosper. We see God apparently silent or indifferent. So it must have seemed in the long dark years for France before the tide of war turned. It is difficult for us to gain perspective on everyday events, for we do not have the advantage of seeing how things turn out in the end. That is why the lessons of history can be so valuable for us: they provide a chance to see purpose where those involved saw only confusion.

Pluck a flower and the bloom will soon fade. We have plucked freedom, democracy, rule of law, civil society and countless other good things from the soil of faith that nourished them. Without the Almighty, they are but empty forms and will wither as sure as night follows day. For years, we have lived on the legacy of the past, but this inheritance is fast being spent. We need to breathe fresh life into the empty forms of our society and for that we need the help of the God who will "save" (Proverbs 2:12), "guard" (Proverbs 2:8 and 11) and "protect" (Proverbs 2:8 and 11).

The Lord has a vision for England. It needs to be our vision, too.

12. Two tribes

Jeremiah 8:1-12.

Key word: destiny.

There is nothing like comprehensive defeat in war to sow dissent and discord. So it was in England as her gains in France were steadily eroded. Henry VI came of age in 1437, and proved a pitiful king. Military disaster overseas was compounded by incompetence at home, where his wife Margaret of Anjou dominated government. So appalling was the monarch that he was twice deposed (and once reinstated) before eventually being murdered in 1471.

A weak sovereign and a disputed succession ushered in the dynastic contest known since Victorian times as the Wars of the Roses, comprising over a quarter century of tribal strife under the banners of the white rose of York and the red rose of Lancaster. From 1450 onwards England was laid low as rival armies pressed the claims of competing candidates for the throne, each descended from Edward III: Henry VI for Lancaster and for York first its duke Richard and then his son Edward, Earl of March (later Edward IV).

Battles were fought the length and breadth of the land, from small and scrappy skirmishes to great set-pieces. The pendulum swung first one way and then the other. Richard, duke of York gained brief ascendancy after the battle of St Albans in 1455 before the Lancastrians recovered control and the upstart duke was slain in battle at Wakefield in 1460. The tide turned again with comprehensive Lancastrian defeat at Towton in 1461, where the outcome was decided by the late arrival of Yorkist reinforcements under the Duke of Norfolk. After the battle the earl of March, who had already taken the title Edward IV, was formally crowned king and Henry VI fled overseas. In 1469 it was the usurper's turn to be shunted aside in favour of a reinstated Henry VI, but Edward returned to win decisively at Tewkesbury in 1471 and thereafter held the throne until his death over a decade later.

All the while, the country and the common people suffered. So weak did royal authority become that for long periods the balance of power was held by Richard Neville, Earl of Warwick. Such was his influence that he was known as Warwick the Kingmaker. It was his support that enabled Richard of York in 1460 to force Henry VI into recognising him as heir. In 1469, it was Warwick's changing sides that led to Henry VI being restored to the throne the following year. The earl remained a force in the land until he was defeated and killed at the battle of Barnet in 1471.

Edward IV died in 1483. Two years later, the wretched conflict came at last to an end when Henry Tudor defeated Edward's brother Richard III at Bosworth. As Henry VII, the new monarch wisely did all in his power to make sure that a line was drawn under the war. Symbolically, the Tudor Rose included both the white of York and the red of Lancaster.

Fall from grace.

A mere forty years passed between England routing the flower of French chivalry at Agincourt in 1415 and the battle of St Albans, with a defeated and divided realm consuming itself in civil war. It would be difficult to believe that a country could fall so hard and fast, were it not that the lives of both nations and individuals provide countless examples of such precipitate decline: "Since they hated knowledge and did not choose to fear the LORD, since they would not accept [God's] advice and spurned [his] rebuke, they will eat of the fruit of their ways and be filled with the fruit of their schemes." (Proverbs 1:29-31). England's fall from grace was neither unique nor inevitable. It was the result of choices made by human beings and their consequences. The nation misused the blessings that God had given it. She became "clay marred in [the potter's] hands; so the potter formed it into another pot, shaping it as seemed best to him." (Jeremiah 18:4). The flaw was in the clay itself, not in the potter's skill.

The Lord told Jeremiah: "Go down to the potter's house, and there I will give you my message." (Jeremiah 18:2). As the prophet "saw [the potter] working at the wheel" (Jeremiah 18:3), so he learnt of God's sovereignty (Jeremiah 18:5-6), of how nations fall and rise (Jeremiah 18, passim) and of how his own land would be broken and chastised (Jeremiah 19:10-13).

Changing fortunes.

Scripture shows us that the Lord works to a plan: a plan to rescue mankind from the consequences of rebellion and sin, to restore the broken relationship between God and man and to bring about a perfect re-creation. In doing so, he will at all times be true to his own character. Were that the end of the story, we might have difficulty accounting for the fact that God has given man free will, so that he can opt for right or wrong, line up on the side of good or evil, choose to love God or to reject him. Jeremiah, however, tells us that our personal destiny is neither fixed nor immutable: it is instead the result of a combination of forces – of God's activity in our lives and of our own choices.

This combination appears clearly in the message that Jeremiah brings from God to the Israelite kingdom of Judah shortly before the final cataclysm of defeat and enslavement at the hands of the Babylonians. The Israelites are told that, if only they will turn back to God, this fate can still be averted: "If at any time I announce that a nation or kingdom is to be uprooted, torn down and destroyed, and if that nation I warned repents of its evil, then I will relent and not inflict on it the disaster I had planned." (Jeremiah 18:7-8).

In the same way that we can bring God's renewed blessing by turning afresh to him, we can lose that blessing by turning away from the Almighty: "if at another time I announce that a nation or kingdom is to be built up and planted, and if it does evil in my sight and does not obey me, then I will reconsider the good that I had intended to do for it." (Jeremiah 18:9-10).

In each case, repeated use of the word "if" shows that God's promises and threats are conditional on man's actions.

God has so designed things that, whilst there are certain fixed points, whilst the end result and the principles involved remain constant, he can in large degree accommodate our choices and the different outcomes that come from them. Science hints at the tension that thus exists in the universe between being and becoming, actual and potential: we cannot know with absolute certainty since what is to be depends wholly or partly on choice. In particle physics, for example, Heisenberg's uncertainty principle states that it is not possible to know both the position and the momentum of a sub-atomic particle at the same time, since the very act of measuring would invalidate the result by changing what is being measured. In mathematics, Gödel's two Theorems of Undecidability or Incompleteness state that any mathematical system based on axioms[27] contains statements that can be neither proved nor disproved within the system – coming perilously close to saying that, in the strictest scientific sense, we cannot know with certainty that two plus two equals four. In short, our choices are real: what happens is neither scientifically determined nor subject to blind chance.

Choice.

Of course, human choice can only operate within the framework that God has set: "'can I not do with you as this potter does?' declares the LORD. 'Like clay in the hand of the potter, so are you in my hand'" (Jeremiah 18:6). There is no point complaining about this. It is just the way things are. The issue is what we do with the circumstances that confront us.

Our first step must be to recognise who we are and from whence we come: nobody can expect to find their way without correctly identifying their starting

---

[27] An axiom in this context is an assumption used as a basis for deductive reasoning. Goedel's first Theorem of Undecidability states that, if axiomatic set theory is consistent, there exist theorems that can neither be proved nor disproved. Goedel's second Theorem of Undecidability states that there is no constructive procedure that will prove axiomatic set theory to be consistent. The impact of these theorems was so profound that when they were published they led to the immediate abandonment of the so-called Hilbert programme (named after German mathematician David Hilbert), which had aimed to establish an agreed foundation of fundamental assumptions underpinning mathematics.

point. The starting point for humanity is that we were created by God. The image of clay in the hands of the potter harks back to the making of the first human. The Bible describes our bodies as "houses of clay" (Job 4:19) and "jars of clay" (2 Corinthians 4:7), referring to the time when "the LORD God formed the [first] man from the dust of the ground" (Genesis 2:7). The fact that we are creatures, not the Creator, has implications for every aspect of our lives and all our relationships – with our fellow creatures and with the world around us, as well as with God. We should thus begin by acknowledging: "Yet, O LORD, you are our Father. We are the clay, you are the potter; we are all the work of your hand." (Isaiah 64:8).

By denying this most fundamental aspects of our being, we make everything topsy-turvy. "You turn things upside down, as if the potter were thought to be like the clay! Shall what is formed say to him who formed it, 'He did not make me'? Can the pot say of the potter, 'He knows nothing.'?" (Isaiah 29:16). For centuries, western thought has aimed either at dethroning God and putting man in his place or, to the extent that the existence of God has been admitted, at making him seem either powerless, indifferent or malign. These efforts are not just intellectually incoherent. They twist us into shapes we were never meant to form.

Fate.

Christianity is not a fatalistic religion. It celebrates man's free will and affirms the difference that we each can make in the world. It trumpets the possibility of change. It holds out the prospect of a wholesale transformation of individuals, of societies and of nations. It permits and indeed encourages dialogue with God. There are, however, proper limits to our ability to question the Almighty: "Does the clay say to the potter, 'What are you making?' Does your work say, 'He has no hands.'?" (Jeremiah 45:9).

We come back time and again to this: man has a limited grasp of reality. Limited by reason of intellect, limited by being within time instead of outside it and limited in breadth and depth of vision. It is simply unrealistic for us to imagine that we can know enough to see the whole picture as God sees it. This means that we need to learn acceptance. There are things that we need to take on trust from God. This is part of what faith involves.

St Paul puts it thus: "One of you will say to me: 'Then why does God still blame us? For who resists his will?' But who are you, O man, to talk back to God? Shall what is formed say to him who formed it, 'Why did you make me like this?' Does not the potter have the right to make out of the same lump of clay some pottery for noble purposes and some for common use? What if God, choosing to show his wrath and make his power known, bore with great patience the objects of his wrath – prepared for destruction? What if he did this to make the riches of his glory known to the objects of his mercy, whom he prepared in advance for glory – even us, whom he called, not only from the Jews but also from the Gentiles?" (Romans 9:19-24).

Shakespeare's Hamlet confronts issues of free will, fatalism and the desirability of action: "To be or not to be, that is the question. Whether 'tis nobler in the mind to suffer the slings and arrows of outrageous fortune, or to take arms against a sea of troubles, and by opposing end them?" Each generation must grapple with these issues anew. In doing so, we should remember that acceptance is not fatalism. We are not the playthings of fate, but children of a loving God.

Conclusion.

In a snowstorm on Palm Sunday, 29 March 1461 was fought one of the grimmest of all battles. There fell an estimated twenty to thirty thousand Englishmen, a greater proportion of the population than perished on the first day of the Somme offensive in 1916 – one in every hundred, the equivalent of over six hundred thousand today. Towton is the largest, longest and most murderous armed contest ever to take place in these islands. Its closest rival, another Yorkshire bloodbath at Marston Moor in 1644, had only a quarter of the casualties. Shakespeare did not exaggerate when he wrote in *Richard II* of the coming Wars of the Roses: "the blood of England shall manure the ground and future ages groan ... disorder, horror, fear and mutiny shall here inhabit, and this land be called the field of Golgotha and dead men's skulls." The carnage was the culmination of disastrous choices by the nation and its leaders.

We, too, live in an age when our nation has consistently made bad choices over many decades. We have not yet gone so far down the track that we are mired in murderous civil war, but our condition is parlous nevertheless. We live in a land formerly blessed by God to an unprecedented degree, of which the Lord would now be justified in saying: "it does evil in my sight and does not obey me, [so that] I will reconsider the good I had intended to do for it." (Jeremiah 18:10). The words spoken to the Israelites through Jeremiah apply equally to us: "Look! I am preparing a disaster for you and devising a plan against you. So turn from your evil ways, each one of you, and reform your ways and your actions." (Jeremiah 18:11).

We have a choice. We must not succumb to despair and say: "It's no use." (Jeremiah 18:12). God clearly tells us that disaster is not fixed and certain, but that if our nation "repents of its evil ... [he] will relent and not inflict on [us] the disaster [he] had planned." (Jeremiah 18:8). We need to seize this opportunity of forgiveness. We must not refuse to turn back to God, nor say: "We will continue with our own plans; each of us will follow the stubbornness of his evil heart. " (Jeremiah 18:12). We can choose our destiny. It is in our hands.

13. A tongue of our own

1 Corinthians 13.

Key word: love.

The Bible is consistently rated one of the best-selling books in the world. It has been translated into over 1,600 languages. Year by year, more and more people gain access for the first time to the Word of God. It is therefore chastening to reflect that this is a comparatively recent phenomenon. For the best part of three out of every four years that have passed since Jesus died on the cross, the vast majority of Christians did not have the privilege of reading the Scriptures. Most were in any event illiterate, but even those who could read had no text in their own language. In the west of Europe, the Latin Vulgate was to all intents and purposes all that was available and for the common man certainly it was all that was sanctioned by the church.[28]

Into this world came a man driven by passion: a desire for learning, a longing for the Word of God and a yearning to share that Word with others. This compelling force led him to burst out one day to a clergyman whom he considered a disgrace to the cloth: "If God spare my life, I will cause a boy that driveth the plough to know more of Scripture than thou dost." So he did.

William Tyndale was not the first translator of the Bible into English – Wycliffe had already produced an English version of a large part of both Old and New Testaments. Yet Tyndale's translation was influential far beyond his predecessor's. To some degree this was the consequence of being in the right place at the right time: the Protestant Reformation was sweeping Europe, undermining traditional church hierarchies and emphasising the right of every man to examine the Bible for himself. To some extent it was the result of new technology: the invention of the printing press meant that large numbers of Bibles could be printed on the continent and smuggled into England. To some extent it was the result of changes in the language that were already rendering Wycliffe's version unintelligible. Yet Tyndale also deserves credit for his courage and self-sacrifice, his diligence and scholarship, perhaps above all for his economy and elegance of expression. Like King Solomon, he "searched to find just the right words, and what he wrote was upright and true" (Proverbs 12:10).

---

[28] The Bible was originally translated into Latin by St Jerome from AD 382, though subsequently several times revised. In 1546 the Council of Trent promoted the Vulgate as the official translation.

So accurate and felicitous was the result that the Authorised Version produced in the reign of King James I (1603-1625) was in overwhelming proportion based on Tyndale's work. Many phrases that have passed from the Bible into common usage are pure Tyndale. Together with the works of William Shakespeare and the Book of Common Prayer, he has been one of the central influences on the formation of modern English.

For his pains, this scholar of Latin, Greek, Hebrew and Aramaic was forced to flee his own country and to live in hiding overseas. There he adopted various disguises and aliases, rightly fearful that agents of the English king were in search of him. Henry VIII (reigned 1509-1547) had earlier been awarded the title Defender of the Faith[29] by the Pope for authoring a pamphlet defending traditional orthodoxy and had no desire to let writings that were banned by the church into his realm. Indeed, Sir Thomas More (who became Henry's Lord Chancellor – or chief minister – following the downfall of Cardinal Wolsey in 1529) seems to have developed something of a fixation with Tyndale and pursued him unremittingly.

Words.

St Paul encourages his readers to pursue spiritual gifts unremittingly, and these form the subject of chapters 12-14 of his first letter to the early church in Corinth. One of the greatest gifts that God has given us is his Word in the Bible. St Paul says elsewhere that: "All Scripture is God-breathed and is useful for teaching, rebuking, correcting and training in righteousness, so that the man of God may be thoroughly equipped for every good work." (2 Timothy 3:16). Little wonder that when English language Bibles first became widely available, there was a tremendous clamour for them as people yearned to be able to read God's Word for themselves.

The ability to communicate through language is one of the things that set man apart from animals. Once, "the whole world had one language and a common speech." (Genesis 11:1). Since the days of the Tower of Babel, however, there have been myriad languages, for "The LORD said ... 'Come, let us go down and confuse their language so they will not understand one another.'" (Genesis 11:6-7). The result is miscommunication and lack of communication, but this gulf was bridged in miraculous fashion at the first Pentecost. When the Holy Spirit came on Jesus' followers at that time, "a crowd came together in bewilderment, because each one heard them speaking in his

---

[29] Fidei Defensor in Latin. The initials F.D. still appear on British coins. Henry wrote *Assertio Septem Sacramentorum* in response to Martin Luther's *De Captivitate Babylonica*. In May 1521 Henry ordered that all Luther's books be burned.

own language." (Acts 2:7). They exclaimed: "we hear them declaring the wonders of God in our own tongues!" (Acts 2:11). It is scarcely straining sense to draw a comparison with the appearance of English language Bibles in large numbers. For the first time most Englishmen were able to read and hear "the wonders of God" (Acts 2:11) in the vernacular.

Our ability to give utterance to thought does not exist merely to enable communication between human beings. It exists also to enable communication between man and God. In the same way that free communication between different linguistic groups has been hindered and disrupted as a result of our sinfulness, so has our communication with God. The gift of tongues (the ability to speak in languages that we have not learned or in non-human languages) exists in part to aid this. St Paul says that when someone speaks in tongues, it is our spirit which communicates with God: "For if I pray in a tongue, my spirit prays" (1 Corinthians 14:14). The result is that "anyone who speaks in a tongue does not speak to men but to God ... [and] edifies himself." (1 Corinthians 14:2 and 4).

St Paul encourages his readers that they should "eagerly desire spiritual gifts" (1 Corinthians 14:1). However, he makes it clear that these gifts are a means to an end rather than the end itself. He presages his exhortation with the instruction: "Follow the way of love" (1 Corinthians 14:1).

Attitudes.

Our speech, thoughts and actions should all be governed by love. The manner of our communication matters, as does the motive for our action. It is not just a question of what we do or the words that we speak, but also of what is in our hearts. Without love, all else is worthless: "If I speak in the tongues of men and of angels, but have not love, I am only a resounding gong or a clanging cymbal. If I have the gift of prophecy and can fathom all mysteries and all knowledge, and if I have a faith that can move mountains, but have not love, I am nothing. If I give all I possess to the poor and surrender my body to the flames, but have not love, I gain nothing." (1 Corinthians 13:1-3). Even the most spectacular manifestations of spiritual gifts are nothing unless they are motivated by love. This should hardly surprise us, for "God is love" (1 John 4:8).

The love that St Paul talks of is the same kind of love that Jesus speaks about when he tells us to "Love your neighbour as yourself." (Luke 10:27). Love in this sense is not what we often tend to mean when we use this word in English. In our highly sexualised society, words such as love and passion tend to have an overlay of romantic connotation. We are not helped by the fact that in this instance (unusually for a tongue normally so rich in nuance) English has only one word to convey many different shades of meaning.

By contrast, Greek (in which St Paul's letters are written) has various words to distinguish different kinds of love: thus *eros* for sexual love and *philia* for friendly love, affection and friendship. The word that St Paul uses is *agape,* which conveys selfless concern for the welfare of others: brotherly love or charity, the love of God for man and of man for God. From a human point of view, the person loved in this way may not be very lovable. The important distinction between *agape* and other kinds of love is that it is a product of the will: it results from a decision to love in obedience to the Lord's command. Christian love is based not on warm feelings but on God's love in action, on an attitude of mind rather than on the vagaries of emotion. The passion that should drive us is the same compelling force that drove Tyndale – not a worldly thing, but a godly.

The characteristics of this kind of love are described as follows: "Love is patient, love is kind. It does not envy, it does not boast, it is not proud. It is not rude, it is not self-seeking, it is not easily angered, it keeps no record of wrongs. Love does not delight in evil but rejoices with the truth. It always protects, always trusts, always hopes, always perseveres." (1 Corinthians 13:4-8). These echo the fruits of the Spirit: "But the fruit of the Spirit is love, joy, peace, patience, kindness, goodness, faithfulness, gentleness and self-control." (Galatians 5:22). The passion that Christian love involves and evokes is the very opposite of the passions engendered by our earthly appetites. Those things, indeed, give rise to "The acts of the sinful nature" (Galatians 5:19).

This *agape* is the "love [that] never fails." (1 Corinthians 13:8). It is the thing of which St Paul writes: "And now these three remain: faith, hope and love. But the greatest of these is love." (1 Corinthians 13:13).

Deeds.

If we are to practise this love and to project it throughout our nation, passion must be balanced with restraint, patience and self-control. This has a number of aspects. We must recognise that our lives on earth necessarily involve:

Impermanence: "But where there are prophesies, they will cease; where there are tongues, they will be stilled; where there is knowledge, it will pass away." (1 Corinthians 13:8).

Limitation: "For we know in part and we prophesy in part, but when perfection comes, the imperfect disappears." (1 Corinthians 13:9-10).

Immaturity: "When I was a child, I talked like a child, I thought like a child, I reasoned like a child. When I became a man, I put childish ways behind me." (1 Corinthians 13:11).

Obscurity: "Now we see but a poor reflection as in a mirror; then we shall see face to face." (1 Corinthians 13:12).

Incompleteness: "Now I know in part; then I shall know fully, even as I am fully known." (1 Corinthians 13:12).

The consequence is that we need faith to make good the deficiency. Through faith we lean on the rock of God's unchanging nature, access the Lord's insight, supplant our foolishness with his wisdom, gain glimpses of his vision and tap into his knowledge. If we do these things, we will overcome our limitations and immaturity, we will be able to see beyond and through the things of this world, we will build a lasting treasure on sure foundations and we will take part in the process whereby God brings all things to completeness.

There is no telling what God has in store for each one of us here on earth. We seldom see more than a few steps ahead, nor do we fully grasp the meaning of what we are involved in day to day. For some there are tasks monumental and epic, like those of Tyndale. For most, the daily round is rather more mundane. Yet if we truly bring to bear *agape* love in all that we think and do, people cannot fail to be affected and the world cannot fail to be changed. This land has become a temple to self-interest, self-promotion, self-regard and self indulgence. The result is rottenness at the core of our society and in our very hearts. The antidote is *agape*. We need to apply the antidote swiftly and in large doses.

Conclusion.

The date of Tyndale's birth is uncertain[30] and much detail of his life obscure, the result of his living under assumed names and in disguise in Europe during his time as translator of the Bible and writer of Protestant tracts. The time and manner of his death, however, are well documented. He was strangled and burnt at the stake as a heretic in Brussels in 1536, having been tracked down and entrapped by an agent probably sent by Sir Thomas More, then handed to the local authorities for sentencing and execution. He refused to save himself by abjuring his life's work and went bravely to his death. As flames licked about him, he cried, "Lord, open the king of England's eyes."

In pursuit of his life's work Tyndale gave up everything: friends, home, wife, family, country, security and eventually his life. He did it because he was consumed by passion. The effort was not wasted and his final prayer was answered. Just one year after his death a complete English language Bible, two thirds translated by Tyndale and the remainder by his associate Miles de Coverdale, was published by royal permission. It was put on display in St Paul's cathedral and a spontaneous public reading of the entire text soon began. To this day, the Church of England is required by law to keep a complete, accessible Bible in all its places of worship.

Today, it is not merely the eyes of a king and his ministers that need to be opened, but the eyes of an entire nation. We need to feel the same desire that our

---

[30] Thought to be 1494 or thereabouts.

forebears had for the Word of God. We need to recover some of the same passion that drove William Tyndale. We need to experience the same love that inspired St Paul. If we will only allow a little of this same zeal to fire us, we will be astounded at the result. Our land needs to be set ablaze again with passion, a passion the source and object of which is God himself.

14. Martyrs

Hebrews 10:32-39.

Key word: confidence.

William Tyndale's death was just the start. During the reign of Queen Mary (1553-1558) nearly three hundred Protestants were burnt at the stake for their faith. Amongst the martyrs were Archbishop Cranmer and Bishops Hooper, Ridley and Latimer. The last words of the Archbishop of Canterbury and of the Bishop of Worcester in particular have resonated down the centuries. Together, they found a degree of resolve and confidence that made a deep impression on all who heard them.

Latimer, burnt alongside Ridley at Oxford in 1555, called out to his friend as the flames licked about him: "Courage, Master Ridley. With God's good grace we shall this day light such a fire in England as shall never be put out."[31] A year later Cranmer, author of the greater part of the Book of Common Prayer and thus instrumental in establishing the Calvinist orthodoxy of the Church of England, who had earlier recanted of Protestantism and then thought better of it, held his right arm to the flames and said: "For as much as my hand hath sinned, by writing contrary to my heart, it shall be the first to burn."

The queen who had these men put to death, devout and sincere as she undoubtedly was, is the Bloody Mary of infamy. When she died childless after a reign of six years, the popular support that had accompanied her accession and enabled her to weather the usurpation of Lady Jane Grey had evaporated. Her passing was unlamented, her only lasting legacy the loss of England's last piece of territory in France. She said that she died "with Calais engraved on my heart."

Standing our ground.

The words addressed to early Jewish Christians by the writer of the book of Hebrews apply equally to the Protestants martyrs of Queen Mary's day: "Remember those earlier days after you had received the light, when you stood your ground in a great contest in the face of suffering. Sometimes you were publicly exposed to insult and persecution; at other times you stood side by side with those who were so treated. You sympathised with those in prison and

---

[31] Latimer had not always been so brave. In 1532 (during the reign of Henry VIII) he saved himself from burning by signing a full recantation of Protestant views.

joyfully accepted the confiscation of your property, because you knew that you yourselves had better and lasting possessions." (Hebrews 10:32-34).

These words should resonate with us just as did those of Latimer and Cranmer amongst previous generations. We, too, should remember "those earlier days after [this nation] had received the light," for our forefathers are amongst those who "stood [their] ground in a great contest in the face of suffering." (Hebrews 10:32). If they could do it, so can we. The book of Hebrews tells us how. It tells us how to respond to attack, how to deflect blows and how to build confidence.

Responding to attack: when "publicly exposed to insult and persecution" (Hebrews 10:33), we should not be blown off course and neither should we respond in like manner. Our duty then is not to give way but to stay put: to stand our ground and to stand "side by side with those who [are] so treated." (Hebrews 10:33).

Deflecting blows: the harm that others seek to do us will be robbed of its power if we give each other help and support and if we put material possessions in their proper place. If we are able to "[sympathise] with those in prison and joyfully [accept] the confiscation of [our] property" (Hebrews 10:34) much of the hold that others have over us will simply evaporate.

Building confidence: our trust and confidence in God will increase if we put our faith into practice, for in this way we will come to "[know] that [we ourselves] have better and lasting possessions." (Hebrews 10:34). Once we gain that perspective, then like St Paul we will "consider everything a loss compared to the surpassing greatness of knowing Jesus Christ [our] Lord, for whose sake I have lost all things. [We will] consider them rubbish, that [we] may gain Christ and be found in him" (Philippians 3:8-9).

The writer of Hebrews draws a contrast between the things of this world and the things of heaven. On one side stands "suffering ... insult and persecution ... prison ... confiscation of your property" (Hebrews 10:32-33). On the other stands sympathy, joy, "better and lasting possessions" (Hebrews 10:34), rich reward and the promises of God.

The advice given to the readers of Hebrews holds true for us as well: "So do not throw away your confidence; it will be richly rewarded. You need to persevere so that when you have done the will of God, you will receive what he has promised." (Hebrews 10:35-36). Over recent decades, this nation has progressively thrown away her confidence and dismantled the solid platform upon which she had built. We have thrown away the ultimate ground for all confidence – trust in God – and in doing so we have lost confidence in everything else. We no longer seem to have confidence that ours is a society worth fighting for. Neither do we seem to have confidence that, for all its manifest faults, this society remains one of the best in the world, where there is a greater chance of happiness and fulfilment than in most parts of the globe, where decent values continue to be upheld and where corruption both personal and corporate is less firmly rooted than in most countries. These are things on which our forebears once stood their ground. They cannot continue to be things that distinguish the life of this nation unless we do likewise.

A great contest.

We are engaged in a great contest no less than were former generations. The writer of Hebrews speaks of "a great contest in the face of suffering" (Hebrews 10:32). In this land we do not currently face outright persecution in the sense that we are the victims of physical violence, but there is an intellectual climate that is distinctly hostile and a determined attempt to erode the Christian fabric of the nation by removing its underpinnings from all walks of life. For a large proportion of Christians overseas, however, the picture is very different. Many labour under persecutions that range from relatively minor administrative inconvenience to direct attack. Each day increases the number of martyrs. We have signally failed in our duty so stand "side by side with those who [are] so treated." (Hebrews 10:33). We need to be far more active and vocal in our support of the persecuted church worldwide.

Nor is it only fellow believers who need our care, sympathy, support and prayer. The world around us is groaning under the weight of suffering and injustice. This is a direct consequence of human behaviour, itself a result of what men believe and hold in their hearts, which in turn comes back to being for God or against him. If we open our eyes, we will not need to look far to find the "great contest in the face of suffering" (Hebrews 10:32), on our doorstep or further afield. In those circumstances, just like the Christians of former times we need to:

"Persevere" (Hebrews 10:36). To persevere means to persist in or with any undertaking, design or course. In a later Christian context it means continuance in a state of grace. Our perseverance means that we will continue on our own personal journey of faith, but it must not stop there. Until we take our faith out into the world we will be doing less than we can and should.

"Live by faith" (Hebrews 10:38). To live by faith means that we will slough off the false beliefs and perspectives of the world around us, cease to place our trust in those things which are worthless and instead put all our trust in God: for guidance, health and wellbeing, for all the necessities of life and ultimately for salvation.

Not shrink back. To shrink back involves giving way, recoiling or flinching. It is in effect a form of denial, just as Peter shrank back when asked if he were one of Jesus' followers (see Matthew 26:69-75, Mark 14:66-72, Luke 22:54-62 and John 18:15-18 and 25-27). Hence: "those who shrink back ... are destroyed" (Hebrews 10:39). They are contrasted with "those who believe and are saved." (Hebrews 10:39). We must remember that "if he shrinks back, I [the Lord] will not be pleased with him." (Hebrews 10:38).

We should not retreat into a Christian ghetto, nor allow Christianity to be absent from the public sphere. To do so would be to shrink back and to fail to live out Christ's Great Commission. When he tells us to: "go and make disciples of all nations, baptising them in the name of the Father and of the Son and of the Holy Spirit, and teaching them to obey everything I have commanded you" (Matthew 28:19-20), that command applies to our own nation just as to any other. This is our "great contest": a battle for souls between the Kingdom of Heaven and the forces of darkness. We each have a part to play in the fight.

Coming glory.

It is a fight that we can undertake with confidence, knowing that:

"[Our] confidence ... will be richly rewarded." (Hebrews 10:35).

"[When we] have done the will of God, [we] will receive what he has promised." (Hebrews 10:36).

"For in just a very little while, 'He who is coming will come and will not delay. But my righteous one will live by faith'" (Hebrews 10:37-38).

The "better and lasting possessions" (Hebrews 10:34) and the rich reward that the writer of Hebrews speaks of include our salvation in Christ and our future reward in heaven. Like Abraham, we can "[look] forward to the city with foundations, whose architect and builder is God." (Hebrews 11:10). Daily we need to remind ourselves to focus on eternity rather than on what is transient: "For here we do not have an enduring city, but we are looking for the city that is to come." (Hebrews 13:14).

St Paul says: "I consider that our present sufferings are not worth comparing with the glory that will be revealed in us." (Romans 8:18). Jesus says: "Rejoice and be glad, because great is your reward in heaven, for in the same way they persecuted the prophets who were before you." (Matthew 5:12).

The prospect of glory to come has motivated, inspired, comforted and thrilled Christian martyrs throughout the ages. It has enabled them to withstand persecution, torture and every kind of ill. Set alongside them, what is required from us seems small indeed. We are not yet grown so lazy, slack, self-satisfied and seduced by worldly things that the necessary effort is beyond us, but it will not be long before it is so. When the prophet Jonah was sent to preach to wicked

Nineveh, all who heard him believed and turned from their wrongdoing with repentance: "When God saw what they did and how they turned from their evil ways, he had compassion on them and did not bring upon them the destruction he had threatened." (Jonah 3:10). Yet just a generation later the city had slipped back into its bad old ways and consequently was destroyed. This happened because those who heard Jonah failed to keep alive his message and to pass it on to the next generation. We must not be guilty of the same.

Conclusion.

For centuries, every Anglican parish kept John Foxe's *Book of Martyrs* (first published in 1563) on display alongside the Bible and Book of Common Prayer. The martyrs whose lives and deaths it recorded were not solely English, but included Protestants from other lands. Yet inevitably, by keeping alive the memory of those who had died in England for the reformed faith, it contributed to the country's growing identity as a self-consciously Protestant nation. The example of the great men and women of the past was a powerful force in building and strengthening the beliefs of generations to come. It is a lesson we need to learn all over again. We need a dollop of the confidence that inspired the martyrs of years gone by. It was not delusion that led to their self-sacrifice, but a reasoned and well-founded assurance.

Bishop Hugh Latimer had tremendous and unshakeable confidence: in the power of God to save, in his own deliverance and the rich reward that was his in consequence, in the cause for which he was martyred and in the future of England. That same confidence can be ours. Archbishop Cranmer overcame the fear of hurt and death that we all experience, and in the end was true to all that he believed and held dear. His initial cowardice was redeemed in deepened courage and renewed assurance. We can do likewise.

Whether we be amongst the rare few like Latimer whose conviction never seems to fail or amongst the majority like Cranmer who quake and tremble before the trials and tribulations of life, we can learn from the past and from the example of others. In doing so, we will be strengthened for what lies ahead. Like the martyrs of old, we need to respond in the right ways to the attacks we face, so that we deflect the blows that are aimed at us and above all so that we grow in confidence in the one who is our "help and shield" (Psalm 115:9). We must ensure that "we are not of those who shrink back and are destroyed, but of those who believe and are saved." (Hebrews 10:39).

England must not be another Nineveh. The blood of martyrs must not have been shed in vain. We need to take our stand, in whatever ways we are able. With God's good grace each one of us can this day add our little spark to what will then become a mighty conflagration.

15. Protestant wind

Hosea 8:7.

Key word: recompense.

In the sixteenth century Spain was not just a European power of the first rank, but a world power beyond compare. Under her control came all South America bar Brazil, the whole of Central America and much of the Caribbean, together with what are now the southernmost parts of the United States. In the Far East, she held the Philippines. Within Europe, her Habsburg kings were also rulers of the Spanish Netherlands and much of Italy.[32] Her resources of manpower and of bullion from the New World seemed inexhaustible. It was not realised at the time that the yearly import of vast quantities of gold and silver was the source of rampant inflation, nor that the illusion of bottomless wealth was encouraging severe imperial overstretch. In 1588 only her strength was apparent.

For years England had provoked Spain: through raiding of Spanish treasure fleets, through support for Dutch rebels and through her unrepentant Protestantism. King Philip II determined that enough was enough. A mighty fleet was equipped: seventy three fighting vessels, attended by over fifty freighters and lighter craft, together carrying 2,400 guns, crewed by eight thousand sailors and carrying in addition seventeen thousand soldiers. Their orders were to sail up the Channel, pick up a further sixteen thousand men of the Duke of Parma's forces from the Netherlands and land these, together with the Armada's own complement of troops, in the southern shires. Little serious resistance was expected to Parma's battle-hardened force and in truth the raw recruits of the English army cut a sorry sight alongside the veterans of the Spanish *tercios*, then acknowledged as the finest infantry in Europe.

The words of Elizabeth I as she addressed her troops at Tilbury in Kent were defiant: "I know that I have the body of a weak and feeble woman, but I have the heart and stomach of a king, and of a king of England, too; and think foul scorn that Parma or Spain, or any prince of Europe, should dare to invade the borders of my realm." The reality was that, unless the Spanish could be prevented from landing, the outlook was bleak. All depended on the outcome of

---

[32] From 1580 Philip II of Spain was also king of Portugal, herself the ruler of a considerable overseas Empire, which included Brazil as well as possessions in Africa and the East Indies and trading posts in India. The two countries remained united under the Spanish Crown for the next sixty years.

the war at sea. As Drake shrewdly observed, "The advantage of time and place in all practical actions is half a victory; which being lost is irrecoverable."

Elizabeth had at her command some of the most talented sailors England has ever produced. The Lord High Admiral (Lord Howard) was not an experienced seaman, but he was a good chief and a wise judge of men. With Drake, Hawkins, Frobisher and others at his side, he was able to achieve a deliverance that seemed almost miraculous. As the Armada sailed up the Channel, scores of English ships clustered around it, dodging Spanish attempts to grapple at close quarters and pouring broadside after broadside at the enemy. The image is glorious, the truth rather more prosaic. Despite a prodigious expenditure of powder and shot, by the end of the third day of fighting the English had only succeeded in capturing, sinking or disabling two Spanish vessels.[33] Whilst Howard's fleet had suffered little damage, the Armada was still a formidable force and its formation remained intact.

A turning point came on 28 July 1588. Eight fire ships were sent amongst the Spaniards by night as they lay at anchor off Calais. In the event, these did not destroy a single vessel and burnt themselves out harmlessly on the sandbanks east of the town, but they did something that the English had been unable to achieve hitherto: they broke the Armada's cohesion. Scattering into the North Sea pursued by an adversary with his tail up, the Spaniards took a terrible pounding from shot and shell and were driven beyond the point at which wind and currents made junction with Parma impossible. Their enemy continued to harass them along the North Sea coast as far as the Scottish border and then left them to the mercy of the elements. The battered remnants of the once-proud force limped home several months later. Only some sixty ships returned, with a loss of perhaps fifteen thousand men killed, captured and dying. Many vessels that were not lost in action were sunk in storms around the coasts of Scotland and Ireland.[34] The jubilant English and Dutch spoke unashamedly of the part played by the so-called Protestant Wind. In their eyes, Catholic Spain had

---

[33] Neither was lost as a direct consequence of English action. The *Nuestra Señora del Rosario* collided with another Spanish vessel, facilitating her subsequent capture by Drake, whilst the *San Salvador* accidentally caught fire and exploded.

[34] The Spaniards' misery was increased by the fact that many of the casks in which food and drink were stored were made of unseasoned wood, with the result that they leaked and their contents spoiled. (Large quantities of seasoned wood that had been intended for the Armada were destroyed by Sir Francis Drake during his attack on Cadiz in 1587, an event that he termed "singeing the King of Spain's beard.") Even when shipwrecked crews made it ashore, their safety was not assured. Whilst some were treated hospitably, others were butchered by the local inhabitants.

"[sown] the wind and [reaped] the whirlwind." (Hosea 8:7). There was great rejoicing.

Sowing and reaping.

The prophet Hosea was sent to the northern Israelite kingdom of Israel in the middle of the eighth century BC, during its last days of independence before the Assyrians invaded and it was destroyed. He was told to depict the unfaithfulness of Israel to God and to warn of the consequences. He told the Israelites: "Do not rejoice, O Israel, do not be jubilant like the other nations. For you have been unfaithful to your God" (Hosea 9:1). The phrase "They sow the wind and reap the whirlwind" (Hosea 8:7) was echoed by the prophet when he said: "Sow for yourselves righteousness, reap the fruit of unfailing love, and break up your unploughed ground; for it is time to seek the LORD until he comes and showers righteousness on you. But you have planted wickedness, you have reaped evil, you have eaten the fruit of deception. Because you have depended on your own strength and on your many warriors, the roar of battle will rise against your people, so that all your fortresses will be devastated" (Hosea 10:12-14). These words chime also with those of the prophet Nahum: "The LORD is slow to anger and great in power; the LORD will not leave the guilty unpunished. His way is in the whirlwind and the storm, and clouds are the dust of his feet." (Nahum 1:3).

In phrase and counterpoint we see the Lord's instructions for right living and, by way of contrast, the reality of human conduct. On one side sowing righteousness, breaking up unploughed ground and reaping unfailing love. On the other, sowing the wind and reaping the whirlwind. In both good and bad we see in operation the inexorable laws that govern our behaviour, by which the consequences of our actions are multiplied. Hence our righteousness will lead to unfailing love, whilst wind will turn to whirlwind. There is no mystery here. We can test it for ourselves. History and our own experience show it to be the case that small beginnings lead to something greater. As the saying has it: "Sow a thought, reap an action. Sow an action, reap a habit. Sow a habit, reap a character. Sow a character, reap a destiny." In this nation we been sowing the wind for many a long year. We are already experiencing the inevitable consequences. If we carry on, we will reap the whirlwind just as surely as did Israel in the days of Hosea.

Fruitfulness.

Hosea pictured a land and a people that were unfruitful: "The stalk has no head; it will produce no flour. Were it to yield grain, foreigners would swallow it up." (Hosea 8:7). God demands fruitfulness. He demands it from nature and he demands it from man.[35] The only miracle of destruction performed by Jesus was when he cursed the fig tree for failing to bear fruit, saying, "May you never bear fruit again!" (Matthew 21:19) and causing it to wither. He told his hearers that "I am the true vine and my Father is the gardener. He cuts off every branch in me that bears no fruit ... If anyone does not remain in me, he is like a branch that is thrown away and withers; such branches are picked up, thrown into the fire and burned ...This is to my Father's glory, that you bear much fruit, showing yourselves to be my disciples." (John 15:2, 6 and 8).

Israel was in a critical condition. Without grain there would be no flour and without flour there would be no bread, the staple food. Starvation beckoned. The lack of physical nutriment points to spiritual hunger, for "man does not live on bread alone, but on every word that comes from the mouth of the LORD." (Deuteronomy 8:3). Jesus describes himself as "the bread of life." (John 6:35). It is no coincidence that he was born in Bethlehem, which means 'place of bread.' As formerly in Israel, so here today: the long roll-call of things with which we seek to fill the emptiness inside shows the deep spiritual hunger that grips our land. We are starving, slowly but surely, and the harvest from what we have sown will not feed us. We desperately need to "break up [our] unploughed ground" (Hosea 10:12) and to "sow for [ourselves] righteousness" (Hosea 10:12). Then we will harvest a crop worthy of the name: "unfailing love" (Hosea 10:12). As it is, our land is unploughed. If we leave it lying fallow, no crop will come from it.

St Paul writes that "when the ploughman ploughs and the thresher threshes, they ought to do so in the hope of sharing in the harvest." (1 Corinthians 9:10). Things had reached such a pass in Israel, however, that benefit accrued not to the nation, but to foreigners who "swallow it up" (Hosea 8:7). Again, the parallels with our situation are too close for comfort. A tremendous amount of effort is being and has been expended by the state, by individuals and by the church, but it is to no avail if it is lavished on unploughed ground, for then effort will be wasted and benefit will not go where it is intended. In large measure the post-war attempts to right injustice, create a more equal society and

---

[35] The Lord's very first command to the newly created Adam and Eve was to "Be fruitful ..." (Genesis 1:28). The same command was earlier given to the animal kingdom (Genesis 1:22) and was later repeated both to Noah and his sons when mankind was given a new start after the Flood (Genesis 9:1 and 7) and to Jacob as a representative of the "nation and ... community of nations [that] will come from you" (Genesis 35:11).

help those at the bottom of the heap have demonstrated the law of unintended consequences in precisely this way. It has happened because this has been almost entirely a secular project, divorced from God, carried out without reference to his will and often in direct contravention of his laws. We have indeed "eaten the fruit of deception" (Hosea 10:13).

Unploughed ground can only be broken up by prayer, by walking in the ways of the Lord and seeking his will, by obedience to his commandments and demonstrating the love of Jesus. Until this is done, we will be whistling in the wind.

Righteousness.

Hosea emphasised the need for righteousness: "Sow for yourselves righteousness ... for it is time to seek the LORD until he comes and showers righteousness on you." (Hosea 10:12). The recompense for our righteousness is an even greater abundance of righteousness showered upon us by God. As in all our endeavours, the Lord will take what we bring and multiply it beyond our wildest imaginings. Correspondingly, the recompense for unrighteousness and "wickedness" (Hosea 10:13) is the "whirlwind" (Hosea 8:7), a "stalk [with] no head ... [producing] no flour ... [or] grain [which] foreigners swallow up" (Hosea 8:7), "evil" (Hosea 10:13) and "the roar of battle" (Hosea 10:14).

If we reject God we remain under his judgment. In that event, the Lord says: "I will repay them according to their deeds and the work of their hands." (Jeremiah 25:14). In other words, we get what we deserve. However, if we place our trust in Jesus as our Lord and Saviour we obtain mercy and forgiveness. In that event "[The LORD] does not ... repay us according to our iniquities." (Psalm 103:10). Then instead of reaping the punishment that is rightfully ours, we gain salvation – made possible by the death of Jesus on the cross, a free gift given in spite of what we have done, not because of it. Ultimately, the only way for us to obtain true righteousness is by having imputed to us the righteousness of Christ.

When we think in terms of recompense we tend instinctively to imagine payment for services rendered. The dictionary definition includes making a return or giving an equivalent for something, requiting or repaying, indemnifying, compensating or making up for something, making satisfaction for a service or injury. To this frame of mind belongs insistence on our own rights, on what is our due, on revenge and retribution, on the letter of the law rather than on its spirit. This viewpoint is prevalent in present-day Britain. Jesus calls us to something different: to forgoing what we think is owing to us, to putting others before ourselves, to having regard to what is in our hearts rather than merely to outward forms of speech or behaviour. Above all, we should recollect that we have been forgiven when we did not deserve it and that we should therefore be forgiving towards others.

Conclusion.

The triumphalism of English and Dutch Protestants over the defeat of Catholic Spain sits ill with our society's current values. The readiness of people of that age to see God as being on their side and against their enemies is something that nowadays makes us uncomfortable. We have, thankfully, learnt something in the intervening centuries (though it is fair to say that we have forgotten much of worth as well). Such attitudes also run counter to what Scripture teaches. In truth, we have no reason to be smug: "Do not rejoice, O Israel, do not be jubilant like the other nations. For you have been unfaithful to your God" (Hosea 9:1). We "have depended on [our] own strength and on [our] many warriors" with the consequence that "the roar of battle will rise against your people, so that all your fortresses will be devastated" (Hosea 10:12-14). Instead of patting ourselves on the back for our cleverness, we should recognise that we are under the judgment of God for ignoring him, for relying on our own strength and imagining that we can do without him.

God will recompense us for our actions unless we bring ourselves under the umbrella of his forgiveness by repenting of what we have done and putting our faith (trust) in him. There is still time for us to turn, so that we reap unfailing love. If not, the whirlwind will be upon us. "It is time to seek the LORD until he comes" (Hosea 10:12).

16. Secret lives

Deuteronomy 29:29.

Key word: focus.

During the war with Spain the dog that did not bark was the feared fifth column within England: its Roman Catholic minority.[36] Those who remained loyal to the Pope had been driven underground, but a network was kept alive to enable them to continue worshipping in secret. Country houses up and down the land still proudly show their 'priest's holes' where the celebrant of Mass could be hidden during searches by government agents. Those who declined to embrace state-sponsored religion were called recusants (from the Latin *recusans*, meaning refusing).

Adherents of the old faith lived a curious double life, often mixing outward conformity to Anglican rites with their inner allegiance. One such was the composer William Byrd (1543-1623). He was able to walk the tightrope with such skill that in 1563 he became organist at Lincoln cathedral. Thereafter Elizabeth I appointed him joint organist of the Chapel Royal with his co-religionist Thomas Tallis, with whom he was granted a licence to print and publish music and whom he succeeded in 1585.[37] For all his success, however, Byrd never forgot where his heart lay: his treatment of Psalm 137 is in effect a coded statement of continued loyalty to Rome.

The expectation that religious allegiance would trump national feeling made this embattled group dangerous in the eyes of government and people alike. Nor was the danger wholly illusory. In 1605 a group of Roman Catholics, of whom Guy Fawkes remains in popular imagination the central figure, conspired to blow up King James I during a sitting of Parliament. The plot was discovered before the intended date of its execution: 5 November, still celebrated with bonfires and fireworks each year as the date of the Gunpowder Plot. Fawkes and the other conspirators were executed, not for their religious beliefs, but for treason.

---

[36] Queen Elizabeth had been excommunicated by the Pope in February 1570. As far as the Papacy was concerned, this absolved Englishmen of any duty of loyalty to her. There were in fact various Catholic plots during her reign. A number of these centred on plans to put Mary, Queen of Scots on the throne in place of Elizabeth, who reluctantly authorised Mary's execution on 8 February 1587.

[37] The poet John Donne was another famous recusant. Catholicism did not prevent his taking part in two expeditions against the Spanish sponsored by the Earl of Essex in 1596 and 1597. He eventually took Anglican orders in 1615.

The link between Roman Catholicism and treason thereafter became so fixed in the minds of most Englishmen that the merest hint of suspicion was capable of producing hysterical overreaction. In 1678 Titus Oates invented the so-called Popish Plot, supposedly involving Jesuit plans to depose Charles II in favour of his Roman Catholic brother James (later James II). Despite evidence that no such plot existed, the resulting feverishness encouraged efforts to exclude James from the throne and helped prepare the ground for his eventual expulsion in favour of William and Mary.

Resentment and suspicion of Roman Catholics continued for generations. In 1780, during what became known as the Gordon riots, Protestant extremists led by Lord George Gordon marched on Parliament to protest at the passing two years beforehand of the Catholic Relief Act, which lifted some restrictions on Roman Catholics. The march degenerated into a week-long disturbance in which some four hundred and fifty people were killed. These were hardly glory days of religious toleration and freedom of worship. Until the late nineteenth century Roman Catholics (and indeed Nonconformists, too) would still find a career in the civil service or as an officer in the armed forces closed to them. They would risk censure, loss of a job and possibly attack. Small wonder, then, that many preferred to live secret lives.

Things kept secret.

Christianity is not a religion of secrets. All that we need to know for our salvation, for right living on earth and proper service and worship of our Lord can be read plainly in the words of the Bible. All Christians are equal in the sight of God. There is no class of adepts who are superior to the rank and file. There is no set of knowledge that is accessible to the few but not to the many. There is no group that has access to texts that are denied to others. The Protestant Reformation emphasised that all believers have access to God without the mediation of a priestly caste, since those who confess that Jesus Christ is the Son of God form "a chosen people, a royal priesthood, a people belonging to God." (1 Peter 2:9).

One of the early heresies that the apostles went to great lengths to refute was Gnosticism (from the Greek *gnosis*, meaning knowledge). St Paul addresses it in his letter to the Colossians and both Peter and John deal with it in their letters. Gnosticism taught that there were those who had become perfect by being possessors of the secrets or knowledge boasted of by the sect concerned. The Bible quite clearly refutes such claims and ascribes them to the work of the forces of darkness: Revelation speaks of "Satan's so-called deep secrets" (Revelation 2:24).

God likes things above board and undisguised. Jesus says: "For whatever is hidden is meant to be disclosed, and whatever is concealed is meant to be brought out into the open" (Mark 4:22). He affirms that "There is nothing concealed that will not be disclosed, or hidden that will not be made known. What I tell you in the dark, speak in the daylight; what is whispered in your ear, proclaim from the roofs." (Matthew 10:26-27). To go by night is a sign of being furtive, of having a guilty conscience and of being in opposition to God: "Everyone who does evil hates the light, and will not come into the light for fear that his deeds will be exposed. But whoever lives by the truth comes into the light, so that it may be seen plainly that what he has done has been done through God." (John 3:20-21).

It is our duty to shine the light of God's truth wherever we go and to "speak in the daylight" (Matthew 10:27), but we are not possessors of all knowledge. There are things that remain unknown by man: "the secret things [that] belong to the Lord our God" (Deuteronomy 29:29). What these secret things might be is by definition beyond our ken: some will be unknowable by reason of our human limitations, some unknown because God chooses not to reveal them at this point.

Things revealed.

Rather than fret about what the secret things might be, we should rejoice that "the things revealed belong to us and to our children for ever" (Deuteronomy 29:29). These should be our focus. Our knowledge of God, his character, his ways and his plans would be limited indeed had he not chosen to reveal these through his prophets and ultimately through his Son. In his love and his desire to draw us back to him, God has always taken the initiative in revealing himself to mankind.

What God told his people at various stages in redemption history was sufficient for them to believe and do all that he required of them. The same remains true today. The Lord certainly can and does continue to speak to us in various ways, but we cannot on our own initiative add to what he has already said. It follows that, in our doctrinal and ethical teaching, we should emphasise the same things that Scripture emphasises. Where one portion of Scripture is stressed at the expense of another or undue attention given to particular verses divorced from their context there is a great likelihood that we will take a wrong turn.

Similarly, we should be content with what God has told us in Scripture. There are some things about which the Bible says little or nothing. The correct response is to acknowledge that God has revealed exactly what he deems right for us, neither too much nor too little. We should accept this and not regard the Bible as somehow incomplete, nor wish that God had given us more information than there appears. Neither should we treat any part of the Bible as irrelevant or surplus to requirements.

The fact that there are areas on which the Bible places relatively little emphasis should cause us to be humble with regard to doctrinal differences that are of a minor nature. The central truths of Christianity are non-negotiable and should not be traded away or watered down on any account, but there are other areas where Christians can and do differ in good faith. We should be gentle and understanding with each other in relation to these, preferring always to emphasise the things that we share and which unite us, rather than those points on which we disagree.

Things mysterious and paradoxical.

The fact that God has made his revelation plain to mankind does not mean that there are no mysteries connected with it. Even within the confines of what has been revealed, there are certain things that are known only to God and certain things that are knowable only by him. So, for example, the precise timing of events is usually beyond us. Jesus says that: "No-one knows about that day or hour, not even the angels in heaven nor the Son, but only the Father. Be on guard! Be alert! You do not know when that time will come." (Mark 13:32-33). So, too, "the Son of Man will come at an hour when you do not expect him." (Matthew 24:44). This is as it should be. Were we to know when things will happen, it would tend to paralyse our day-to-day activity and replace dynamism with fatalism. It would sap our energies and make a mockery of free will.

In the same way that God's revelation encompasses mysteries, it also contains paradoxes. From a human point of view, living according to the values of the kingdom of God is paradoxical, precisely since the ways of God are so different from those of man. Paradox exists in attitudes, behaviour and their outcomes. For example:

"Blessed are you when people insult you, persecute you and falsely say all kinds of evil against you because of me." (Matthew 5:11).

"Do not resist an evil person. If someone strikes you on the right cheek, turn to him the other also." (Matthew 5:39).

"Love your enemies and pray for those who persecute you." (Matthew 5:44).

"For whoever wants to save his life will lose it, but whoever loses his life for me will find it." (Matthew 16:25);

"Therefore, whoever humbles himself like this child is the greatest in the kingdom of heaven." (Matthew 18:4).

"Instead, whoever wants to become great among you must be your servant, and whoever wants to be first must be your slave" (Matthew 20:26-27).

"So the last will be first, and the first will be last." (Matthew 20:16);

We may not fully understand these paradoxical attitudes and types of behaviour intellectually, but we can test them by the simple process of living them out and observing the result. Those who do so are witness to the blessing that flows and the power of God that is thereby unleashed.

Paradox also exists in the way in which the kingdom of God breaks into the world. We are told that it will come, has come, is coming immediately and will be delayed. Jesus says:

"The kingdom of God does not come with your careful observation, nor will people say, 'Here it is' or 'There it is,' because the kingdom of God is within you." (Luke 17:20-21).

"The kingdom of God is near." (Mark 1:15 and Luke 10:9, 10:11 and 21:31).

"But if I drive out demons by the Spirit of God, then the kingdom of God has come upon you." (Matthew 12:28 and Luke 11:20).

"Then the King will say to those on his right, 'Come, you who are blessed by my Father; take your inheritance, the kingdom prepared for you since the creation of the world'" (Matthew 25:34).

This is not nonsensical and it is not contradictory. It is instead a function of the fact that Jesus has come once and will come again. Applying the proper focus resolves any confusion.

Conclusion.

When we think in terms of secrets, we would do well to remember that the Lord "knows the secrets of the heart" (Psalm 44:21), that there will come a "day when God will judge men's secrets" (Romans 2:16) and that "the secrets of [man's] heart will be laid bare." (1 Corinthians 14:25). The Lord is the one "who sees what is done in secret" (Matthew 6:18) and "Everything is uncovered and laid bare before the eyes of him to whom we must give account." (Hebrews 4:13). We should not live secret lives, but be open with God and with our fellow men.

In doing so, it is important to recognise that the "things revealed" belong to us for a purpose: in order that we "may follow all the words of this law." (Deuteronomy 29:29). Whilst they belong to us and our children, like any possession they can be lost, broken or forgotten. It is our obligation to retain their memory and to teach our young people about them. This is something that we have neglected in recent years. Now is the time to make amends. The spiritual longing in our nation is tangible. If we do not satisfy this need with the gospel, other things will fill the vacuum. We see this already. In words commonly attributed to G. K. Chesterton, "Once people cease to believe in God, they don't believe in nothing. They believe anything." It is time we let England into a secret: there is a God in heaven and the Lord God Almighty is his name. He and he alone should be the focus of our nation.

17. A nation chooses (1)

Exodus 23:20-33.

Key word: preparation.

Nowadays we read with distressing frequency of young men killed in knife fights. These have a long pedigree. In 1593 a twenty-nine year old died in a pub brawl in Deptford, stabbed to the heart. The area was then part of that collection of taverns, brothels, bear-pits and theatres south of the Thames that was beyond the control of the City of London authorities and consequently a haunt for all manner of dubious characters and pursuits. The man who breathed his last proved to have a warrant out for his arrest on charges of atheism and blasphemy, and there were rumours that he was a government agent of some kind. Such things were certainly somewhat uncommon compared to the more run-of-the mill criminality and intrigue of the age, but hardly enough to cause later generations to take note. This murder victim, however, also left behind works of erratic genius. He was Christopher Marlowe: poet, playwright and songwriter.

Marlowe's play *Doctor Faustus* takes a subject later explored by Goethe in *Faust,* dramatising a medieval tale of a man who sells his soul to Satan. Marlowe makes his protagonist a man of arrogance and ambition, who leagues himself with the devil Mephistopheles in order to become "great Emperor of the world." Early in the play, Faustus questions Mephistopheles as to whether hell really exists. The latter replies: "Why, this is hell, nor am I out of it. Think'st thou that I who saw the face of God and tasted the eternal joys of heaven am not tormented with ten thousand hells in being deprived of everlasting bliss?" Ironically, a great paean of religious orthodoxy is put in the mouth of a fiend by a man who denied the existence of God. The dramatic vision of the English atheist is bleaker than that of the German Romantic: Goethe's Doctor is claimed by heaven, Marlowe's by hell.

In *The Jew of Malta*, Marlowe includes a statement more in keeping with his atheism: "I count religion but a childish toy, and hold there is no sin but ignorance." It is a sentiment that chimes with many in modern-day England. For such as these, religion has nothing to offer to any but the retarded or deluded and the future belongs to science, with its promise to dispel ignorance.[38] For those who retain belief in the Almighty, all too often we feel ourselves surrounded by uncertainties and unsure which way to turn, latter-day Israelites wandering in the wilderness.

Preparing our hearts.

In his goodness and mercy, God provides the remedy for our situation: "See, I am sending an angel ahead of you to guard you along the way and to bring you to the place I have prepared ... My angel will go ahead of you and bring you into the land of the Amorites, Hittites, Perizzites, Canaanites, Hivites and Jebusites" (Exodus 23:20 and 23). The fact that God has prepared a place for us, will guard us along the way and will provide the help we need to get there should be a cause of joy and confidence. We will not reach this place without effort on our part, however. There are three things that we need to do as we follow God's way:

"Pay attention to him [the angel, God's representative and messenger] and listen to what he says." (Exodus 23:21).

"Do not rebel against him [the angel]. He will not forgive your rebellion, since my Name is in him." (Exodus 23:21).

"[Listen] carefully to what he [the angel] says and do all that I say" (Exodus 23:22).

In other words, we need to prepare our hearts to receive God's direction and hence his blessing. Each of the three things we are told to do is deceptively simple. Sadly, they are things that we seem to find tremendously difficult to do at all, and even more difficult to do consistently. Paying attention, being obedient and listening carefully do not come easily to a society that increasingly replaces reasoned argument with sound-bites, considered reflection with instant gratification and deference with insubordination. We will have to make an extra effort to overcome these tendencies in our dealings with God.

---

[38] The extent to which modern science increasingly corroborates the existence of God is conveniently overlooked. For example, we can now measure the microwave radiation generated since the universe began. Like a musical note, the wavelength of this radiation has harmonics associated with it which reflect the shape of the object in which the waves were generated. Using these observations, researchers at the Paris Observatory deduce that the universe is shaped like a dodecahedral space and that it is finite. The obvious questions are: if the universe is finite, what came before it and what lies beyond it?

Preparing for blessing.

In order to experience blessing, we must root out what is bad and turn to what is good. Rooting out what is bad has two aspects. First, we need to turn from false gods and the behaviour that accompanies their worship: "Do not bow down before their gods [those of the pagan nations round about] or worship them or follow their practices. You must demolish them and break their sacred stones to pieces." (Exodus 23:24). Second, we are told, "Do not make a covenant with them or with their gods. Do not let them live in your land, or they will cause you to sin against me, because the worship of their gods will certainly be a snare to you." (Exodus 23:32-33).

In a multiracial, multicultural, multi-faith society, we may think that this places us in some difficulty. It is one thing to be told not to worship false gods, quite another to be told to "demolish [them and their practices] and break their sacred stones to pieces ... [and] not [to] let them live in your land." (Exodus 23:24, 33). Of course, many of the false gods of the present day are secular in form, but the fact remains that our land is also host to many non-Christian religious groups. The steady erosion of the Christian fabric of our society in the name of fairness and equality between different faiths and a tendency to 'pick-and-mix' religious views amongst the population at large may well seem evidence that "the worship of [other] gods will certainly be a snare to [us]." (Exodus 23:33).

We need to feel our way carefully at this point, remembering that things that are played out in physical form in the Old Testament are more often played out in a spiritual dimension in the New Testament. We must also take to heart the overarching message of love that runs throughout the Gospel. We are certainly called to preach the good news of Jesus Christ fearlessly amongst all groups and can expect that its power will indeed metaphorically "break their sacred stones to pieces" (Exodus 23:24), but our duty is always to tell the truth in love. We are specifically told not to use physical violence, but to "turn ... the other [cheek]" (Matthew 5:39 and Luke 6:29), for victory will come "'Not by might, nor by power but by my Spirit,' says the LORD Almighty." (Zechariah 4:6).

Humility is also required. We should get our own house in order first. Jesus told us: "first take the plank out of your own eye, and then you will see clearly to remove the speck from your brother's eye." (Matthew 7:5). Our primary duty, therefore, is to make sure that we turn to what is good. This means first and foremost that we must: "Worship the LORD your God" (Exodus 23:25). When we do this properly, everything else will fall into place and, like the walls of Jericho (Joshua 6:20), all the strongholds of the enemy will come a-tumbling down.

Rooting out the bad and turning to the good will bring blessing. This will involve health and long life, fruitfulness and enjoyment of all the good things that the earth has to offer. God says that:

"[Blessing] will be on your food and water." (Exodus 23:25).

"I will take away sickness from among you" (Exodus 23:25).

"[None] will miscarry or be barren in your land." (Exodus 23:25).

"I will give you a full life span." (Exodus 23:26).

An end to sickness and premature death seems like an impossible dream, a vision of the Promised Land indeed, but this is what the Lord holds out to us. These words are not idly spoken, neither is the prospect a mirage: "For the LORD your God will bless you as he has promised" (Deuteronomy 15:6).

Preparing the ground.

The Promised Land points ultimately to heaven, but there is also territory that God requires us to take hold of here on earth. The place that God has prepared for us is a land that is already occupied. The Israelites found the land of Canaan settled by a variety of different tribes. These included "the Amorites, Hittites, Perizzites, Hivites and Jebusites" (Exodus 23:23), peoples noted for their worship of false gods and for their barbarous practices, including child sacrifice and ritual prostitution. In the same way, the spiritual ground we must seize for God is also occupied by those who stand in settled and wilful opposition to him and his ways. Whichever areas we consider, both public and private, there we will find dark forces as well as good: in media, education, health policy and such like. These are the modern equivalents of the tribes that confronted the Israelites, those being physical manifestations and playthings of the spiritual forces that stood behind them.

We might imagine that God will drive out these dark forces in one fell swoop, but that is not so. They will be driven out to an extent and at a pace that is commensurate with our ability to occupy, hold and profitably use the ground that is won. God tells the Israelites that "I will not drive them [the pagan nations] out in a single year, because the land would become desolate and the wild animals too numerous for you. Little by little I will drive them out before you, until you have increased enough to take possession of the land." (Exodus 23:29-30).

This is a healthy reminder for us. The fact that there are so many areas of our national life that are under the control of forces inimical to God is in large measure a reflection of the fact that we do not have godly people ready, able and willing to move into them. If we truly wish to see these aspects of the country's life won for the Lord, we must recruit, equip and train for the job. Up to now, we have shown little appetite for this task, let alone the necessary aptitude and application. Unless and until we do, these areas will remain foreign territory. An awful lot of preparation will be necessary if we are to move forward in the way God wishes.

We should ask God to prepare the ground, but we should not neglect the preparation that we need to undertake: preparing our hearts, preparing for blessing and preparing people to settle territory that the enemy vacates.

Preparing for victory.

We also need to change our attitudes and mentality so that we prepare for victory. God says that: "I will be an enemy to your enemies and will oppose those who oppose you." (Exodus 23:22). He promises victory to his people: "I will send my terror ahead of you and throw into confusion every nation you encounter. I will make all your enemies turn their backs and run. I will send the hornet ahead of you to drive the Hivites, Canaanites and Hittites out of your way." (Exodus 23:27-28).

However, no-one will achieve victory who believes victory to be impossible. Regrettably, that appears to be our present situation. There is in fact no excuse for defeatism. When God makes a promise, that promise can be relied on. What we need to concentrate on are the conditions we need to fulfil in order to be able to claim the promise.

The Lord extends Israel's territory: "I will establish your borders from the Red Sea to the Sea of the Philistines and from the desert to the River. I will hand over to you the people who live in the land and you will drive them out before you." (Exodus 23:31). He will do the same for us if we "pay attention ... do not rebel ... [and] listen" (Exodus 23:21-22). In similar fashion will he extend our spiritual territory, if and to the extent that we are able to cope with the added responsibility that this will bring.

Conclusion.

The England of Marlowe's day was a place of uncertainty. There was uncertainty about the political future, as an ageing and childless queen neared the end of her days; about the uneasy compromise that governed religious affairs, with Puritans at one end of the spectrum, Roman Catholics at the other and the Church of England in between; about economic disruption resulting from closure of the monasteries, the enclosure of common land and a new class of indigent poor thereby created. The country was coming by degrees to that fork in the road that led eventually to civil war.

We, too, feel ourselves beset by uncertainty. Our fears are understandable, but illusory. Jesus says: "So do not worry, saying, 'What shall we eat?' or 'What shall we drink?' or 'What shall we wear?' For the pagans run after all these things, and your heavenly Father knows that you need them. But seek first his kingdom and his righteousness, and all these things will be given to you as well. Therefore do not worry about tomorrow, for tomorrow will worry about itself. Each day has enough trouble of its own." (Matthew 6:31-34). Somehow we have to find the ability to set aside fear and worry and to concentrate on what is truly important. We must prepare our hearts, prepare for blessing, prepare the ground and prepare for victory. Like Marlowe's Faustus, we can choose the road we take: to be ambitious, like him, for worldly things or for the things of God. Our choices will help determine whether the people of this land are claimed by heaven or by hell. This is a time of preparation. Let us use it wisely.

18. A nation chooses (2)

2 Thessalonians 2:1-12.

Key word: delusions.

Macbeth is one of Shakespeare's finest tragedies. In the opening scene, three witches prophesy that the victorious general will become thane of Cawdor and thereafter king of Scotland. When the first prediction comes to pass, Macbeth's wife persuades him to murder King Duncan so as to make the realm his. Remorse, despair and madness unfold against a background of further killing before the usurper dies in battle and the rightful order is restored.

The play was probably finished in 1606, by which time the first Stuart king of England, James, had been three years in London (after already reigning more than thirty years in Scotland). This "wisest fool in Christendom" was the reputed author of the *True Law of Free Monarchies*, published in the year of his accession to the English throne. The book responds to the contention that a king is elected by and is responsible to the people and makes the countervailing argument: that kings are established by God and are responsible to him alone.

Being a foreigner in England, James trod carefully. His son was less circumspect. As the reign of Charles I progressed it became increasingly obvious that Parliament and the king had competing and mutually exclusive concepts of government. The former looked to the privileges it had won from often reluctant monarchs in preceding reigns and sought to protect and augment them, the right to vote taxes being particularly jealously guarded. The latter proclaimed with increasing stridency the so-called divine right of kings and sought to free administrative purse-strings from the unwelcome control of elected representatives. The contest increasingly acquired a religious overlay as Puritans sided with Parliament, whilst high Anglicans and Roman Catholics aligned with the king.

For eleven years the monarch dispensed with Parliament altogether, using ingenious and ever more desperate schemes to raise the money he needed. At last, however, the need for cash was so acute that he could not avoid recalling elected representatives to vote new taxes. The result was uproar as pent-up resentments burst in a torrent against the king and his ministers. The stage was being set for civil war. Shortly, the nation would be forced to choose: between Parliament and the king, between rebellion and loyalty, between competing visions of right and wrong.

Counterfeits.

In his second letter to the early church in Thessalonica, St Paul wrote "Concerning the coming of our Lords Jesus Christ and our being gathered to him" (2 Thessalonians 2:1). His aim was to scotch false reports, to uncover forged letters and to lay bare false prophecy, which had made people "unsettled or alarmed" (2 Thessalonians 2:2). The difficulty arose from "some prophecy, report or letter supposed to have come from us, saying that the day of the Lord has already come." (2 Thessalonians 2:2). St Paul advised: "Don't let anyone deceive you in any way, for that day will not come until the rebellion occurs and the man of lawlessness is revealed, the man doomed to destruction." (2 Thessalonians 2:3).

The Thessalonians were confronted by counterfeits – perversions and parodies of the truth. This is one of the tricks of the enemy: if we were presented with things that were wholly bad, we would straight away see them for what they are and reject them without further ado. Instead, "Satan himself masquerades as an angel of light. It is not surprising, then, if his servants masquerade as servants of righteousness." (2 Corinthians 11:14-15). The forces of darkness leaven what they dangle before us with just enough of what appears worthy or desirable for us to mistake it for something good. They show a seemingly glamorous beginning but never a degraded end. They manipulate our weaknesses and even our best intentions for evil purposes. Thus loyalty is transposed into gang mentality, the desire for a father's love and approval into obedience to dictators large and small, a longing for closeness and affection into promiscuity. "The work of Satan [is] displayed in all kinds of counterfeit miracles, signs and wonders, and in every sort of evil that deceives those who are perishing." (2 Thessalonians 2:9).

The protagonists in *Macbeth* utter many of the counterfeits that beset our age:

That what is good is really bad and vice versa: "Fair is foul and foul is fair."

That there is no moral absolute: "This supernatural soliciting cannot be ill, cannot be good."

That there is no God to judge us: "What need we fear who knows it, when none can call our power to account?"

That life is meaningless and there is no existence after death: "Life's but a walking shadow, a poor player, that struts and frets his hour upon the stage, and then is heard no more; it is a tale told by an idiot, full of sound and fury, signifying nothing."

That nothing and nobody can touch us: "I bear a charmed life."

That we are imprisoned by our past, with no hope of acceptance by God: "They have tied me to the stake; I cannot fly. But bear-like must fight the course."

These are siren voices. They are just as misleading and just as dangerous as those against which St Paul warned. We must recognise them for what they are, look honestly at where they lead and call a spade a spade.

Rebellion.

The power that Satan and his counterfeits have over mankind is ultimately the consequence of our rebellion: rebellion not against an earthly ruler, but against the High King of Heaven, the Lord God Almighty. St Paul writes of "those who are perishing" that "They perish because they refused to love the truth and to be saved. For this reason God sends them a powerful delusion so that they will believe the lie and so that all will be condemned who have not believed the truth but have delighted in wickedness." (2 Thessalonians 2:10-12). To "believe the lie" (2 Thessalonians 2:11) is a choice, not something that is imposed upon us.

We are not helpless in the face of the counterfeits that surround us. For all that they may take the form of "miracles, signs and wonders" (2 Thessalonians 2:9), we do not have to be deceived by them. These counterfeits will always be shown up for what they are when they are exposed to the light of God's truth[39]. The issue is whether we are prepared to accept this truth, adopt it for our own and shine it upon areas of darkness. If we are to do so we must forgo our rebellion against God, cease our refusal "to love the truth and be saved" (2 Thessalonians 2:10) and no longer be amongst those who "delighted in wickedness" (2 Thessalonians 2:12). In short, we must turn again to the Lord.

Lawlessness.

In our present society, as in all others at every stage of history, those who are on the side of right live amongst those who would rather do wrong. St Paul describes both this and something more than this, an active rebellion that comprises the supreme opposition of evil to the things of God. Instrumental in

---

[39] As a starting point we should apply the same tests that hold good in other walks of life when seeking to discern truth from falsehood, by looking to (1) first-hand evidence, preferably from eyewitnesses and corroborated by a number of independent sources, (2) correspondence between assertion and attested fact, (3) consistency between words and deeds, (4) unity of theory and practical experience, and (5) ultimate outcomes rather than initial results. Christianity passes such tests with flying colours. Other religions do not.

such rebellion is "the man of lawlessness ... the man doomed to destruction. He will oppose and will exalt himself over everything that is called God or worshipped, so that he sets himself up in God's temple, proclaiming himself to be God." (2 Thessalonians 2:4). This individual is not Satan (he is clearly distinguished from Satan in verse 9) and neither is he merely a military or political leader. Instead he claims a place above every god and everything associated with worship. He even claims to be the one true God.[40]

At the time when St Paul wrote, the work of the man of lawlessness was under some kind of restraint: the apostle talks of "what is holding him back" (2 Thessalonians 2:6) and of "the one who now holds him back" (2 Thessalonians 2:7). Speculations as to the nature of this curb include the temporal power of the state, the effect of St Paul's missionary work, the work of the Holy Spirit, the activity of the worldwide church, and others. Whatever the source of this check might be, present circumstances do not readily seem to fit the time when "the one who holds [the secret power of lawlessness] back ... is taken out of the way" (2 Thessalonians 2:7) and the full power of "the lawless one" (2 Thessalonians 2:8) is unleashed. Rather, what we experience here and now is "the secret power of lawlessness ... already at work; [with] the one who now holds it back [continuing] to do so until he is taken out of the way. And then the lawless one will be revealed ..." (2 Thessalonians 2:7-8).

In confronting "the secret power of lawlessness ... at work" (2 Thessalonians 2:7), we need to make choices. The choices that faced the nation in the run-up to civil war were momentous, but they were essentially the same ones that we currently face, albeit writ larger. We, too, must choose between competing visions of the kind of society in which we should live. We, likewise, must opt for rebellion or loyalty: rebellion against God or loyalty to him. We, also, must elect between right and wrong. It is of cardinal importance that our choices should not be based on delusions but should instead be firmly rooted in God's truth.

We will be aided in making correct choices if we recollect that "the Lord Jesus will overthrow with the breath of his mouth and destroy by the splendour of his coming." (2 Thessalonians 2:8). This same breath which destroys "the lawless one" (2 Thessalonians 2:8) is the Spirit of God that gives life to, animates and sustains all things: the Lord "breathed into [Adam's] nostrils the breath of life" (Genesis 2:7) and Jesus "breathed on [his disciples]" (John 20:22). Out of

---

[40] As with many prophesies, this may have a number of levels of fulfilment, with each age having its "man of lawlessness." One instance of someone elevating himself to the status of God is provided by Napoleon Bonaparte. Whilst occupying the Roman States, French troops distributed his picture with the inscription: "This is the true likeness of the holy saviour of the world!"

this same mouth "comes a sharp sword with which to strike down the nations." (Revelation 19:15). Jesus warns: "Repent therefore! Otherwise, I will soon come to you and will fight against them with the sword of my mouth." (Revelation 2:16). As St Paul advised, we should "not let anyone deceive [us] in any way." (2 Thessalonians 2:3).

Conclusion.

Macbeth's actions were based on delusions: that murder could go unpunished, that a malign power might truthfully foretell, that a crime was needed to bring about what had been foretold, that good could be founded on evil. Instead, as he later wearily acknowledges, "Things bad begun grow worse by ill."

Charles I's attempts to secure untrammelled power were similarly beset by delusions. He imagined that he could with impunity ride roughshod over the accumulated freedoms of the English, that he could dispense with Parliament and rule by decree and that his resort to force was justified. On 22 August 1642, he made what was effectively a declaration of war by raising his standard outside the walls of Nottingham castle. The place is called Standard Hill to this day. There he called on loyal subjects to join his army. In fact, few did, for Nottingham's sympathies lay with Parliament. Nevertheless, the king had set his people on the road to a calamitous conflict, in which perhaps as many as one in twenty of the population may have died. He did it ultimately in pursuit of the delusion of power.

We may smile at the delusions of those long dead and gone. We may be diverted by the delusions portrayed upon the stage. We may even be alert to the delusions of others. We are less apt to spot our own delusions. This land is at present in the grip of delusions of many kinds, but their ultimate source is the same: a denial of and rebellion against God. It is the greatest and most fatal delusion that any human being can entertain. From it springs all manner of evil. Amongst other outgrowths of this evil, we see in England an increasing lawlessness, apparent not just in crime statistics but in the erosion of habits of kindliness, politeness and consideration for others. It is time to wake from our long nightmare and start to repair the damage that this has done to the fabric of our society and to individual lives.

In setting about this task, we should be mindful of "the coming of our Lord and our being gathered to him" (2 Thessalonians 2:1). The knowledge of Christ's return is a balancing doctrine. It gives perspective to both present and future, thereby helping us to set priorities that honour God. It combats any tendency to fatalistic resignation, withdrawal from society and neglect of worldly duties. The fact that Jesus' coming is imminent but is not yet should cause us to be alert and watchful. It should inspire us to be eager and active in working for the kingdom of God. It should caution us to be on our guard against delusions and to take to heart the teaching of our Saviour, to "keep the way of the LORD by doing what is right and just" (Genesis 18:19), to be "doers of the word, and not hearers only, deceiving [our] own selves." (James 1:22, KJV).

In the *Tempest*, the latest of his completed works, Shakespeare observed that "We are such things as dreams are made on." The statement encompasses and illumines two competing sides of human nature, achievement and aspiration: on the one hand lies an insubstantial and unworthy thing that is flown in the night; on the other, a thing of beauty that soars to the heavenly realms. We once had a dream of England that looked to the latter. There is no need to settle for the former. Rather, we should work with God to make of these islands a place in which the rightful order is restored and of which Caliban might exclaim: "O brave new world, that has such creatures in it!"

19. Brother against brother

Judges 5:19-23.

Key word: partnership.

Oliver Cromwell was a divisive figure in life and remains so in death. For many, his memory is indelibly stained by massacres at Drogheda and Wexford during his Irish campaign of 1649. For some he is the archetype of the Puritan bigot: a sanctimonious kill-joy and a hypocrite. Others remember him as the killer of his king, a war-monger and dictator whose standing army and rule through major-generals forever inoculated England against militarism. This Cromwell was a man whose religion was but a fig-leaf for ambition and expediency.

There is another Cromwell. Ireland excepted, in war he was humane. In private life he was warm and fun-loving, readily showing emotion and crying easily, a caring father and a loving husband. He was a man who enjoyed music, dancing and practical jokes. He was at first in favour of accommodation with the monarch, until Charles I provoked the second civil war in 1648 and drove many to the conclusion that there would be no end to bloodshed as long as he lived. For Cromwell, the execution of the sovereign was a "cruel necessity," not something that he deliberately sought from the start.[41] The king gone, he tried repeatedly to fashion a parliamentary form of the godly government he craved, until bitter experience proved this a chimera. As Lord Protector he steered a remarkably even course in the stormy post-war years, acknowledged abroad as a statesman and a man to be reckoned with. Far from seeking power for its own sake, after much agonising he turned down the crown when it was offered to him. Far from unbridled bigotry, he was in some respects notable for his toleration. He it was who was responsible for Jews being readmitted to England for the first time in more than three and a half centuries.[42] Far from being a doctrinaire Puritan zealot, he was usually pragmatic, responding to complaints about the religious affiliations of some of his appointees: "Sir, the State, in choosing men to serve it, takes no notice of their opinions."

We each inevitably bring prejudices to bear upon the past. Whatever those may be, the facts of this man's life are arresting. At the outbreak of civil war in

---

[41] At the Army Debates in 1647 (see chapter 27) Cromwell vetoed demands for overthrow of the monarchy.

[42] Jews were expelled in 1290, during the reign of Edward I.

1642, he was a relative nobody, well into middle age[43] and with no previous military experience. Yet within two years force of personality, coupled with fearsome tactical and organisational abilities, saw him command the Parliamentary cavalry at Marston Moor. The next year (1645) he was made second-in-command to Sir Thomas Fairfax, helped to form the New Model Army and, following decisive victory at Naseby, emerged as the leading voice of the army faction. From 1648 he was sole commander, and as such never lost a battle.

New Model army.

Cromwell's record shows that he was not in general a bloodthirsty man, though in Ireland he seems to have given way to what he afterwards regarded as a godly rage. Undoubtedly he viewed war as a proving-ground and a means of testing God's will. Of his part in the victory at Marston Moor he wrote, "We never charged but we routed the enemy ... God made them as stubble to our swords." Nevertheless, where possible he sought to avoid armed conflict. Thus at the outset of his Scottish campaign he pleaded with the General Assembly of the Scottish Kirk: "I beseech you, in the bowels of Christ, think it possible you may be mistaken." Only when it became clear that a breach was inevitable did he lead his forces into Scotland in order to spare northern England from invasion. In his hands, the New Model army proved what a superbly disciplined instrument of warfare it had become. His victory over the Scots at Dunbar on 3 September 1650 was one of the most shattering ever won by England: some twenty or so men killed against thousands of the enemy dead and taken prisoner. Exactly a year later he routed the forces that the future Charles II had led into England at the battle of Worcester, effectively ending any serious royalist military threat.

As a soldier, Cromwell's professionalism and preparation were always outstanding. He made great efforts, for instance, to ensure that his men were well mounted: "Then thundered the horses' hooves – galloping, galloping go his mighty steeds." (Judges 5:22). Good equipment, however, was only the starting point. He wanted an army that was not just well-equipped and well-led, but one whose soldiers were godly men. He sought "such men as had the fear of God before them and as made some conscience of what they did ... the plain russet-coated captain that knows what he fights for and loves what he knows."

Cromwell did not take needless risks in war, but neither did he flinch if the odds seemed against him. If victory were won in such circumstances, it was all

---

[43] Cromwell was 42 in 1642. Life expectancy at the time made this a fairly advanced middle age.

the more evidence of God's favour. Typically, as he raised himself in the saddle to unleash his cavalry at the start of the battle of Dunbar, he bellowed the opening words of Psalm 68: "Let God arise and let his enemies be scattered." (Psalm 68:1). As far as Cromwell was concerned, the battles that he fought on earth were but mirrors and extensions of battles fought in heaven. This is a view endorsed by Scripture. The book of Judges pictures the very Creation as being involved in the battle between Israel and her Canaanite oppressors under the general Sisera. First is described the earthly battle: "Kings came, they fought; the kings of Canaan fought at Taanach by the waters of Megiddo, but they carried off no silver, no plunder." (Judges 5:19). In parallel is the spiritual dimension: "From the heavens the stars fought, from their courses they fought against Sisera. The river Kishon swept them away, the age-old river, the river Kishon." (Judges 5:20-21).

New Model citizens.

This spiritual aspect applies equally to civilian as to military matters. Immediately before and during the Civil War, Puritan preachers were fond of taking as their theme 'Meroz accursed.' The point they wished to drive home was that it was not possible to be neutral in the conflict between king and Parliament. The duty of all people was to "come to help the LORD, to help the LORD against the mighty." (Judges 5:23). In the event, substantial numbers of Englishmen disagreed with them: in various areas of the country groups called Clubmen flourished, equally opposed to both warring factions and prepared to use violence against either in order to keep the conflict away from their locality.

The preachers had a point, however. Jesus said, "Do not suppose that I have come to bring peace to the earth. I did not come to bring peace, but a sword. For I have come to turn 'a man against his father, a daughter against her mother, a daughter-in-law against her mother-in-law – a man's enemies will be the members of his own household.'" (Matthew 10:34-36, referring to Micah 7:6). Whilst Christ came to bring peace – peace between men and peace between men and God – the inevitable result of his coming was and is conflict. There is conflict between Christ and anti-Christ, between light and darkness, between God's children and the devil's. This conflict is a kind of civil war. It encompasses even members of the same family.

Like the writer of Judges, Jesus emphasised that spiritual neutrality is not possible, telling his disciples that "He who is not with me is against me, and he who does not gather with me, scatters." (Luke 11:23). At first blush this might seem to sit uneasily with the fact that Jesus also says of "a man driving out demons in [his] name ... 'Do not stop him ... for whoever is not against you is for you.'" (Luke 9:49-50). In fact, the context readily clarifies the issue. On both occasions, Jesus is speaking in relation to the driving out of demons. Now, we may not be entirely comfortable with it in our modern western culture, but the fact is that the Bible very clearly tells us that there is not just a personal God, but a personal devil as well. This personal devil, Satan (the accuser, the adversary) has legions of fallen angels (demons) in his service. Sometimes these demons have human beings so much in their power that we can speak of someone being 'possessed' by them.

Jesus is telling us something of great moment: although like the Clubmen we may wish to sit on the sidelines, this simply is not possible. If we align ourselves with the Lord and honestly do our best to act in accordance with his teaching, we are on the side of good. If we do not, then our silence, our failure to act and complicity in the wrongdoing of others is as much help to the forces of darkness as if we actively took up arms in their cause. It is indeed the case that, for evil to prosper, it is only necessary that good men do nothing.

New Model nation.

This may sound melodramatic, so it is worth exploring. Jesus says: "he who does not gather with me, scatters." In the cosmic conflict between God and the devil, the human soul is a battleground. God gathers souls to him: "[The Son of Man – Jesus] will send his angels and gather his elect from the four winds, from the ends of the earth to the ends of the heavens." (Mark 13:27). The gifts of God's Holy Spirit are things that build partnership and community, that gather people together in fellowship and love. St Paul tells us that "the fruit of the Spirit is love, joy, peace, patience, kindness, goodness, faithfulness, gentleness and self-control." (Galatians 5:22-23).

By contrast, Satan tries to scatter, to disrupt the work of God and to prevent our gaining salvation. His objective is the opposite of God's: that instead of gathering to God and drawing near him, we will be scattered and estranged from him.[44] Accordingly Satan's works, the "works of the flesh," destroy community and fellowship with God and amongst men through "sexual immorality, impurity and debauchery, idolatry and witchcraft, hatred, discord, jealousy, fits of rage, selfish ambition, dissensions, factions and envy, drunkenness, orgies and the like." (Galatians 5:19-21)

We need to nail our colours to the mast. What we do, every minute and second of every day, has eternal significance. We may feel like people of no consequence, we may think that we cannot affect the world, but that just is not true. With small steps, soft words and hearts that belong to Jesus, we can move mountains. If we wish to see our nation restored, we must work for the things

---

[44] Compare God's words as recorded by the prophet Zechariah and quoted by two of the gospel writers: "I will strike the shepherd and the sheep of the flock will be scattered." (Zechariah 13:7, Matthew 26:31 and 56, Mark 14:49-50)

that belong to God, to help rebuild partnership and community and thereby see our people gathered together in fellowship and love. There is no option but to engage ourselves fully in this work. If we do not, then the words spoken in the book of Judges will apply equally to us: "'Curse Meroz', said the angel of the LORD. 'Curse its people bitterly, because they did not come to help the LORD, to help the LORD against the mighty.'" (Judges 5:23).

Conclusion.

Opinions of the Lord Protector tend to tell as much about the holder of the opinion as about the man they purport to describe. The very convolutions that he went through in trying to discern God's will in trying circumstances were seen by those of his contemporaries who were against him as evidence that he acted in bad faith. The extraordinary turns of events that brought him to prominence and then to power were read as showing that he must always have acted through selfish ambition, for otherwise his rise was inexplicable. His acts of mercy, generosity and tolerance were deliberately overlooked to emphasise the instances that mar an otherwise fine record. He was undoubtedly a great man, but for all that he represents division rather than partnership.

After the cold certainties of war, Cromwell found the messiness and compromise of politics frustrating. No longer was it possible to see God's judgment delivered swift, sure and certain as on the battlefield. Such is the arena in which we must fight, murky and confusing though it may often be. For this we need a New Model Army to come into the battle zones of this land, bringing not death and the sword but the Word of God, his healing, cleansing power and his salvation: an army to fight not physical battles, but spiritual ones. Creating an army of this kind will mean amongst other things reclaiming men for God and making more room in our concept of what the Christian life entails for virtues that we regard as masculine as well as those that we regard as feminine. We need to relearn how to fight for our faith, how to suffer and if need be die for what is right and good and true. We have to rediscover the need for taking personal responsibility, not just for our own spiritual health but for that of the land in which we live.

An army needs leaders and it needs followers. We should ask God to raise up his spiritual army in this nation, to commission its officers and to enlist its rank and file, to form them into squads, companies and regiments, to drill and equip them so that they will be able to reclaim ground that the enemy has held unopposed for too long. We should pray for him to give us the impetus no longer to sit on the sidelines like the people of Meroz, but to engage fully in the battles ahead, "strong in the Lord and in his mighty power." (Ephesians 6:10).

Civil war marks the final breach of those bonds that hold us in one polity. Instead of cleaving together, nations cleave asunder. Instead of togetherness and understanding, there is discord and hatred. Instead of partnership, there is faction and the pursuit of selfish gain. Mercifully, there is no civil war in present-day England, but there is a distinct loosening of the ties that should bind us together in the bundle of life. A healthy land involves partnership at all levels of society. Sadly, that sense of mutual affection and responsibility is becoming weaker and rarer. God wishes to work in partnership with us to mend this brokenness. It is for us to proclaim this joyous message to our land, and to match our deeds to our words.

20. Commonwealth

Leviticus 11:44-45.

Key word: holiness.

The years of the Commonwealth prove how difficult it is for flawed human beings to achieve holiness. The experiments in government that the army council and then Cromwell alone conducted during this time were an ever more despairing attempt to make the rule of the saints a reality in England. Again and again there was disappointment. Hand-picked groups proved just as fractious as those they replaced. The franchise was restricted and then pared again, but still there was no end to the capacity of men for pursuing self-interest and creating faction.

At the end of the second Civil War the Long Parliament, which had first been called by Charles I in November 1640, was still sitting. It did not much outlast the peace. On 6 December 1648 about 140 members were expelled on the orders of the army council, an event known as Pride's Purge from the name of the colonel whose men carried it out. The aim was to rid the House of Commons of any still anxious to negotiate with Charles I. Those who remained were called the Rump Parliament. They survived for a further five years, unrepresentative and quarrelsome, until Cromwell had had enough. Sick of their failure to produce political and religious reforms, he acted decisively. On 20 April 1653 he descended on Westminster at the head of a troop of soldiers and addressed the shocked assembly thus:

"It is high time for me to put an end to your sitting in this place, which you have dishonoured by your contempt of all virtue, and defiled by your practice of every vice; ye are a factious crew, and enemies to all good government, ye are a pack of mercenary wretches, and would like Esau sell your country for a mess of potage, and like Judas betray your God for a few pieces of money; is there a single virtue now remaining among you? Is there one vice you do not possess? Ye have no more religion than my horse; gold is your God; which of you has not bartered your conscience for bribes? Is there a man amongst you that has the least care for the good of the Commonwealth? Ye sordid prostitutes, have you not defiled this sacred place, and turned the Lord's temple into a den of thieves, by your immoral principles and wicked practices? Ye are grown intolerably odious to the whole nation; you who were deputed here by the people to get grievances redressed, are yourselves become the greatest grievance. Your country therefore calls upon me to cleanse this Augean stable by putting a final period to your iniquitous proceedings in this house; and which by God's help, and the strength he has given me, I am now come to do; I command ye therefore, upon the peril of your lives, to depart immediately out of this place; go, get you out! Make haste! Ye venal slaves, be gone!"

Despite this outburst, Cromwell still sought to work through the House of Commons (the House of Lords having by this time been abolished). In July 1653 he instituted a body composed of men hand-picked by him and other army chiefs. The resulting group was known as the Barebones Parliament from the name of a prominent member, Praise-God Barebone. It was also called the Parliament of the Saints. Cromwell initially had high hopes for it, but in the event it was crippled by religious disputes. Within six months it voted its own dissolution and handed over power to Cromwell as Lord Protector, which he remained until his death five years later.

Teaching.

Even allowing for the fact that Cromwell was in a towering rage as he addressed the Rump Parliament in April 1653 and that his charges might therefore be exaggerated, there is clearly at least an element of truth in them. It is a sorry commentary on the weakness and sinfulness of human beings. Our best intentions and most carefully designed institutions are no protection against our fallen nature. As the subsequent tale of the Barebones Parliament illustrates, even a group composed entirely of those we consider most godly is not immune from this taint.

Against that background, Leviticus makes uncomfortable reading. Holiness is its central theme. The word "holy" appears more often in this book than in any other of the Bible. Leviticus makes clear that Israel was to be totally consecrated to God. Her holiness was to be expressed in every aspect of life, to the extent that all of life had a ceremonial quality. As a result of God's nature and because of what he has done, his people must dedicate themselves fully to him. Hence the Lord tells them: "therefore be holy, because I am holy." (Leviticus 11:45).

The same concept is echoed by Jesus (and, typically, given an extra twist) in the Sermon on the Mount when he says: "Be perfect, therefore, even as your heavenly Father is perfect." (Matthew 5:48). Both the Old Testament injunction to holiness and New Testament one to perfection are breathtaking. We know from history and even more from personal experience that it is impossible by human efforts alone to live up to the righteous demands of a holy God, still less to be holy or perfect ourselves.

Rather than frustrate us, however, God wants to teach us. The Law of Moses was designed to lead the Israelites to be dependent on God. Just as the Lord provided rituals and sacrifices for cleansing a sinful people, so he wants us to learn that only through the supernatural provision of a sinless Saviour can we hope to achieve holiness. God does not set us up to fail, but he does want us to reach a proper recognition of what we are and who he is. Only then can we fully appreciate that we need to depend upon him in all things. As St Paul puts it: "So then, just as you have received Christ Jesus as Lord, continue to live in him, rooted and built up in him, strengthened in the faith as you were taught, and overflowing with thankfulness." (Colossians 2:6).

Dedicating.

Chapters 11-15 of Leviticus set out rules and regulations concerning diet (Leviticus 11), childbirth and related matters (Leviticus 12), leprosy and other skin diseases (Leviticus 13-14) and bodily discharges (Leviticus 15). In each case there is a description of what causes defilement, followed by instructions on how to regain purity. The instructions are lengthy and detailed, since holiness demands attention to detail.

Leviticus 11 concerns purity in diet and thus addresses issues of avoidable defilement. The Israelites are told: "Do not defile yourselves ... do not make yourselves unclean ... Do not make yourselves unclean" (Leviticus 11:43-44). It is at the end of the section of dietary instructions that God also tells them: "I am the LORD your God; consecrate yourselves and be holy, because I am holy." (Leviticus 11:44).

To consecrate means to set apart as sacred, to devote to the service of someone or something (usually divine or sacred), to dedicate or to hallow. It is appropriate that the instruction to "consecrate yourselves" comes within a section dealing with avoidable defilement since the issue is one of choice. We can choose a lifestyle that will lead to defilement or we can choose to follow Jesus. If we opt for the latter, Jesus will cover us with his own holiness, purity and perfection so that we are treated as righteous in the eyes of God, no matter what we have done or failed to do. If we do not follow him, we will have nothing to fall back on but our own endeavours, and these will not avail.

We no longer live in the period of the temple and sacrificial system that applied to the Israelites of old. Nor are we subject in full to the Law of Moses. We have a new freedom by virtue of the death of Jesus on the cross, albeit that this freedom should never descend into licence: "It is for freedom that Christ has set us free ... But do not use your freedom to indulge the sinful nature; rather, serve one another in love." (Galatians 5:1 and 13). "Live as free men, but do not use your freedom as a cover-up for evil; live as servants of God." (1 Peter 2:16).

When we consider what it means for us to consecrate ourselves, therefore, in the modern context we are talking about dedicating ourselves to Jesus and to the way that he taught. This dedication must be accompanied by attention to detail just as it was for the Israelites. Every aspect of our lives has the potential to affect our destiny and the destiny of others. Every little action or inaction contributes on one side of the equation or the other.

These are not just words or thoughts without practical application. At the most mundane level it is not difficult to imagine things that would transform this land. If nobody were to drop litter or spray graffiti, how much better our environment would be and what resources would be released for use elsewhere. If all were to display courtesy, how much needless hurt would be avoided. If every man did a fair day's work for a fair day's pay, how much better off we would be. These things are hardly the apogee of holiness or perfection. They are simple everyday things that are readily within our reach. The issue is one of choice.

Seldom is the issue put before the nation in this way. We need to start making the case for holiness. We need to start making the case for God.

Setting apart.

God's desire for us goes further: "I am the LORD who brought you up out of Egypt to be your God; therefore be holy, because I am holy." (Leviticus 11:45). The Lord has brought us out of slavery for a purpose. He wishes us to be his people and this means that we should be holy, for his "eyes are too pure to look on evil." (Habbakuk 2:13). When we do things that are wrong in God's sight, we "grieve the Holy Spirit of God" (Ephesians 4:30). We should do everything in our power to express our love and gratitude to him, not do things that cause him pain. To seek holiness is thus one way of expressing what we feel for our Saviour.

To be holy means to be made sacred, set apart for the service of God or other sacred use, morally pure, free from sin or sinful affections, of high spiritual excellence. The injunction to holiness is found time and again: see Leviticus 19:2, 20:7 and 26, 21:8 and 15, 22:9, 16 and 32. We reflect too little on what this setting apart might mean in modern-day Britain. Clearly it cannot mean that we are to hive ourselves off from our fellow men. Quite the contrary: we are to be "the salt of the earth ... [and] the light of the world" (Matthew 5:13-14) and for this we need to be actively engaged in and part of society, not separated from it.

Our setting apart is therefore to be of a moral and spiritual nature. We are not to follow the ways of the world but the ways of God. We are to set a different example of how life can and should be lived. We are to have different dynamics in our relationships and different ways of acting, so that we "do not conform any longer to the pattern of this world, but [are] transformed by the renewing of [our] mind." (Romans 12:2). We are to be a "voice calling in the wilderness" (Isaiah 40:3 and Mark 1:3) by offering the good news of Jesus Christ to family, friends, neighbours, colleagues and fellow-citizens. We are to "prepare the way for the Lord [and] make straight paths for him." (Isaiah 40:3 and Mark 1:3).

The Lord clearly tells us that we are not on our own in the pursuit of holiness. It is he who makes holiness possible for us and for others. The message is repeated lest we miss it first time round. Its application to all people is shown by use of the second person (twice), the third person singular and the third person plural (twice): "Consider them holy, because I the LORD am holy – I who make you holy ... I am the LORD, who makes him holy ... I am the LORD, who makes them holy ... I am the LORD who makes them holy ... I am the LORD who makes you holy." (Leviticus 21:8 and 15, 22:9, 16 and 32). For sinful human beings to become holy is a tall order, but incredibly God makes it possible.

Conclusion.

The Commonwealth and the Protectorate were ultimately times of great disappointment for those who had supported Parliament in the Civil War. They were disappointing because their experiments failed. They failed to implement Puritan principles on a spiritual level through durable nationwide church reform or on a practical level through a workable parliamentary form of government. They failed to create an enduring institution in the office of Lord Protector. They failed to remould the English people in a new and godlier image. They failed to bring about the rule of the saints on earth. There must have seemed a terrible irony in the words that Cromwell spoke during his parting address to the Rump Parliament: "It is not fit that you should sit here any longer! ... You shall now give place to better men." They were forced to confront the fact that the "better men" were just as prone to error as those they replaced. They were forced to confront the fact that they could not bring about holiness.

This might seem discouraging, but the fact that we might fall short of an ideal does not mean that the ideal is worthless. Still less does it mean that we should make no effort to reach it. For all his personal faults and the many twists and turns of policy in the post-war period, when Oliver Cromwell died in 1658 the country was again wealthy and at peace. Though none could then know it for sure, the foundations of constitutional government had in fact been laid.

In a speech to Parliament on 12 September 1654, Cromwell said: "Necessity hath no law. Feigned necessities, imaginary necessities ... are the greatest cozenage [deception or cheating] that men can put upon the Providence of God, and make pretences to break known rules by." We are great ones for creating so-called necessities to override God's laws and the pursuit of holiness. We must lay these aside. If we can only make all the pressing concerns of life give way to having hearts that yearn for God, then we will begin to make progress.

21. Cauldron

Philemon.

Key word: kinship.

The years following the Civil War were times of great upheaval. Groups such as the Fifth Monarchy Men, the Ranters, the Levellers and their even more extreme offshoot the Diggers propounded views that seemed to strike at the very fabric of society. In 1647 the Leveller leaders, of whom 'Freeborn John' Lilburne was one, presented a constitution to Oliver Cromwell. When their demands were not met, a series of mutinies broke out in the army. These were put down, but agitation continued. Writing to Parliamentary General Lord Fairfax in 1649 after the Diggers' take-over of St George's Hill in Surrey, the Digger theorist Gerard Winstanley asserted: "None ought to be lords or landlords over another, but the earth is free for every son and daughter of mankind to live free upon." In *Law of Freedom* (published in 1652) Winstanley proposed that property be held in common in order to create social equality. The basis for this was biblical – that there had been no distinction of class or ownership in the Garden of Eden and that amongst the first Christians "No-one claimed that any of his possessions were his own, but they shared everything they had" (Acts 4:32) – but the millenarianism and egalitarianism of these and other groups collided with hard political reality. All were eventually suppressed.

The life of John Bunyan, former Parliamentary soldier, tinker, author, preacher and gaolbird illustrates something of the turmoil and its effects on the country at large. It shows, too, how hard life remained for ordinary people. After discharge from the army, in 1653 he joined a Nonconformist church in Bedford, preached there and came into conflict with the Quakers, against whom he published a number of pamphlets. In 1655, two of those to whom he was closest died: his first wife and his pastor John Gifford. It was in this year that he began to preach. The great Puritan theologian John Owen later said of him: "Could I possess the tinker's abilities for preaching, I would willingly relinquish all my learning." Bunyan remarried, to Elizabeth, but further personal sadness lay in wait: Mary, his blind daughter by his first wife (also Mary), died young.

Upon the return of Charles II to England in 1660, the official attitude to Nonconformists changed and in November of that year Bunyan was arrested for preaching without a licence. He was kept in prison without trial for the following twelve years. After his release he was again put in gaol for a short while and it was then that he wrote *Pilgrim's Progress from this World to that which is to come*, the work for which he is today best known. It was finished in 1678 and first published in 1684. It has been described as "the greatest book, other than Scripture, which an Englishman has given to mankind."

John Bunyan lived until 1688, long enough to experience further turns of the wheel in England's long political and religious tussles. His dying words were, "Take me, for I come to thee."

Thanksgiving.

Like John Bunyan, St Paul knew plenty about arbitrary arrest. He was put in gaol in Philippi (Acts 16:22-24) and in Jerusalem (Acts 21:33) before being transferred to Caesarea (Acts 23:23-35) and from thence to Rome. His period of house arrest in the imperial capital is described in Acts 28:16-31. Several of his letters contain references to imprisonment: "Pray also for me, that whenever I open my mouth, words may be given me so that I will fearlessly make known the mystery of the gospel, for which I am an ambassador in chains" (Ephesians 6:20); "So do not be ashamed to testify about our Lord, or ashamed of me his prisoner" (2 Timothy 1:8) and "May the Lord also show mercy to the household of Onesiphorus, because he often refreshed me and was not ashamed of my chains." (2 Timothy 1:16).

The charges that St Paul faced, like those of the English tinker, were trumped up and unjust. He was often beaten. He records that: "I have been in prison more frequently [than the false teachers who seek to undermine the gospel], been flogged more severely, and been exposed to death again and again. Five times I received from the Jews the forty lashes minus one. Three times I was beaten with rods" (2 Corinthians 11:23-25).

St Paul's letter to Philemon, a Christian in the Greek town of Colosse in Asia Minor, was almost certainly written from a Roman gaol at the same time as his letter to the Colossian church, which ends with the words: "Remember my chains" (Colossians 4:18). To Philemon "our dear friend and fellow worker" (Philemon :1) he describes himself as being "a prisoner of Christ Jesus" (Philemon :9) who is "in chains for the gospel" (Philemon :13). Given these circumstances, it is extraordinary to find that the apostle is nevertheless able to give thanks, not just occasionally but always: "I always thank my God as I remember you in my prayers, because I hear about your faith in the Lord Jesus and your love for all the saints." (Philemon :4-5). He practices what he preaches elsewhere, namely that we should "Be joyful always; pray continually; give thanks in all circumstances, for this is God's will for you in Christ Jesus." (1 Thessalonians 5:18).

This does not mean that we are necessarily called to express gratitude for terrible events, but that we should look beyond such happenings and see the things that manifest God's activity and blessing. If we concentrate only on the troubles of daily life, we will miss much that is good. In the midst of tribulation, St Paul focuses on the positive: Philemon's "faith ... [and] love" (Philemon :5), which have "refreshed the hearts of the saints" (Philemon :7) and which in turn "has given me great joy and encouragement" (Philemon :7).

St Paul's desire is that Philemon should build on this foundation of faith and love by "[being] active in sharing your faith, so that you will have a full understanding of every good thing we have in Christ." (Philemon :6). An intriguing truth lies at the heart of these words: it is through the act of sharing our faith that we gain "full understanding of every good thing we have in Christ." (Philemon :6). Faith cannot just remain an internal, intellectual or theoretical thing. It needs to be acted out and it needs to be shared: shared in the sense of telling others and shared in the sense of being given practical expression. Real understanding comes only through doing so, for until the message is lived it cannot be fully appreciated.

Appeal.

St Paul offers Philemon the chance to "be active in sharing your faith" (Philemon :6) in a remarkable way. What he asks is that Philemon should display three qualities that are central to the Christian life and message: forgiveness, love and brotherhood. Philemon is asked to take his former slave Onesimus back into his household "no longer as a slave, but better than a slave, as a dear brother." (Philemon :16). This is against every social convention and legal obligation. Onesimus was a runaway slave and as such could face the death penalty. Some surmise that he may have stolen from his master and that this is why St Paul says: "If he has done you any wrong or owes you anything, charge it to me." (Philemon :18). Even if he were taken back into the master's household, everything would appear to militate against his being freed, still less that he should thereafter be treated as a "dear brother." (Philemon :16).

Philemon is under no requirement of law or convention and St Paul deliberately avoids putting him under any hold by virtue of his own authority and standing within the church, for love and compulsions of these kinds do not mix. Rather, the apostle says that whilst he "could be bold and order you to do what you ought to do, yet I appeal to you on the basis of love ... I did not want to do anything without your consent, so that any favour you do will be spontaneous and not forced." (Philemon :8 and 14). Far from pulling rank, St Paul deliberately puts his relationship with Philemon on an equal footing, calling him "partner" (Philemon :17).

Instead, the apostle draws on the impetus that comes from love and adherence to the gospel. He draws a parallel between what Philemon has already done for others and what St Paul now asks to be done for him. When he asks for "some benefit from you in the Lord; refresh my heart in Christ" (Philemon :20) this mirrors the earlier mention of Philemon being one who "refreshed the hearts of the saints." (Philemon :7). He also reminds Philemon that "you owe me your very self" (Philemon :19): that, but for St Paul having preached the gospel to him, he would still be dead in his sins and cut off from salvation.

The appeal to Philemon shows how we can continue to make steady progress in the Christian life as our understanding of the implications of the gospel for ourselves and those around us deepens. Although Philemon is a sufficiently committed Christian that there is a "church that meets in [his] home" (Philemon :2), clearly he had never previously considered that he had any obligation to free a slave. Now he is brought to that realisation through being challenged by a fellow believer and being forced to confront the implications of the things in which he believes. In the same way, we need to challenge ourselves and our fellows about the implications of our beliefs for our own lives and those of others. We should do this in a loving way, without pulling rank or giving orders, but we must not shy away from it. If we do not grasp the nettle, we will fail to grow, the gospel will fail to gain ground as it should and our society will remain under unnecessary burdens.

Family.

The letter to Philemon is a personal one. Unlike those that are addressed to an entire church community, it was not designed for public consumption by being read out to the whole assembly. Its tone is intimate and familial. Indeed, its every reference to people is shot through with family analogies. St Paul writes of "Timothy our brother" (Philemon :1), "Apphia our sister" (Philemon :2) and Philemon his "brother" (Philemon :20).

The most fulsome family references are to the former slave, who is described as being related both to St Paul and to Philemon. To St Paul he is "my very heart" (Philemon :12), "my son ... who became my son while I was in chains" (Philemon :10) and "is very dear to me" (Philemon :16). To Philemon he is "even dearer ... both as a man and as a brother in the Lord." (Philemon :16) and can be restored "no longer as a slave, but better than a slave, as a dear brother." (Philemon :16). There is something deeper at work here than the straightforward story of a runaway slave. The repeated references to family relationships are not just an elaborate conceit on the part of a skilled orator to win trust, build sympathy and compel obligation. Family relationships between all Christians exist by virtue of our all being adopted into God's family.

We do not know why Onesimus ran away from his master. There is no telling what hurts, injustices and cruelties were on one side or what measure of broken trust on the other. For these individuals, as for us, it is not the past that matters, however, but the present and the future. Both Onesimus and Philemon had to put their former relationship behind them in order to experience the kinship that they share by being children of a loving God. We need to do the same, especially in those areas of our lives that have been scarred by bad experiences.

The story of Philemon and Onesimus is no less than an acting out in real life of the story of the Prodigal Son (Luke 15:11-32) and hence the story of our own redemption by God. Loss and separation are to be made good. What has been marred or mislaid is to be replaced by something even better than before. Human beings are to be transformed: "Formerly he was useless to you, but now he has become useful both to you and to me." (Philemon :11) – a pun on the name Onesimus, which means 'useful.' Thanks to the work of the Holy Spirit in his life, a slave is set free and is made into the person that God intended him to be. This is a story that our nation needs to hear again.

Conclusion.

John Bunyan experienced repeated loss: the death of wife, daughter, friend and mentor was compounded by enforced separation from family during long years in gaol. There is a world of pain in this life, but through such a cauldron he was fired, moulded and transformed. Indeed, the very trials he suffered were used so that they became the occasion for something great and beautiful to see the light of day. Perhaps *Pilgrim's Progress* could not have been written without years behind bars. This is not to fall into the facile argument that "everything is for the best in the best of all possible worlds."[45] It merely recognises the way that God is able to work extraordinary things through ordinary people and bring spiritual triumph from circumstances of desolation and despair. Although we often have difficulty accepting it in times of hardship, it is indeed the case that "in all things God works for the good of those who love him, who have been called according to his purpose." (Romans 8:28). With the benefit of hindsight, we can often say as Joseph did to his brothers: "You intended to harm me, but God intended it for good to accomplish what is now being done, the saving of many lives." (Genesis 50:20).

We have kinship with God and kinship with each other. We must start to put this into practice. We need to challenge each other, gently and lovingly but also firmly so that we may continue to grow and so that our nation may be transformed by the power of God working through us. The things we experience, alone and collectively, can be our cauldron. We have the option of concentrating on our pain and anguish, of allowing ourselves to be caught up in the injustices of the past, or of looking beyond these things to where God is at work. To quote Oscar Wilde: "We are all lying in the gutter, but some of us are looking at the stars." God calls us to "shine like stars in the universe as [we] hold out the word of life" (Philippians 2:15). With his help, we can all do so.

---

[45] Leibnitz, as lampooned by Voltaire in *Candide*.

22. Restoration

Key word: humility.

It is a measure of the misery brought about by civil war, the selectiveness of human memory and the amiable nature of the occupant of the throne that the Restoration retains the aura of "good king Charles' golden days." Reality belies the rosy image. Charles himself had talent and charm, for sure. With the exception of trying and executing the surviving regicides early in his reign, he was remarkably free of vindictiveness towards supporters of the Commonwealth. The 'Merry Monarch' was a keen tennis player, yachtsman and hunter. He started horse-racing at Newmarket, which in turn gave rise to the new sport of fox-hunting. People generally welcomed such pursuits after years of Puritan moralising and petty restrictions on traditional pastimes.

Yet the sovereign was also deeply cynical in both private and public affairs. He set the tone for a court that was a byword for corrupt morals, some of whose attitudes and witticisms are preserved in the Restoration comedies penned by the fashionable playwrights of the day. At one point, he arguably betrayed his own country by negotiating the extraordinary secret Treaty of Dover (1670) with Louis XIV. This provided for Charles to receive annual payments, and in return he agreed both to help the French ruler and to become a Roman Catholic. The subsidies enabled the king to dissolve Parliament on 28 March 1681, in an uncomfortable echo of his father.

Perhaps most notable of all is that he presided over three consecutive years of disasters, any one of which might have been enough to darken the remembrance of a reign less flattered by the internal strife that preceded and followed it. In 1665 bubonic plague struck, first in London and then throughout the country. Scenes reminiscent of the Black Death were played out, highlighting the same mixture of human virtue and vice. At Eyam in Derbyshire, an entire village chose to die rather than risk infecting others, but plenty had no such qualms.

London was still recovering from plague when the Great Fire (1666) caught hold. It burned for four days. In that time it devastated 400 streets and lanes, 13,200 houses, 89 parish churches, 52 halls, old St Paul's cathedral, the Guildhall, gaols, markets and other public buildings. The area affected comprised 373 acres within the old city walls and a further 63 acres outside. Some 200,000 people were made homeless, but remarkably there was little loss of life. The fire caused enormous damage to property, but in destroying the filthy alleys and narrow thoroughfares of the city, it cleansed it of the last traces of plague.

Through disease and fire the country was at war with former allies and fellow Protestants, the United Provinces of the Netherlands. They inflicted one of the most ignominious defeats in English naval history. In 1667 their admiral de Groot sailed up the Medway, broke the defensive chain across the river and burned the English fleet at anchor, towing away some ships as prizes. In the event, the war was fought to a stalemate and peace brokered later that same year, but the blow to English pride and prestige was heavy. In *Last Instructions to a Painter*, the poet Andrew Marvell (a former tutor to the daughter of Parliamentary general Lord Fairfax and a fierce critic of Charles II) wrote indignantly of "our ships unrigg'd, our forts unmanned."

Yet Charles breezed blithely through it all, for all the world without a care to his name.

Authority.

In truth human lives, even those of kings and princes, are seldom without care. The apostle Peter writes to early Christians who experience "anxiety" (1 Peter 5:7) and whose "brothers throughout the world are undergoing the same kind of sufferings." (1 Peter 5:9). He cautions them to "Be self-controlled and alert. Your enemy the devil prowls around like a roaring lion looking for someone to devour." (1 Peter 5:8).

At a time of difficulty and persecution, Peter has advice for how we should conduct ourselves. The way in which he phrases his exhortations to those in positions of authority in the early church is revealing. The apostle is a man who lived with Jesus for more than three years during his earthly ministry, was a participant in many of the major events of those days, was "a witness of Christ's sufferings" (1 Peter 5:1) and was the leading figure at the first Pentecost. At the time of writing this letter he remained one of the acknowledged principals of the new faith.

Nevertheless, he does not give orders, though he might be considered to have every right to do so. Rather he says: "I appeal to you" (1 Peter 5:1). He puts himself on the same level as those to whom he writes, calling himself "a fellow-elder ... and one who will also share in the glory to be revealed." (1 Peter 5:1).

Peter gives a good example of the way in which we are to exercise authority: through persuasion and encouragement, relying on the power of example rather than "lording it over those entrusted to you" (1 Peter 5:3).The watchword is humility. To both young and old, Peter counsels: "All of you, clothe yourselves with humility towards one another, because 'God opposes the proud but gives grace to the humble.' Humble yourselves, therefore, under God's mighty hand ..." (1 Peter 5:5-6).

Peter practices what he preaches. This no-nonsense fisherman, by turns rash, courageous, cowardly, and foolhardy, has learnt just as Jesus predicted: "You do not understand now what I am doing, but later you will understand."

(John 13:7). This should encourage us that we, too, might grow in understanding. It should also guide us towards humility, for there will always be much that we "do not understand now" (John 13:7).

Advice.

Humility is not the same as weakness, though many confuse the two. The humility that we are to practice is to enable God to clothe us with his power and strength: our attempts to do things on our own and according to human understanding get in the way. When once we start to exercise humility, we allow God to work in us "to will and to act according to his good purpose" (Philippians 2:13). We are told to "humble yourselves ... that God may lift you up in due time." (1 Peter 5:6). The word "that" in this sentence makes it clear that there is a connection between our humility and God's lifting us up. Far from our being weak, the Lord "will himself restore you and make you strong, firm and steadfast." (1 Peter 5:10). This is the bedrock on which we are to build.

The values of the kingdom of heaven seem topsy-turvy by comparison with those of the world. Humility and its corollary, service, are amongst the central kingdom values. With that in mind, Peter has advice for both the leadership and the rank and file of the church. "To the elders among you" (1 Peter 5:1) he counsels:

"Be shepherds of God's flock that is under your care" (1 Peter 5:2). Leaders act under the delegated authority of "the Chief Shepherd" (1 Peter 5:4): the flock is not ours, but belongs to the Lord God Almighty. We are to be mindful that the flock is "entrusted" (1 Peter 5:3) to us, for with trust comes a special duty of care and responsibility.

"[Serve] as overseers – not because you must, but because you are willing, as God wants you to be" (1 Peter 5:2). In the kingdom of heaven, compulsion is replaced by willingness and service becomes a joy. It is impossible to serve in the way that God truly desires without humility.

Be "not greedy for money, but eager to serve" (1 Peter 5:3). In this we are to follow the example of Jesus: "The Son of Man came not to be served but to serve." (Matthew 20:28). In doing so, we recall that: "No-one can serve two masters. Either he will hate the one and love the other, or he will be devoted to the one and despise the other. You cannot serve both God and Money." (Matthew 6:24).

"Not lording it over those entrusted to you, but being examples to the flock" (1 Peter 5:3). The earthly ministry of Jesus is a prime instance of teaching by example rather than through the heavy-handed exercise of power and authority.

God is "the King of kings and Lord of lords" (1 Timothy 6:15) and as such he has every right to compel obedience. Instead, he allows us to exercise choice.

Each of these pieces of advice reminds us that it is right for us to be humble, in submission to God and in submission to others. The followers, the "young men" (1 Peter 5:5) are told: "In the same way be submissive to those who are older" (1 Peter 5:5).

Sheep and shepherds.

Humility is one of the qualities to be expected of those who "will share in the glory to be revealed" (1 Peter 5:1). When Peter speaks of this glory, he is not just talking in figurative terms. Neither is his an intellectual understanding divorced from experience. He himself saw something of it through being present at the Transfiguration of Jesus: "There [Jesus] was transfigured before them. His face shone like the sun, and his clothes became as white as the light." (Matthew 17:2). So what Peter says deserves the closest attention:

"When the Chief Shepherd appears, you will receive the crown of glory that will never fade away." (1 Peter 5:4).

"God's mighty hand [will] lift you up in due time." (1 Peter 5:6).

"[The] God of all grace, who called you to his eternal glory in Christ, after you have suffered a little while, will himself restore you and make you strong, firm and steadfast. To him be the power for ever and ever. Amen." (1 Peter 5:10-11).

These are promises of great things to come. They will come at God's appointed time and in fulfilment of his plan to "restore" (1 Peter 5:10): to restore us and to restore Creation, to mend what has been broken and to reconfigure what has been marred. We can scarcely fail to be humble in the face of our Lord's thereby redeeming what we have damaged through our sin and rebellion.

Peter's description of Christ as the Chief Shepherd recalls the recurring imagery of sheep and shepherds throughout the Bible. The patriarch Jacob speaks of "the God who has been my shepherd all my life to this day" (Genesis 48:15) and describes the Lord as "the Shepherd, the Rock of Israel" (Genesis 49:24). The condition of the people when they are "harassed and helpless, like sheep without a shepherd" (Matthew 9:36) invites the compassion of Jesus. The Lord comes to be "the shepherd of my people" (Matthew 2:6) and Jesus says: "I am the Good Shepherd" (John 10:14). The book of Hebrews picks up the image by talking of "that great Shepherd of the sheep" (Hebrews 13:20).

Jesus himself tells the parable of the Lost Sheep, in which the love of the shepherd is so great that he "leaves the ninety nine on the hills and [goes] to look for the one that wandered off" (Matthew 18:12). He uses the story to illustrate

131

the point that: "In the same way your Father in heaven is not willing that any of these little ones should be lost." (Matthew 18:14). It is not just empty rhetoric, therefore, when Peter encourages his readers to "Cast all your anxiety on [the Lord] because he cares for you." (1 Peter 5:7). At the same time, the image of the shepherd reminds a people undergoing persecution of how they may be called upon to respond: "The good shepherd lays down his life for the sheep." (John 10:11).

Conclusion.

In 1660 the publication of the Declaration of Breda, promising religious toleration and an amnesty for supporters of the Commonwealth, led directly to Charles II's being restored to the throne in May that year. It was a pale shadow of the amnesty that God makes available and of the restoration that he plans for us and for his Creation, but it was nevertheless cause for rejoicing amongst a majority of the population.

During the Restoration the great Puritan poet John Milton, who had been Oliver Cromwell's secretary when he was Lord Protector and continued in that post despite becoming blind in 1652, completed two of his finest works: *Paradise Lost* and *Paradise Regained*. They read as epitaphs for the Puritan dream. Milton was arrested shortly after the return of Charles II and fined (losing the greater part of his fortune), but released. Thereafter, he wisely lived in hiding: as the author of a pamphlet excusing regicide[46] he was scarcely likely to be in favour with the new regime. *Samson Agonistes*, published in 1671, mirrors the circumstances of the poet's own life as it recounts the blindness of Samson, held prisoner by the Philistines (see Judges 16).

Charles II and John Milton are a study in contrasts, yet in a curious way they share a certain humility. Milton's was a product of his blindness and deep Christian faith, Charles' of his long years of exile and a determination "never to go on my travels again." His quarter century on the throne reminds us that the way in which we act has a profound impact. The tone set by the king influenced every aspect not just of the court but of the country at large. The widespread influence of what we do makes it of the utmost importance that we practice humility in our lives. Our recent conduct as a nation has disclosed the opposite, for we have sought to put ourselves above God. Now, more than ever, we need to "humble [ourselves] ... under God's mighty hand" and pray that he will indeed "lift [us] up in due time." (1 Peter 5:6).

---

[46] *The Tenure of Kings and Magistrates*, published in 1649 following the execution of Charles I.

23. Revolution

1 Timothy 2:1-8.

Key word: authority.

On one level the Glorious Revolution was neither much of a revolution nor particularly glorious. On another it was a profound shake-up of the political order in England which finally drew a line under the long conflict between king and Parliament. Fearful that James II (reigned 1685-88) intended to impose Roman Catholicism on the country and goaded by the monarch's intemperate actions (such as the charging of seven bishops with seditious libel in June 1688) a number of prominent Protestant noblemen offered the Crown to the ruler of the Netherlands, William of Orange. A fig leaf to propriety was provided by the fact that William's wife Mary Stuart, herself a Protestant, was James' daughter and hence in the line of succession. The offer was accepted. William landed in England at the head of an army and was greeted warmly. At this, James lost his nerve and fled London for France. Constitutional theorists conveniently if improbably treated flight as abdication, smoothing the way for what was in truth usurpation. James sought to make a comeback and with French help invaded Ireland, but William's victory at the battle of the Boyne on 11 July 1690 put the matter beyond doubt.

The offer of the Crown to William III and Mary II came with strings attached. Royal prerogative powers were curtailed: there was to be freedom from laws and taxes passed without the consent of Parliament, freedom to elect members of Parliament and freedom of speech. The passing of the Bill of Rights in 1689 meant that from then onwards Britain had for the first time a genuinely constitutional monarchy. Supreme power thenceforth resided in the king in Parliament. The administration of justice, too, was placed above the will and whim of the sovereign. Indeed, the primacy and independence of the rule of law was one of the hallmarks of this innovative and wholly unprecedented form of government.

An independent judiciary proved itself a redoubtable defender of freedom. In its Lord Chief Justice William Murray, Lord Mansfield, it had a champion of fire and intellect. In 1772 he delivered one of the landmark judgments of English law in Somersett's case, concerning the status of a black slave who had been brought to England. The judge was in no doubt: "Every man who comes to England is entitled to the protection of English law, whatever oppression he may heretofore have suffered, and whatever may be the colour of his skin, whether it is black or whether it is white." The effect was that any slave who set foot on English soil was immediately free.

On another occasion his lordship considered an appeal by the radical John Wilkes against a sentence of outlawry.[47] The overriding authority of the law was again clearly stated: "We must not regard political consequences, however formidable they may be; if rebellion was the certain consequence we are bound to say, *Justicia fiat, ruat coelum*' [Let justice be done, though the sky fall]." This same judge said: "English law is Christian law." It is not generally appreciated that right up to the modern era almost every aspect of English law came about specifically in response to Christian teaching: remove this and its foundation is gone.

Regulations.

The law of the land has authority. It is an authority that our constitution makes independent of and in some respects even above that of monarch and Parliament. It is an authority that is backed implicitly and explicitly by the power of the state. Yet if that were the sole pillar on which it rested, the law would be weak indeed. The true authority of law derives from its moral content: men will readily obey rules that are just but will chafe under those that are unjust. Moral content, of course, is ultimately linked to our obedience to God's laws, which he has written in our hearts through our innate sense of right and wrong. Hence faithfulness to God is the rule above all others that we must keep.

With justice comes prosperity: "When the righteous prosper, the city rejoices; when the wicked perish, there are shouts of joy." (Proverbs 11:10). Bad laws and poor enforcement promote wrongdoing and allow the guilty to go scot free. They undermine the foundations of society, proper relations between men and regard for God. It thus might come as something of a surprise that St Paul is so emphatic in saying: "I urge then, first of all, that requests, prayers, intercessions and thanksgiving be made for everyone – for kings and all those in authority" (1 Timothy 2:1-2). This was not penned in balmy moments of personal and religious freedom. It was written when Nero was Emperor of Rome (54-68 AD), a man whose debauchery and cruelty are legend. His was one of the worst regimes of all time. What St Paul says thus cannot be premised on the assumption that the "kings and those in authority" (1 Timothy 2:2) are good and wise rulers.

---

[47] Amongst other things that caused him to fall foul of the authorities, Wilkes published the scurrilous broadsheet *The North Briton*, issue number 45 of which implied that it would be a sacrilege if King George III were to attend a thanksgiving service at St Paul's cathedral. It was called *The North Briton* since all references to Scotland were forbidden following the 1745 Jacobite uprising in favour of the last Stuart claimant to the throne, Young Pretender Charles Edward Stuart (otherwise known as Bonnie Prince Charlie).

St Paul's urging is so "that we may live peaceful and quiet lives in all godliness and holiness. This is good, and pleases God our Saviour, who wants all men to be saved and to come to a knowledge of the truth." (1 Timothy 2:2-4). There are several strands to this. It shows that Christianity does not aim at the undermining of earthly authority and hence gives no excuse for persecution on those grounds. It acknowledges that "kings and all those in authority" (1Timothy 2:2) hold their positions on God's sufferance. It affirms that all are treasured by God and consequently are worthy of our prayers. It admits the possibility of salvation for each, no matter how improbable that may seem to human eyes. Such an attitude accepts and proclaims that the rule and authority of God exist at all times and at all places. His is the supreme power to command. Our role is not to challenge the dispositions of the Almighty but to draw as close as we can to him. For this reason St Paul says that: "I want men everywhere to lift up holy hands in prayer, without anger or disputing." (1 Timothy 2:8).

Proceedings.

The Lord's authority is shown in his judgments and in his dealings with man. These are not based on whim, but on due process. There is:

Advocacy: "For there is one God and one mediator between God and men, the man Christ Jesus" (1 Timothy 2:5-6). We are not left without representation, but instead have a mediator to plead our case and to "make [our] righteousness shine like the dawn, the justice of [our] cause like the noonday sun." (Psalm 37:6). The apostle John expresses the same sentiment: "But if anybody does sin, we have one who speaks to the Father in our defence – Jesus Christ, the Righteous One." (1 John 2:1). The concept can be traced back at least as far as Job, who avers that: "my advocate is on high" (Job 16:19).

Evidence: St Paul speaks of "the testimony given in its proper time." (1 Timothy 2:5-6). The evidence for the truth of the gospel and in favour of our salvation is provided by the life, death and resurrection of Jesus. Christianity is not based on supposition, nor on blind acceptance but on evidence and the testimony of eyewitnesses. It is rooted in historical fact and its truth can be tested.

Oath: witnesses in English courts take an oath to swear solemnly that their evidence "shall be the truth, the whole truth and nothing but the truth." St Paul makes a similar solemn statement in giving his evidence: "I am telling the truth, I am not lying" (1 Timothy 2:7).

Order: things do not occur randomly and the working out of God's plan is not attended by chaos and confusion, however much it might sometimes seem so to us. Instead, each event happens "in its proper time" (1 Timothy 2:6).

Due compensation: St Paul reminds us that "Christ Jesus ... gave himself as a ransom for all men" (1 Timothy 2:5-6). There is a penalty to be paid for the wrongdoing of mankind and God's justice demands that this be paid. Justice is administered impartially, which means that the penalty cannot be waived. The judgment was enforced and the sentence served on our behalf by Jesus through his death on the cross. Through this we have been redeemed, bought back and set free.

This same regard for due process, truth and the impartial administration of justice is one of the hallmarks of English law, hallmarks that are now widely copied but which once were rare. Indeed, there are still many parts of the world where these concepts remain foreign, or honoured more in the breach than in the observance.

We should never overlook the value of our laws and our system of justice. Moreover, we should bear in mind that the laws we proclaim and administer here on earth are shadows of the justice that God wishes for mankind. The Lord reminds his people of this repeatedly: "Hate evil, love good; maintain justice in the courts" (Amos 5:15). When our laws start to diverge from what God has ordained, justice will suffer and the authority of the law will be undermined. We forget this at our peril.

Proclamations.

Judgments in open court under English law are not kept secret. They are published and can be read by anyone. In the same way, God has made known his plan for the salvation of mankind. He has done so openly and has clothed with authority those who make his determinations known. St Paul says: "And for this purpose I was appointed a herald and an apostle – I am telling the truth, I am not lying – and a teacher of the true faith to the Gentiles." (1 Timothy 2:7). St Paul, the great apostle to the Gentiles, was to proclaim that Jesus has bridged the gap between man and God and made salvation available to all through his death on the cross. "For this purpose" (1 Timothy 2:7) the Lord clothed him with a three-fold authority: as "a herald and an apostle ... and a teacher of the true faith to the Gentiles." (1 Timothy 2:7). The authority was not something that St Paul took upon himself. It came because he "was appointed" (1 Timothy 2:7) by God. The three roles that St Paul was given follow a logical order:

As herald: to announce and to proclaim publicly.

As apostle: to establish the church and to be a witness. When the eleven apostles were looking for someone to replace Judas Iscariot, they said that: "one of these must become a witness with us of [Jesus'] resurrection." (Acts 1:22).

As teacher: to ensure that converts learn properly, truly understand the gospel that they have heard proclaimed and grow in the faith.

To this day, the Lord continues to clothe people with his authority to perform the ministries that he has allocated to them: he gives "some to be apostles, some to be prophets, some to be evangelists, and some to be pastors and teachers, to prepare God's people for works of service, so that the body of Christ may be built up until we all reach unity in the faith and in the knowledge of the Son of God and become mature, attaining to the whole measure of the fullness of Christ." (Ephesians 4:11-13). In a land where substantial re-evangelisation is necessary, we each need to search diligently to discover the ministry to which God calls us. Every one of us needs then to exercise our ministry to the praise and glory of our Lord and Saviour.

Conclusion.

There is all too little appreciation at present of the underlying basis for our system of government and our laws. It is not merely that these were instituted in an age when Christian belief was taken for granted: they have been self-consciously Christian in inspiration and application. It simply is not the case that any society might have conceived them and that only chance brought them about in a particular place and time. Neither can the prosperity, influence and security that the nation has experienced for generations be divorced from them. Flawed though they might often be in concept and administration, they give a glimpse of the benefits that flow from the practical application of Christianity.

England has never been perfect, but for centuries she set an example of good government and impartial justice to the world. This is no idle boast: murder statistics, which are the best proxy we have for comparative levels of violence and disorder across societies and across ages, bear it out.[48] As others have applied the same principles and habits that were pioneered in England, so these benefits have spread across the world. The influence of this country, both in spreading the gospel and in propagating the institutions and behaviour which the gospel inspired, has been incalculable. We have acted under the authority of God in doing so.

God's authority is seen at each stage of human life and experience: in his laws, in his ordering of the universe, in the evidence for and the proclamation of the gospel. A nation that accepts the good news of Jesus Christ and puts it into practice will attain earthly benefit as well as salvation and everlasting life for its people. By the same token, a land that neglects these things will forgo blessing

---

[48] See Appendix 1, page 384

and will take the way of death. We must turn back onto the straight path, and quickly, both for our own sakes and for the sake of the world around us.

24. New horizons

2 Peter 1:1-21.

Key word: promises.

The output of Isaac Newton (1642-1727), mathematician, astronomer and philosopher, was by any measure prodigious. He developed theories of mechanics and gravitation that survived unchallenged until the twentieth century. He showed that white light is made up of the colours of the spectrum and proposed a particle theory of light.[49] In the early 1670s he built the first reflecting telescope. With Leibnitz he shares the honour of discovering calculus, the branch of mathematics that deals with continuously changing quantities. This was of prime importance for engineering and for future scientific development. Differential calculus is used to find the slopes of curves and rates of change of one quantity with regard to another. Integral calculus is used to find the area enclosed by curves. Without calculus, the industrial revolution would have been a starveling child.

Newton sat twice as a Member of Parliament, was Master of the Mint from 1698 and president of the Royal Society for Improving Natural Knowledge from 1703, in both cases until his death. In 1705 he became the first person to be knighted for scientific work. He bestrode the scientific firmament like the proverbial colossus, at the side of whom even such men as William Harvey (1578-1657), the discoverer of blood circulation, and Robert Boyle (1627-91),[50] the father of modern chemistry, appear pale shadows.[51] The renowned scientist was not known for his modesty, but he did say this: "I do not know what I may appear to the world, but to myself I seem to have been only a boy playing on the seashore, and diverting myself in now and then finding a smoother pebble or a

---

[49] Modern science acknowledges light to be both waves and particles.

[50] Boyle was born in Ireland.

[51] So highly was Newton regarded by contemporaries that the poet Alexander Pope wittily proclaimed in an intended epitaph: "Nature and Nature's laws lay hid in night; God said, *Let Newton be!* And all was light." The path to the top was not smooth, however. Newton was born in the year civil war broke out, left school the year Cromwell died, went to Cambridge University as the monarchy was restored, graduated in the year of the Great Plague and was elected Fellow of the Royal Society as war broke out with the Dutch. He was of modest means and was only able to study at Cambridge through receiving financial help from his college.

prettier shell than ordinary, whilst the great ocean of truth lay all undiscovered before me."

Knowledge.

Newton pursued scientific knowledge. In doing so, he gained enough of an inkling of the divine power that lay beyond the horizon of his discoveries to acknowledge that he had "been only a boy playing on the seashore." The author of 2 Peter is "Simon Peter, a servant and apostle of Jesus Christ" (2 Peter 1:1). He was an uneducated fisherman, whom we may presume to have been largely ignorant of scientific matters, but he developed deep wisdom and understanding by virtue of his long association with Jesus. This association began during the latter's earthly ministry and continued throughout the apostle's faithful service of the church following Jesus' resurrection. This "rock [on which] I will build my church" (Matthew 16:18) writes that: "His [God's] divine power has given us everything we need for life and godliness through our knowledge of him who called us by his own glory and goodness." (2 Peter 1:3).

Peter, more than almost any man before or since, knew what he was talking about when he spoke of divine power. He reminds his readers that he personally saw the transfiguration of Jesus: "We did not follow cleverly invented stories when we told you about the power and coming of our Lord Jesus Christ, but we were eye-witnesses of his majesty. For he received honour and glory from God the Father when the voice came to him from the Majestic Glory, saying, 'This is my Son, whom I love; with him I am well pleased.' We ourselves heard this voice that came from heaven when we were with him on the sacred mountain." (2 Peter 1:16-18). The knowledge that Peter celebrates is not scientific, nor is it worldly. It does not consist in knowledge of things, but of a person. That person is Jesus, the one "who called us by his own glory and goodness." (2 Peter 1:3). What Peter writes about cannot be known by science, still less proved by it, any more than the personality of a human being can be known and proved scientifically.

The means by which Peter recommends that we pursue and increase in such knowledge is similarly unknown to the scientific method: "For this very reason, make every effort to add to your faith goodness; and to goodness, knowledge; and to knowledge, self-control; and to self-control, perseverance; and to perseverance, godliness; and to godliness, brotherly kindness; and to brotherly kindness, love. For if you possess these qualities in increasing measure, they will keep you from being ineffective and unproductive in your knowledge of our Lord Jesus Christ." (2 Peter 1:5-8). Peter tells us that, if our aim is to increase in knowledge of and closeness to a person, we do so best by emulating the qualities of that person. As we progress from one quality to the next, so we grow in the quality that is nearest the essence of that person. In the case of God, that quality is love. As the apostle John said: "Whoever does not love does not know God, for God is love." (1 John 4:8).

What Peter says goes to the heart of much modern discourse about the relationship between science and religion. Since he writes about things that cannot be known by science or proved by it and since he propounds means that are unknown to the scientific method there are those who would count all that he says as worthless. Such an attitude treats Christianity as harmless fantasy at best and wicked falsehood at worst. The difficulty with this approach is that it fails to describe accurately or completely[52] what goes on in the physical world and has no basis at all on which to account for things of a spiritual nature. After the Roman Catholic Church forced him to recant his statement that the earth revolved around the sun, the astronomer Galileo Galilei is said to have remarked: "But nevertheless it does move." One might be tempted to echo those words: the fact is that a spiritual dimension exists, whether we like it or not, and a theory that does not take account of this is not much of a theory.

Participation.

Christianity involves participation: in "Grace and peace ... in abundance through the knowledge of God and of Jesus our Lord." (2 Peter 1:2). Peter writes to participants in this grace and peace, "To those who through the righteousness of our God and Saviour have received a faith as precious as ours." (2 Peter 1:1). Such people are also participants in and recipients of the promises of God, and thereby become participants in the nature of God himself: "Through these [his own glory and goodness] he has given us his very great and precious promises, so that through them you may participate in the divine nature and escape the corruption in the world caused by evil desires." (2 Peter 1:4). The fact that human beings might be able to "participate in the divine nature" (2 Peter 1:4) is a startling concept. Peter sets out the progression that takes us there:

"Through the righteousness of our God and our Saviour Jesus Christ [we] have received a faith as precious as ours." (2 Peter 1:1). That is to say, salvation comes by grace through faith alone.

---

[52] The present consensus amongst cosmologists is that less than 5% of the universe is comprised of the matter that we see around us (of which only a minute proportion has been explored). The remainder is said to be composed either of 'dark energy' or 'dark matter.' Nobody currently knows what either of these is. On this hypothesis, it follows that more than 95% of the universe consists of things of which we are entirely ignorant. In view of that, the atheist's confident assertion that the non-existence of God is definitively proven seems curious.

"[God's] divine power has given everything we need for life and godliness" (2 Peter 1:3). Through the power of the Holy Spirit working in us, we are enabled to "work out [our] salvation with fear and trembling." (Philippians 2:12).

"Through [his glory and goodness] he has given us his very great and precious promises" (2 Peter 1:4). These promises include the giving of the Holy Spirit: "I will ask the Father, and he will give you another Counsellor to be with you for ever – the Spirit of truth." (John 14:16).

"[Through these promises] you may participate in the divine nature" (2 Peter 1:4). By the power of the Holy Spirit working in us, we "are being transformed into [the Lord's] likeness with ever-increasing glory" (2 Corinthians 3:18).

As well as enabling our participation in the divine nature, the promises of God also enable us to "escape the corruption in the world caused by evil desires." (2 Peter 1:4). Again, the concept is striking. Christians live in the world and are subject to all its vicissitudes and temptations. They are often on the receiving end of persecution for their faith and, like everyone else, have to deal with the consequences of a world that is marred and broken by sin. Peter does not say that we are able to avoid such things. What we can avoid, however, is "the corruption ... caused by evil desires" (2 Peter 1:4). This comes about because "it is God who works in [us] to will and to act according to his good purpose." (Philippians 2:13). That is to say, the activity of the Holy Spirit in our lives begins to change us so that we increasingly desire the things that God wants.[53] Hence we are more and more able to break free from the desires of the sinful nature and thus from the corruption that such desires bring. Evil desires will instead be replaced by faith, goodness, knowledge, self-control, perseverance, godliness, brotherly kindness and love.

Possession.

Peter tells us that possessing faith, goodness, knowledge, self-control, perseverance, godliness and love will make us effective and productive, "But if anyone does not have them, he is short-sighted and blind, and has forgotten that he has been cleansed from his past sins." (2 Peter 1:9). At first blush, this statement might seem a leap of logic, but it is not. What Peter is driving at is that being cleansed from past sins gives us a clean slate and a fresh start. Failure to

---

[53] The qualities that Peter lists in 2 Peter 1:5-7 are similar to the fruits of the Spirit that St Paul enumerates in Galatians 5:22. Peter includes knowledge, perseverance and godliness, which St Paul does not. St Paul includes joy, peace, patience and gentleness, which Peter does not. They have in common faith, goodness, self-control, kindness and love.

take advantage of this by building godly qualities on the ground thus cleared is indeed "short-sighted and blind" (2 Peter 1:9).

Neither should we stand still. Our aim should be to "possess these qualities in increasing measure" (2 Peter 1:8). We are encouraged to press on continually along the road towards attaining the likeness of Christ. This takes discipline and practice. It involves action, for the things that Peter talks about can only be developed by exercising those very qualities through an act of will: we become kind through being kind, develop perseverance through persevering and so forth. In this way we will build on the foundation of faith: "Therefore, my brothers, be all the more eager to make your calling and election sure. For if you do these things, you will never fail, and you will receive a rich welcome into the eternal kingdom of our Lord and Saviour Jesus Christ." (2 Peter 1:10-11).

We must be always on our guard against the possibility of backsliding, either on our own part or by others. It is for this reason that Peter says: "So, I will always remind you of these things, even though you know them and are firmly established in the truth you now have. I think it is right to refresh your memory as long as I live in the tent of this body, because I know that I will soon put it aside, as our Lord Jesus Christ has made clear to me. And I will make every effort to see that after my departure you will always be able to remember these things." (2 Peter 1:12-15). We too readily forget even the things that we seem to know and to have taken to our hearts, and continual reminders are therefore needed. We are all apt to be "short-sighted and blind, and [to have] forgotten that [we have] been cleansed from [our] past sins." (2 Peter 1:9).

Conclusion.

Newton's work opened up new scientific horizons. His discoveries held out great promise for the future advancement of mankind, yet he himself realised their limitations. He was canny enough to recognise that there were many things that he did not know, even though by definition the full extent of what remains to be discovered is always beyond our ken. He was also wise enough to see the hand of God at work. He said: "In the absence of any other evidence, the existence of the human thumb alone would persuade me of the existence of God."

Science and religion are not implacable enemies. When properly understood and applied, they are two sides of the same coin. God delights in our scientific investigation when it is undertaken for his praise and glory. To search out and discover the wonder and beauty of Creation through science is part of what is involved in the command to "fill the earth and subdue it" (Genesis 1:28). We must beware, however, of making a god out of science. The promise of scientific advancement is as nothing beside the promises of God. Our speculations about the world change as fashions come and go and as fresh discoveries are made. By contrast, "Jesus Christ is the same yesterday and today and for ever" (Hebrews 13:8) and his Word does not change: "And we have the word of the prophets made more certain, and you will do well to pay attention to it, as to a light shining in a dark place, until the day dawns and the morning star rises in your hearts. Above all, you must understand that no prophecy of Scripture came about by the prophet's own interpretation. For prophecy never had its origin in the will of man, but men spoke from God as they were carried along by the Holy Spirit." (2 Peter 1:19-21).

As Peter advises, we "will do well to pay attention to [the word of the prophets]" (2 Peter 1:19). Or, as the writer of Hebrews puts it: "We must pay more careful attention, therefore, to what we have heard, so that we do not drift away. For if the message spoken by angels was binding, and every violation and disobedience received its just punishment, how shall we escape if we ignore such a great salvation?" (Hebrews 2:1).

25. Balance of power

Nahum 2:1-6.

Key word: splendour.

For much of the last thousand years, France and England have been rivals and, often, enemies. Wars between them have been fuelled by different ideologies, from the dynastic concerns of the Angevin and Hundred Years' Wars to the religious fervour that drove conflict between Protestant and Catholic in a later age, but the logic of geographic proximity has remained constant. Sometimes England has had the upper hand, sometimes France. Yet throughout there is one fact perhaps above all others that demands explanation: in times when land, wealth, population and power were closely linked, how could England even begin to compete with France, whose cultivable area, numbers of inhabitants and resources were so much greater? In 1346 (the year of Crécy) England had a population of some 3 millions, France 12 millions. In 1715, at the close of the War of the Spanish Succession, the United Kingdom (into which England was by then subsumed) had somewhat less than 10 millions, France 19 millions. In 1815, at the end of the Napoleonic Wars, the United Kingdom had 19 millions, France 30 millions. Indeed the population of the United Kingdom did not overtake that of France until the dawn of the twentieth century.[54]

It is of course true that, during some of her conflicts with France, England was able to build effective coalitions against her rival. There were, however, times when it was she who was isolated. It is equally the case that being an island power meant that England was able to fight on her opponents' territory rather than her own, though this held good only so long as England controlled the Channel and this was less of a certainty than hindsight might make it appear.[55] Occasionally England had the advantage of better military technology – with the

[54] The difference in the second half of the nineteenth century is partly accounted for by emigration. In the thirty years after 1850 some six and a half million people left the British Isles. Most went to Canada, South Africa, Australia or New Zealand.

[55] That British naval supremacy could not be taken for granted was shown in the closing years of the American War of Independence, when France drew Spain into alliance with the colonists and organised the so-called 'League of Armed Neutrality' involving Russia, Sweden, Denmark and the Netherlands. Britain was temporarily isolated and surrounded by hostile or unfriendly powers. In consequence, the French were able to achieve temporary naval superiority off the American coast, leading directly to British defeat at Yorktown in 1781 and consequent loss of the Thirteen Colonies.

longbow, for example, during the Hundred Years' War – although more often she did not. Sometimes English tactics were superior, though again it was not always so: use of the line instead of the column during the Napoleonic Wars was distinctly old hat, and only British troops consistently employed this formation successfully against Bonaparte's armies. Certainly, in the latter period Britain was able to bring greater financial resources to bear: a reliable legal system and secure property rights made her national debt (though larger) less costly to service than that of France, whose capricious rulers merited a higher risk premium. By definition, however, this was not a factor in earlier ages.

In truth none of these things, either alone or collectively provides a complete answer. The plain fact is that, time and again, England seemed to have just the right man in just the right place at just the right time. So great are the coincidences and so oft repeated that even the most ardent atheist might be tempted to say that Providence herself took a hand.

The career of John Churchill, later Duke of Marlborough, is a case in point. He was promoted by a fluke: the fact that his wife Sarah happened to be a close friend of Queen Anne and the era was one of unashamed nepotism. Yet he was undoubtedly the man for the hour: a general of genius and consummate diplomat, able to hold together the fractious coalition that strove to hobble the ambitions of Louis XIV and pen France within her existing borders. Marlborough never fought a battle he did not win nor invested a stronghold he did not take. The roll-call of his victories includes Blenheim (1704), which saved Vienna and led to Bavaria's being taken by the allies; Ramillies (1706) which compelled the French to give up the whole of the Spanish Netherlands; Oudenaarde (1708) which drove Louis XIV to make peace overtures; and Malplaquet (1709) which routed the French on home soil. The reward bestowed on him by a grateful nation, the enormous house and gardens that comprise Blenheim Palace in Oxfordshire, might nowadays seem excessive but is the measure of how contemporaries viewed his achievements. Working closely with his friend and colleague, the Austrian general Prince Eugène of Savoy, Marlborough ensured that the vaulting ambition of the Sun King did not upset the balance of power in Europe.

Contrasts.

The reign of Louis XIV represents the apogee of French royal power and achievement. In culture and military might France was by some distance pre-eminent amongst European nations. The splendour of the Sun King's court and his breathtaking palace at Versailles held up a mirror to her grandeur. Indeed, the Hall of Mirrors was a fitting metaphor: dazzling in its light and display, magnificent to behold, awesome in conception and execution, but ultimately lacking real substance. As with all dominion built on tyranny and oppression, a hard surface masked what was fragile and brittle. Like Nineveh before her, she was vulnerable: "An attacker advances against you, Nineveh. Guard the fortress, watch the road, brace yourselves, marshal all your strength!" (Nahum 2:1).

When the prophet Nahum spoke in the middle of the seventh century BC, the mighty Assyrian empire and its capital Nineveh seemed in every way beyond comparison with the puny Israelite kingdom of Judah. Small and weak, with little to boast of in terms of architectural or cultural achievement, she must have seemed almost beneath contempt to the haughty Assyrians, who had already overrun the northern kingdom of Israel and become the "destroyers [who] have laid them waste and have ruined their vines." (Nahum 2:2). Under Ashurbanipal (669-627 BC) Assyria reached a new peak of power and brutality. Yet: "The river gates are thrown open and the palace collapses." (Nahum 2:6). Nineveh, whose mighty walls and moat were built to withstand a long siege, was taken after just a few months in 612 BC when floodwaters from a tributary of the Tigris swept away a vital section of the defensive ramparts. The fate of this once great city is a timely reminder of the fragility of human achievement.

The example of the Assyrians should also stand as a warning to all who seek to impose their will on others through force. Our desire to dominate and oppress is the source of conflict and ultimately of our own downfall. In the same way that the threat from Louis XIV helped stir a coalition against France, so Scythians, Medes and Babylonians united to attack Assyria. Nineveh was quite literally wiped off the map. Likewise the impressive edifice built by Louis XIV did not long outlast his death in 1715. Within the space of one lifetime all was similarly swept away by floodwaters, this time a tide of oppressed subjects who rose up in revolution on 14 July 1789.

By contrast, God promises that Judah will not be swept away entirely. Instead: "The LORD will restore the splendour of Jacob like the splendour of Israel" (Nahum 2:2). The fact that God's way of looking at things is different from ours is emphasised by the twofold repetition of the word 'splendour.' From a human point of view, there was little splendour in the Israelite kingdoms by comparison with the mighty empires that surrounded them: Egypt, Assyria, Babylon and (later) Persia, Greece and Rome. Yet she nevertheless had splendour of a different kind: her worth in the eyes of God. We should compare and contrast, drawing wise conclusions from the lessons of the past as to the kind of splendour that we wish to see exhibited in our own lives and in our nation. History teaches that only the splendour that derives from God is worthwhile, and that all other splendours inevitably fade, being at best a curiosity to succeeding generations.

Comfort.

The "restore[d] splendour of Jacob" (Nahum 2:2) means that, as a result of God's provision, the entire nation of Israel is to be reunited and brought back. Given that the northern Israelite kingdom was at this time under the Assyrian yoke and that Judah herself would in due course face a similar fate at the hands of the Babylonians, this is an extraordinary prophecy. The contrast between such eventual restoration and the complete obliteration of Nineveh could not be starker. For all that the Israelites had fallen short of the splendour that God wished to see in their individual lives and in the life of the nation as a whole, still he would not desert them. Nor will he desert us. The promise of restoration holds good for us just the same.

To sustain his people through dark years to come, the Lord sent words of comfort[56] about the future destruction of Nineveh and eventual reinstatement of "the splendour of Jacob" (Nahum 2:2). For us too, these words should be a source of support and assistance in time of weakness and waiting. To comfort involves giving cheer, succour, encouragement, consolation, ease, strengthening and freedom from anxiety and Nahum's prophecy works these things on several levels: destruction of a corrupt and evil regime shows God's justice; fulfilment of prophecy confirms the reliability of God and his promises; breaking the stranglehold of an oppressor makes freedom possible; reversing the oppressor's policies of deportation and exile allows homecoming; return to the Promised Land involves inheriting God's covenant blessings; whilst restoration brings unity with God and amongst those who love him.

For Israel and for us, the ultimate comfort is God's assurance of eventual redemption, both physical and spiritual.

Chastisement.

The Assyrians have no such comfort, for they neither know nor acknowledge the one true God and hence are exposed to the full force of his judgment. They reap as they have sown, with death, violence and the sword: "The metal on the chariots flashes on the day they are made ready; the spears of pine are brandished. The chariots storm through the streets, rushing back and forth through the squares. They look like flaming torches; they dart about like lightning." (Nahum 2:3-4).

In the face of attack, the military might on which the Assyrians have always relied proves pitifully inadequate: "He [the Assyrian leader] summons his picked troops, yet they stumble on their way" (Nahum 2:5). Human agency is shown to be fallible. So are the defences that we throw up to keep God out: "They dash to the city wall; the protective shield is put in place." (Nahum 2:5). It is all in vain,

---

[56] Nahum means 'comfort.' The name of this prophet who spoke of restoration is related to the name of another Israelite who was to play a large part in catalysing rebuilding of the nation after the return from exile in Babylon: Nehemiah, which means 'The Lord comforts' or 'comfort of the Lord.'

for the Lord works out his purposes regardless of the barriers and objections put in place by man. This should give us pause: since resistance to God is impossible, how much more sensible it would be to line up on the side of the Almighty and to seek splendour in the things that he values rather than in the illusory riches of the world. It is a proposition so easy to state, but which sinful human beings find so difficult to implement.

For reasons that are difficult to fathom, we have trouble recognising that setting ourselves against God can only bring destruction. The prophet describes the troops besieging Nineveh thus: "The shields of his soldiers are red; the warriors are clad in scarlet." (Nahum 2:3).[57] They are avengers and chastisers, the ones who carry out God's judgment against an unrighteous nation. It is an intriguing coincidence that since the days of Oliver Cromwell English soldiers wore red uniforms. The tradition was continued by the British army, which adopted bright scarlet in part to disguise bloodstains. These same redcoats were the ones who were instrumental in checking French designs in Europe and further afield.

Conclusion.

The nation which did so much to frustrate the plans of Louis XIV was a new creation.[58] Right from the start, maintaining the continental balance of power was a primary aim of her foreign policy. She was largely content to stay aloof from European affairs so long as no one Power threatened to dominate the mainland, preferring to be left alone to pursue her commercial interests and the concerns of Empire. Such was the danger posed by Louis XIV, however, that isolation was neither feasible nor desirable. With perfect timing and to the dismay of their enemies, England and Scotland, which had passed large parts of the seventeenth century in self-absorption and civil war, were able to take the field at the start of the eighteenth united as never before.

The Sun King was arrayed in pride and splendour, the focal point and the very embodiment of the nation: he it was who said, "I am the state." The sun is the centre of our solar system, the object around which the planets orbit. It is undoubtedly splendid, but it is a created thing. The pride was misplaced, the splendour illusory. In due course, it all came crashing down.

---

[57] It is likely that 'his' in this verse refers to the commander of the attacking forces. Since the attack is brought about by God working through human agency the reference can ultimately be seen as being to the Lord himself.

[58] The Act of Union to merge England and Scotland into the United Kingdom was passed in 1707.

Our pride is similarly misplaced and our splendour just as illusory. Instead of giving room to things of such little worth, we should rather "ascribe to the Lord the glory due to his name. Bring an offering and come before him; worship the LORD in the splendour of his holiness." (1 Chronicles 16:29). If we do not, then all that we set such store by will come crashing down, too.

26. Revival

Zephaniah 3:9-17.

Key word: purity.

For all her success on the battlefield, for all her grandiose Palladian mansions, for all the exquisite music of Georg Friedrich Händel (1685-1759), behind an elegant facade England in the early years of the eighteenth century was in a sorry state. Painter and engraver William Hogarth (1697-1764) chronicled widespread moral and spiritual decay in works such as the *Rake's Progress*, the *Harlot's Progress*, *Gin Lane* and *Marriage à la Mode*. The themes of these and others of Hogarth's works are all too familiar: untimely death, drunkenness, violence, addiction, child abuse, sexual immorality, crime, materialism and corruption of all kinds. What is portrayed is the very opposite of purity. The nation was become a sink and a cesspool. Many abandoned themselves to wickedness. Justice and mercy seemed in short supply.

Yet though people abandoned themselves and abandoned God, the Almighty did not abandon them. He sent men to preach his word and he sent the power of his Spirit. Two in particular were channels of the Great Awakening that resulted: John Wesley and George Whitefield.

Wesley began his lifetime habit of hard work and early rising whilst still an Oxford undergraduate. He and the group that gathered around him and his younger brother Charles prayed incessantly, took communion weekly instead of the three times a year which then was usual at that university, fasted, preached in gaols, helped the poor and lived austerely. They were mockingly called 'The Holy Club' or, in revival of a term applied to earlier Puritans, the 'Methodists' (because they strove to live by a certain method or rule of life). Wesley in the end adopted the nickname and gave it a simple definition: "A Methodist is one who lives according to the method laid down in the Bible."

In 1739, at the age of thirty-five, Wesley began the campaign of preaching that he pursued until his death. Over the next fifty-two years he travelled nigh on 5,000 miles a year, by foot and on horseback, preaching all over the country. He covered a total of almost a quarter of a million miles and delivered over forty thousand sermons, an average of more than fifteen each week. After the first year he spoke almost always in the open air, for the church establishment disapproved of the emotional scenes at his meetings and consequently churches were usually shut against him. Indeed, gatherings were sometimes broken up by violent mobs and Wesley himself was at times in danger of his life. Nevertheless, his audience often ran into thousands.

If anything, George Whitefield was an even more inspired preacher. He had been with the earliest Methodists at Oxford and continued to work alongside

Wesley for many years. Eventually he split from mainstream Methodism, though he remained an active participant in the religious revival that was by then sweeping the country. By the time he and Wesley ceased their work, the spiritual landscape of the country had changed almost beyond recognition.

Deceit.

At a time when our nation has sunk low, it is encouraging to be reminded that there have been similar periods in our history and that the Lord, ever loving and faithful despite our weakness and wrongdoing, has time and again sent his Spirit amongst us to cleanse, renew and purify. This should not be cause for complacency, however. Great men of God need to be nurtured and need to be heeded. Revival requires that we turn our ears and turn our hearts. It needs us to recognise the deceitful lives we lead and to see the blandishments of the world for the worthless toys they are.

The prophet Zephaniah was a contemporary of Jeremiah, Nahum and (perhaps) Habbakuk. He was sent to the Israelite kingdom of Judah when that nation, too, had wandered far from God. He prophesied early in the reign of King Josiah (640-609 BC), when the Israelites were still reaping what had been sown during the rule of two apostates, King Manasseh and King Amon. The deliverance that God promises for the future points up the shortcomings of the present by way of contrast: the Lord "will remove from this city those who rejoice in their pride. Never again will you be haughty on my holy hill ... The remnant of Israel will do no wrong; they will speak no lies, nor will deceit be found in their mouths. They will eat and lie down and no-one will make them afraid." (Zephaniah 3:11 and 13). The picture is of a nation mired in pride, wrongdoing, deceit, fear and blasphemy.

Like them, we live at a time of great deceit. All around us are lies: about God and our relationship to him, about the means to our salvation, about the meaning of our lives and the way in which we should live. The consequences are just as they were in Zephaniah's day. We are surrounded by "those who rejoice in their pride" (Zephaniah 3:11) and are "haughty" (Zephaniah 3:11). There is rebellion against God, wrongdoing, fear and blasphemy. The Lord would be entitled to punish us severely for "all the wrongs you have done to me" (Zephaniah 3:11).

Deceit can take the form of telling a lie or of suppressing the truth. Both are prevalent in modern Britain. In addition to outright lies, we have suppressed the truth of God's Word in the Bible by allowing it to be forgotten. The Israelites did the same. It was only "in the eighteenth year of [King Josiah's] reign" (2 Kings 22:3 and 2 Chronicles 34:8) that "the Book of the Law [was rediscovered] in the temple of the LORD." (2 Kings 22:8 and 2 Chronicles 34:15). Whether this comprised the entire five books of Moses or Deuteronomy alone in unclear, but at all events the effect was electrifying. The king instituted religious reforms to do away with pagan worship and to turn the people back to the Lord. The reforms and their results are described in 2 Kings 23:1-25 and in 2 Chronicles 34:1-13 and 35:1-19.

In the same way, we need to rediscover God's Word and to reform our land on the basis of it. If we will only do this, God will bring deliverance.

Deliverance.

Through the prophet Zephaniah the Lord tells us what his deliverance will look like: "The LORD has taken away your punishment, he has turned back your enemy. The LORD, the King of Israel, is with you; never again will you fear any harm. On that day they will say to Jerusalem, 'Do not fear, O Zion; do not let your hands hang limp.'" (Zephaniah 3:15-16). Deliverance will bring purification, gathering, cleansing, rebuilding and revival:

The nation will be purified so as to allow relationship and fellowship with God to be restored: "Then I will purify the lips of the peoples, that all of them may call on the name of the LORD." (Zephaniah 3:9).

There will be a gathering of believers, who will come to faith even from the most physically and spiritually distant places to join in true worship: "From beyond the rivers of Cush my worshippers, my scattered people, will bring me offerings." (Zephaniah 3:10).

There will be cleansing from sin: "On that day you will not be put to shame for all the wrongs you have done to me." (Zephaniah 3:11).

Those who remain in opposition to God, who do not acknowledge him or give him the glory that is his due, will be marginalised: "I will remove from this city those who rejoice in their pride." (Zephaniah 3:11).

God's people will be restored and rebuilt so that they are characterised by their faith and by proper attitudes: "But I will leave within you the meek and humble, who trust in the name of the LORD." (Zephaniah 3:12).

Right action will flow from right attitude: "The remnant of Israel will do no wrong; they will speak no lies, nor will deceit be found in their mouths." (Zephaniah 3:13).

In consequence of right attitude and right action, society will be harmonious: "They will eat and lie down and no-one will make them afraid" (Zephaniah 3:13).

This deliverance will not occur without our involvement, nor will it be either right or possible for us to be inactive in the face of it. We are to "call on the name of the LORD and serve him shoulder to shoulder." (Zephaniah 3:9). We are to work alongside God, joining in his activity and being available for use as his instruments.

Similarly, we are told: "do not let your hands hang limp." (Zephaniah 3:16). On one level this is simply a way of telling people not to be discouraged, but more is at work in this image. It brings to mind Moses at the battle between Israel and the Amalekites: "As long as Moses held up his hands, the Israelites were winning, but when he lowered his hands, the Amalekites were winning. When Moses' hands grew tired, they [Aaron and Hur] took a stone and put it under him and he sat on it. Aaron and Hur held his hands up – one on one side, one on the other – so that his hands remained steady till sunset. So Joshua overcame the Amalekite army with the sword." (Exodus 17:11-13).

Raising our hands is a symbol of praise, prayer and worship. It reminds us that we need to come before God and be available to be used by him. It warns us also that this can be tiring work and that we often need the help of others to see it through to completion. When we play our part to the full, the result is that the enemy is overcome and we are delivered.

Delight.

Our deliverance will bring delight: delight to us and delight to God. Our delight is described first: "Sing, O Daughter of Zion; shout aloud, O Israel! Be glad and rejoice with all your heart, O Daughter of Jerusalem!" (Zephaniah 3:14). The deliverance that God brings is not something that we are to keep to ourselves. We are to share our joy and give expression to our delight in praise and thanksgiving to our Lord and Saviour.

More extraordinary still is the delight of God and what will come in its wake: "The LORD your God is with you, he is mighty to save. He will take great delight in you, he will quiet you with his love, he will rejoice over you with singing." (Zephaniah 3:17). Our society is disquieted and discomforted. It desperately needs to know that there is the chance of being quieted with God's love and that the Lord holds out a wonderful promise of peace, wholeness and wellbeing amongst all our brokenness. In hearing that God will "rejoice over [us] with singing" (Zephaniah 3:17) we are reminded that "there will be more rejoicing in heaven over one sinner who repents than over ninety-nine righteous persons who do not need to repent." (Luke 15:7).

Turning back to God is not a weary road of grovelling apology, hair-shirt misery and endless reminders of all that we have done wrong. It is the path of delight. It is the highway to purity.

Conclusion.

More than two hundred years ago our forefathers turned back to God. They repented of wrongdoing and changed their ways. One of the most momentous results was seen in changing attitudes towards slavery. The British, who previously had shown few qualms about treating other humans as chattels, suddenly started granting slaves their freedom. Many were shipped back to Africa to form a new colony of freedmen in Sierra Leone, whose capital is still called Freetown. Eventually the slave trade itself was outlawed and suppressed.[59] It is now generally acknowledged that slavery was not abolished because it had ceased to be profitable. Both slave trading and slave ownership remained lucrative, and for precisely that reason the British government paid compensation to slave owners who suffered financial loss from slavery's abolition. Human bondage was done away with for no other reason than because it was unethical. This was a national change of heart so dramatic, a moment of collective recognition so startling and so different from what went before that many have been at a loss to account for it.

The facts certainly defy prosaic explanation, but there is in truth no mystery. The Word of God and the Spirit of God worked in the lives of individuals and of a whole nation. The High King of Heaven, who "is mighty to save" (Zephaniah 3:17) stretched forth his arm and did these things. He it was who "[purified] the lips of the peoples" (Zephaniah 3:9) of these islands, who caused them to "call on the name of the LORD and serve him shoulder to shoulder." (Zephaniah 3:9). From the depths of squalor, the nation was lifted to new heights by the activity of God.

If we truly wish to see an end to the troubles that currently plague us, there is only one way. There is only one thing that will go to the root and address the underlying cause rather than the myriad symptoms. It is no secret what this is. It can be read as plain as day in our history. Not until we turn back to God, worship him in spirit and truth, "keep his commands and obey him; serve him and hold fast to him" (Deuteronomy 13:4) will we have rest.

God longs to bring revival. The issue is whether we will turn our hearts and make ourselves receptive to being purified by his Spirit. At things stand, we are still fiddling whilst Rome burns. If we delay much longer, we will have nothing but cinders and ashes left.

---

[59] See chapter 31. The Act to abolish the slave trade was passed in 1807, an event all the more remarkable given that at the time Britain was still fighting for her life against Napoleon.

27. Beacon

Genesis 2.

Key word: paradise.

It is almost impossible to emphasise too greatly the impact that the first two chapters of Genesis have had on English society and culture. The statement that man is made "in the image of God" (Genesis 1:27), the relationship portrayed between man and God (see for example Genesis 2:7) and the charge given by God to man to "work [the land] and take care of it" (Genesis 2:15) have influenced every aspect of our lives. Genesis is central to the most fundamental freedoms that Englishmen have held dear for generation upon generation. Three examples give a flavour.

John Wycliffe (first translator of the Bible into English) and his followers the Lollards pointed to Genesis when they railed against church corruption and the lot of the poor. It was a theme echoed by their contemporary, rebel preacher John Ball. In a sermon at Blackheath in spring 1381 (just prior to the Peasants' Revolt of June that year) he said: "From the beginning all were created equal by nature. Slavery was introduced through the unjust oppression of worthless men, against the will of God; for if God had wanted to create slaves, he would surely have decided at the beginning of the world who was to be slave and who master."

Following the end of the first Civil War, Cromwell and Ireton chaired the so-called Army debates, held at St Mary's church in Putney, south-west London. Although Parliament had won the war its supporters were divided as to what form the government should take, leading to ferment in the ranks of the New Model Army. So, each regiment was invited to send delegates to Putney to put the men's case. There, soldiers argued from Scripture that there should be democracy based on one man, one vote – for, they said, it was obvious from Genesis that no man was born to have dominion over another and that each is of equal worth in the sight of God.[60] Even Cromwell, who started out sceptical, began to be swayed by the compelling nature of the argument.

---

[60] The debates took place over three days from 28 October 1647. Colonel Rainsborough, the highest-ranking Leveller sympathiser, said in the course of them that: "the poorest he that is in England hath a life to live, as the greatest he; and therefore truly, Sir, I think it's clear that every man that is to live under a government ought first by his own consent to put himself under that government ..."

The radical Thomas Paine (1737-1809), whose book *The Rights of Man* (published in 1791) was one of the catalysts of the French Revolution wrote: "The error of those who reason by precedents drawn from antiquity, respecting the rights of man, is that they do not go far enough into antiquity. They do not go the whole way. They stop in some of the intermediate stages ... But if we proceed on, we shall at last come out right; we shall come to the time when man came from the hand of his Maker. What was he then? Man. Man was his high and only title, and a higher cannot be given him."

The influence of Genesis extends yet further. Already in its opening chapters we see a relationship-oriented God, who comes "walking in the garden in the cool of the day" (Genesis 3:8) and who speaks to man. We encounter a covenant-making God, who does not merely make demands of man, but commits himself to certain courses of action and allows us to call on him to honour the words he has spoken: God commits himself to allowing Adam and Eve to remain in the garden to enjoy all the good things it has to offer, so long as they do not break their side of the bargain by eating "from the tree of the knowledge of good and evil."(Genesis 2:15-17). We glimpse a God who cares intimately for man and for his wellbeing: thus he says, "It is not good for the man to be alone. I will make a helper suitable for him." (Genesis 2:18). We experience, moreover, the extraordinary structural unity of the Bible. The tale begins with a perfect creation that sees man placed in a garden, enjoying the occasional presence of God and the created light of sun, moon and stars. The book of Revelation tells us how the story will end, with a perfect re-creation that sees man welcomed into the city of God, where he will enjoy the continual presence of his Lord and thus need no created light.

Man made in the image of God, a God who makes covenants and a caring God. It is no accident that democracy, freedom and the rule of law were the fruits of a Christian country: we will look in vain in the holy texts of other religions for the words that gave them birth and nurtured them. These are the very things that made England for centuries a beacon to the world. They are England's greatest gifts to the world. They are things through which much that is best in the world has come about. If we are tempted sometimes to imagine that England has little that makes her culturally distinctive, we should remember that this is because so much of the world has aspired to those things that were England's first. We have exported across the globe not only our methods of manufacture and ideas about the role and responsibility of the state, but our forms of government and our laws, together with their underlying concepts of human dignity, freedom, justice and fairness.

The breath of life.

The early chapters of Genesis tell us about the creation of the universe and of life on earth.[61] Genesis 1 gives a concise overview of the process of creation, climaxing in the creation of man on the sixth day. Genesis 2 provides a close-up of what happens on the sixth day, with the start of human history and the giving of life to man: "the Lord God formed the man from the dust of the ground and breathed into his nostrils the breath of life, and the man became a living being." (Genesis 2:7).

Man was formed from existing materials: he is "dust" (Genesis 2:7). Yet he has unique dignity and worth because he is made in the image of his Creator. This is emphasised by the language of Genesis. The word *bara'* describes the creation of man. This word is used at three stages of the creation process, each time to describe an act of divine production that brings into being something entirely new. The wording thus makes clear that man is something more than just another animal. More than that, we are told that God "breathed into [Adam's] nostrils" (Genesis 2:7). The Hebrew word that is used for breath (*ruach*) is the same word that is used for the Spirit of God. It is the Spirit of God that animates and gives life to man. It is the Spirit of God that is designed to be our guide and comforter. It is the Spirit of God that we need in our lives, for without it we are less than we were created to be. When we forget these basic things about what we are, we go against the fundamental nature of our being and we start to go astray. We need to remember where we came from and for what we were created.

The river of life.

The Spirit of God is not just breathed into man, but courses through the whole creation: "streams came up from the earth and watered the whole surface of the ground ... A river watering the garden flowed from Eden; from there it was separated into four headwaters." (Genesis 2:6 and 2:10). The water that flows through the earth is a symbol of God's Spirit. The prophet Ezekiel likens the Spirit of God to a river: "I saw water coming out from under the threshold

---

[61] The First Law of Thermodynamics (otherwise known as the law of conservation of mass and energy) states that matter and energy can neither be created nor destroyed: matter can be converted into energy and energy into matter, but their sum total must remain the same. The law is sometimes expressed in the Latin dictum *Ex nihilo, nihil fit* (nothing comes out of nothing). Isaac Asimov called it "the most powerful and fundamental generalisation about the universe that scientists have ever been able to make." It confirms the need for a divine act of creation to form the universe.

of the temple ... [becoming] a river that no-one could cross ... I saw a great number of trees on each side of the river ... When it empties into the Sea, the water there becomes fresh. Swarms of living creatures will live wherever the river flows" (Ezekiel 47:1, 5, 7-9). Likewise, Jesus talks about "a spring of water welling up to eternal life." (John 4:14).

The water that flowed through Eden also flows through the city described in Revelation: "Then the angel showed me the river of the water of life, as clear as crystal, flowing from the throne of God and of the Lamb down the middle of the great street of the city." (Revelation 22:1). Wherever we turn, we cannot escape the Spirit of God. Nor should we: instead, we should invite the Spirit to fill us afresh every day, to empower and equip us for the life that God wishes us to lead.

The tree of life.

The earth described in Genesis is well-watered. It is also a place of lush vegetation: "And the LORD God made all kinds of trees grow out of the ground – trees that were pleasing to the eye and good for food. In the middle of the garden were the tree of life and the tree of the knowledge of good and evil." (Genesis 2:9). So well-known is the story of Adam and Eve eating the fruit of the one tree in the garden that was forbidden them that we are apt to overlook that another tree was right beside it: the tree of life. God's will for man is and always has been that we should have life. The tree of life appears again in God's perfect re-creation, the City of God described in Revelation: "On each side of the river stood the tree of life, bearing twelve crops of fruit, yielding its fruit every month. And the leaves of the tree are for the healing of the nations." (Revelation 22:2).

In a land that increasingly embraces a culture of death, it is up to us to point the way to life. It is up to us to show that when human beings go against God's laws, the result is that "[we] will surely die." (Genesis 2:17). All around we see the consequences of misusing the good things that God has given us: we were given "wine [to] gladden the heart of man" (Psalm 104:15), not become drunkards; we were given sex to enjoy between man and wife and bind them close, not to be promiscuous; we were given drugs to cure disease and alleviate pain, not to seek escape from reality.

The sharing of life.

We have also been given each other, so that we may share life, so that we may comfort one another, share our joys and bear one another's burdens. Man was made to be a social being. He was made for relationship with God and he was made for relationship with his own kind: "It is not good for the man to be alone. I will make a helper suitable for him." (Genesis 2:18). In a land where so many feel alone and friendless, we are to reach out to the helpless and the lost.

159

We are to provide an example of the love that Jesus commanded us to have for one another (see John 15:12). We are to point the way back to community and fellowship for a nation that craves it but does not quite know how to get there.

The unity of life.

Furthermore, we are to remind ourselves and others that man is designed to live a life that reflects the fact that he is made in the image of his Creator: "Then the LORD God made a woman from the rib he had taken out of the man, and he brought her to the man. The man said, 'This is now bone of my bone and flesh of my flesh; she shall be called woman, for she was taken out of man.' For this reason a man will leave his father and mother and be united to his wife, and they will become one flesh." (Genesis 2:22-23). There is unity in life and there is unity in human beings. This does not mean that we are to be carbon copies of each other. It does not mean that we have to pretend that male and female are in all respects identical. It does not mean that every Christian has to worship in precisely the same way. The unity that God has created and wants us to display in our lives is unity in diversity, a unity that mirrors his own nature. The Hebrew word that is used to describe one flesh ('ehad) is never used in the Bible to describe a stark singular entity. It means not one in isolation, but one in unity. It is the same word that is used when the Bible tells us that: "The LORD our God, the LORD is one." (Deuteronomy 6:4).

We are given the example of the unity in diversity of man and wife in order to show us how human beings are intended to interact, and also to help us understand better the unity in diversity of God himself: one God, Father, Son and Holy Spirit.

The purpose or meaning of life.

God created man to have purpose and meaning in his life: "The LORD God took the man and put him in the Garden of Eden to work it and take care of it ... Now the LORD God had formed out of the ground all the beasts of the field and all the birds of the air. He brought them to the man to see what he would name them; and whatever the man called each living creature, that was its name. So the man gave names to all the livestock, the birds of the air and the beasts of the field." (Genesis 2:15 and 2:19).

We need to work out what God's purpose for us is. We need to work out whether the tasks in which we are currently engaged are still the ones that the Lord wants us to pursue, or whether he wishes to take us in new directions. Discerning what God is saying to us about these things is something we do primarily through prayer and reading the Bible, but there may be other ways in which he is guiding us, too. We need to make time to listen to what he is saying, and then to act.

Conclusion.

There is a message in this for us, as individuals and as a body. We need to remember where we came from and for what reason we were created (the breath of life); to seek continually to be filled by the Spirit of God (the river of life); to point out the way to a lost and hurting world (the tree of life); to reach out to the helpless and lost (the sharing of life); to work for reconciliation – in church, society, family, friendships, marriage and other relationships (the unity of life, a unity that allows for the diversity that God created); and to seek the purpose that God has in mind for our lives (the meaning of life). When we do these things, we will find reconciliation, community and wholeness. We will again have purpose and meaning as a nation.

This is hard work. These are not tasks that can be completed overnight. For sure, the road will often be difficult. We will need "perseverance ... character and ... hope" (Romans 5:3), but with the Lord's help the end is attainable. This land was once a beacon to the world. With the grace of God, it can be so again.

28. Slough of despond

John 20:24-30

Key word: assurance.

There was once a young man so overcome with feelings of doubt, fear and worthlessness that he resolved to take his own life. Placing a loaded pistol to his temple, he pulled the trigger. Nothing happened. He tried again, and a second time the weapon failed to fire. At that point, trembling, he laid the gun aside and said to himself: "It seems that I am meant for something after all; I will live." The place was Madras, the date was 1744 and the young man was Robert Clive (1725-74), otherwise known as Clive of India. In the years following this incident, he went on to gain famous victories against great odds at Arcot (1751), Plassey (1757) and Buxar (1764). The first of these was won when he was only twenty-six years old.

Together these magnificent feats of arms broke French power in India, entrenched the influence of the East India Company and made it ruler over millions of Bengalis instead of merely a trading entity. In doing so, they set the stage for almost two hundred years of British rule in the subcontinent. How many times the victorious general, who became governor of Bengal and a baron of the realm, must have thought back to the day he tried to kill himself and said again: I was meant for something.

Absence.

Doubt can be a terrible thing. It can cripple us so badly that we are incapable of anything. It can blind us to any meaning in life. It can make us want to deny the life in us, perhaps not with a loaded pistol, but with destructive behaviour that may have much the same result in the end. Doubt can bring loneliness, isolation and despair. Yet there is another kind of doubt that can lead us to question, explore and ultimately to encounter God. The story of Jesus' disciple Thomas shows us how.

Thomas' life-changing meeting with Jesus after the latter's resurrection did not take place in a vacuum. By the time that the disciple came face to face with the Christ, most of those who were closest to Jesus during his earthly ministry had already seen the risen Lord. On the morning that Jesus' empty grave was discovered, Jesus appeared to Mary Magdalene whilst she was still standing outside the tomb: see John 20:14. During the same day, Jesus appeared to Cleopas and another disciple on the road to Emmaus: see Luke 24:13-35. That very evening, he appeared to a number of disciples as they met together behind locked doors: see John 20:19-23. We are not told exactly how many disciples were gathered together on this occasion, but we are told that Thomas was not amongst them: see John 20:24. It is a point we need to remember whenever we are tempted to doubt: it was Thomas who was absent, not Jesus.

Not surprisingly, the disciples who had been present excitedly related to their comrade what had happened. They told him: "We have seen the Lord!" (John 20:25). Thomas was thus faced with a body of testimony from a significant number of people. Not from strangers, but from people he knew well. These included those with whom he had spent three years or more of his life whilst they accompanied Jesus on his journeys through Galilee, Judea and Samaria. They had shared times of joy and wonder, but also times of challenge, stress and fear. They had seen each other under pressure, and when we see people in those circumstances we tend to have a pretty good idea of whether we can rely on what they say.

Over and above all that, Thomas would have been present when Jesus performed miracles. He had seen Jesus raise people from the dead: Lazarus (John 11:38-44), the widow of Nain's son (Luke 7:11-17) and the ruler's daughter (Matthew 9:18-26). For good measure, Thomas would have heard Peter affirm that Jesus is "the Christ, the Son of the living God" and Jesus not rebuke him for blasphemy but reply, "Blessed are you, Simon son of Jonah, for this was not revealed to you by man, but by my Father in heaven." (Matthew 16:13-17).

Proof positive.

Thomas was a man for our times, a hard-headed rationalist: if you cannot drop it on your foot, it does not exist.[62] When he heard the disciples report their sightings of Jesus and their conversations with him, this man did not allow any past experience to spoil his scepticism. He wanted hard facts, and not someone else's hard facts. He wanted to see for himself: "Unless I see the nail marks in his hands and put my finger where the nails were, and put my hand into his side, I will not believe it." (John 20:25). This is a telling phrase. With millions of others, Thomas says: I will not believe, I refuse to believe, I will make a conscious effort not to believe, and I will disregard everything that is inconvenient or contrary to my not believing. Double standards abound, with different levels of proof being set for the Bible from those that are applied to other sources. To take just one

---

[62] Immediately prior to his crucifixion, Jesus comforted his disciples by telling them that "I am going [to my Father's house] to prepare a place for you ... You know the way to the place where I am going." (John 14:1-4). Quick as a flash, Thomas gave a no-nonsense reply: "Lord, we don't know where you are going, so how can we know the way?" (John 14:5). To this, Jesus responded in turn that "I am the way and the truth and the life." (John 14:6).

example: much of the life and achievement of Julius Caesar is known through his own telling of the story. Yet that is taken at face value whilst some will twist and turn every which way rather than accept the evidence of eyewitnesses to the miracles of Jesus – eyewitnesses who were so convinced of the truth of what they related that they went on to suffer and die for it.

Too often, we do not apply consistent standards. To give Thomas his due, however, when Jesus appeared and spoke to him there was no longer the shadow of a doubt in his mind. His response was direct and to the point: "My Lord and my God!" (John 20:28). Incidentally, there is nothing to tell us for sure that Thomas took up Jesus' invitation to "Put your finger here; see my hands. Reach out your hand and put it into my side." (John 20:27). Maybe in the end merely seeing Jesus was enough for him, despite all his earlier bravado.[63] At all events, the encounter fundamentally changed both his attitude and his future. Tradition has it that Thomas became a missionary, founded the church in Parthia (modern Iran), later travelled to India and in due course was martyred.

Presence.

The story of Thomas is of a man overcoming doubt. It is about the presence of God, not his absence. It shows us how to grapple with doubt that comes through our isolation, how to address legitimate doubt and how to eschew wilful doubt.

There is nothing like being isolated to increase doubt. When we no longer have strength in numbers or any source of support it is easy for us to become prey to all sorts of fears and imaginings. We do not know why Thomas was not with the other disciples on the evening when Jesus first appeared to them as they cowered behind locked doors. Maybe his tendency to doubt had something to do with it, maybe not. Maybe the reckless courage that he showed when told of the death of Lazarus led him to be out and about as everyone else skulked inside. Whatever the reason, Thomas must have felt isolated. Every other apostle (with the exception of Judas Iscariot) had had a personal encounter with the risen Jesus. Thomas would not have been human had he not wondered why he should be the odd one out, and whether it was some lack or unworthiness in him that was the reason. We all go through this, when we look around and others seem to

---

[63] The apostle John, at least, does not seem to have held back. He speaks of "That which ... we have seen with our eyes, which we have looked at and our hands have touched" (1 John 1:1). Presumably he took advantage of Jesus' invitation when the risen Lord said: "Why are you troubled, and why do doubts rise in your minds? Look at my hands and my feet. It is I myself! Touch me and see; a ghost does not have flesh and bones, as you see I have." (Luke 24:38-39).

have so much more faith, assurance or experience. So there is something here from which we can each take heart. For despite his doubt and isolation, Jesus came and met Thomas, inviting him to explore the things that lay behind his doubt and to experience for himself. In truth we are never alone and never abandoned by God.

Not all doubt is bad. There is nothing inherently wrong in questioning and investigating, as long as it is done in the right spirit. Shortly before the crucifixion, Thomas had said to Jesus: "Lord, we don't know where you are going, so how can we know the way?" (John 14:5). For many, that will not sound an unreasonable question. Given what the disciples knew at that point and had experienced up till then, it seems more like a sensible request for clarification, which is precisely how Jesus treated it. He did not censure Thomas, but gave further explanation of what he meant. We are reminded, not for the first time, that God does not ask us to leave our brains behind in order to become Christians: far from it. He asks us to use the intellect he has given us to test and investigate. The prophet Isaiah, writing some seven hundred years before the birth of Jesus, records God as saying: "Come, let us reason together." (Isaiah 1:18). The apostle John, writing a letter to early Christians, told them: "do not believe every spirit, but test the spirits to see if they are from God" (1 John 4:1).

Yet there comes a time when we need to get off the fence and make a leap of faith. Thomas' opinionated assertion that "I will not believe" (John 20:25) shows wilful doubt, an entrenched refusal to believe, come what may. In answer to this, Jesus gives Thomas a straightforward command: "Stop doubting and believe" (John 20:27) and then goes on to say: "Because you have seen me, you have believed, blessed are those who have not seen and yet have believed." (John 20:29). This latter statement, of course, applies to us. We have not seen in the way the disciples were able to see, in a flesh and blood physical sense. We can have real experiences of God's presence and power, sure enough, but we are not able to put our hands in the holes made in Jesus' body by nail and spear.

Vanquishing doubt.

All too often, our response is to say of the disciples' experience: that was then and this is now, we have doubts and we cannot just wish them away – no amount of telling us to believe can change that. Somehow we have to get beyond this, to overcome the things that are stumbling blocks for us and to unstop the things that dam up our relationship with God. There are simple practical things that each of us can do:

Reflect and pray. We can ask God to resolve doubts for us and to give us insights. In one of his letters to Timothy, St Paul advises: "Reflect on what I am saying, for the Lord will give you insight into all this." (2 Timothy 2:7).

Turn doubt into something positive. Instead of allowing doubt to cripple, blind and destroy, we can make it a spur to question and explore. When we do this, however, we owe it to ourselves (and to God) to be consistent and to apply the same standards of proof that we use in other areas of life.

Test and examine. Some take at face value the assertion that the Bible is full of stories that are fit only for children, which never really happened. Yet we cannot know one way or the other unless we read and investigate. Many are astonished to learn that events similar to those of Jonah and the whale or Joshua leading the Israelites through the parted waters of the River Jordan have been observed and attested beyond contradiction in modern times. At the height of commercial whaling in the nineteenth century a seaman was swept overboard and swallowed by the animal his crew were trying to harpoon. Some while later that same creature was cut open and the man found inside its stomach, still alive.[64] In 1927 there was an upstream blockage of the River Jordan that interrupted the flow of water so that the river could be forded easily. Of course, this kind of thing does *not* show that equivalent events recorded in the Bible are not miracles, merely that God does not need to break natural laws in order to bring miracles about.

Build up a picture. We will never be able to check personally every single fact and circumstance recounted in the Bible for the simple reason that we were not present at the time of the events in question. What we can do is to build up a picture from what we are able to check that allows us to treat with confidence those things that we cannot.

Work at it. It is unrealistic to expect that doubts will be resolved without hard work. We need to read the Bible. We may need the help of Bible commentaries and courses, too.

Solomon wrote that "there is nothing new under the sun." (Ecclesiastes 1:9). So it proves, for centuries ago the prophet Isaiah had words for those in doubt: "Do you not know? Have you not heard? Has it not been told you from the beginning?" (Isaiah 40:21). Like Thomas, we need to get off the fence, stop doubting and believe.

---

[64] See chapter 61.

Conclusion.

The story of Thomas shows how God responds to our doubts. In isolation, loneliness and despair, Jesus meets us. In legitimate questioning and exploring, Jesus answers us. In wilfulness, Jesus challenges us.

Robert Clive overcame doubt and realised that he was meant for something.[65] A message that resonates throughout the Bible is that we are *all* meant for something. We are all called to be the people that God created us to be. We all have meaningful work to do in the service of our Lord. Our forefathers were not uniformly zealous Christians, but many made a leap of faith and allowed God to work wonders in their lives. They turned doubt to assurance. We can do the same. Indeed, we must if there is to be hope for our nation.

---

[65] He was no paragon. In his *Historical Essays*, Macaulay pronounced him: "A savage old Nabob, with an immense fortune, a tawny complexion, a bad liver and a worse heart."

29. Colossus

Joshua 5:10-15.

Key word: steadfastness.

The Seven Years' War began in 1756, a contest that pitted Britain and Prussia against a coalition comprising France, Austria, Sweden and Russia. Its outcome was as surprising as the match was on paper unequal. In mainland Europe, the brilliant Prussian king Frederick the Great consistently out-fought his opponents, whilst Britain concentrated her efforts largely at sea and in the colonies. Prussia not only survived but retained control of Silesia, which she had seized at the outset of hostilities. The Treaty of Paris in 1763 confirmed her ally supreme in North America and India. By the war's end Britain was the foremost maritime and colonial power.

This position was won on the back of extraordinary success in every theatre where the nation's arms were engaged. So momentous were the attainments in 1759 in particular that this was known as the Year of Victories: Quebec was captured, a French invasion fleet destroyed at Quiberon Bay off Brittany, Guadeloupe taken, a Dutch naval expedition vanquished, and to cap it all the French were defeated at Minden on the Weser, where six British infantry regiments earned fame and glory for their advance under fire.[66] These victories were almost miraculous in extent and execution. At Quiberon Bay, Admiral Hawke did not merely maul his opponents. They were utterly shattered. Two thirds of the French fleet was wrecked, burned or captured.

Beyond compare was the taking of Quebec, key to control of Canada and the Great Lakes, without which French dominion in the vast western territories of Louisiana was ultimately unsustainable. Before she fell, France seemingly had the upper hand in North America, for the Thirteen Colonies of British North America were in danger of being penned to the eastern seaboard. At the time, French dreams of entirely overrunning or extinguishing them did not appear fantastic.

Quebec was an exceptionally hard nut to crack. Her natural defences were considerable, girt as she was by steep cliffs, dense forest and the swift-flowing St Lawrence river (then largely uncharted, never before navigated by large men-of-war). The soldier who undertook her conquest was, at thirty-two years of age, the youngest major-general in the British army. To those who did not know him he

---

[66] These were afterwards known as the 'Minden Regiments.'

made an unlikely "mighty warrior" (Judges 6:12) to equal or surpass Gideon. He was pallid and gangly, of poor health and fitful physical strength. During the Quebec campaign he was frequently confined to a sick bed[67] and had presentiments of impending death. Depending on one's viewpoint, the plan which he conceived for taking the capital of New France was the product either of genius, desperation or folly. It was made possible by the fact that, to the amazement of the enemy and through a surpassing feat of seamanship, a British fleet had made its way up the St Lawrence without loss. The Royal Navy was thus on hand to help execute a night landing on the north shore of that river close to the city and astride her vital supply lines.

The place chosen for the assault was at the foot of the Heights of Abraham, a cliff so high and steep that the French thought it impassable to an attacker and had posted only a token picket line to defend it. Of those taking part, Admiral Holmes described the operation as "the most hazardous and difficult task that I was ever engaged in" whilst Admiral Saunders considered the achievement of reaching the cliff top above the beachhead as "scarce credible." In the battle that took place on the plain above the Heights as day broke after the landing, numerically superior French troops were put to flight by what Christopher Lloyd in *The Capture of Quebec* called "the most perfect volley ever fired on a battlefield." A few days later, the city surrendered and within a year all Canada fell into British hands. Wolfe did not live to savour his triumph. During the battle he was thrice wounded, the last blow proving fatal.[68] So departed this life a man to rank alongside "the heroes of old, men of renown." (Genesis 6:4).

Taking responsibility.

Like Wolfe, Joshua was a general of genius, a man who inspired his troops, led from the front and saw opportunity where others saw only difficulty. He had been hardened by experiencing slavery under Pharoah, tempered by witnessing God's miracles during Israel's departure from Egypt and whilst wandering in the wilderness, honed by apprenticeship alongside Moses. Together with Caleb, he was the only one of the twelve spies sent into Canaan by Moses who returned with a positive report and was eager to follow God's instructions by taking immediate possession of the land: see Numbers 14:26-34. He was an experienced commander, having already led the Israelites to victory against the Amalekites:

---

[67] The likelihood is that Wolfe was suffering from rheumatic fever. Without proper treatment, this would have produced a heart condition that would have proved fatal in a matter of months.

[68] His French opposite number, Marquis Louis-Joseph de Montcalm, a wily and able foe, also suffered a mortal wound and died the day after the battle.

see Exodus 17:8-13. He was known for his deep trust in God and is described as "a man in whom is the spirit" (Numbers 27:18). Reflecting this, "Moses gave Hoshea son of Nun the name Joshua." (Numbers 13:16).[69]

God does not ask us to take on things that are beyond us or to carry more than we can bear. He prepares us for what is ahead. In precisely this way, Joshua was equipped for the task of leading the Israelites into the Promised Land of Canaan and defeating the tribes that were already settled there. God told him what was required: "After the death of Moses the servant of the LORD, the LORD said to Joshua son of Nun, Moses' assistant, 'Moses my servant is dead. Now then, you and all these people, get ready to cross the Jordan River into the land I am about to give to them – the Israelites. I will give you every place where you set your foot, as I promised Moses.'" (Joshua 1:1-3).

Joshua received both a divine commission and a divine promise. He and his people symbolically accepted the former and claimed the latter. They did so through:

Preparing their hearts by undergoing circumcision (see Joshua 5:2-5 and 7-8) – the outward sign of God's covenant with Abraham and a mark of the inner disposition that devotion to the Lord requires.

Accepting and celebrating God's free gift of deliverance and salvation: "On the evening of the fourteenth day of the month, while camped at Gilgal on the plains of Jericho, the Israelites celebrated the Passover." (Joshua 5:10).

Taking hold of what was promised: "The day after the Passover, that very day, they ate some of the produce of the land: unleavened bread and roasted grain." (Joshua 5:10-11).

This did not mean that all would thereafter be plain sailing. Nor did it mean that the Lord would hand everything to them on a plate. Quite the contrary: "The manna stopped the day after they ate this food from the land; there was no longer any manna for the Israelites, but that year they ate of the produce of Canaan." (Joshua 5:12). During their time in the wilderness, the Israelites were dependent on God's miraculous provision of food and water. This now ceased. Henceforth, the people were required to stand on their own two feet and to take responsibility for their own futures. This is a lesson about which we often need to remind ourselves. God can and does provide for us miraculously, but much more often he requires us to provide for ourselves and for others through using the strength and intelligence that he has given us. If we will not

---

[69] Hoshea means 'salvation.' Joshua means 'the Lord saves.'

take responsibility for our lives, it is unrealistic to expect that God will step in and fill the gap when all that is lacking is a proper degree of human application.

Taking sides.

Joshua did not fail to take responsibility. There were times when he received specific guidance from God, for example in relation to the taking of Jericho (see Joshua 6:2-5), but there were also times when he had to use his own skill to discern how best to give effect to divine instructions. At no point was the Israelite general able to dispense with basic military preparations and precautions merely because he was acting in accordance with the will of God. We would hardly expect otherwise, for that simply is not the way the Lord works.

Having led his people across the Jordan, Joshua therefore did what any good commander would do in similar circumstances. He set out from his base at Gilgal to scout the land around Jericho, which was his intended objective and would shortly become the first Canaanite town to be taken by the Israelites. Whilst conducting this reconnaissance, the general had an encounter of a kind that is unique in Scripture: "Now when Joshua was near Jericho, he looked up and saw a man standing in front of him with a drawn sword in his hand. Joshua went up to him and asked, 'Are you for us or for our enemies?'" (Joshua 5:13). Joshua's reaction is instructive. In hostile territory, confronted by a man with weapon drawn, accompanied probably by only a small scouting party, most would be tempted to instant fight or flight. Showing the calm deliberation that no doubt helped make him an outstanding battlefield leader, Joshua did neither. He did not leap to conclusions, but realised that appearances can be deceptive: hence his question.

The answer was certainly unexpected: "'Neither,' [the man] replied, 'but as commander of the army of the LORD I have now come.'" (Joshua 5:14). In times of war especially, we are wont to see God as being on our side and against our enemies. Here we are given quite a different perspective. It is not a question of God's being on our side. It is rather a question of whose side we take. Our obligation and our responsibility is to be part of "the army of the LORD" (Joshua 5:15), to fight battles for and on behalf of the Almighty. Lest we forget, Joshua's encounter reminds us that our actions on earth are but a reflection and a part of battles that are being fought in the heavenly realms.

It is thus a delusion to ask whether God was on the side of England during the Seven Years' War, or at any other point in her history. The correct question is to ask what England was and is doing to fight for and advance the kingdom of God.

Taking position.

If we are to be of maximum use in combat for God, we need to take up the right position. Any general knows that the disposition of forces before a battle has an overwhelming impact on its outcome: to quote the Chinese military strategist Sun Tzu,[70] author of *The Art of War*, "Every battle is won before it is fought." The way in which Joshua responds to his meeting with the "commander of the army of the LORD" (Joshua 5:14) is a model for us. It leads him by stages to where God ultimately wants him to be, through:

Prostration before the Almighty: "Then Joshua fell face down to the ground in reverence ..." (Joshua 5:14).

Seeking the will of God: "[Joshua] asked him, 'What message does my Lord have for his servant?'" (Joshua 5:14).

Heeding and acting on what is said: "The commander of the LORD's army replied, 'Take off your sandals, for the place where you are standing is holy.' And Joshua did so." (Joshua 5:15).

Joshua is then given instructions for the forthcoming campaign against Jericho: see Joshua 6:2-5. If we follow the same path we will be led in the same way.

Often we bemoan the fact that we do not hear from God. We can hardly expect to do so if we flee from or resist his messengers, nor if we fail to approach him with reverence to ask his will. Neither can we complain if our inability to hear is a consequence of our failure to listen and give effect to what God tells us. We live in a land where the great majority have long been guilty of all these failings. We need to reposition ourselves so that we are once again able to take God's side in the battles to come. We need first of all to start taking responsibility for ourselves and to stop acting like petulant children.

Conclusion.

The Year of Victories was an astonishing watershed in the history of this nation, and a turning point in the long struggles with France. At the outbreak of the Seven Years' War, all dispassionate analysis would have concluded that the advantage in every theatre of conflict lay with France. For sure, the Royal Navy was preponderant in both numbers of ships and quality of seamanship, yet

---

[70] Sun Tzu is commonly thought to have lived around 500 BC, though both the date and even the fact of his existence are open to doubt.

important as sea power might be to stave off invasion and project influence overseas, it could not of itself gain territory: the battles for India and Canada were fought and won on land.

The future of our nation is in the balance as never before. As in previous ages, circumstances might at present seem to favour the enemy. The ground is difficult and a hard campaign lies ahead. That is no reason to give up the fight. Like Joshua and James Wolfe, we need strength of will and purpose. We need to be steadfast in the face of troubles, obstacles and disappointments. The Heights of Abraham may seem to tower above us, but they can be scaled, "For nothing is impossible with God." (Luke 1:37).

30. New lands

Numbers 13.

Key word: optimism.

Captain James Cook (1728-79) was the son of a Yorkshire farm labourer. He went to sea at the age of 18 in a Whitby collier, thereafter enlisting in the Royal Navy. Though he had little in the way of formal schooling, such was his industry, intelligence and passion for learning that he earned a master's warrant by the time he was 29. During the British campaign to conquer Canada from the French he played an important part in surveying the estuary of the St Lawrence and in ferrying General Wolfe's men along that river to attack Quebec. Following the end of the war, he mapped the islands of St Pierre and Miquelon, together with the coasts of Newfoundland and Labrador. Over the years he became a navigator of genius, almost entirely self-taught.

In 1768 he was commissioned as a lieutenant in command of the 368-ton *Endeavour*. At the instance of the Royal Society and the Admiralty, he then undertook three voyages of exploration over the next eleven years. Thanks to his indomitable leadership, these revolutionised knowledge of the southern seas. Cook and his crew charted the shores of New Zealand and Australia and laid claim to those lands on behalf of the Crown, preparing the way for Britain's first Antipodean colony at Botany Bay a mere eighteen years after his visit in 1770. On return from his second expedition in 1775 he was promoted to captain, elected a member of the Royal Society and awarded its gold medal. He is generally regarded as the greatest European explorer of the Pacific in the eighteenth century. His reach extended to within a day's sailing of Antarctica and brought him inside the Arctic Circle. To this day, few have sailed further north or south.

The voyages that Cook led were testament not only to his skills and those of his crews, but also to the growing scientific and technological prowess of Britain. His men had a diet supplemented by sauerkraut to stave off scurvy and development of reliable marine chronometers by Harrison enabled greater precision in navigation than ever before. The aims of his voyages were not only exploratory but also scientific: he observed a transit of Venus in 1769[71] and brought back specimens of previously unknown flora and fauna. His voyages led to the identification and drawing of thousands of new plants, animals and birds by his talented passengers, whilst their astronomical and horological work advanced those sciences immeasurably. So highly valued was this undertaking for the betterment of mankind in days of peace that during the American War of Independence both French and Americans gave Cook's ships immunity from interference.

On 17 January 1779 the great sea captain was killed by natives at Kealakekua Bay on Hawaii (then called the Sandwich Islands). There his remains were buried and there a memorial stands, close to the water's edge where he fell. He was aged 50. The expedition was piloted through the remainder of its term and on the long journey home by sailing master William Bligh, later Captain of the *Bounty* during the mutiny led by Fletcher Christian.

Exploration.

There was great competition amongst European nations with regard to voyages of discovery. These promised not merely geographical and scientific knowledge, but also opportunities for trade and colonisation. Consequently, it was by no means a foregone conclusion that Britain would be the first to settle Australia and New Zealand. France in particular was active in the south Pacific. Her eighteenth century navigators Louis Antoine de Bougainville, Marc-Joseph Marion du Fresne, Jules Crozet, Yves-Joseph de Kerguelen-Trémarec and Jean-François-Marie de Surville came within a hair's breadth of beating Cook to it. Once again, France was pipped at the post by her arch rival.

Unlike the competing Powers of Europe, the Israelites did not undertake their survey of Canaan according to human timing and desires. They did so at the behest of God: "The LORD said to Moses, 'Send some men to explore the land of Canaan, which I am giving to the Israelites. From each ancestral tribe send one of its leaders.' So at the LORD's command Moses sent them out from the Desert of Paran. All of them were leaders of the Israelites." (Numbers 13:1-3). God does not expect us to act in ignorance, nor does he want us to shun enquiry

---

[71] Observing the transit of Venus across the sun was significant because, by triangulating measurements taken from different points across the globe, it enabled the distance to the planets to be measured accurately. Transits occurred in 1761 and 1769. The next transit was in 1882, with none in the twentieth century and two in the first decade of the twenty-first century. It was thus of prime importance that Cook was in position on time to observe the transit. Dithering by the Royal Society meant that he left England with few hours to spare.

and investigation. On the contrary, he wishes us to test and examine: hence we are told to "Taste and see that the LORD is good" (Psalm 34:8) and to "Test everything" (1 Thessalonians 5:21).[72] Christianity has nothing to fear from honest and open-minded searching. The problem in our present society is that these qualities are so often lacking from our approach to things spiritual.

The instructions Moses gave were similar to those given to Cook: "'See what the land is like and whether the people who live there are strong or weak, few or many. What kind of land do they live in? Is it good or bad? What kind of towns do they live in? Are they unwalled or fortified? How is the soil? Is it fertile or poor? Are there trees on it or not? Do your best to bring back some of the fruit of the land.' (It was the season for the first ripe grapes.)" (Numbers 13:18-20). There was to be a thorough investigation of the country, its topography, its inhabitants and its produce. This is arresting. God had already told the Israelites that he would give them a land flowing with milk and honey and that he would enable them to vanquish their opponents. He did not expect them to take his word for it, however. He allowed them to see the reality for themselves.

On his first voyage, Cook was accompanied by botanist Joseph Banks, who later helped establish the Royal Botanic Gardens at Kew, London. As well as cataloguing and drawing plants and animals, Banks and his team also brought samples back with them. The Israelites did the same: "So they went up and explored the land from the Desert of Zin as far as Rehob, towards Lebo Hamath ... When they reached the Valley of Eshcol, they cut off a branch bearing a single cluster of grapes. Two of them carried it on a pole between them, along with some pomegranates and figs." (Numbers 13:21-23). They thus brought back with them proof positive that what God said about the fruitfulness of the land was correct. There comes a point, however, when we have to move beyond what is known and what can be examined. There are times when we need to step out in faith, without precise knowledge of what lies ahead, relying on God rather than on the things of this world. If we are to do this effectively, we need to assess accurately the information we have and how this fits into what God is asking us to do.

Assessment.

The Israelites started this process in the right way: "They [the spies] came back to Moses and Aaron and the whole Israelite community at Kadesh in the

---

[72] Legitimate testing and examination of the kind described in these verses is not to be confused with a disrespectful attitude towards God and his servants: "Do not test the Lord your God as you did at Massah [where the Israelites grumbled against Moses and doubted God's promises]" (Deuteronomy 6:16).

Desert of Paran. There they reported to them and to the whole assembly and showed them the fruit of the land." (Numbers 13:26). At first, the evidence was presented correctly: "They gave Moses this account: 'We went into the land to which you sent us, and it does flow with milk and honey. Here is its fruit.'" (Numbers 13:27). Then things began to go awry:

Difficulties were magnified: "But the people who live there are powerful, and the cities are fortified and very large. We even saw descendants of Anak there. The Amalekites live in the Negev; the Hittites, Jebusites and Amorites live in the hill country; and the Canaanites live near the sea and along the Jordan." (Numbers 13:28-29).

Defeatism grew: "But the men who had gone up with [Caleb] said, 'We can't attack those people; they are stronger than we are.'" (Numbers 13:31).

Risks were exaggerated or misrepresented: "And they spread among the Israelites a bad report about the land they had explored. They said, 'The land we explored devours those living in it. All the people we saw there are of great size. We saw the Nephilim there (the descendants of Anak come from the Nephilim).'" (Numbers 13:32-33)

A feeling of helplessness and inferiority took hold: "We seemed like grasshoppers in our own eyes, and we looked the same to them." (Numbers 13:33).

Most glaringly of all, God's promise and the evidence that proved its truthfulness were completely overlooked. We do not need to reflect long to see these same tendencies at work around us. There are two sure ways to reach a wrong result, and we are currently indulging each of them: failing to gather evidence properly and drawing wrong conclusions from what evidence we do have. One of the commonest errors is to assume that the future will be like the past by extrapolating a trend forward on a straight line. Life does not work like that. More to the point, any assessment that leaves God out of the equation is almost bound to be flawed.

Attitude.

Cook's voyages were tremendous feats of courage and endurance. Crews were away from home for extended periods: his first and second expeditions each lasted a shade under three years, his third for four years and three months. In uncharted waters the dangers of the deep were magnified and the attitude of natives was always uncertain. Even those who were initially friendly often proved volatile. On the second voyage, Cook in the *Resolution* became separated from the accompanying *Adventure* in foul weather. Lacking the firm hand and good judgment of his leader, the captain of the *Adventure* subsequently had eleven of his men eaten by Maoris, notwithstanding that Cook had "always found them of a brave, noble, open and benevolent disposition" (though he added that "they are a people who will never put up with an insult if they have an opportunity to resent it."). There were difficulties and dangers aplenty, as there are bound to be in the most worthwhile of human endeavours. If we focus only on those, however, we are guaranteed to fall short of what we can and should achieve. We are sure to be less than God created us to be. Like so much else in life, what we make of our situation and of ourselves as we "work out [our] salvation in fear and trembling" (Philippians 2:12) is a question of attitude.

Cook always took great care over the health of his crews. He insisted on a regime of strict cleanliness and provision of fresh fruit and vegetables (or sauerkraut when these were not available) to ward off scurvy. This habitually decimated crews on long ocean voyages. On vessels where he was in personal command, Cook never lost a man to the disease. He regarded it as an unnecessary evil and took the necessary steps to combat it. The success of his methods led to their soon being adopted by navies throughout Europe, saving countless lives in consequence.

The attitude of Caleb and Joshua was similarly positive: "Then Caleb silenced the people before Moses and said, 'We should go up and take possession of the land, for we can certainly do it.'" (Numbers 13:30). This was not misguided optimism. Nor was it foolhardiness. It was sober reflection based on facts. The Israelites did not lack evidence, for the exploration of Canaan had been conducted thoroughly "through the Negev and on into the hill country" (Numbers 13:17) over an extended period: "At the end of forty days they [the spies] returned from exploring the land." (Numbers 13:25). The number forty is spiritually significant.[73] When this period had passed, the people were faced with a choice: to do as God told them or to take a different path. They got the wrong answer.

Conclusion.

It is especially poignant that Cook should have died at the hands of angry islanders, for on his first two voyages he was noted for a civilised and

---

[73] Before the Flood it rained for forty days and forty nights (Genesis 7:12). Moses was forty years old when he killed the Egyptian and fled to Midian (Acts 7:23-24), and a further forty years passed before God called him to return and free his people from bondage (Acts 7:30). Joshua was forty when Moses sent him to spy out the land of Canaan (Joshua 14:7). The Israelites wandered in the wilderness for forty years (Exodus 16:35). Jesus fasted for forty days and nights in the wilderness (Matthew 4:2). Jesus ascended to heaven forty days after his resurrection. There are many other examples.

understanding attitude to the peoples he encountered. The novelist, dramatist and diarist Fanny Burney, whose brother sailed with the captain, described him as "the most moderate, humane and gentle circumnavigator that ever went upon discoveries." There are indications, however, that by the time of his third voyage Cook was suffering from an internal parasite that, amongst other things, was starting to affect his moods and judgment. All started well on Hawaii, where the explorer was taken for *Orono makua*, god of the season of abundance. Local tradition said that this deity would one day appear in a great canoe, being greeted by the waving of white banners and sailing all around the island before alighting at Kealakekua[74] to take part in religious ceremonies there. Uncannily, all happened as legend predicted. Then things went wrong. Cook's previously sound judgment and sure handling of native peoples deserted him. He overreacted badly to theft by the islanders and in the resulting fight he was killed.

We need good judgment and clear thinking if we are to see our way through to where God wants us to be. These things have been sadly lacking in our recent past. We must put aside the attitudes that were the undoing of the Israelites – the tendency to disregard evidence, to magnify difficulties, to defeatism, to exaggerate or misrepresent risks, to feelings of helplessness and inferiority. We have every reason for optimism, since God's promises are as sure and as reliable today as they were in the days of Moses. If we look about us, there is no want of evidence to prove it.

---

[74] Kealakekua means 'path of the gods.'

31. Jubilee

Colossians 4:1-6

Key word: proclamation.

25 March 2007 marked the two hundredth anniversary of the passing of an extraordinary piece of legislation: an Act to outlaw the slave trade in Britain and her Empire. It became law only after years of relentless petitioning, extensive gathering of evidence and several failed attempts. Dreary hours of unremitting slog were put in by William Wilberforce, Thomas Clarkson and others of the so-called Clapham sect. At the start, their campaign seemed quixotic at best and downright crazy at worst. Yet, against all odds, they won. They won against the power of self-interest, they won against the voices of bigotry and they won against an initially hostile establishment.

Nor did they stop there. The campaign against slavery in all its forms and wherever it was practiced continued throughout the early part of the nineteenth century. It was a campaign so successful that in response the Royal Navy undertook to wipe the high seas clear of slave traders. They proceeded to do so, at considerable cost in British blood and treasure. About five thousand Britons died in the process. This was altruism on a grand scale, inspired by the Word of God. For Wilberforce and his fellow campaigners were devout Christians. John Newton, himself a former slave trader, was the man who persuaded Wilberforce that he could best serve God by entering Parliament rather than becoming a clergyman. He was also the man who wrote the hymn "Amazing Grace" and in its words we can hear the agony of someone who came to see that his former life was wrong and deeply displeasing to God. ("... How sweet the sound that saved a wretch like me. I once was lost and now am found, was blind but now I see ...")

That Wilberforce and his supporters campaigned so long and hard against the slave trade might seem all the more remarkable given that the Bible does not state unequivocally that slavery must be abolished. Understanding how they reached the conclusions they did thus touches on something very fundamental about what it is to be a Christian, to live as a Christian and to aspire to the holiness that God desires.

Christian principles.

In his letter to the early church at Colosse, St Paul tells his readers about how to live a holy life. He reminds them that in their behaviour towards others they should always be mindful of the way that God treats them, and aspire to reflect God's righteousness and holiness in their dealings with their fellow men: "Masters, provide your slaves with what is right and fair, because you know that you also have a Master in heaven." (Colossians 4:1). He returns to the theme when writing to the church at Ephesus: "And masters, treat your slaves in the same way. Do not threaten them, since you know that he who is both their Master and yours is in heaven, and there is no favouritism with him." (Ephesians 6:9). Ultimately, of course, providing slaves with what is right and fair involves providing them with their freedom, just as God provides "freedom for the captives and release from darkness for the prisoners" (Isaiah 61:1).

One of the things that distinguish Christianity from other religions is that daily life is not based on rules and regulations. Judaism and Islam in effect give a list of things to do and to refrain from doing: by obeying these Jews and Muslims believe that they will get right with God. By contrast, Christianity is not about rules and regulations, because sinful human beings on their own will never be able to earn salvation from a just and holy God. We will never be able to measure up to God's standards. We know what God's standards look like: Jesus showed them in his life and teaching, from the Sermon on the Mount to his endless care and compassion for the suffering. If we ever want to know how far short of divine excellence we human beings fall, we only have to read chapters 5, 6 and 7 of Matthew's Gospel. This is where Jesus tells his listeners, amongst other things, to "be perfect, therefore, as your heavenly father is perfect." (Matthew 5:48).

When we reflect on God's standards, we recognise the great truth of what Jesus came to show us. There is only one way that salvation for anybody is possible and that is because Christ paid for our sins when he died on the cross, making it possible for God to be both just and forgiving towards us. So what we see being set out throughout the New Testament teaching by Jesus, by St Peter, by St Paul and by all the other New Testament writers are not rules and regulations, but principles. That makes living the Christian life at the same time both easier and much more demanding than living according to the systems that other religions put in place. It is easier because we do not have to put up with the inconvenience of adhering to strict rules on diet, dress and what-have-you. It is more demanding because we need constant work, prayer and reading of Scripture to understand how the principles that God has set down for us in the Bible are to be acted out in our daily lives.

The debate about slavery illustrates this. In his letter to the Colossians, St Paul does not in terms condemn slavery. Instead, he neither condones it nor sanctions revolt against masters, but calls on both slaves and masters to show Christian principles in their relationship and thereby bring about change in the institution of slavery from within. Yet there is absolutely no doubt about what St Paul thinks of slavery and of those who profit from it or perpetuate it. In his first letter to Timothy he lumps slave traders with: "lawbreakers and rebels, the ungodly and sinful, the unholy and irreligious; ... those who kill their fathers or mothers ... murderers ... adulterers and perverts ... liars and perjurers" (1Timothy 1:10). In addition, St Paul roundly proclaims the common humanity and dignity of all human beings when he tells the Colossians that "there is no

Greek or Jew…slave or free, but Christ is all, and is in all." (Colossians 3:11). It was left to later generations of Christians, however, to work out how this and the teachings of Jesus were to be put into practice in their own generation. They did not invent new doctrine, but they did apply what had always been there in a new and better way.[75]

The distinction between rules and principles goes a long way towards explaining why the Muslim world has never produced the equivalent of William Wilberforce and his colleagues in the abolitionist movement. Put simply, the thinking seems to be that the Koran does not condemn slavery, so it must be all right – indeed Mohammed himself condoned slavery on condition that slaves were treated as members of their owner's family (a condition honoured far more often in the breach than in the observance). In Islam as practised by the majority, there appears little room for principles or working out how God wants us to respond in a given situation: the Muslim's job is just to submit to the immutable will of Allah as expressed in the Koran. The sad truth is that Muslims were enslaving their fellow men before the British had even thought of the idea and continued to do so long after the British had outlawed it.[76] Slavery still exists in many parts of the Muslim world.

Working out our salvation.

The Christian's calling is to "…work out [our] own salvation with fear and trembling, for it is God who works in [us] to will and to act according to his own good purpose." (Philippians 2:12-13). In chapter three of his letter to the Colossians St Paul encourages this Christian community to cooperate with God in making themselves holy, in sanctifying themselves and in working out their salvation. In chapter four, he tells them what they should be doing as part of that process of working out their salvation. He does not claim to give them an

---

[75] The Old Testament makes it clear that people were not to be enslaved for generation upon generation: "Even if he is not redeemed in any of these ways [described above, the slave] and his children are to be released in the Year of Jubilee, for the Israelites belong to me as servants." (Leviticus 25:54). Each fiftieth year was to be a Jubilee (see Leviticus 25:11), when debts were to be forgiven, land left untilled, certain alienated property restored and slaves freed.

[76] Between 1662 and 1807 some three and a half million Africans were shipped westwards in British ships. Almost two million more were transported to the New World by other Europeans after the British ban. Figures for those trafficked by Muslim slave traders are much harder to come by, though it is commonly reckoned that some two million African slaves were transported to Arab states between 1800 and 1870 alone. There was also a significant trade in European slaves, particularly from Russia and the Balkans.

exhaustive list, but identifies seven things for them to do. It is good advice and holds true for all believers at all times:

First of all, we should pray – and not just occasionally or in a lukewarm fashion. We should instead "devote [ourselves] to prayer." (Colossians 4:2). To devote oneself to something means to dedicate oneself to it or give oneself up to it wholeheartedly. It is very typical of St Paul that he should put prayer first and give it such emphasis. He does this because he is so conscious of the spiritual and cosmic significance of prayer: he knows that it is through prayer "that God may open a door" (Colossians 4:3). Prayer is the mechanism by which we invite God to engage with us and with our world, and the means by which we release his power in us and through us. When that door is open, amazing things happen. In the book of Revelation, St John sees "a door standing open in heaven" (Revelation 4:1) and is ushered into the very throne-room of God.

Secondly, St Paul tells us to be "watchful and thankful." (Colossians 4:2). It is intriguing how much Jesus had to say about watchfulness. "Therefore keep watch, because you do not know on what day your Lord will come" (Matthew 24:42). "Watch and pray so that you will not fall into temptation." (Matthew 26:41). "What I say to you, I say to everyone: 'Watch'" (Mark 13:37). "It will be good for those servants whose master finds them watchful when he comes." (Luke 12:37). The message is repeated again and again throughout both the Old and New Testaments: we are not to sleepwalk through life, but to be on our guard against danger and alert to opportunities. We should also be thankful for all that is done for us, all the wonders that God works day by day that are so often ignored because we are not watching properly and are tuned into the earthly rather than the spiritual.

Thirdly, the apostle exhorts us to "proclaim the mystery of Christ [and to] proclaim it clearly" (Colossians 4:3-4). It is interesting that St Paul should use the word 'mystery' here, for a mystery is something beyond human understanding, a divine truth partially revealed. We get a better idea of what St Paul means elsewhere in his writing. He talks about "the mystery of godliness" in his first letter to Timothy and there he describes what that mystery is by using what may be a quotation from an early hymn: "He [that is, Jesus] appeared in a body, was vindicated by the Spirit, was seen by angels, was preached among the nations, was believed on in the world, was taken up in glory" (1 Timothy 3:16). In his first letter to the church at Corinth, St Paul stresses what he has also emphasised to the Colossians – the supremacy and sufficiency of Christ: "I resolved to know nothing while I was with you except Jesus Christ and him crucified." (1 Corinthians 2:2). This is the mystery that we need to proclaim: the crucifixion of Jesus, his resurrection from the dead, primacy and sovereignty over "all things ... in heaven and on earth, visible and invisible" (Colossians 1:6) and his sufficiency for our salvation.

Fourthly, we are to "be wise in the way [we] act towards outsiders" (Colossians 4:5). The Bible has a very particular slant on the concept of wisdom. In Proverbs, the Psalms and elsewhere in the Old Testament, wisdom is often equated with godliness, with the way of thinking and acting that comes from being in tune with God, and it is contrasted with what the world considers to be wisdom: "I will destroy the wisdom of the wise; the intelligence of the intelligent I will frustrate" (Isaiah 29:14) and "Has God not made foolish the wisdom of the world?" (1 Corinthians 1:20). It is this godly wisdom that we are called on to show, the wisdom that comes from knowing God's Word and adhering to it.

Fifthly, St Paul advises us to "make the most of every opportunity" (Colossians 4:5). We are, after all, called to fullness of life. Jesus says that he has "come that you may have life, and have it to the full." (John 10:10). We are not to be shrinking violets, but people who know how to seize the moment, and who do so with joy and courage and assurance. Easily said and less easily done, but this is what St Paul encourages us to do.

Sixthly, he admonishes us to "Let [our] conversations always be full of grace, seasoned with salt" (Colossians 4:6). Salt is something that gives flavour, something that preserves and is precious.[77] We are called to be salt and light: "You are the salt of the earth. But if the salt loses its saltiness, how can it be made salty again?" (Matthew 5:13) and "let your light shine before men" (Matthew 5:16). The Spirit should shine out from us.

Lastly, we should "know how to answer everyone." (Colossians 4:6). We should naturally prepare ourselves as best we can, but not fret unduly about it. Jesus told his disciples: "do not worry about how you will defend yourselves or what you will say, for the Holy Spirit will teach you at that time what you should say." (Luke 12:12).

Seven things: pray, keep alert, proclaim the message, be wise, seize the moment, let the Spirit shine and let the Spirit speak.

Conclusion.

The example of the slave trade shows how, long after the New Testament writers lived, later generations of Christians were able to take their teachings and give them a force and direction that their forebears had not foreseen. This shows

---

[77] In biblical times, salt was so valuable that Roman legionaries were even paid in it: this was their '*salarium*' and hence the word 'salary'.

us the way forward: not necessarily to become giants like Wilberforce, but in our own small, quiet ways to make a difference in the lives of those around us. There is no reason for us to imagine that we cannot do it. St Paul tells us how. If we were to apply this to the life of our country, we would see a tremendous difference in a very short space. We have a job to do: to "proclaim the mystery of Christ ... [and to] proclaim it clearly, as [we] should." (Colossians 4:3-4). We need to roll up our sleeves and set to work.

32. New power

Ephesians 6:10-20.

Key word: equipping.

As a young boy, Richard Trevithick (1771-1833) was told by a schoolteacher that he would never amount to anything. The Cornishman proved him wrong. Developing work that had already been carried out by William Murdoch, the budding engineer made a model steam engine so successfully that he took it to London and put it on show. He proceeded to construct the world's first railway engine, which pulled ten tons of iron along primitive tracks in south Wales. In the event, two difficulties scuppered the project: rails kept breaking under the weight and workers refused to let his machine run, fearing for the jobs of those who minded the horses which hitherto had been used. Discouraged, Trevithick left to try his luck in America, but left behind a foundation on which others built to great effect.

The explosion of engineering activity in Britain during the latter part of the eighteenth century and throughout the nineteenth was wholly unprecedented. It was not just that men of energy and invention abounded, but that there was for the first time a sufficiently wide canvas for all to display their prodigious talents. Men like canal builder James Brindley (1716-1772), bridge and harbour designer John Rennie (1761-1821), bridge and aqueduct builder Thomas Telford (1757-1834), railway pioneers George (1781-1848) and Robert Stephenson (1803-1859) and polymath Isambard Kingdom Brunel (1806-1859)[78] reshaped the nation and the world. They provided machines and infrastructure to drive the nascent industrial revolution to new heights. Many were entirely self-taught and from humble backgrounds: George Stephenson, for example, worked as a shepherd and colliery fireman before building his first locomotive in 1817.

Nor was experiment and exploration restricted to industry. Charles Babbage (1791-1871) compiled the first actuarial tables and planned a mechanical calculating machine that is widely regarded as the fore-runner of the modern computer – only lack of funding prevented its full construction.[79] In 1808 John Dalton outlined atomic theory in his *New System of Chemical Philosophy* and in 1843

---

[78] Rennie and Telford were Scots, Brunel the son of a Frenchman.

[79] A working model has since been made using Babbage's plans.

James Joule established the First Law of Thermodynamics. [80] It was a time when new discoveries were made and new power was harnessed: power from water and steam, power to drive machinery and run locomotives, power for new industrial processes, together enabling a rapid equipping of the nation for the industrial age.

Power for good.

In his letter to the church at Ephesus, St Paul tells his readers how they can best equip themselves for the age of the Spirit. He, too, is interested in the harnessing of power: "Finally, be strong in the Lord and in his mighty power." (Ephesians 6:10). This power is to be used not for human activity but for the spiritual battles ahead: "For our struggle is not against flesh and blood, but against the rulers, against the authorities, against the powers of this dark world and against the spiritual forces of evil in the heavenly realms." (Ephesians 6:12).

We live at a time when many in the western world do all they can to deny a spiritual dimension to life. Physical events are seen as proceeding from physical causes in a chain of causation that starts and ends with what is physically manifest. Much scientific advancement and much good for mankind have come from application of the scientific method in this way. It has enabled us to explore and to understand better the workings of Creation and the mechanisms and laws that God has put in place. Without it, the great engineering achievements of the nineteenth century and beyond would not have been possible. To acknowledge the importance of this approach and the benefits that have come from it, however, does not mean that we have to be its slaves, nor that we must perforce deny a dimension above and beyond the physical. If we do, we will hand victory on a plate to "the spiritual forces of evil in the heavenly realms." (Ephesians 6:12).

Instead, we need to be realistic about what confronts us and to: "Put on the full armour of God so that [we] can take [our] stand against the devil's schemes." (Ephesians 6:11). So important is the message that St Paul repeats it just two sentences later: "Therefore put on the full armour of God, so that when the day of evil comes, you may be able to stand your ground, and after you have done everything, to stand. Stand firm then ..." (Ephesians 6:13-14). The Lord's

---

[80] See note 60. The Second Law of Thermodynamics was formulated by German physicist Rudolph Clausius in 1850. It states that any physical system becomes less ordered and more random over time. Applied very simply and generally, this means that the entire universe is running down. As the rotation of the heavenly bodies slows and stars burn out, matter grows increasingly disorganised as its energy is dissipated. This is consistent with a universe that is neither infinite nor eternal: see note 38.

aim is that we should not give way to the enemy nor flee the battlefield, neither that we should bury our heads in the sand and pretend that no fighting is taking place, but that we should occupy the position in the line of battle that he has assigned to us. This is not intended to be a suicide mission: if we make proper use of the equipment we are given, then "after [we] have done everything, [we will] stand." (Ephesians 6:13). The equipment has been bestowed for a purpose and it is intended to be used. We should not leave it gathering dust, but put it on and employ its power for good.

Power for ill.

It is of the utmost importance that we take part in this battle, for there are plenty who use their power for ill. We do not need to look to the relations between nations to see how human beings misuse the power they have. Examples are all around us, in homes, workplaces and schools, through media and the institutions of public life. The fact that evil of this kind might start on a small scale does not make it any less damaging in the long run. One blighted life affects another and another, spreading the effects far and wide. The experience that Richard Trevithick had at school is a common one. To be told that we are worthless, that we will never achieve anything of value or that we are useless can crush us and break our spirit. It is no less an attack for being delivered through words than by blows. It is a form of spiritual warfare and a type of curse. Many labour under curses of this kind for years, their lives crimped and misshapen and their potential unfulfilled.

To be cursed robs us of power. The Lord does not want to curse us, but to bless. In the eyes of God, no-one is on the scrap-heap. No-one is without value. No-one lacks inner beauty and worth. The Lord longs to free us from the curses which have been placed on us. He wishes to break the cycle that results in those abused so often becoming abusers themselves. He wants to ensure that we bless others instead of cursing them. By contrast, the devil is delighted if we continue to allow such things to exercise power over us. His desire is for us to be enslaved by things that harm us and rob us of power. He rejoices when we misuse the power we have so that it hurts rather than bringing pleasure and so that it tears down rather than building.

We cannot break the stranglehold of a curse on our own. Nor can we alone undo the effects of generations of harm and neglect. If we want proof of this, we need look no further than the shortcomings of our own society: sixty years of the Welfare State and the expenditure of countless billions have made little discernible impact on child abuse, educational under-achievement and any number of other ills. If it were otherwise, we would hardly be awash with charities and government initiatives designed to tackle such things. For decades we have been akin to a giant laboratory, a showcase of man's ability to better himself through changing his environment. The experiment has failed: we have proved beyond a shadow of a doubt that we do not have power to deal with the root cause of our problems on our own and that, without God, we are adrift and helpless.

If we are to make progress, we need to access the power of God through his Spirit. This we do through prayer. St Paul therefore tells his readers: "And pray in the Spirit on all occasions with all kinds of prayers and requests. With this in mind, be alert and always keep on praying for all the saints." (Ephesians 6:18). To be alert is especially necessary: alert to where the enemy seeks to do harm, alert to the support that our fellows need in the fight, alert to the need to counter the work of evil and alert to the part that we can play in doing so.

Power to advance.

In the battles to come there is no reason for us to fear defeat, for we have been given all that we need to prevail. We need to take hold of this equipment and use it. There are six items listed by St Paul. They all have a defensive capability, but can equally be used to attack:

"... with the belt of truth buckled round your waist" (Ephesians 6:14). Jesus tells us that "Satan was a murderer from the beginning, not holding to the truth, for there is no truth in him. When he lies, he speaks his native language, for he is a liar and the father of lies." (John 8:44). What Satan proclaims cannot stand against truth. To hold fast to truth is both a protection against being undermined by falsehood and also takes the battle to the very heart of the enemy's territory.

"... with the breastplate of righteousness in place" (Ephesians 6:14). A breastplate protects the heart. If we are righteous, our heart will be in the right place and will not be subverted. We will want the things that God wants and will be able to steer clear of the things that the devil offers.

"... with your feet fitted with the readiness that comes from the gospel of peace." (Ephesians 6:15). If our feet are properly shod we will be able both to flee danger and to advance quickly against the foe. The gospel brings this readiness because with knowledge of God's Word we will never lack guidance as to the right way to behave, nor understanding of what we should embrace and what we must shun. Furthermore, through knowledge of the gospel, we will "Always be prepared to give an answer to everyone who asks [us] to give the reason for the hope that [we] have." (1 Peter 3:15).

"In addition to all this, take up the shield of faith, with which you can extinguish all the flaming arrows of the evil one." (Ephesians 6:16). The devil's first line of attack is to undermine faith: by undermining belief in God, in what God has said and in what God has told us will be the consequences that flow from actions both good and ill. In the Garden of Eden, the serpent's first words to Eve tried to do precisely this by putting doubt in her mind: "Did God really say ...?" (Genesis 3:1). Faith is a shield against attacks of this kind.

"Take the helmet of salvation" (Ephesians 6:17). A helmet protects the head, and thus both brain and mind. Reflecting on our salvation will protect our thinking. Our intellects are constantly assailed by supposedly rational and scientific attempts to debunk Christianity. These are the product of confused thinking and a twisting or misinterpretation of facts. We need clear heads to see them for what they are.

"Take ... the sword of the Spirit, which is the word of God." (Ephesians 6:17). The Word of God is a weapon that cuts through all that is wrong and misleading, slices apart all falsehood, lays bare all vanity and forestalls each attack of the enemy: "For the word of God is living and active. Sharper than any double-edged sword, it penetrates even to dividing soul and spirit, joints and marrow; it judges the thoughts and attitudes of the heart." (Hebrews 4:12).

No-one sensible undertakes a task without the equipment they need. Still less do people go into battle deliberately lacking kit. We are rightly outraged when unnecessary casualties result from our troops having improper or inadequate equipment. Yet every day we fail to don the armour that God has made available for our protection. Little wonder that we seem to lack power in facing down the enemy.

Conclusion.

None of this is not to be glib about the reality of spiritual warfare. Just as we forget too readily the human cost of the great engineering achievements of the nineteenth century, we are apt to overlook the price of fighting in the spiritual realm. The toll exacted by the former was ghastly. Just one example will serve by way of illustration: construction of Brunel's Great Western Railway involved the digging of Box Tunnel, at that time the longest railway tunnel yet attempted. Work began in September 1836 and was not completed until June 1841, using solely the muscle power of navvies and horses. Over 247,000 cubic yards of spoil were excavated and 30 million bricks used. About a hundred men died in this work alone. There were many more deaths in the fight for material progress. As regards spiritual warfare, to this very day Christians are being imprisoned, maimed and martyred as they labour in the work of construction, and toil to build the kingdom of God.

There will always be casualties. No-one relishes deaths, injuries and suffering, but equally no army expects to escape battle scot free and an army that will not fight is little use. In other spheres we readily acknowledge that attack is the best form of defence. Yet in the spiritual realm we too often seem paralysed and inactive, waiting for the next assault from the enemy and prepared at every stage to hand him the initiative. It is time that we stopped cowering in our dugouts and emerged to do battle. What St Paul asked his readers to pray for him, we can just as well pray for ourselves: "Pray also for me, that whenever I open my mouth, words may be given me so that I will fearlessly make known the mystery of the gospel, for which I am an ambassador in chains. Pray that I should declare it fearlessly, as I should." (Ephesians 6:19-20).

33. Band of brothers

Acts 9:1-22.

Key word: realisation.

"England expects that every man this day will do his duty." Nelson's signal to the fleet immediately before the battle of Trafalgar on 21 October 1805 has become everyday currency. As with all that becomes over-used or over-familiar, there is a tendency in the process for real meaning to be lost. In fact, duty was a recurrent theme for this younger son of a Norfolk parson. Even as he lay dying he several times repeated, "Thank God I have done my duty." Nowadays it is a concept that we find difficult to grasp, for we live in a society whose sense of duty is diminished. Still more have we abandoned the deep Christian commitment that infused and inspired someone who was described by Sir Gilbert Elliot, a witness of the battle of Cape St Vincent in 1797, as "a hero beyond Homer's or any other possible inventions." In his day Nelson was both an international celebrity and recognised as one of the greatest naval commanders of all time, but he was more. The poet Robert Southey wrote: "The death of Nelson was felt in England as something more than a public calamity; men started at the intelligence and turned pale, as if they had heard of the loss of a dear friend."

On the morning of the battle of Trafalgar, Nelson wrote a prayer: "May the Great God, whom I worship, grant to my country, and for the benefit of Europe in general, a great and glorious victory; and may no misconduct in anyone tarnish it; and may humanity after victory be the predominant feature in the British fleet ..." The same sentiment was translated into the orders issued to each crew. These ensured that British sailors risked their lives in foul weather after the battle (and in some instances even during the battle itself) to rescue drowning French and Spanish seamen. The conduct of the Royal Navy in the aftermath of one of the most crushing victories in naval warfare stands as a model for magnanimous treatment of a defeated foe.

Nelson's Christianity did not come out of thin air, nor was it based on unquestioning acceptance of all he had been taught. It was instead the result of a profound mystical experience. Invalided home from India in 1774, the youngster (then only 16) experienced what he termed a "light from heaven." He said that, from this moment, "a sudden glow of patriotism was kindled within me" and often spoke afterwards of the "radiant orb" suspended in his mind's eye. In 1793 he wrote in his private journal: "When I lay me down to sleep I recommend myself to the care of Almighty God. When I awake I give myself up to his direction. Amidst all the evils that threaten me, I will look up to Him for help, and question not but He will either avert them or turn them to my advantage.

Though I know neither the time nor the manner of my death, I am not at all solicitous about it because I am sure that He knows them both, and that He will not fail to support and comfort me under them."

Preparation.

Thus the Lord prepared the future admiral for the work ahead. In the same way he prepared St Paul for his work as "my chosen instrument to carry my name before the Gentiles and their kings and before the people of Israel." (Acts 9:15). In the same way, he will prepare us. This does not mean that we will necessarily see "a light from heaven ... and [hear] a voice" (Acts 9:3-4), nor see a "vision" (Acts 9:10 and 12), for the manner of our preparation will differ from person to person. In general, we can expect that the more we are asked to do and the greater the change that is needed in our lives, the more dramatic will be the divine intervention. What we can all expect, however, is to encounter Jesus. It is our response to this that holds the key to what happens next. Whatever form our meeting with the Lord may take, the lessons from what St Paul experienced on the road to Damascus hold good for us, too:

In the presence of the Almighty, the only proper response is to fall on our knees in wonder and worship, being alert to what he wants to say: "He fell to the ground and heard a voice say to him, 'Saul, Saul, why do you persecute me?'" (Acts 9:4).

We should recognise our Lord and Saviour for who he is, and obey his commands, acknowledging that often we may have to wait before we are shown the next step[81]: "'Who are you, Lord?' Saul asked. 'I am Jesus, whom you are persecuting,' he replied. 'Now get up and go into the city, and you will be told what you must do.'" (Acts 9:5).

It should be no surprise if those who lack a godly perspective fail to see God at work and have nothing worthwhile to say on matters spiritual: "The men travelling with Saul stood there speechless; they heard the sound but did not see anyone." (Acts 9:7).

There is no shame in accepting help when we need it, as long as it is taking us in the right direction: "Saul got up from the ground, but when he opened his eyes he could see nothing. So they led him by the hand into Damascus." (Acts 9:8).

---

[81] From 1787 Nelson spent more than five years ashore on half pay. He was thirty-five before he had his first real sea fight and was twenty-four years in the service before experiencing his first fleet action.

There will be times of trial, points at which we may not hear from God and occasions when it is right to fast. These should be taken as part and parcel of life, not allowed to undermine our faith or to deflect us from our course: "For three days he was blind, and did not eat or drink anything." (Acts 9:9).

Prayer is the key to unlocking the power and activity of God: "[Saul] is praying. In a vision he has seen a man named Ananias come and place his hands on him to restore his sight." (Acts 9:12).

God's activity in our lives requires a reaction on our part, and this involves giving priority to the spiritual over the physical – only in this way can we achieve insight into the ways of God: "Immediately, something like scales fell from Saul's eyes, and he could see again. He got up and was baptised, and after taking some food, he regained his strength." (Acts 9:18-19).

Fellowship with other believers is vital for our wellbeing and growth: "Saul spent several days with the disciples in Damascus." (Acts 9:19).

Proclaiming the gospel is a duty for all: "At once he began to preach in the synagogues that Jesus is the Son of God." (Acts 9:21).

The more closely we walk with God and do our utmost to obey him, the greater will be our spiritual strength: "Yet Saul grew more and more powerful and baffled the Jews living in Damascus by proving that Jesus is the Christ." (Acts 9:22).

Others' failure to accept what is staring them in the face should neither alarm nor discomfort us: although St Paul's preaching of the gospel "baffled the Jews living in Damascus by proving that Jesus is the Christ" (Acts 9:22), this apparently did not lead to their all becoming Christians. Some were resistant to truth, then as now.

On the road to Damascus St Paul reached a point of realisation. It involved realisation in the sense of perceiving as true what had previously been hidden and apprehending clearly and vividly what had previously been obscured. Thus he saw that what he had been doing up to then in the belief that he was serving God was wrong, he came to see exactly who Jesus Christ is and, most importantly, to know that this Jesus was not dead, but alive. It also involved realisation in the sense of bringing into existence and making actual the fullness of his destiny. From this moment he was no longer Saul, known everywhere for his "persecuting of the church" (Philippians 3:6), but began the process of transformation by which he became Paul, the great apostle to the Gentiles.

Collaboration.

Usually God involves others in our preparation and transformation: "The Lord told [Ananias], 'Go to the house of Judas on Straight Street and ask for a man from Tarsus named Saul, for he is praying. In a vision he has seen a man named Ananias come and place his hands on him to restore his sight.'" (Acts 9:11). It may be only one in a million who is called to exercise the kind of ministry that St Paul undertook or to perform the deeds of an Admiral Nelson, but every Christian is called to exercise the ministry of Ananias. He was "a disciple" (Acts 9:10) who gave practical effect to what he believed:

He was responsive to God: "The Lord called to him in a vision, 'Ananias!' 'Yes, Lord,' he answered." (Acts 9:10).

His dialogue with God was respectful – he put the facts as he knew them before God but did not attempt to substitute his judgment for that of the Almighty: "I have heard many reports about this man ..." (Acts 9:13).

He did what God told him, even though it made no sense from a human point of view, and he acted promptly: "But the Lord said to Ananias, 'Go!' ... Then Ananias went to the house and entered it." (Acts 9:15 and 17).

He showed love and acceptance to the unlovable: "Placing his hands on Saul, he said, 'Brother Saul ...'" (Acts 9:17).

He corroborated what Saul had heard and experienced in a way that authenticated his own mission and gave encouragement to the future apostle: "the Lord – Jesus, who appeared to you on the road as you were coming here – has sent me" (Acts 9:17).

He was a channel for healing and the work of the Holy Spirit: "Placing his hands on Saul, he said, '... Jesus ... has sent me so that you may see again and be filled with the Holy Spirit.'" (Acts 9:17).

If we want to have people like Saul of Tarsus at work in our land and to see people changed so that instead of "persecuting the church" (Philippians 3:6) they become its most powerful advocates, if we long to witness deeds like those of the heroes of old, we must each do as Ananias did.

Jubilation.

At Trafalgar Nelson won a victory which was beyond almost any in the annals of naval warfare. So overwhelming was it, both physically and psychologically, that no enemy dared challenge the Royal Navy in battle for a century.[82] The turnaround in the nation's fortunes in the years immediately following was spectacular. Hitherto Napoleon's armies had been everywhere victorious. England had been isolated and beleaguered. Triumph at sea freed her from the threat of invasion and gave new hope to those fighting tyranny. With the start of the Peninsular War in 1808, the long process of rolling back French conquests on the continent began.

The experiences of St Paul on the road to Damascus brought about an equally sharp switch in direction for him, with momentous consequences for the future spread of Christianity. The man who up to then had been "breathing out murderous threats against the Lord's disciples" (Acts 9:1), who wanted to "take [any he found] as prisoners to Jerusalem" (Acts 9:2), who was known for "all the harm he has done to [the] saints" (Acts 9:13) and who had "come [to Damascus] with authority from the chief priests to arrest all who call on [the] name [of Jesus]" (Acts 9:14) was utterly changed. He was transformed because he met Jesus and thereby experienced a moment of realisation.

Conclusion.

The Lord has a disconcerting habit of using those who have been great sinners to do some of his mightiest work. Moses, David and Saul were all murderers, either killing with their own hands or having others kill on their behalf and with their approval.[83] God also tends to choose those we might regard as unprepossessing, even puny. Nelson was small in stature and weak in constitution, suffering recurrent illnesses. At the time of his greatest victory, he was middle-aged, blind in one eye and his right arm was only a stump. Reflecting on such things should build us up. No matter what we have been, what we have done or what we lack, Jesus can use us. If we allow the moment of realisation to come upon us, we will be changed. The greater our past sin, the more obvious our limitations and infirmities, the more powerful will be our witness: "All those who heard him were astonished and asked, 'Isn't he the man who caused havoc in Jerusalem among those who call on this name? And hasn't he come here to take them as prisoners to the chief priests?'" (Acts 9:21).

A man like Horatio Nelson did not come about by chance any more than the world was formed by chance. He was prepared by God and placed by the

---

[82] Not until Jutland in 1916 did Nelson's heirs again fight a general engagement, this time against the Imperial German Navy.

[83] Moses slew the Egyptian who was beating an Israelite slave (Exodus 2:12), David had Uriah the Hittite placed in the front rank of battle so that he would be killed (2 Samuel 11:15) and Saul watched with approval whilst Stephen was stoned to death (Acts 8:1).

Almighty where he could best be used, just as each of us will be if we allow our Creator to mould, shape and guide us. The Lord's signs and wonders are visible in this land today, just as they have been in years past. The reason they are not better known is that too many "heard the sound but did not see anyone" (Acts 9:7): events take place without our recognising who is behind them. We need to look for our heavenly Father at work and pray that the scales will fall from our eyes and those of our fellow countrymen. Then realisation will come upon us and we will live in a land where: "Everyone was amazed and gave praise to God. They were filled with awe and said, 'We have seen remarkable things today.'" (Luke 5:26).

34. Titans

Zechariah 12:1-6.

Key word: strength.

On the morning of Sunday 18 June 1815 some 140,000 soldiers faced each other across the fields of Flanders. The French army under Napoleon was slightly the larger, with 71,947 men and 246 guns to the 67,655 men and 156 guns commanded by the Duke of Wellington. In practice, the Duke's army was considerably weaker: only 24,000 of its number were British, the remainder being German or from the United Provinces of the Netherlands. These latter were of doubtful loyalty. Many had previously fought under French colours and in the battle to come an entire brigade under General-majoor van Bijlandt fled at the first French advance on their position. By contrast, Bonaparte's troops were seasoned veterans willing to die for their Emperor. He for one had no doubt as to the relative merits of forces from different nations. At the outset of the campaign, he declared: "A French soldier would not be equal to more than one English soldier, but would not be afraid to meet two Dutchmen, Prussians or soldiers of the Confederation [of the Rhineland]." French victory over Blücher's Prussians at Ligny a few days earlier seemed to confirm that assessment.

Such was the position immediately before the first shot was fired at Waterloo. The contest started late in the morning, as the French waited for the ground to dry after the soaking rain of previous days. Once battle was joined, however, it raged until evening, when at last the arrival of Marshal Blücher's army put the issue beyond doubt. In retrospect, many have found it difficult to understand how Napoleon lost, and every attempt to recreate the contest has ended with French victory. There is no doubt that Wellington chose his ground with great skill and that his British and German troops fought with tenacity. Yet it is uncertain whether that alone would have been enough. Three elements in particular stand out on the French side. The Emperor, who had been so vigorous in mustering his troops and who had conducted them adroitly and energetically as recently as 15 June, was unaccountably lethargic at key points. Marshal Grouchy, who commanded 32,000 men and 96 guns just a few miles from the battlefield, failed to join the main French force although his staff pleaded with him to do so and the sound of gunfire from Waterloo was clearly audible. Perhaps most inexplicable of all, Marshal Michel Ney, a commander well aware of the capabilities of cavalry, persistently committed unsupported horsemen to fruitless charges against defensive squares of British infantry.

So the allies prevailed, by the skin of their teeth. Wellington said of it afterwards: "It has been a damned serous business – Blücher and I have lost 30,000 men. It has been a damned nice thing – the nearest run thing you ever saw in your life ... I do not think it would have done if I had not been there." Of his French opponent, he commented: "He is just an old pounder, after all."

Napoleon tried his strength for the first time against Wellington at Waterloo, and his strength was found wanting.

The source of strength.

Human beings tend to have a view of their own strength and importance that is at one and the same time too elevated and not elevated enough. It is too elevated in that we do not give the proper respect and glory to God, failing to recognise that his hand is in all things and that even evil can only persist because, for a time of his choosing, the Almighty allows it to be so. It is not elevated enough in that we do not ascribe to our deeds the eternal significance which they in fact have, and nor do we take proper account of the influence which we can wield for good or ill.

The sovereignty of God, over heaven and earth, over man and all his doings is emphasised by the prophet Zechariah in words spoken over two thousand five hundred years ago. The Almighty is: "The LORD, who stretches out the heavens, who lays the foundation of the earth, and who forms the spirit of man within him" (Zechariah 12:1). He is the source of our strength and of our very being, the one who created and sustains the universe. The point is repeatedly emphasised in Scripture: "In the beginning, you laid the foundations of the earth, and the heavens are the work of your hands. They will perish, but you remain; they will all wear out like a garment. You will roll them up like a robe; like a garment they will be changed. But you remain the same, and your years will never end." (Psalm 102:25-27 and Hebrews 1:10-12). God is in charge, whatever we might think.

Similarly, the impact and intervention of God in the affairs of men is clearly described: "'On that day I will strike every horse with panic and its rider with madness,' declares the LORD. 'I will keep a watchful eye over the house of Judah, but I will blind all the horses of the nations." (Zechariah 12:4). So it was during the battle of Waterloo, as Ney's French cuirassiers and Polish lancers hurled themselves repeatedly upon massed bayonets. It was madness, and any dispassionate observer knew it.

The prophet recounts what human experience repeatedly affirms: that God can turn our weakness to good account and can bring us low for all that we seem to be mighty.

Strength in numbers.

The French fought bravely at Waterloo, but it was not enough. As the tide of battle turned, retreat turned to rout. So complete was the wreck that within a week it was clear that the Emperor's cause was beyond salvage.

So ended the Hundred Days and so ended the Napoleonic Wars. The conflict was one in which France enlisted the soldiers of many nations: Poles and Italians in large numbers, Germans, Belgians, Dutchmen and Spaniards, inspired by the slogans of the Revolution and a desire for national self-determination, or simply conscripted. Whole nations were dragooned into an attempt to blockade Britain through the Continental System and a mighty army gathered at the Channel ports for a planned invasion of these islands. At times it might well have seemed to the people of this land that "all the nations of the earth are gathered against her" (Zechariah 12:3) and that she was indeed "besieged" (Zechariah 12:2). Yet for all that her enemies had strength in numbers, they did not prevail.

In the event, crushing victory over the combined French and Spanish fleets at Trafalgar in 1805 made a Channel crossing impractical. Britain proved "an immovable rock for all the nations [on which] all who try to move it will injure themselves" (Zechariah 12:3), whilst continued British resistance became the hope of those who wished to cast off French vassalage. Frustrated, Napoleon unleashed the Grande Armée elsewhere, to eventual ruin in the snows of Russia. The strength of France ebbed away, encouraging the formerly cowed peoples of Europe to rise in revolt. The Emperor was driven slowly but surely back to his own borders and from thence to his first exile on Elba.

Growing strength.

Waterloo set the seal on European freedom from French domination. It also confirmed Britain's place in the world. The decades-long preoccupation of France with Europe, an obsession reinforced by British blockade, caused not only her own but also her satellites' overseas empires to waste away. Some colonies were captured by the British, some fell to local insurrections. Others were simply too expensive or too far away to maintain: hence Napoleon's sale of Louisiana to the United States for US $6 million. The result was to leave Britain at the war's end by far and away the mightiest imperial power. By the second quarter of the nineteenth century her dominance was clear to all. The great contest with France, which had smouldered and flamed intermittently for a century through the Wars of the Spanish and Austrian Successions, the Seven Years' War, the Revolutionary Wars and the Napoleonic War was effectively decided in her favour. It may not have been comfortable for others to admit it, but "Then the leaders ... [said] in their hearts, 'The people of Jerusalem are strong'" (Zechariah 12:5). Waterloo marked Britain's growing strength and the start of her long ascendancy.

It is important that we place this period of British power and influence in its rightful setting. Zechariah describes the people of Jerusalem as being strong for no other reason than "because the LORD Almighty is their God." (Zechariah 12:5). To apply this to the circumstances of a particular people at a particular phase in history does not mean that we have to assert the ludicrous claim that all

Englishmen were models of godly virtue and those of all other nations the opposite. Neither does it mean that we have to make the equally preposterous statement that the British state was the archetype of all that is good. The slightest familiarity with the times will show that neither proposition can hold water.

Yet if we wish to weigh the picture in the round, to consider the type of men that came to the fore under one system as opposed to another, we can do worse than consider the attitude of the commanders at Waterloo towards casualties. When *le petit caporal*, supposedly the soldiers' soldier, spotted French corpses at Eylau in 1807 he remarked: "Small change, small change. One night in Paris will soon make good these losses." The depths of cynicism, the sheer disregard for human life that this conveys is beyond expression. By contrast, shortly after the battle of Waterloo had ended Wellington, so often a reactionary in politics, wrote: "My heart is broken by the terrible loss I have sustained in my old friends and companions, and my poor soldiers. Believe me, nothing except a battle lost can be half so melancholy as a battle won; the bravery of my troops has hitherto saved me from the greater evil; but to win such a battle as this of Waterloo, at the expense of so many gallant friends, could only be termed a heavy misfortune but for the result to the public."

Strength of ground.

Great events often turn on apparently small happenstances, yet there is nothing that comes about by chance or unplanned by God. It was no accident that Wellington gave battle at Waterloo. Moving a vote of thanks to the Duke in the House of Lords after victory was won, Lord Bathurst recalled that when passing through Flanders in the summer of 1814 Wellington had particularly remarked the strength of this position. The general made a note of it at the time, telling those who were with him that, if ever he were to fight in that area for the protection of Brussels, this would be his chosen ground. Its strength allowed optimum deployment of his troops just one year later.

We place ourselves on the strongest of grounds when we put ourselves under the guidance and protection of God: "On that day I will make the leaders of Judah like a brazier in a woodpile, like a flaming torch among sheaves. They will consume right and left all the surrounding peoples, but Jerusalem will remain intact in her place." (Zechariah 12:6). Like the Israelites of old, however, we appear to have forgotten this simple maxim and to be seeking strength everywhere but through our Lord. This is foolishness of the highest degree, a confusion of cause and effect, of the source with what is derived from that source. We need once more to seek out the strong ground so that we can stand firm in the battle for our nation and prevail as our forebears did one June day almost two hundred years ago.

Conclusion.

Napoleon Bonaparte abdicated for the second time on 22 June 1815 for a lifetime's exile on St Helena. Looking back, he had little doubt that victory at Waterloo would have seen him secure in power: "If the English army had been beaten at Waterloo, what would have been the use of those numerous bodies of troops, of Prussians, Austrians, Germans and Spaniards, which were advancing by forced marches to the Rhine, the Alps and the Pyrenees?" This was not just wishful thinking: such was the tactical superiority of the French over continental armies that at Auerstadt in 1806 Marshal Davout's 26,000 men had attacked, enveloped and destroyed 63,000 Prussians. In the years before and since Austrians, Russians and Spaniards had each been trounced in their turn. There is no reason to believe that it could not have happened again.

Waterloo was not one of the largest battles of all time. Neither was it the longest, nor the bloodiest. It was, however, one of the most influential. It is no exaggeration to say that allied victory saved Europe from the man who had been its peace-breaker and mischief-maker for a generation, whose proclamations of good intent on his return to France were, to put it neutrally, of uncertain reliability. Many times had he sent "the surrounding peoples reeling." (Zechariah 12:2). Given that record, nobody could risk letting him loose again.

Napoleon remains one of the greatest generals of all time, a man who understood how to apply overwhelming strength at the critical time and place. For many Frenchmen he remains a powerful symbol of glory and national pride, a titan amongst men. On one occasion this same Bonaparte, so talented and so driven, reflected not just on battles won and lost, but on the nature of power and dominion. He said: "I know men; and I tell you that Jesus Christ is no mere man. Between Him and every other person in the world there is no possible term of comparison. Alexander, Caesar, Charlemagne and I myself have founded empires; but upon what do these creations of our genius depend? Upon force. Jesus alone founded his empire upon love; and to this day millions would die for him."

Napoleon's nemesis at Waterloo, Arthur Wellesley, Duke of Wellington, never lost a battle. After the contest that is forever associated with his name was over, he said, "I do not think it would have done if I had not been there." In doing so, he touched upon the personal responsibility that we each have to be a channel of God's strength and a force for good in our nation and in the world. Free will means that our decisions affect how the future will play out. Our diligence or negligence, our ability to apply God-given reason with appropriate wisdom and foresight, our temporising or prompt action all have an impact. It would not do if we were not there either, in whatever situation God has placed us. We must start to act as though we really believe it.

35. Aftermath

Ezekiel 37.

Key word: regeneration.

The years immediately following the battle of Waterloo were hard. There was little in the way of post-war boom and soon there was full-scale slump. Agitation was widespread. Luddites smashed machines in country areas as well as in the towns. Fearful of a repeat of the French Revolution, regimes of all stripes were swift to stamp out any signs of incipient revolt. In 1817, for example, hundreds of Manchester weavers set out on a protest march to London, but were dispersed after the arrest of their leaders. [84] Just two years later the charged atmosphere contributed to an appalling and unnecessary outrage: eleven members of a peaceable demonstration in Manchester were killed by a charge of the Yeomanry – the so-called Peterloo Massacre. Far from sparking contrition in high places, this was followed by the passing of the Six Acts designed to restrict public meetings and demonstrations.

Antipathy to the organisation of labour continued for decades. In the wake of further rural unrest, including rick-burning and machine-breaking, in 1834 Home Secretary Lord Melbourne decided to make an example of six labourers from a village in Dorset. They were tried and found guilty under an Act of Parliament which forbade the administering or taking of unlawful oaths for seditious purposes. Despite no evidence of any seditious intent, they were given the maximum sentence: transportation to Australia for seven years. There were vigorous protests at the harsh treatment of these 'Tolpuddle martyrs', partly in consequence of which the men were given a free pardon in 1836 and gradually made their way home. Yet reaction and repression remained the order of the day, whilst large numbers of ordinary people continued to suffer from bad living conditions, long hours of work, low wages and lack of a political voice. For those at the bottom of the heap, workhouses were so dreaded that they were known as 'Bastilles.'

Against this background, the People's Charter was published in 1838. It made six demands: annual Parliaments, manhood suffrage, vote by ballot, abolition of property qualifications for MPs, payment of MPs and equal electoral districts. Mass petitions were organised in its favour. A whiff of uprising was in the air. In various areas working men armed and drilled, and in 1839 some three

---

[84] Since they carried blankets or coats, they are known as the Blanketeers.

thousand miners tried unsuccessfully to seize Newport in Monmouthshire to release an imprisoned Chartist leader. At length the movement collapsed, undermined by poor leadership and disunity, unable to gain the necessary support for a programme which was too far in advance of its time. The 'hungry forties' gave way to better times, whilst the working classes turned increasingly to what became the trade union movement.

Back to back.

It is easy to forget that, whilst Britain forged ahead of her rivals to become the dominant political and economic power of the nineteenth century, there was a battleground at home. In a world where there were precious few democracies, she was increasingly admired abroad for her freedoms and representative government, even as many of her own people experienced little of either. So deeply entrenched were the social divisions that in 1845 Benjamin Disraeli could write: "I was told that the Privileged and the People formed Two Nations."

God takes the prophet Ezekiel to a battleground: "The hand of the LORD was upon me, and he brought me out by the Spirit of the LORD and set me in the middle of a valley; it was full of bones ... Then he said to me, 'Prophesy to the breath; prophesy, son of man, and say to it, 'This is what the Sovereign LORD says: Come from the four winds, O breath, and breathe into these slain, that they may live.'" (Ezekiel 37:1 and 9). What God has in mind is mind-numbing in scope, wondrous in beauty and awesome in extent. He intends not merely to bring back to life those who were killed in battle and to make good all that has been marred by human sin, but also to bring about a new era in the relationship between man and God. Hence:

Unity will replace division: "This is what the Sovereign LORD says: I am going to take the stick of Joseph - which is in Ephraim's hand – and of the Israelite tribes associated with him, and join it to Judah's stick, making them a single stick of wood, and they will become one in my hand ... I will make them one nation in the land, on the mountains of Israel" (Ezekiel 37:19 and 22).[85]

Gathering will replace dispersal: "This is what the Sovereign LORD says: I will take the Israelites out of the nations where they have gone. I will gather them from all around and bring them back into their own land." (Ezekiel 37:21).

---

[85] Ephraim and Judah are especially favoured since from these tribes came Joshua and Caleb, the only spies who reported faithfully following their exploration of Canaan: see Numbers 13:6 and 8.

Godly government will replace misrule: "There will be one king over all of them and they will never again be two nations or be divided into two kingdoms ... My servant David will be king over them, and they will all have one shepherd." (Ezekiel 37:22 and 24).

Righteousness will replace sin: "They will no longer defile themselves with their idols and vile images or with any of their offences, for I will save them from their sinful back-sliding and I will cleanse them." (Ezekiel 37:23).

Obedience will replace rebellion: "They will follow my laws and be careful to keep my decrees." (Ezekiel 37:24).

Security will replace uncertainty: "They will live in the land I gave to my servant Jacob, the land where your fathers lived. They and their children and their children's children will live there for ever, and David my servant will be their prince for ever." (Ezekiel 37:25).

Peace will replace war: "I will make a covenant of peace with them; it will be an everlasting covenant." (Ezekiel 37:26).

Fellowship with God will replace separation: "They will be my people and I will be their God ... I will put my sanctuary among them for ever. My dwelling-place will be with them; I will be their God, and they will be my people. Then the nations will know that I the LORD make Israel holy, when my sanctuary is among them for ever." (Ezekiel 37:23 and 26-28).

Today, we are as much two nations as ever we were in the time of Disraeli. This is not how God wishes us to be. He wants us to stand back to back in brotherhood and unity. If we turn to him, he will restore, revive, renew and rebuild.

Back from the dead.

On many occasions the fight for union recognition and a political voice for the working classes seemed a lost cause. Thought of present-day renewal for our nation might seem equally hopeless, but we should take heart. God's words through the prophet Ezekiel have particular resonance for lost causes and for the hopeless, for he speaks of coming back from the dead. Too often, we say: "Our bones are dried up and our hope is gone; we are cut off." (Ezekiel 37:11). God reminds us: "This is what the Sovereign LORD says: O my people, I am going to open your graves and bring you up from them; I will bring you back to the land of Israel. Then you, my people, will know that I am the LORD, when I open your graves and bring you up from them. I will put my Spirit in you and you will live, and I will settle you in your own land. Then you will know that I the LORD have spoken, and I have done it, declares the LORD." (Ezekiel 37:12-14).

God will do as he has promised, but he will do it through human agency. It is the activity of the prophet Ezekiel, responding to divine command, which is the catalyst for what happens in the valley of dry bones: "So I prophesied as he commanded me, and breath entered them; they came to life and stood up on their feet – a vast army." (Ezekiel 37:10). It will be the same in our day. Unless we offer ourselves as God's agents, regeneration will not come. Above all, we need to "prophesy" (Ezekiel 37:4 and 9) – in other words, to tell forth the word of God and to foretell in accordance with what he reveals to us – and we need to "hear the word of the LORD" (Ezekiel 37:4).

Back together.

If we play our part, God will mend and bind up. He will bring things back together. He will do this on an individual basis as "bones [come] together, bone to bone." (Ezekiel 37:7). He will do it on a corporate basis by making us "one nation in the land" (Ezekiel 37:22). He will do it through physical renewal by "[attaching] tendons to [us] and [making] flesh come upon [us] and cover [us] with skin" (Ezekiel 37:6). He will do it through spiritual rebirth by "[putting] breath in [us so that we] will come to life." (Ezekiel 37:6). The result will be the creation of a "vast army" (Ezekiel 37:10). This should cause us to reflect on lessons from the clash of armies past.

One such has particularly resonance. Astride almost sheer cliffs hundreds of feet above the Judean desert stand the remains of a hilltop palace and fortress complex called Masada, built by Herod the Great. Here hundreds of Jewish rebels committed suicide in AD 73 rather than surrender to the Roman legions which were besieging them. The last of the Zealot defenders left alive was their leader, Eleazar ben Yair. Before falling on his own sword he cut Ezekiel 37 from a scroll of Scriptures and buried it with great care. He did so to send a message to succeeding generations: that the nation was not irredeemably vanquished, but would rise again. God has given us a similar message of renewal and regeneration. We need to pass it on.

Conclusion.

To the repressive regimes of continental Europe, all forms of collective activity were deeply suspect: trade associations, friendly societies, co-operatives, clubs and even informal cafe discussion groups. This did not just hinder political activism and trade unionism. It struck at the heart of civil society and the creation of a developed economy. It prevented political, social and economic renewal by peaceful means and made violent revolution more likely, not less. There were interests in Britain that opposed these things, too, but despite stubborn resistance they were eventually forced to give way. They could not forever hold against the things for which Britain claimed to stand: either they must yield or the nation would have to concede that her vaunted ideals of democracy, freedom and justice were nothing but a sham. The ideals won.

The inter-connectedness of life should never cease to strike us. The fact that Britain became a world economic and political power cannot be ascribed to one cause alone. It is indeed almost impossible to disentangle the threads that made this possible. Without constitutional monarchy, tenuous would have been the independence of the judiciary. Without rule of law, there would have been no secure property rights and less impetus for innovation. Without freedom of association, there would have been no Lloyds of London insurance market (whose members first met in coffee houses) and hence less trade, which in turn would have meant less wealth and less capital to finance industrial expansion. Without political stability and due regard for creditors, higher interest would have been charged on government debt, making it harder to finance the wars whose successful outcome helped secure British dominion in Canada, India, South Africa and elsewhere. Without a free press, abuse of executive power would have lacked an important check and the free flow of information that is needed for relationships of trust between strangers (vital for development of business outside tight family-held groups) would have been hindered. Without representative government, there would have been no safety valve for political grievances.

All this was subordinate to and dependent on right relationship with God. It is no accident that so many successful businessmen of the era were committed Christians. Strangers were happy to do business with them because they were trustworthy, and they were trustworthy because their Christian faith made it impossible for them to be otherwise. [86] We are presently hollowing out all the institutions and structures of our nation, removing the Christian underpinnings that gave them life and breath, without which they are empty and meaningless. Remove Christianity from capitalism and it becomes only vulgar money-making and an opportunity for exploitation. Remove it from law and we are at the mercy of expediency and the utilitarian. Remove it from our sense of morality and any excess becomes possible and even justifiable. The skeleton on which the life of the nation hangs is becoming nothing but bones that are "very dry" (Ezekiel 37:2). They are lifeless, for there is "no breath in them." (Ezekiel 37:8).

Things behave according to their natures. If we let a stone drop we do not need to watch to know that it will fall: it is in its nature that it will do so in

---

[86] In *The Protestant Ethic and the Spirit of Capitalism*, German sociologist Max Weber (1864-1902) theorised that capitalism developed from Protestantism (in particular, Calvinism). He cited the disproportionate numbers of Nonconformists amongst leading British businessmen, including families such as the Clarks (shoes), Rowntrees (chocolate), Frys (cocoa), Gurneys (banking), Barclays (banking) and Levers (soap).

obedience to the natural laws which govern the universe. So it is with mankind and so it is with God. We are each true to our natures. If we persist on our present course, only ruin awaits. Sinful human beings will always make a hash of things when left to their own devices. If we really want to see renewal and regeneration, our only option is to turn again to our Creator.

36. Furnace

Daniel 3:13-30.

Key word: fire.

Round the back streets of old Nottingham is a pub called the Bendigo, the only one in England to bear this name. It commemorates a local man, William Thompson, born in 1811 and a boxer by trade. His career in the ring lasted almost twenty years (1832 to 1850) and for six years (1839 to 1845) he was champion prize fighter of all England. He was nicknamed Abednego, and Bendigo is a corruption of that name.

To be a prize fighter was almost unimaginably hard. There were no Queensberry rules (these only became standard in 1889), no gloves, no limits on the number of rounds fought. Not surprisingly, some were literally bludgeoned to death during the most brutal bouts. The existence of prize fighting and the fact that men would contemplate becoming a prize fighter at all, let alone spend almost twenty years at it, shines an unflattering light on life in England. It is testament to grinding poverty.[87] It speaks of a precarious existence: women died in childbirth in large numbers, many children did not live to see their fifth birthday and deadly diseases were commonplace. There were Europe-wide cholera epidemics, for example, from 1830-35, 1847-48, 1853-56, 1865-67, 1869-74, 1883-87 and 1893-95. In Britain, 53,000 died of cholera in 1848 alone.

Prize fighting is also testament to the dark side of human nature, to our willingness to make sport of others and take amusement from their suffering. It is the spirit of the amphitheatre and the reality TV show. That spirit is alive and well now just as it has always been. The story of Bendigo, however, is one of hope. He survived his trial by fire in the ring, became a Christian and eventually a Methodist minister.[88] Thereafter he worked with another Nottingham man, William Booth, writer of the hymn Send the fire!, founder of the Salvation Army and great minister to the urban poor, in bringing the message of God's grace and love to those whose lives were hardest. The old boxer died on 23 August 1880,

---

[87] Bendigo was born into an impoverished family of 21 children. When his father died, he and his mother were sent to the workhouse.

[88] Since prize fighting was considered a breach of the peace, Bendigo was arrested after most of his bouts. During one of his terms in gaol he heard a sermon by the prison chaplain that led him to change his life.

well stricken in years (he was aged 69) after a life full of incident and pleasing to God.

What's in a name?

The protagonists in Daniel 3 include Bendigo's namesake Adenego and his companions Shadrach and Meshach. Of mature years in this story, they were young men when they were led with Daniel as captives from the Israelite kingdom of Judah after Nebuchadnezzar's invasion of 605 BC, prior to his eventual conquest in 586 BC. In Babylon, they were given new names[89] and Babylonian education. In the ancient near east, taking away an old name and substituting a new one was a way of exercising authority, expressing overlordship and setting a new direction in life. God frequently renames people in this way: thus Abram became Abraham (Genesis 17:5), Sarai became Sarah (Genesis 17:15) and Jacob became Israel (Genesis 32:28 and 35:10).[90]

As far as the Babylonians were concerned, renaming aimed to mark the captives out for service of pagan gods: the new names referred to Aku, a Sumerian moon-god, and Nabu, one of the major Babylonian deities. As events showed, this was a forlorn hope, for the men remained loyal to the one true God. As the tale unfolds and they undergo their own literal trial by fire, their original Hebrew names are shown to be particularly apt.

Remaining true.

When king Nebuchadnezzar learnt that these three would not bow down and worship a golden image that he had caused to be made, he was "furious with rage ... [and] summoned Shadrach, Meshach and Abednego" (Daniel 3:13), who by this time had risen to high office. They are said to have been "set over the affairs of the province of Babylon" (Daniel 3:12).

What follows shows the unbridled, unprincipled but ultimately futile exercise of human force, set alongside the saving power of God. It also shows tremendous courage, faith and integrity on the part of "Shadrach, Meshach and Abednego [who] replied [to the king's threats], 'O Nebuchadnezzar, we do not need to defend ourselves before you in this matter. If we are thrown into the

---

[89] Hananiah (meaning God is my judge) became Shadrach (meaning Command of Aku), Mishael (meaning Who is what God is?) became Meshach (meaning Who is what Aku is?) and Azariah (meaning The Lord helps) became Abednego (meaning Servant of Nabu).

[90] Abram means 'exalted father,' Abraham 'father of many.' Sarai and Sarah both mean 'princess.' Jacob means 'he grasps the heel,' Israel 'he struggles with (or for) God.'

blazing furnace, the God we serve is able to save us from it, and he will rescue us from your hand, O king. But even if he does not, we want you to know, O king, that we will not serve your gods or worship the image of gold that you have set up'" (Daniel 3:16-18).

In a rage, the king promptly ordered the men to be bound and thrown into a furnace, which was "heated seven times hotter than usual" (Daniel 3:19). The spiritual depravity of Babylon is clear. This nation was not a neutral force, but stood in opposition to the High King of Heaven. There are echoes of pagan methods of sacrifice: "They have built the high places of Baal to burn their sons in the fire as offerings to Baal – something I did not command or mention, nor did it enter my mind. So beware, the days are coming, declares the Lord, when people will no longer call this Topheth or the Valley of Ben Hinnom, but the Valley of Slaughter." (Jeremiah 19:5-6). The Lord's strictures against such behaviour are clear: "Let no-one be found among you who sacrifices his son or daughter in the fire" (Deuteronomy 18:10).

Like Shadrach, Meshach and Abednego, we need to remain true to God and his ways, even though we live in a society that no longer honours them and which so often goes deliberately counter to them. This takes courage, whether the threats we face are physical or whether they take other forms. When we are undergoing trial by fire, we need to remind ourselves of the important truths that were spoken to Nebuchadnezzar by Daniel's friends. They acknowledged the possibility that God, although able to pluck them from "this hour" (John 12:27) might not do so: "the God we serve is able to save us ... But even if he does not ... we will not serve your gods or worship the image of gold that you have set up." (Daniel 3:17-18). Alongside this they had the certainty that, come what may, "he will rescue us" (Daniel 3:17). Our bedrock is that we will be rescued (through our ultimate salvation) even though we may not be kept from the particular trial that is at hand.

Images of gold.

The three Jews were punished because they would not worship a golden image. We live in a land that has images of gold aplenty. United States President Calvin Coolidge said: "Prosperity is only an instrument to be used, not a deity to be worshipped." Sadly, we have ignored such sound advice. We have taken consumerism and materialism to levels previously undreamt of. We have made gods out of the pursuit of pleasure and the cult of celebrity. We have drunk deep from the wine of unbelief and elevated mere men to the place that belongs to God.

The lure of such things is seductive. There is "the sound of the horn, flute, zither, lyre, harp, pipes and all kinds of music" (Daniel 3:15). Society would have us believe that to esteem such things is not wrong: "If you are ready to fall down and worship the image I made, very good." (Daniel 3:15). We risk being objects of scorn, ridicule and even persecution if we do not follow the crowd. We need to know when to draw a line in the sand. Shadrach, Meshach and Abednego had faithfully served the Babylonian state for years, to such good effect that they had been promoted to positions of trust and influence. They had been able to do this in a way that was consistent with and true to their faith. When they were asked to step over the line, however, they had the insight, wisdom and courage to know that this was a bridge too far and to refuse. We have to live and work in the society around us, just as these men did. We can be effective and influential without compromising our principles, but we need to make sure that we recognise images of gold when we see them and that we refuse to bow down before them. If we are able to do this, we will proclaim the power and glory of the Lord and it will lead others to say of him that "no other god can save in this way." (Daniel 3:29).

Trial by fire.

Trial by fire is an awful thing to contemplate. None would willingly submit to it. Fire can burn, scald, scar and kill. It has another side, however. Fire cleanses, purifies and cauterises. It provides heat and light. It transforms through its touch: wood into charcoal, raw ingredients into cooked delicacies. Fire is an element in which God is often revealed: to Moses in the burning bush (Exodus 3:2), to the Israelites in a pillar of fire during the flight from Egypt (Exodus 13:21), to Elijah on Mount Carmel (1 Kings 18:38) and to the first Christians at Pentecost (Acts 2:3). We are reminded that "our God is a consuming fire" (Hebrews 12:29), that Jesus will baptise "with the Holy Spirit and with fire" (Matthew 3:11) and that we should "not put out the Spirit's fire" (1 Thessalonians 5:19).

Similarly, God is revealed in the fiery furnace: "Then King Nebuchadnezzar leaped to his feet in amazement and asked his advisers, 'Weren't there three men that we tied up and threw into the fire?' They replied, 'Certainly, O king.' He said, 'Look! I see four men walking around in the fire, unbound and unharmed, and the fourth looks like a son of the gods.'" (Daniel 3:24-25). Some identify the fourth person in the furnace as Christ. Nebuchadnezzar calls him an "angel". (Daniel 3:28). Whichever it may be, the Lord is clearly powerfully present. He not only keeps the three companions alive but a divine presence accompanies them, frees them from their shackles and undergoes the same trial that they experience. We need to remember that God is right alongside us in our troubles in just the same way.

The furnace provides an image of hell. It is a place of flame and torment. It is thus no surprise that it "killed the soldiers who took up Shadrach, Meshach and Abednego" (Daniel 3:22) but did not harm the three Jews: "Nebuchadnezzar then approached the opening of the blazing furnace and shouted, 'Shadrach, Meshach and Abednego, servants of the Most High God, come out! Come here!'

So Shadrach, Meshach and Abednego came out of the fire, and the satraps, prefects, governors and royal advisers crowded around them. They saw that the fire had not harmed their bodies, nor was a hair of their heads singed; their robes were not scorched, and there was no smell of fire on them." (Daniel 3:26-27). Again, there is something for us to learn from this: others may create hellish conditions for us, but they cannot consign us to eternal damnation. We are kept free from the bonds of hell by the blood and sacrifice of Jesus, who went through the fire precisely so that we should not have to do so.

Even the pagan king acknowledged that Lord has been at work. The result was glory for God and honour for his faithful servants: "Then Nebuchadnezzar said, 'Praise be to the God of Shadrach, Meshach and Abednego, who has sent his angel and rescued his servants! They trusted in him and defied the king's command and were willing to give up their lives rather than serve or worship any god except their own God. Therefore I decree that the people of any nation or language who say anything against the God of Shadrach, Meshach and Abednego be cut into pieces and their houses be turned into piles of rubble, for no other god can save in this way.' Then the king promoted Shadrach, Meshach and Abednego in the province of Babylon." (Daniel 3:28-30). Nebuchadnezzar remained to the end a cruel despot with only the faintest glimmer of spiritual understanding. The decree with which the story ends is as harsh as any that he has hitherto pronounced against the people of God, yet despite himself the man who formerly trampled the name of the God of Israel ended up raising that name on high. This is what we can expect to happen when we remain true and faithful witnesses to our Lord.

Conclusion.

The England of Bendigo's day was a furnace. She was the workshop of the world, a place of fire and smoke billowing from foundries. She was also the crucible of a new kind of living, as towns gathered ever more people from the countryside to feed burgeoning factories and people adjusted to new working practices, to the rhythm of the shift and the clock instead of that of the seasons. She was a place where old certainties and old ways of doing things no longer applied. We, too, live in a land where the ground is shifting under our feet. When the environment is uncertain and potentially hostile, it is all the more important to know when we can safely compromise with the society in which we live and when we cannot.

Shadrach, Meshach and Abednego provide an example of how to be faithful to God in an unbelieving environment. The pagan king put it thus: they "trusted in God ... defied the king's command and were willing to give up their lives rather than serve or worship any god except their God." (Daniel 3:28). To defy the command of the rightful ruler or to disobey the law of the land is something we should only do as a last resort. The Bible teaches us that we are to "obey [our] earthly masters" (Colossians 3:22, Ephesians 6:5). On the other hand, "We must obey God rather than men!" (Acts 5:29). We must not "serve or worship any god except [the one true] God." (Daniel 3:28). The men who stood up to Nebuchadnezzar had fire in their hearts. We need to kindle the same fire in ourselves and in England. Or, more correctly, we need God to fan us into flame through the activity of his Spirit. This can only happen if we call on him and if we make ourselves available for his service. Bendigo did precisely that and fought for God with the same fire that he fought in the ring. With only a little of the same glow, we can be instruments through which God will transform our nation.

37. Sisters of mercy

Ruth 2.

Key word: favour.

Attitudes changed greatly between the eighteenth and nineteenth centuries. The religious revival begun in the days of Wesley and Whitefield spread gradually throughout the land, bringing with it a new seriousness. By the 1850s many households had revived family prayers and a strict Sunday routine. Emphasis was placed on hard work and eagerness to acquire knowledge. Within the Church of England the influence of evangelicals such as William Wilberforce and Lord Shaftesbury (author of the Factory Acts, which restricted the hours of work for women and children) increased. Such people believed in austere living, works of charity, in the importance of personal faith and of the individual conscience. With the Bible as their ultimate source of authority, they attached correspondingly less weight to the sacraments and to priestly ministrations. Women as well as men worked to improve conditions. Two in particular stand out for their fearless efforts on behalf of different types of outcast: criminals and prostitutes.

Elizabeth Fry (1780-1845) was born into a Quaker family. In 1813 she visited Newgate gaol. Horrified by what she saw, she set out champion prison reform and an association was established under her guidance. She agitated for more humane treatment of women prisoners and of convicts transported to Australia. She was also involved in attempts to improve working conditions for nurses and facilities for women's education. Largely in response to her work (and that of her predecessor John Howard in the eighteenth century) Prime Minister Sir Robert Peel took steps to reform the larger prisons: female prisoners were no longer supervised by male warders and gaolers were paid instead of living on fees from prisoners.

Josephine Butler (1828-1906) championed a group even less likely to elicit sympathy amongst those hunkered in well-to-do respectability. She worked first alongside vagrant women in the Brownlow Hill Workhouse in Liverpool and took prostitutes into her home to care for them there. The more she discovered about prostitution, however, the more she realised that it was not merely a matter of reclaiming individuals. She began to tackle the double standards which held women entirely to blame for the evils of that profession and excused the conduct of men, together with the economic conditions that forced so many to sell their bodies in the first place. In doing so, she confronted the ugly underbelly of life in Victorian England. She came increasingly to the view that the entire position of women in society needed to be changed and as such she was a precursor to later generations of feminists.

Her campaigns for raising the age of consent and for repeal of the Contagious Diseases Act (which effectively allowed any woman to be subjected to forcible examination for venereal disease), were without precedent and courageous in the extreme. Many times she addressed public meetings of men on a subject about which most then considered that a woman of good repute should be wholly ignorant, and of which a lady most certainly should not speak. The audiences were often bawdy or hostile. The medical profession and the Establishment (each almost exclusively male) were against her. The Anglican Church and the Liberal Party, both of which might have been thought natural allies, were unhelpful. There was no quick victory. The campaign against the Contagious Diseases Act began in 1869. Not until seventeen years later was a Repeal Bill passed.

Favour in tragedy.

Josephine Butler was born to privilege amongst a family of landowners in Northumberland. She was related to Lord Grey, who was Prime Minister (1830-43) when slavery was abolished throughout the British Empire and the Great Reform Act passed.[91] She might easily have passed her life in comfort and obscurity had not one of her daughters died in a childhood accident. This tragedy was a spur to action rather than self-pity. Of it she wrote:

"I felt possessed with an irresistible desire to go forth, and find some pain keener than my own – to meet with people more unhappy than myself (for I knew that there were thousands of such). I did not exaggerate my own trial; I knew only that my heart ached night and day, and that the only solace would seem to be to find other hearts which ached night and day."

The book of Ruth describes a time of tragedy: "In the days when the judges ruled, there was famine in the land" (Ruth 1:1). Despite moving to Moab to save her family, Naomi loses her husband and two sons: "Now Ehimelech, Naomi's husband, died ... after they had lived [in Moab] about ten years, both Mahlon and Killion also died, and Naomi was left without her two sons and her husband." (Ruth 1:3). Naomi's reaction to her loss was rather different from that

---

[91] The Great Reform Act (1832) redistributed seats in the House of Commons to include large cities that were previously unrepresented. It also extended the franchise to adult males occupying premises worth at least £10 per year. Further extensions of the male franchise were enacted by the Reform Acts of 1867, 1884 and 1885. Women over thirty gained the vote in 1918 and universal adult suffrage was introduced by the Representation of the People (Equal Franchise) Act 1928.

of Josephine Butler, but is one with which anyone can sympathise: "'Don't call me Naomi,' she told them. 'Call me Mara, because the Almighty has made my life very bitter. I went away full, but the LORD has brought me back empty. Why call me Naomi? The LORD has afflicted me; the Almighty has brought misfortune on me.'" (Ruth 1:20-21).[92] To blame God when things go wrong is a very human reaction. Rarely are we able to see good things at such times, nor to consider that God might in fact be showing his favour both during our tragedies and even through them. Yet the book of Ruth describes precisely that: God's favour shown through one human being (Boaz) to another (Ruth) and, through her, to yet another (Naomi). Ultimately this favour extends to all mankind, for Boaz and Ruth became great-grandparents to King David and thus ancestors of Jesus: see Ruth 4:21-22.

Our reaction to tragedy is of critical importance, for every human life contains heartache. This can crush us and turn us from God, or it can increase our understanding of and sympathy for others. Instead of sitting on our hands feeling sorry for ourselves, we need to react as did Ruth, one of Naomi's two daughters-in-law, who stayed beside her mother-in-law throughout all the trials to come: "And Ruth the Moabitess said to Naomi, 'Let me go to the fields and pick up the leftover grain behind anyone in whose eyes I find favour.'" (Ruth 2:2). Josephine Butler went into the fields and picked up leftovers, the young women spurned and rejected by the society that spawned and used them. Perhaps God spoke to her words similar to those spoken to Ruth by Boaz, her kinsman-redeemer[93]: "My daughter, listen to me. Don't go and glean in another field and don't go away from here. Stay here with my servant girls." (Ruth 2:8).

Favour in hardship.

Ruth is shown favour: "At mealtime Boaz said to her, 'Come over here. Have some bread and dip it in the wine vinegar.' When she sat down with the harvesters, he offered her some roasted grain. She ate all she wanted and had some left over. As she got up to glean, Boaz gave orders to his men, 'Even if she gathers among the sheaves, don't embarrass her. Rather, pull out some of stalks for her from the bundles and leave them for her to pick up, and don't rebuke her.'" (Ruth 2:14-16). Blessing is pronounced upon her: "May the LORD repay you for what you have done. May you be richly rewarded by the LORD, the God of Israel, under whose wings you have come to take refuge." (Ruth 2:12).

---

[92] Naomi means pleasant. Mara means bitter.

[93] The kinsman-redeemer was responsible for protecting needy members of the extended family.

Neither favour nor blessing means that life is easy for Ruth, nor are her troubles over in an instant. Gleaning is hard labour. It is work for those at the very bottom of the heap, the destitute and the outcast. The Law of Moses required landowners to leave what had not been gathered during harvesting so that the poor, the alien, the widowed and the fatherless could glean and thereby provide for their needs: see Leviticus 19:9 and 23:22, Deuteronomy 24:19. Ruth "worked steadily from morning ... except for a short rest in the shelter" (Ruth 2:7). After a full day's toil in the fields there was more for her to do when she got home: "So Ruth gleaned in the field until evening. Then she threshed the barley she had gathered, and it amounted to about an ephah. She carried it back to town, and her mother-in-law saw how much she had gathered." (Ruth 2:17-18).

Ruth "left [her] father and mother and [her] homeland and came to live with a people [she] did not know before." (Ruth 2:11). Often, we are called to do the same, in a metaphorical if not a literal sense. When Josephine Butler went to minister amongst the prostitutes of Liverpool she entered a world as different from her own as if it had been a foreign country. The fields in which she worked were places of hard labour. There was no ease or softness for her there and her family suffered by reason of what she did. Her husband had to resign his position as Principal of Liverpool College. Her eldest son found his career at the Bar untenable. Doubtless her other children also faced disapproval and rejection. At such times we need great sense of purpose and we need great faith to remind ourselves of God's favour and blessing. It can be hard for us to recognise that God might be showing us these things even in times of hardship. Yet paradoxically, it is often precisely when the going is toughest that God's favour and blessing is greatest.

Favour in suffering.

Naomi and Ruth faced not merely hardship but real suffering. Quite apart from having lost those nearest and dearest to them, life for a woman without an adult male to protect and provide for her was precarious and dangerous: "Naomi said to Ruth her daughter-in-law, 'It will be good for you, my daughter, to go with his [Boaz'] girls, because in someone else's field you might be harmed.'" (Ruth 2:22). The days of the judges were lawless, for "In those days Israel had no king; everyone did as he saw fit." (Judges 21:25). Ruth was both a widow and a foreigner, hence doubly vulnerable. Yet without its being apparent straightaway, God is in fact protecting and providing. He does so through:

Place: "As it turned out, [Ruth] found herself working in a field belonging to Boaz" (Ruth 2:3).

Timing: "Just then, Boaz arrived from Bethlehem and greeted the harvesters" (Ruth 2:4).

Repute: "I've been told all about what you have done for your mother-in-law since the death of your husband" (Ruth 2:11).

People: "The name of the man I worked with today is Boaz" (Ruth 2:19).

Opportunity: "So Ruth stayed close to the servant girls of Boaz to glean until the barley and wheat harvests were finished. And she lived with her mother-in-law." (Ruth 2:23).

In the same way, the Lord protects and provides for us. He enables us, moreover, to be protectors and providers for others, as Boaz is for Ruth: "Watch the field where the men are harvesting, and follow along after the girls. I have told the men not to touch you. And whenever you are thirsty, go and get a drink from the water jars the men have filled." (Ruth 2:9). We therefore need to make sure that we search out the place that God allocates to us for our work, are sensitive to God's timing, build a reputation that will bring honour, are alert to the people that God has placed in our path and thereby take full advantage of the opportunities that God gives. If we do all this, we will find favour even as Ruth did.

Like Ruth, Josephine Butler suffered greatly – not just through the untimely death of her daughter but also as a result of the awful things that she confronted during her campaigns. Of her suffering she said:

"[As] we get nearer to God, all prayer resolves itself into communion. To the Holy of Holies, face to face with Jesus, all perplexities vanish. No difficulties can live. If I may dare to tell a little of what He has taught me, even in days and weeks of bodily suffering, it is this; that in prayer I am still, silent, waiting for the Spirit and the Spirit is granted, so that He prompts every request."

We, too, need to be still and silent so that we allow God's Spirit to work in our lives.

Conclusion.

Josephine Butler set out to reclaim individuals but found herself trying to reclaim a nation. Through the Ladies' National Association she oversaw the first effective political campaigning movement led by women. The tasks are as pressing now as they were then. Though we try to fool ourselves into thinking otherwise, we are no less prone to double standards than the Victorians. Our society has no lack of abuses and victims. It does not want for tragedy or brutality. The difference between present and past is that once large numbers of English men and women were prepared to do something about it in the name of Almighty God.

We are called to be the instruments of God's favour to our fellow men. Unbelief and false belief grow because of our failings, nothing more or less. It is we who give the message that Christianity is a lukewarm confection of the fabulous and the irrelevant, a bland mess of meaningless stories. It is because of us that our countrymen regard it as indistinguishable from any other faith and lacking in power. If we wish to experience divine favour for ourselves and for our land, we need to take refuge under the wings of the God of Israel. We need to work in his power and tell forth his Word. We need to stop wallowing in self-pity and self-absorption and instead "go to the fields and pick up the leftover grain behind anyone in whose eyes [we] find favour." (Ruth 2:2).

38. The Great Game

Ecclesiastes 9:11-18.

Key word: remembrance.

In the heart of central Asia lies a city that once was deservedly called the Noble. She sits astride the old Silk Route from China and amongst the memories of her former greatness, an oasis town that on every side is compassed by desert. She was and remains a place of palaces and monuments, of bath-houses and pleasure gardens. Her story also has a darker side. Here on 24 June 1842 two figures were dragged from the dungeon where they had been held captive. Filthy and half-starved, their bodies covered with sores and their hair infested with lice, they were ordered to dig their own graves. To the sound of drums and reed pipes from atop the citadel wall, a crowd watched as they were then beheaded.

Such executions normally attracted scant attention, being all too commonplace in Bokhara under its despotic emir Nasrullah Khan. The victims in this case were unusual, however, for they were British officers. Colonel Charles Stoddart had arrived three years earlier on a mission to reassure the emir about British intentions following their invasion of Afghanistan and to seek his alliance against the Russians, who were daily advancing further east. The notoriously depraved ruler, who had ascended the throne in 1826 by killing his brothers and 28 other relatives, promptly threw the Englishman in gaol. When Captain Arthur Conolly arrived in 1841 to negotiate Stoddart's release, he was similarly treated. The officers were kept in a dark, stinking pit beneath the citadel, alive with rats and other vermin. Eventually, British withdrawal from Afghanistan convinced Nasrullah that he could kill them with impunity: "As fish are caught in a cruel net, or birds are taken in a snare, so [they were] trapped by evil times that fell unexpectedly on them." (Ecclesiastes 9:12).

These largely forgotten heroes were victims of what the British called the Great Game and the Russians the Tournament of Shadows. It was a game for high stakes, a contest of lofty principle and low cunning, of daring and deceit. The British aim was the protection of the jewel in the crown of their Empire: India. Whether or not the Russians were really aiming at the subcontinent is open to debate, but certainly their appetite for conquest in Asia was insatiable. It is conservatively estimated that between 1683 and 1914 the territory of their empire was expanding at an average of 55 square miles per day. For over a century the two powers squared off across a steadily shrinking no-man's-land. In the event, a developing threat from Germany turned rivals into allies before the game was fully played out. The Tournament of Shadows officially ended with the signing of the Anglo-Russian Convention of 1907, to resume in another form during the Cold War.

Remembering and reflection.

In the book of Ecclesiastes, King Solomon examines various aspects of human experience. He explores the meaninglessness of life on earth if it is lived apart from or in denial of God, before presenting "the conclusion of the matter: fear God and keep his commandments, for this is the whole duty of man." (Ecclesiastes 12:13).

The Great Game might seem an anachronism: a meaningless conflict played out by people who are strangers to us, for purposes that appeared worthwhile to them but which seem illusory nowadays. We may think it difficult to discern what good, if any, came from such heavy investment of idealism, courage and self-sacrifice. Looking at this and reflecting on the bravery and talent of many of those involved, we might agree that, since people do not always get what they deserve, this means that our actions are of no account: "The race is not to the swift or the battle to the strong, nor does food come to the wise or wealth to the brilliant or favour to the learned; but time and chance happen to them all." (Ecclesiastes 9:11). We might conclude from the uncertainty which characterises human affairs that nothing but blind chance is involved: "Moreover, no man knows when his hour will come." (Ecclesiastes 9:12). If so, we would plunge all too easily into nihilism, apathy and despair.

It is of the greatest importance, therefore, that we ponder deeply on such things and reach considered conclusions about them. This involves a process of remembrance: to remember facts so that we have a proper basis on which to make our assessment, to remember the wisdom of our forefathers so that we do not forget the lessons of ages past and to remember God so that we have a proper perspective on events.

Remembering facts.

In the process of trying to make sense of life, Solomon recalls facts and reflects on them: "I also saw under the sun this example of wisdom that greatly impressed me: There was once a small city with only a few people in it. And a powerful king came against it, surrounded it and built huge siegeworks against it. Now there lived in that city a man poor but wise, and he saved the city by his wisdom." (Ecclesiastes 9:13-15).

Solomon recounts an extraordinary series of events, making several pointed contrasts. In circumstances that should have been ones of utter hopelessness, the weak stood against the strong, the few in number against a mighty army, and a poor man outwitted a powerful king. Thus was a small city enabled to withstand huge siegeworks. Not surprisingly, Solomon says that this "greatly impressed me" (Ecclesiastes 9:13) and it should greatly impress us, too. If anything should cause us to doubt that our deeds are of no effect, events of this kind should do so. Life is neither deterministic nor mechanistic. The triumph against all odds of countless English men and women down the ages proves the opposite to be true.

Sadly, "nobody remembered that poor man."(Ecclesiastes 9:15). In failing to remember him, those he had saved showed disrespect and rank ingratitude. They also harmed themselves, for in forgetting their saviour, the real lessons to be learnt from what had befallen them would have been overlooked: that no situation is ever hopeless, that victory does not always go to those who appear strongest or are greatest in number, that insight and discernment are not monopolies of the wealthy or powerful and that wisdom can overcome a mighty army.

These lessons apply not just to the physical world, but to the spiritual. In failing to remember our Saviour, the Lord Jesus Christ who gave his life for us and who has blessed our nation so abundantly, we are guilty of the most appalling disrespect and ingratitude. We have also turned our backs on the most important lessons and the greatest gifts of all. In seeking modernity, in elevating relevance to current circumstances over timeless truth and in trying to be progressive, inclusive and tolerant whatever the consequences we have thrown the baby out with the bathwater.

We need to remember the wisdom of our forefathers. In a land where nihilism, apathy and despair abound, we must remind our fellow countrymen that Christianity stands for the very opposite of such attitudes. The gospel brings a message hope and a call to a lifetime of meaningful activity in the service of God and our fellow men.

Remembering past wisdom.

In reflecting on the past, Solomon draws a number of conclusions. These are as important for what he does not say as much as for what he does. He does not conclude that the poor man's actions were of no account because they are now forgotten by those he saved. Neither does he say that these actions were of no effect. Nor does not say that the events he describes came about through blind chance. Instead he extols the virtues of the godly and the results of their deeds:

"Wisdom is better than strength." (Ecclesiastes 9:16).

"The quiet words of the wise are more to be heeded than the shouts of a ruler of fools." (Ecclesiastes 9:17).

"Wisdom is better than weapons of war" (Ecclesiastes 9:18).

Correspondingly, he acknowledges the harm that can be done by just one unrighteous person. We see all around us the truth of the saying that "one sinner destroys much good" (Ecclesiastes 9:18): whilst the vast majority of Englishmen remain decent and law-abiding, disproportionate mayhem is caused by a relatively small number. We are complicit in this by failing in our duty to instruct people in the truth, by failing to uphold proper values and most of all by allowing God to be marginalised.

The result is a society that signally lacks wisdom and the blessings that flow from it. Elsewhere, Solomon strongly identifies wisdom with godliness: "The fear of the LORD is the beginning of wisdom and knowledge of the Holy One is understanding. For through me your days will be many and years will be added to your life. If you are wise, your wisdom will reward you; if you are a mocker, you alone will suffer." (Proverbs 9:10-12). St Paul reminds us: "Do not be deceived: God cannot be mocked. A man reaps what he sows. The one who sows to please his sinful nature, from that nature will reap destruction; the one who sows to please the Spirit, from the Spirit will reap eternal life." (Galatians 6:7-8). We are presently holding God up to mockery and scorn. We are suffering for it, and will suffer further unless we desist. We are trampling the gift of eternal life in the dust.

Remembering God.

We should thus remember God for our own sakes, as well as because duty and gratitude demand it. Without God we cannot expect to see clearly, neither to be wise nor to draw proper conclusions from the facts. The same circumstances that, without God, might seem cause for despair and confirmation that life lacks meaning become with him sources of hope and the inspiration for action. Hence the very things that Solomon talks about can be turned on their heads to strike a note of hope rather than of despair. If "The race is not to the swift or the battle to the strong" (Ecclesiastes 9:11) it follows that the mailed fist will not always triumph nor might always be right. If "nor does food come to the wise or wealth to the brilliant or favour to the learned" (Ecclesiastes 9:11) it follows that someone who lacks these qualities yet is godly can still aspire to good things. If "time and chance happen to [us] all" (Ecclesiastes 9:11) it follows that there is a level playing field between men, regardless of outward appearances.

What makes the difference is whether we invite God to come close or keep him at arm's length. He yearns to be part of our lives. If he is not, it is only because we do not allow him to be. If once we genuinely turn to him and ask him to be with us, he will come. Jesus says: "Here I am! I stand at the door and knock. If anyone hears my voice and opens the door, I will come in and eat with him, and he with me." (Revelation 3:20).

Conclusion.

Between 1848 and 1871 the population of the Russian Empire increased by twenty millions, or more than a quarter. By 1910, her people numbered over 155 millions. Between 1835 and 1914 her railway network grew from nothing to be larger than that of Britain, France and Germany. In an age when power was measured by the size of conscript armies and the ability to deploy them quickly, this represented an exponential increase in military might.

Russia's rapid progress eastwards showed that she had no inhibitions about using force against whoever stood in her way. One by one the khanates of what had once been the territory of the Golden Horde fell under her sway: Kazan, Astrakhan, Bokhara, Khiva and Khokand.[94] Her Cossacks seemed unstoppable and her ambitions boundless. With hindsight we may conclude that she overreached herself and that she had no realistic prospect of taking India, but that was not how it appeared to contemporaries. Imperial Russia hid her weaknesses just as effectively as the Soviets were to do generations later. In the context of the times, Britain had no choice but to deflect and oppose the ambitious power growing ever nearer her sphere of influence.

Many brave men played the Great Game, and many died in doing so. There is no telling what would have been without their sacrifice. They have left us a legacy not just in their deeds but in their attitudes: in their courage, sense of duty, unashamed patriotism, decency and honour, but most of all in the Christian faith that was then so strong in these islands. When we look at what these men undertook, it is sometimes difficult to avoid the conclusion that they were quite simply of greater stature than we.

Old attitudes and old ways of doing things can be outmoded, old-fashioned and out-of-date. Yet that should not blind us to the fact that sometimes the wisdom of our forefathers has more to commend it than any number of new-fangled suppositions. Sir Edward Coke, Lord Chief Justice of England in the early seventeenth century, said: "We have a maxim in the House of Commons ... that old ways are the safest and surest ways." We need to feed on the wisdom of the past and to keep alive the remembrance of former things. If this becomes a land where "the poor man's wisdom is despised, and his words are no longer heeded" (Ecclesiastes 9:16), we are the ones who will be impoverished. When we reject our history and forget those who had a hand in making it, we set at naught all that God has done for us in years gone by. This should be a cause for shame and outrage amongst us. There is one the remembrance of whose deeds and character should always be foremost: the Lord God Almighty, maker of heaven and earth. In recovering our past, let us lift his name on high.

---

[94] Kazan was taken in 1553, Astrakhan in 1555, Bokhara in 1868, Khiva in 1873 and Khokand in 1875.

39. Lady of the Lamp

1 John 1:1-7.

Key word: light.

On 7 February 1837 a seventeen-year-old girl had a powerful experience of the presence of God. She put it simply: "God spoke to me and called me to his service." From then on, she was consumed with a longing to nurse, but her family forbade it. Such was her passion that she felt it was "eating out my vital strength." At times, she plunged into depression: "I feel myself perishing when I go to bed," she wrote; "I wish it were my grave." She had to wait seventeen difficult years before the Lord's purpose for her life was revealed.

The Crimean war, which pitted Britain, France and Turkey against imperial Russia, broke out in 1853 and raged for three years. Poorly led and inadequately equipped troops suffered appallingly, above all in the harsh winters. Frostbite and disease took an even heavier toll than Russian bullets. Victories at Alma, Balaclava, Inkerman and Sebastopol could not disguise official incompetence from those at home. This was not merely an issue of battlefield blunders, like that which sent the Light Brigade on its suicidal charge at Balaclava. Supplies were mishandled and casualties had minimal medical attention, until press reports galvanised action: the young girl's time had come.

Florence Nightingale (1820-1910) arrived in the Crimea in 1854, bringing with her a staff of 38 nurses. Relentless in her energy, after a full day's work she would nevertheless insist on touring the wards by night. Hence her nickname: the Lady of the Lamp. From the Barrack Hospital in Scutari (modern Uskudur, near Istanbul) she instituted proper care for the sick and wounded. Within four months, the death rate in British military hospitals was reduced from 42% to 2%.

Her achievement, in organising and motivating her nurses, in badgering and hectoring the authorities and in giving succour to the sick and wounded is monumental. Yet arguably her most important work was done upon her return to England, and that when she was almost incapacitated by illness. From her sickbed, she organised the Nightingale School of Nursing at St Thomas' Hospital in London, which was opened in 1860. She was instrumental in setting up training for midwives and for nurses in workhouse infirmaries, helped establish a drainage and sewage system for India, campaigned for improved conditions for the rank and file of the British Army and wrote a work of religious philosophy, *Suggestions for Thought*. She is widely regarded as the founder of modern nursing.

All this was done by the sheltered daughter of a rich country gentleman, every circumstance of whose early life might have seemed inimical to the role that God marked out for her.

Seeing the light.

We talk of having "seen the light." It is another way of saying that we have heard and understood the message. Like the apostle John, whose relationship with Christ was so close that he describes himself as the "disciple whom Jesus loved" (John 13:23, 19:26, 21:7 and 21:20), Florence Nightingale could say: "this is the message [I] have heard from him" (1 John 1:5). God spoke clearly to her and gave her a mission. It seems that she had no doubts about what she was to do, though she had to wait patiently to learn the timing and manner of fulfilment of God's charge.

Many do not have the experience of God speaking so manifestly into their lives. The way is uncertain, the path dim, the light veiled. We grope and search, sometimes with greater success than others. In his letter to the early church, the apostle John helps us to understand how we can nevertheless "walk in the light" (1 John 1:7) and in consequence allow our own light to shine.

Darkness into light.

John was an eyewitness to the miracles and teaching of Jesus. He talks of "That which was from the beginning, which we have seen with our eyes, which we have looked at and which our hands have touched" (1 John 1:1). Speaking of Jesus as the source of life, he says: "The life appeared; we have seen it and testify to it, and we proclaim to you the eternal life, which was with the Father and has appeared to us. We proclaim to you what we have seen and heard" (1 John 1:2-3).

It is important for us to hold on to the eyewitness testimony of John and others like him. When our own eyes do not see, or glimpse but indistinctly, we need to walk in faith. At such times, our hearts are warmed and our trust is increased by hearing the experiences of those whose word we have reason to consider trustworthy. We do not have to delve into distant societies and far-flung realms to find such testimony. It is all about us in the lives of Christians in our own land, both those living today and those who trod the earth in years past.

To "walk in darkness" or "walk in light" (1 John 1:6-7) has nothing to do with physical conditions. Florence Nightingale trod the gloomy wards and corridors of the Barrack Hospital at Scutari but shone light all about her. The light she carried belongs to Jesus, "the light of the world." (John 8:12), whose Word is "a light to our path and a lamp to our feet." (Psalm 119:105). Through him, we are able to say that "my God turns my darkness into light" (Psalm 18:28).

The words of Scripture and the deeds of believers past and present remind us that there is not a single situation that we cannot transform from darkness to light by the power of God working in us. They remind us that there is not a single circumstance that should hold us captive to the power of darkness. Yet somehow we seem to be forgetting this, or at best giving intellectual assent to it without truly believing it in our hearts. We need to change this attitude of mind, to claim the light for our own and thereby to banish the darkness in our land.

Bathed in light.

The characteristics of light are seen in the sun: brightness, heat and radiation. With light we can see clearly, distinguishing truth from falsehood and rooting out what does not belong. With light the darkness is dispersed, bringing cleanliness and purity where before was filth and rottenness. With light comes heat – warming, comforting and sustaining. Light radiates, transmitting energy. The trilogy of light, heat and radiation is indeed an imperfect analogy for the Trinitarian nature of the one true God.

John is in no doubt: "God is light; in him there is no darkness at all." (1 John 1:5). The consequence is this: "If we claim to have fellowship with him yet walk in the darkness, we lie and do not live by the truth." (1 John 1:6). We need to move ourselves physically and spiritually from the side of darkness to the side of light. We need to bathe in the light rather than wallow in darkness. Doing so will bring closeness to God and closeness to other believers: "But if we walk in the light, as he is in the light, we have fellowship with one another, and the blood of Jesus, his Son, purifies us from all sin." (1 John 1:7).

St Paul has practical advice as to how we can bathe in the light. "Finally, brothers, whatever is true, whatever is noble, whatever is right, whatever is pure, whatever is lovely, whatever is admirable – if anything is excellent or praiseworthy – think about such things. Whatever you have learned or received or heard from me – put it into practice." (Philippians 4:8-9).

Shining a light.

As we bathe in the light, we will experience blessing. We will experience "fellowship with [other believers]... fellowship ... with the Father and with his Son, Jesus Christ [and] ... our joy [will be] complete." (1 John 1:3-4). The more we bathe in the light, the more the light in us will increase. We will begin to shine. Moses shone so greatly with the reflected light of God that his face had to be covered, for men could not bear to look at it: "When Aaron and all the Israelites saw Moses, his face was radiant, and they were afraid to come near him." (Exodus 34:30). We may not be able to achieve that degree of holiness and closeness to God – Moses was, after all a man to whom God spoke "face to face, as a man speaks to a friend" (Exodus 33:11) – but we can still shine.

Florence Nightingale shone and thereby discharged the trust that the Lord placed upon her. Her life demonstrates that shining to the fullest possible extent cannot rest solely on our receiving from God without also passing on what we have received. One of the essential truths of the kingdom of God is that we must give away what is given to us: "Freely you have received, freely give." (Matthew 10:8). It is by enriching others that we are most fully enriched ourselves. It is by giving our gifts away that we multiply them for the benefit of others and also ensure that they redound to our benefit: "Cast your bread upon the waters, for after many days you will find it again." (Ecclesiastes 11:1). Our aim must be to turn our personal blessing into a corporate blessing, one that benefits our nation and our fellow men. This requires preparation, obedience and action.

In terms of preparation:

Priming our lamps. A light needs fuel to shine. We are fuelled and fed spiritually by God. Our light will soon dim unless we have "fellowship ... with the Father and with his Son, Jesus Christ" (1 John 1:3).

Keeping our lamps ready. We are told to: "Be dressed ready for service and keep [our] lamps burning." (Luke 12:35).

In terms of obedience:

Using our lamps for their intended purpose. We need to obey the instructions that God gives us: "For this is what the Lord has commanded us: I have made you a light for the Gentiles, that you may bring salvation to the ends of the earth." (Acts 13:47).

In terms of action:

Uncovering our lamps. A light that is "put under a bowl" (Matthew 5:15) will not illuminate anything. This is what we have done in England by treating faith as a private matter, but not for the public arena. The result is that we have been silent when we should have spoken out and our light has been invisible.

Conclusion.

Florence Nightingale's reputation has been under attack virtually from the moment she set foot back in England at the Crimean War's end. The British authorities had made a disastrous mistake in accepting Turkey's offer of the old barracks at Scutari for a hospital. There were no facilities there for landing the sick and wounded who arrived by sea, so men had to be brought ashore in rowing boats and then carried up the steep slopes to the hospital on stretchers. The building itself had no proper water supply or drainage system. Such toilet facilities as there were, wholly inadequate for the numbers concerned and quite without means of flushing or cleansing, stood right alongside the main water storage tank. The supply to this tank was eventually found to be flowing through the rotting carcass of a horse.

Little wonder that a wounded man stood a better chance of recovery by being tended near the front than by being brought to Scutari. The Barrack Hospital became a charnel house packed with men too numerous to receive any effective help. For every one who died of his wounds, three died from the conditions in the hospital itself. When the full extent of the horror became known, her complicity in such suffering almost destroyed Florence Nightingale, but it does not negate her achievements. Rather, these very circumstances magnify the impact of her work and make yet nobler her sheer tenacity in the face of official bumbling and bloody-mindedness.

In 1869 she chided a disaffected colleague: "Do you think I should have succeeded in doing anything if I had kicked and resisted and resented? Is it our Master's command? Is it even common sense? I have been shut out of hospitals into which I had been ordered to go by the Commander-in-Chief – obliged to stand outside the door in the snow till night – have been refused rations for as much as ten days at a time for the nurses I had brought by superior command. And I have been as good friends the day after with the officials who did these things – have resolutely ignored these things *for the sake of the work* ... Who am I that should not choose to bear what my Master chooses to bear?"[95]

Florence Nightingale shone a light in the darkness of the Crimean War. The lamp she carried burned so bright because she herself had seen the light, because she walked in the light and was herself bathed in the light. We all have light to shine. Jesus tells us that we "are the light of the world" (Matthew 5:14), that this light is designed to be used so that it "gives light to everyone in the house" (Matthew 5:15) and that we should "let [our] light shine before men, that they may see [our] good deeds and praise [our] Father in heaven." (Matthew 5:16). We do not have to tend wounded on a battlefield to obey this command. There are casualties and suffering aplenty on our doorstep.

Like the apostle John, we need to "proclaim" (1 John 1:2 and 3), "declare" (1 John 1:5) and "testify" (1 John 1:2) concerning the light. We can do so by words and deeds. The prophet Isaiah put it thus: "Arise, shine, for your light has come, and the glory of the Lord rises upon you." (Isaiah 60:1). Now is the time for us to shine.

---

[95] Despite such forbearance, Florence Nightingale was not above acerbic comment. On hearing that Dr John Hall, the incompetent British Chief of Medical Staff in the Crimea had been awarded the KCB, she remarked: "Knight of the Crimean Burial Grounds, I suppose?"

40. Soldiers of the Queen

2 Corinthians 4.

Key word: treasure.

Around ten past one on 22 January 1879 an eclipse of the sun spread gloom over the southern skies of the Dark Continent. At that very moment British soldiers lay fighting and dying amidst rock and scrub in the foothills of the Drakensberg mountains, which form part of present-day South Africa. Just across the Mangeni River at Isandhlwana, a Zulu impi (army) of 20,000 had surprised one of the outlying units of Lord Chelmsford's command. This column, along with four others, had been sent to secure the northern border of British domains and force the Zulu King Cetewayo kaMapande into submission. The British thereby planned to subdue a proud warrior nation which threatened its territory, had already overrun many tribes in the region and had fought bitterly in bygone years with Boer settlers.

Instead, the redcoats were caught in the open, their camp unfortified. Outnumbered more than twenty to one, the soldiers of Queen Victoria fought and died with characteristic bravery. Little drummer boys of ten or twelve years old stood at their post as the enemy came in wave after wave towards them. Volleys were delivered with customary calm and discipline, to such good effect that at first the Zulus drew back, until a grizzled veteran urged them on again. Under the renewed assault bullets began to run short, for ammunition boxes could not be unscrewed fast enough. The 800 or so British and 500 native troops were overrun and slaughtered almost to a man. It was one of the British Empire's most ignominious defeats.

The blow to Imperial pride and prestige was enormous. In a fever of patriotic excitement, an expeditionary force was immediately raised to teach the Zulus a lesson. It was scarcely needed. Cetewayo's commanders were unable to capitalise on small successes at Ntombe Drift and Hlobane, whilst at Rorke's Drift a British garrison of just 140 was able to hold off repeated attacks by a force more than twenty times their size for the loss of just seventeen men.[96] A thousand and more Zulus lost their lives in that engagement and their warriors' morale was broken by further bloody defeats at Gingindlovu, Kambula and Nyezane. The one-sided conflict was over less than six months after it started: on

---

[96] Chelmsford's blushes over Isandhlwana were at least partially spared by the fact that eleven Victoria Crosses were bestowed on those who had fought at Rorke's Drift, the highest number ever awarded for a single engagement.

4 July 1879 British forces took the Zulu capital of Ulundi following a half-hearted defence, deposed Cetewayo and split the Zulu kingdom into thirteen independent chiefdoms. Civil war ensued and, although Cetewayo was restored to part of his kingdom after a visit to London in 1882, he was subsequently driven from his realm and died a fugitive on British soil on 8 February 1884. The Zulu lands were annexed to South Africa three years later.

Jars of clay.

Although so inferior to the British in technology, the Zulus were doughty warriors. King Chaka, who preceded Cetewayo's father King Mpande on the throne and who unified the Zulu clans into a powerful military force, is said to have made his warriors discard their shoes and dance barefoot on thorns to toughen their feet and increase their mobility. Such men recognised and honoured bravery in their opponents. Their folk history retains eyewitness accounts of the battle at Isandhlwana. These tell that, as the fighting drew to a close, Captain Younghusband and a few comrades were all that remained of the British force. Their ammunition spent, they shook hand, fixed bayonets and charged to certain death amidst the massed ranks of the enemy, yelling defiance. Right to the last, they did not lose heart. One of their opponents said: "We really respected those men. They were men of enormous courage." Another recalled: "Those red soldiers, how few they were, and how they fought! They fell like stones, each man in his place."

The words of St Paul to the Christians in Corinth might almost have been written for these British soldiers: "We are hard pressed on every side, but not crushed; perplexed, but not in despair; persecuted, but not abandoned; struck down, but not destroyed." (2 Corinthians 4:8-9). He continues: "Therefore we do not lose heart. Though outwardly we are wasting away, yet inwardly we are being renewed day by day. For our light and momentary troubles are achieving for us an eternal glory that far outweighs them all." (2 Corinthians 4:16-17).

The picture that St Paul paints is of people brought almost to the last gasp. It is a study in the contrasts and paradoxes that inform the Christian life:

"We are hard pressed on every side, but not crushed" (2 Corinthians 4:8). So often, the forces ranged against us seem overwhelming and our resources pitifully inadequate. It is at precisely such times, when we have come to the end of what we can do on our own and are forced to rely utterly on God, that we see his power most clearly.

"We are ... perplexed but not in despair" (2 Corinthians 4:8). Often we are puzzled by what is happening, bewildered, anxious, embarrassed, confused and unable to understand. None of this should be a cause for despair. The antidote is to look beyond immediate circumstances and keep our eyes fixed on the eternal.

"We are ... persecuted but not abandoned" (2 Corinthians 4:9). The fact that, for a limited period, God allows persecution does not mean that he desires our suffering, still less that he abandons his people. There is no-one who knows more about hardship than Jesus, who took all the pain and wrongdoing of mankind on himself when he died on the cross. We can thus be assured that God is alongside us throughout our trials and suffers with us.

"We are ... struck down, but not destroyed." (2 Corinthians 4:9). Through trials we grow and gain in spiritual strength: "we also rejoice in our sufferings, because we know that suffering produces perseverance; perseverance, character; and character, hope." (Romans 5:3). Through persecution the church expands and renews its vigour, for "unless a grain of what falls to the ground and dies, it remains only a single seed. But if it dies, it produces many seeds." (John 12:24). This is not to belittle the appalling things through which many live. It is merely to recognise God's ability to bring good results even from what is bad.

"Though outwardly we are wasting away, yet inwardly we are being renewed day by day." (2 Corinthians 4:16). Our bodies are "jars of clay" (2 Corinthians 4:7) – weak, subject to failure and ageing, prey to disease and corruption. Yet whatever might happen to this outer shell, when we open ourselves to the work of the Holy Spirit in our lives we are "transformed by the renewing of [our] mind." (Romans 12:2).

Despite everything, St Paul is therefore able to affirm that "our light and momentary troubles are achieving for us an eternal glory that far outweighs them all." (2 Corinthians 4:17).

All-surpassing power.

The key to the apostle's ability to do this is his access to the treasure that consists in "God's light [shining] in our hearts to give us the light of the knowledge of the glory of God in the face of Christ." (2 Corinthians 4:6). Jesus tells us that not just that "The kingdom of God is near" (Luke 10:9) but that "the kingdom of God is within [us]." (Luke 17:21). St Paul elaborates: "But we have this treasure in jars of clay [the human body] to show that this all-surpassing power is from God and not from us." (2 Corinthians 4:7). Moreover, "We always carry around in our body the death of Jesus, so that the life of Jesus may also be revealed in our body. For we who are alive are always being given over to death for Jesus' sake, so that his life may be revealed in our mortal body. So then, death is at work in us, but life is at work in you." (2 Corinthians 4:10-12). In other words, human weakness is the backdrop against which the power of God can be seen in stark relief. The very fact that man cannot measure up to divine standards or gain salvation on his own emphasises the glory, mercy and love of God in all its fullness. The inevitability of our physical death shows beyond a shadow of a doubt that eternal life is from the Almighty.

When the Lord told St Paul that "My grace is sufficient for you, for my power is made perfect in weakness" (2 Corinthians 12:9), the apostle's reaction was to say: "Therefore I will boast all the more gladly about my weaknesses, so that Christ's power may rest on me. That is why, for Christ's sake, I delight in weaknesses, in insults, in hardships, in persecutions, in difficulties. For when I am weak, then I am strong." (2 Corinthians 12:9-10).

The men who fought so gallantly at Isandhlwana won glory and high renown, albeit a glory far below the heavenly glory that St Paul had in mind. Whilst such glory will be brought to final perfection in heaven, it is nevertheless present with us in some degree during our time on earth: "For God, who said, 'Let light shine out of darkness,' made his light shine in our hearts to give us the knowledge of the glory of God in the face of Christ." (2 Corinthians 4:6). We have God's light in us and this reflection of his glory gives us "the knowledge of the glory of God in the face of Christ." (2 Corinthians 4:6).

The confidence that St Paul expresses is thus based not on the passing events of our lives on earth, but on the firm expectation of what is to come: "It is written: 'I believed; therefore I have spoken.' With that same spirit of faith we also believe and therefore speak, because we know that the one who raised the Lord Jesus from the dead will also raise us with Jesus and present us with you in his presence. All this is for your benefit, so that the grace that is reaching more and more people may cause thanksgiving to overflow to the glory of God." (2 Corinthians 4:13-15).

Good conscience.

In pronouncing this message, St Paul makes an appeal to openness and good conscience: "Rather, we have renounced secret and shameful ways; we do not use deception, nor do we distort the word of God. On the contrary, by setting forth the truth plainly we commend ourselves to every man's conscience in the sight of God."(2 Corinthians 4:2). By saying that he "renounced secret and shameful ways", St Paul draws a contrast between himself and the false teachers in Corinth. Unlike them, the apostle says "we do not preach ourselves, but Jesus Christ as Lord and ourselves as your servants for Jesus' sake." (2 Corinthians 4:5). Indeed, wherever we find what is secret, shameful, deceptive or distorting and whenever we come across someone who tries to lord it over others, false teaching is unlikely to be far behind. St Paul instead presents himself as a servant, priding himself on being straightforward and honest in the way that he lays out the treasure of "the light of the knowledge of the glory of God in the face of

Christ." (2 Corinthians 4:6). This approach is what commends itself "to every man's conscience" (2 Corinthians 4:2).

All human beings have an experience at some point of suffering a guilty conscience. The anguish that this can cause makes us treasure peace of mind all the more, but keeping our conscience clear is not always easy. It often involves forgoing things that we would like and even acting against our self-interest. In extreme cases, it might even cost us our lives. Some decades before Isandhlwana, the troopship *Birkenhead* was sent with reinforcements for an earlier war against southern African tribes. On 25 February 1852, not far from her destination, she struck a rock off the southernmost tip of Africa at Cape Agulhas. As the vessel sank, 500 soldiers paraded on deck in perfect order, allowing women and children to be evacuated first. Not a man broke rank. This order of priority is still known as the Birkenhead Drill. Most of the troops drowned, but they did so with a clear conscience, for they had not purchased their lives at the expense of those weaker than they. We need to recover some of the discipline and sense of duty that these men showed. It will help us do so if we "fix our eyes not on what is seen, but on what is unseen. For what is seen is temporary, but what is unseen is eternal." (2 Corinthians 4:18).

Of course, there are some to whom an appeal to good conscience means nothing. Such people will be blind to all calls to duty and incapable of submitting to any discipline that stops them doing precisely as they want. They will be unable and unwilling to understand their need for forgiveness, still less to comprehend and take advantage of the free offer of salvation that Jesus made possible: "And even if our gospel is veiled, it is veiled to those who are perishing. The god of this age has blinded the minds of unbelievers, so that they cannot see the light of the gospel of the glory of Christ, who is the image of God." (2 Corinthians 4:3-4). This is a tragedy, but there is no sense in denying it.

Conclusion.

The soldiers of Queen Victoria were not angels. They were the same mixture of vice and virtue that human beings have ever been. Their campaigns are not always ones that present-day sensibilities find easy to endorse, but it is difficult not to be struck with admiration at what they did. Even allowing for differences in weaponry, the odds that they faced were often stupendous. They showed cool heads and steady nerves. These are qualities that we would do well to emulate, so that "since through God's mercy we have this ministry, we do not lose heart." (2 Corinthians 4:1).

Above all, we should not lose sight of what we aim at, and why it is so precious that we should strain every nerve both to attain it ourselves and to make it an object of striving on the part of our nation. For: "The kingdom of heaven is like treasure hidden in a field. When a man found it, he hid it again, and then in his joy went and sold all he had and bought that field." (Matthew 13:44). To display the beauty and value of this treasure, we need to "[set] forth the truth plainly [and thereby] commend ourselves to every man's conscience" (2 Corinthians 4:2).

41. Grand Old Man

2 John 1.

Key word: obedience.

In 1903 Boer War veteran Erskine Childers wrote the novel *Riddle of the Sands*. It is an adventure yarn with a purpose: to warn about the danger of invasion by Germany. Eleven years later he was gun running for Irish Republicans, a traitor to the very nation about whose defence he had earlier been so concerned. The same trajectory was followed by Sir Roger Casement: though knighted in 1911 for work on behalf of the Crown, by November 1914 he was in Berlin urging Irish prisoners of war to form a brigade to serve against the Allies. Two years later he was caught at Tralee smuggling German weapons and hanged for treason.[97] These two Irishmen are tribute to Britain's extraordinary capacity for taking men of goodwill from that island and turning them into implacable enemies.

For centuries Ireland was a festering sore in the British body politic, a constant reminder of the contradiction at the heart of Empire: that a nation with freedom and representative government as its lodestone denied those very things to its nearest neighbour and supposed partner.

English policy towards Ireland was rarely as deliberately malicious as legend paints it, but it might just as well have been for all the difference it made to those on the receiving end. Negligence, absentee landlords, doctrinaire application of laissez faire economics and visceral anti-Catholicism did tremendous damage. Yet even after the appalling potato famine of 1846-47, it was by no means a foregone conclusion that Ireland would sever completely from Britain. The Easter Rising of 1916 remains a powerful symbol of Irish nationalism, but it was the work of a small minority. Dubliners at first jeered the captured Irish Volunteers who were marched through the streets after the battle, seeing them as traitors, for large numbers of Irishmen were at that moment fighting and dying on the Western Front in British uniform. It took a heavy-handed and inept government response to harden public opinion. Even then, it is doubtful that a majority of Irishmen from the start actively sided with the rebels during the fight for independence that broke out in 1919. Only the ruthless

---

[97] Erskine Childers was Secretary to the Irish delegation in the Treaty negotiations of 1921 that led to creation of the Irish Free State. He was executed by firing squad (by Irishmen, not the British) after siding with extreme Republicans in the Irish Civil War of 1921-23.

genius of Michael Collins and the brutality of the Black and Tans so utterly transformed the political landscape that independence became the only course acceptable to the mass of Irishmen.

Ireland's is a story of what might have been had William Ewart Gladstone, four times Prime Minister and twice Chancellor of the Exchequer, succeeded in his efforts to bring in Home Rule during the closing years of the nineteenth century.

Most tend to become more conservative and less radical with the passing years. Gladstone was exactly the opposite. At the start of his political career he was described by Macaulay as "the rising hope of those stern and unbending Tories." By its end he was leader of the Liberal Party, had been responsible for disestablishment of the Church of Ireland, the passing of two Irish Land Acts[98] and had twice extended the franchise through the Reform Acts of 1884 and 1885. Home Rule Bills were presented in 1886 and 1893. Each failed, though hardly for want of trying on the part of the Grand Old Man, eighty-four when the last of these attempts was made, yet still possessed of extraordinary energy. His endeavours fatally split the Liberal Party, but he would doubtless have considered this a price worth paying. With the benefit of hindsight, we know now what misery resulted from his inability to carry Parliament and the country with him.

Practicing the truth.

Gladstone was a lifelong Christian. He attended church every day of his adult life, sometimes more than once a day. It was obedience to the Christian message that forced him inexorably towards recognising the common humanity of all peoples, and the need for justice towards them whatever his own religious or political preferences might be. This growing conviction found typically eloquent expression during his Midlothian election campaign of 1879-80. In words that still have relevance for today's Britain, on one occasion he told his audience: "Remember that the sanctity of life in the hill villages of Afghanistan is as inviolable in the eye of Almighty God as can be your own. Remember that He who has united you as human beings in the same flesh and blood has bound you by the law of mutual love; that that mutual love is not limited by the shores of this island, is not limited by the boundaries of Christian civilisation, that it passes over the whole surface of the earth and embraces the meanest along with the greatest in its unmeasured scope."

The apostle John talks a great deal, both in his gospel and in his letters, about love. His second letter, addressed "To the chosen lady and her children,

---

[98] The Land Acts enacted fair rents, fixed tenure and freedom of sale.

whom I love in the truth" (2 John 1:1) returns to this theme: "And now, dear lady, I am not writing you a new command but one we had from the beginning. I ask that we love one another." (2 John 1:5). The command to which he refers is taken from Jesus' last discourse with his disciples, when he told them: "A new command I give you: Love one another." (John 13:34). To emphasise the central importance of this message, Jesus repeated similar words a short while later: "This is my command: Love each other." (John 15:17).

John explains what this command involves: "And this is love; that we walk in obedience to his commands. As you have heard from the beginning, his command is that you walk in love." (2 John 1:6). Again, the apostle's words echo those of his Lord: "If you obey my commands, you will remain in my love, just as I have obeyed my Father's commands and remain in his love ... You are my friends if you do what I command." (John 15:10 and 14). Christian love, in other words, requires action. It is not merely or even necessarily a question of warm feelings, but instead is founded on obedience to the teaching of Jesus, with this obedience being put into practice in our daily lives.

Love is intimately bound up with truth. Indeed, taken together these are the measure of the extent and genuineness of Christian faith. The consequence of experiencing and acting out Christian love will inevitably be that we practice the truth and that the truth will be in us. This is more than solely a matter of telling the truth. It goes beyond being unwilling to tolerate any kind of falsehood, deception, concealment or equivocation. It involves taking on a character that is increasingly like that of Christ and thus of God himself. John's second letter helps to show how this can be so and what it means.

Truth and love.

John makes what at first sight might seem a rather unexpected connection between truth on the one hand and love on the other. He describes "the chosen lady and her children" (2 John 1:1) as people "whom I love in the truth ... because of the truth, which lives in us and will be with us for ever." (2 John 1:1-2). This is a highly unusual way for one person to express regard for another, however great that regard might be, and indeed John is doing more than just expressing regard. There are three separate but related elements to what he says:

Loving "in the truth" (2 John 1:1).

Loving "because of the truth" (2 John 1:2).

Having truth "[living] in us and [being] with us for ever." (2 John 1:2).

At first blush, these statements might seem nonsensical or even meaningless. To understand what John is driving at, we need to remind ourselves of the inseparable nature of ultimate truth and Christian love. Jesus – both fully man and fully God – says that he is "the way and the truth and the life" (John 14:6) and John tells us that "God is love" (1 John 4:8). Both truth and love, in other words, are part of who God is. They are aspects of his character, but they are also more than that, for God is the embodiment of each in its greatest fullness and perfection. So, too, is he the yardstick by which each is to be measured. If we want to know what perfect truth and love are, in other words, we look to God (which is to say, to Jesus, who is his earthly representation) for the answer.

Truth is thus portrayed as the source and fount of love, as well as its inevitable outgrowth. The truth and love of which John speaks both belong to and are essential characteristics of a person, within whom truth and love are forever linked. Hence: "Grace, mercy and peace from God the Father and from Jesus Christ, the Father's Son, will be with us in truth and love." (2 John 1:3).

John Keats wrote that "Beauty is truth, truth beauty – that is all ye know on earth and all ye need to know." The Christian might perhaps counter that love is truth and truth is love.

Protecting the truth.

Human beings have a tendency to put difficulties and obstacles in the way of truth. We are fond of painting the world many shades of grey rather than acknowledging that there might be such a thing as straightforward right and wrong. Pontius Pilate asked Jesus: "What is truth?" (John 18:38) and our present age pretends that there are many competing truths, all of which are somehow capable of existing at the same time and being equally 'valid' even when they are contradictory. Such nonsense puts to shame the many fine minds that spout it.

It need not be so. Even children can learn to walk in the truth: "It has given me great joy to find some of your children walking in the truth, just as the Father commanded us." (2 John 1:4). Attaining truth, however, requires humility and obedience. We have to recognise that truth is not something that we can make up for ourselves or bend to fit the demands of circumstances, but that it derives from a standard set by Almighty God.

The ease with which truth can be avoided, distorted and mishandled requires vigilance on our part: "Watch out that you do not lose what you have worked for, but that you may be rewarded fully." (2 John 1:8). It also requires recognition that those who manipulate or trample God's truth thereby act in opposition to the Lord: "Many deceivers, who do not acknowledge Jesus Christ as coming in the flesh, have gone out into the world. Any such person is the deceiver and the antichrist." (2 John 1:7). Our need to be alert is emphasised by the fact that truth is something which can slip from our grasp: "Anyone who runs ahead and does not continue in the teaching of Christ does not have God; whoever continues in the teaching has both the Father and the Son." (2 John 1:9).

Truth is less difficult and problematic than we like to make it, but in human hands it is fragile and needs to be protected. We are reminded to exercise discernment in whom we learn from and to whom we lend our aid: "If anyone comes to you and does not bring this teaching, do not take him into your house or welcome him. Anyone who welcomes him shares in his wicked work." (2 John 1:10-11). As in all things, there is a need for balance: between warning and encouragement, belief and behaviour, doctrinal accuracy and discerning love.

Conclusion.

If we are to be obedient to God's laws and faithful to his commands, truth and love must go hand in hand. We are fooling ourselves if we imagine that we can have one without the other. Of course, every generation has its blind spot. Our Victorian forebears perhaps emphasised hellfire and damnation at the expense of the love of God. We are apt to do the reverse. We need to strive for the most complete understanding that we can achieve, but to recognise at the same time that God is more interested in what is in our hearts than in any doctrinal nuance. The best evidence of what is in our hearts and of the genuineness of our faith consists in our obedience to the commands that God has given us.

Discerning the will of God in our lives and for our nation is rarely completely straightforward, but in its broad outline at least it is a great deal simpler than we often imagine. We do not need direct communication from the Almighty to know that obedience to his commands involves kindness and generosity to others – that is a logical result of Jesus telling us to "do to others as you would have them do to you." (Luke 6:31). Neither do we need much reflection to realise that the injunction not to steal (Exodus 20:15) encompasses all kinds of unlawful taking from others, whether it be skimping on work, overcharging, taking unwarranted sick leave, fiddling a tax return, submitting inflated expenses claims or what have you.

The result is that we have no excuse for disobedience. Of course, there are many aspects of present-day life that throw up complexities we do not find easy to disentangle and there may be particular fields of endeavour in which God wishes us to be involved that we can only know about through his speaking to us directly. When once we set off down the road of obedience, however, there is a tendency over the course of time for such things to be revealed to us. The fact that we may not have the full answer at the outset is no reason to delay putting into practice what we do know. So it was in the life of Gladstone. Only as time wore on did the full implications of applying Christian principles in policy towards Ireland dawn upon him.

The life of the Gladstone family echoes the ups and downs of England's course over the eighteenth and nineteenth centuries. Gladstone's father, a Scottish immigrant to Liverpool, made money from the slave trade, in direct contravention of and disobedience to God's laws. The son did his best to make amends. Our nation has done wrong in the sight of God. Now is the time for us to make amends. We will do so by showing obedience to the commands of our Lord.

42. Besieged

1 Chronicles 29:14-20.

Key word: integrity.

Charles George Gordon (1833-85)[99] fought for his country in the Crimean War, and thereafter was employed by the Chinese government during the Taiping rebellion. From 1877 to 1880 he was Governor-General of the Sudan on behalf of the Khedive of Egypt. Already noted for his reckless courage against the Russians, in China he went into hand-to-hand combat at the head of his troops armed only with a rattan cane. Such exploits earned him the nickname 'Chinese' Gordon. Although he was hardly a youngster when he first came to the Sudan and had never ridden a camel before, within weeks he was delighting in outpacing his escort and arriving long before them in the remote and often hostile outposts that it was his remit to visit. He was by any measure an extraordinary man.

Gordon was a devout Christian. His was a practical faith. During one of his rare tours of duty in England he began taking in foundlings, feeding and clothing them at his own expense and incurring considerable strain to his finances. These informal acts of charity grew in due course into the Gordon Homes for young people.

In 1884 Gordon entered service with the Egyptian government for a second time and returned to Khartoum with instructions to evacuate all Egyptian forces in the Sudan. It was a job no-one else wanted. The country was in the throes of rebellion as a result of an uprising led by Muhammad Ahmad, who claimed to be the Mahdi, the long-awaited 'Rightly Guided One' of Islam.[100] As Ahmad's army closed slowly around Khartoum, Gordon ignored every opportunity to escape and made no real attempt to follow his orders. Despite a considerable disparity in numbers and the poor quality of the Egyptian soldiers under his command, he instead invited a showdown, scorning all idea of surrender or flight. Almost to the last he seems to have hoped that a British column would come to his aid, although Her Majesty's government had made clear its wish to avoid further entanglement in either Egypt or Sudan.

---

[99] Gordon was of Scots descent, but born and brought up in England.

[100] The coming of the Mahdi was first preached in the tenth century. Several have since claimed to be the Rightly Guided One. He is still awaited today.

In the event, public outcry at home ensured that a relief force was finally sent (much against the wishes of Gladstone and his cabinet), but it arrived too late.[101] On 26 January 1885, after holding out for nearly twelve months, Khartoum's walls were breached and its defenders overwhelmed. The victorious dervishes swarmed to the Governor-General's palace from which Gordon emerged alone, clad in white, and faced his attackers calmly. Although he carried a revolver and wore a sword at his belt, he made no attempt to defend himself as spears and swords lacerated his body. The head was cut from the corpse and taken to Ahmad.

After taking Khartoum, Ahmad set up an Islamic state with its capital at Omdurman. His reign lasted only about six months, for he died in 1885, not long after Gordon. Retribution for the latter's death came thirteen years later. On 2 September 1898, witnessed by the young Winston Churchill, a British punitive expedition pulverised the forces of Ahmad's successors in a battle just outside Omdurman. Some 52,000 dervishes were cut to pieces by 20,000 men under Kitchener. Forty-eight British soldiers were killed, together with about four hundred of their Egyptian and Sudanese auxiliaries. The enemy dead, described by Churchill as littering the battlefield like "dirty bits of newspaper" numbered well over 10,000, with many more dying later from their wounds. Ahmad's Islamic Caliphate collapsed, to be replaced by Anglo-Egyptian rule.

Cast out.

Charles Gordon ploughed a lonely furrow. He was not a clubbable man, nor was he easy company. He hated dinner parties and fled attempts to fete him when he became famous. He was more comfortable in lonely overseas postings than in England. Disdainful of all material rewards, he was utterly incorruptible. Single-minded and brave to the point of foolhardiness, he was at the same time cussed and unpredictable. Through the many contradictions of his personality, the constant trait was integrity. Integrity involves probity, rectitude and high principle. Gordon had these qualities in spades. One of the first things he did on being appointed governor of the Sudan was to suggest a reduction in his salary. On arrival in Khartoum, he made strenuous and repeated (but in the event unsuccessful) attempts to stamp out the extensive regional slave trade, though all advisers urged that the task was impossible and it transpired that high officials were heavily implicated in it. Gordon could with justice have said: "I know, my God, that you test the heart and are pleased with integrity." (1 Chronicles 29:17).

---

[101] As a result the Grand Old Man (GOM) became known instead as Gordon's Only Murderer.

In many ways, Gordon was an outsider, an outcast from society by reason of his own character and sensibilities. There is a sense in which every Christian must also be an outsider and an outcast. The Bible consistently talks about the people of God as being strangers in a sinful world, sojourners or temporary residents whose real country and allegiance lie elsewhere: "I am a stranger on earth; do not hide your commands from me" (Psalm 119:19). Jesus said of his disciples: "you do not belong to the world" (John 15:19) and "[you] are not of the world any more than I am of the world." (John 17:14). The contrast with the ungodly could not be greater: "Their mind is on earthly things. But our citizenship is in heaven." (Philippians 3:19-20).

King David acknowledged that human sin and weakness might be said to make us outcasts in the sight of God: "We are aliens and strangers in your sight, as were all our forefathers. Our days on earth are like a shadow, without hope." (1 Chronicles 29:15). All the more remarkable, then, that the death of Jesus on the cross enables us to be treated as righteous in God's sight so that we can come before him with confidence and be adopted into his family. Through the resurrection, the shadow and the hopelessness that David saw are transformed into the light of God's presence and the firm assurance of life everlasting. We are no longer cast out from God, although we remain outcasts in a sinful world.

To be an outcast is not easy. It often involves giving up the pleasurable sensation of being approved by others and being part of the crowd. It involves living in the world but being neither swayed, compromised nor consumed by it. The key to this is integrity. If we are to keep our integrity, we must steer clear of the world's entanglements. Hence the apostle Peter counsels his readers to reject the things of the world: "I urge you, as aliens and strangers in the world, to abstain from sinful desires, which war against your soul." (1 Peter 2:11). However, this is no excuse for failing to engage with the world. We must obey the command to "go and make disciples of all nations" (Matthew 28:19) and we must "Remember that [we] were slaves in Egypt." (Deuteronomy 5:15). That is to say, we should never lose sight of the fact that once we were dead in our sins and that millions upon millions need the saving light of Jesus Christ in their lives. There are practical steps that it is our duty to undertake, too, so as to alleviate the suffering that comes through living in a broken world. St Paul reminds us, for example, that "We should continue to remember the poor." (Galatians 2:10).

Cast off.

Integrity is central to striking the balance between engaging with the world and at the same time distancing ourselves from it. Integrity requires that we cast off the things that belong to our former lives and clothe ourselves with the garments that God wishes us to wear. The former will include those "acts of the sinful nature" that St Paul lists in Galatians 5:19-21 and the latter will include "the fruit of the Spirit" that he describes in Galatians 5:22-23. As he goes on to say, "Those who belong to Christ Jesus have crucified the sinful nature with its passions and desires. Since we live by the Spirit, let us keep in step with the Spirit." (Galatians 5:24-25).

To act with integrity requires that we give generously, not only with material things but with the greatest gift that is ours to bestow: ourselves. Generous giving should be motivated, stimulated and characterised by:

A correct appreciation that the source of what we have is God: "But who am I, and who are my people, that we should be able to give as generously as this? Everything comes from you, and we have given you only what comes from your hand." (1 Chronicles 29:14).

A recognition that, as a result, all that we possess is for God to use and dispose of as he wishes: "O LORD our God, as for all this abundance that we have provided for building a temple for your Holy Name, it comes from your hand, and all of it belongs to you." (1 Chronicles 29:16).

A consequent readiness to place ourselves at God's command without quibble or reserve: "All these things I have given willingly and with honest intent." (1 Chronicles 29:17).

An expectation that others can and should be similarly motivated: "And now I have seen how willingly your people who are here have given to you." (1 Chronicles 29:17).

A level of giving that is at one and the same time unstinting yet realistic, and which does not hold back for selfish motives: "Each man should give what he has decided in his heart to give, not reluctantly or under compulsion, for God loves a cheerful giver." (2 Corinthians 9:7).

In all that he did, Gordon gave wholeheartedly of himself. With hindsight, we may disagree with his methods and perhaps even with his opinions, but there can be no questioning his commitment. Whether he was leading from the front in time of war, seeking freedom for the slaves of the Sudan, confronting what he regarded as the malign pretensions of Muhammad Ahmed or bringing help and opportunity to underprivileged youngsters at home he was unsparing of himself and disdainful of personal reward or safety.

Cast aside.

Integrity necessarily involves loyalty: to truth, justice and other high ideals, and above all to God. King David prays: "O LORD, God of our fathers Abraham, Isaac and Israel, keep this desire [to give willingly] in the hearts of your people for ever, and keep their hearts loyal to you." (1 Chronicles 29:18). Sadly we live in a land where loyalty is a coinage that seems much debased. We too readily cast aside things of real value in favour of worthless baubles. We fail to keep alive the remembrance of what God has done, we fail to acknowledge our dependence on him and we fail to do what he asks of us. We treat those who act with integrity as though they are simply too foolish to look to their own self-interest.

The irony is that, by casting aside God, it is we who end up being cast aside. When God is rejected, we are set adrift from the moorings of his laws and his plan for our lives. Harsh winds drive us from the safe haven of his love into a world that is brutal and uncaring. We lose the secure anchorage of being part of his family and can no longer find the way to the place of our salvation. Loyalty and integrity are not just desirable, therefore. They are essential.

If we are to live with integrity towards God and our fellow men, our faith cannot be something that is practised alone or kept to ourselves. Our duty to engage with the world and to act with integrity brings with it obligations not just to those on earth today, but also to succeeding generations. King David was conscious of this when he prayed: "And give my son Solomon the wholehearted devotion to keep your commands, requirements and decrees and to do everything to build the palatial structure for which I have provided." (1 Chronicles 29:19). It would be the height of cruelty to cast our children and our children's children adrift into the world without giving them guidance for the journey ahead. Yet that is precisely what we are doing at present. In pursuit of what we call fairness and equality we are sending them out like "lamb[s] to the slaughter" (Isaiah 53:7). That is not integrity. It is its opposite.

Conclusion.

It is easy to mock the Victorians for their manifest faults and their blindness to unconscious motivation. Many of those who were used by God then and beforehand were not easy characters, nor were they necessarily even nice people. Charles Gordon and Florence Nightingale were unlikely to have been soothing company. In an earlier era, Robert Clive was a depressive, James Wolfe and Horatio Nelson sickly. Yet that is precisely the point. Flawed characters and weak bodies were enabled to do great things because God worked through them. Thus were they able to outface the opposition that often threatened to overwhelm them. They had something that by and large we lack. They did their best to do the right thing. Although they fell short of perfection, as any human being must, still in the effort they reached higher than we even begin to attempt. At the deepest level, they possessed integrity of a kind that we no longer seem to value.

General Gordon was besieged in Khartoum for nigh on a year. We act as though we were besieged and escape impossible. This just is not so. Once we start to practice integrity on a national level we will see falsehoods of this kind for what they are and break free of them. We should thus do all in our power to hasten the day when God can "test the heart and [be pleased with our] integrity." (1 Chronicles 29:17).

43. Hubris

Obadiah 1-21.

Key word: pride.

The *SS Titanic* was the pride of the White Star Line. She was one of the largest ships of her time, a passenger liner specially built for the transatlantic route, of a construction that was unique in its day. Her double-bottomed hull and series of sixteen watertight compartments, four of which could be flooded without endangering the buoyancy of the vessel, led her makers and owners to claim that she was unsinkable.

On 14 April 1912 the vessel, fitted with every modern luxury and convenience, left Southampton on her maiden voyage to New York. There was every expectation that she might claim the coveted Blue Riband for the fastest transatlantic crossing. It was not to be. In the north Atlantic she struck an iceberg that ripped a long gash in her side beneath the waterline, allowing many of her watertight compartments to be flooded simultaneously. It took hours for the stricken vessel to sink, but unaccountably there was delay in alerting passengers to the danger and in lowering lifeboats. Her band famously played on as the vessel listed ever more alarmingly. When she finally went down, she took some 1,500 passengers and crew with her. Less than half that number survived.

Captain Smith, one of the most experienced of the White Star Line's Master Mariners, subsequently faced criticism of his conduct in sailing too far north and hence too close to seas in which icebergs might be expected, and of failing to keep a proper lookout. Damningly, it was found that insufficient lifeboats had been provided, since they cluttered the deck and spoilt the clean lines of the ship – and anyway, it was never expected that lifeboats might be needed.[102]

Amongst the dead was the campaigning journalist W.T. Stead. It was a melodramatic end to a sensational life. This was a man of whom it might have been said: "We have heard a message from the Lord: an envoy was sent to the nations to say, 'Rise, and let us go against her for battle'" (Obadiah :1), for he brought to England news of dark deeds and of the need to confront an evil at her heart. As editor of the *Pall Mall Gazette*, he worked with Josephine Butler to

---

[102] The disaster led to the calling of the First International Convention for the Safety of Life at Sea. This required passenger vessels to have enough lifeboats for all passengers, to conduct lifeboat drills and to keep a 24-hour radio watch. The International Ice Patrol was also established.

publicise the extent of child prostitution in late nineteenth century England. To that end, in 1885 he arranged for a child called Eliza Armstrong to be bought for £5 by Rebecca Jarrett, a reformed brothel-keeper, and smuggled out of England. His subsequent article *The Maiden Tribute of Modern Babylon* proved to a shocked public that it was possible to procure a child in London for sex.[103] Further horrific revelations followed. In response, Parliament swiftly raised the age of consent from twelve to sixteen and enacted heavy penalties for those guilty of child abuse.

Report.

The prophet Obadiah similarly brings a message "about Edom" (Obadiah :1), a nation that has grown proud and has gloated over Israel's misfortunes at the hands of foreign powers. The envoy to which he refers is unidentified, perhaps being Obadiah himself or perhaps another. An envoy is one who is sent: a messenger, a diplomatic agent, a representative from one government to another. His job is to relay words that have been given him by a higher power and to discharge faithfully a trust that has been placed in him. To be an envoy has traditionally been a dangerous job, for foreign rulers might readily hold hostage, mistreat and even kill those who brought ill tidings. Such has often been the fate of God's prophets.

In this case, the envoy comes from the High King of Heaven, for he is sent at the instance of "the Sovereign LORD" (Obadiah :1). The call that he relays to "the nations" (Obadiah :1) is to: "Rise, and let us go against her [Edom] for battle" (Obadiah :1). An alliance is to be forged against Edom, which will involve even those she had thought to be on her side. In the face of this confederation she will be impotent and helpless. Before it she will be rendered prostrate: "All your allies will force you to the border; your friends will deceive and overpower you; those who eat your bread will set a trap for you, but you will not detect it." (Obadiah :7). Her fate will take her by surprise. Likewise we can often be taken by surprise by the Lord's activity. God's envoys are not always the people we might expect. W.T. Stead is regarded by some as a humbug and a relentless self-publicist, more interested in increasing newspaper circulation than in the justice of the causes he espoused. The Eliza Armstrong case, however, was undoubtedly a call to arms. We must not let our pride stand in the way of heeding similar calls when they come, from however unlikely or unprepossessing a source. We must make sure that we respond as those calls demand.

---

[103] For procuring Eliza Armstrong, Stead was sentenced to three months' imprisonment and Jarrett to two years' penal servitude.

Representation.

Obadiah's call is to earthly nations for an earthly battle: "Your warriors, O Teman, will be terrified, and everyone in Esau's mountains will be cut down in the slaughter." (Obadiah :9). Yet there is also a spiritual dimension. The relationship between Israel and Edom is a family one, the Israelites being descended from the patriarch Jacob and the Edomites from his twin brother Esau: see Genesis 25:21-34. Despite the close bond of blood and the eventual reconciliation between Jacob and Esau described in Genesis 33:4, Edom consistently and from the very first showed hostility to Israel. She is therefore a symbol of those who stand in opposition to God and a representative of the dark forces that must be fought in each age and every place. The charges against her are:

Pride: "The pride of your heart has deceived you, you who live in the clefts of the rocks and make your home on the heights, you who say to yourself, 'Who can bring me down to the ground?'" (Obadiah :3).

Collaboration with evil: "On the day you stood aloof while strangers carried off his wealth and foreigners entered his gates and cast lots for Jerusalem, you were like one of them." (Obadiah :11).

Gloating: "You should not look down on your brother in the day of his misfortune, nor rejoice over the people of Judah in the day of their destruction." (Obadiah :12).

Aggression: "Because of the violence against your brother Jacob, you will be covered with shame; you will be destroyed for ever." (Obadiah :10).

Treachery: "You should not march through the gates of my people in the day of their disaster, nor look down on them in their calamity in the day of their disaster, nor seize their wealth in the day of their disaster. You should not wait at the crossroads to cut down their fugitives, nor hand over their survivors in the day of their trouble." (Obadiah :13-14).

These are indictments that might equally be laid against us: pride in our own cleverness and resources, supine acceptance of what is wrong, pleasure in the misfortune of others, violence and double-dealing. We are no longer on the right side in the battle between good and evil.

Reliance.

Like us, Edom has relied upon her own strength rather than on God, but all sources of false security will be stripped away in turn:

Natural defences will prove inadequate: "The pride of your heart has deceived you, you who live in the clefts of the rocks and make your home on the heights, you who say to yourself, 'Who can bring me down to the ground?'" (Obadiah :3).

Accumulated wealth will prove worthless: "But how Esau will be ransacked, his hidden treasures pillaged!" (Obadiah :6).

Allies will prove false: "All your allies will force you to the border; your friends will deceive and overpower you; those who eat your bread will set a trap for you, but you will not detect it." (Obadiah :7).

Human wisdom will prove illusory: "'In that day,' declares the Lord, 'will I not destroy the wise men of Edom, men of understanding in the mountains of Esau?'" (Obadiah :8).

Armed strength will prove insufficient: "Your warriors, O Teman, will be terrified, and everyone in Esau's mountains will be cut down in the slaughter." (Obadiah :9).

In the end, nothing will be left: "People from the Negev will occupy the mountains of Esau, and people from the foothills will possess the land of the Philistines. They will occupy the fields of Ephraim and Samaria, and Benjamin will possess Gilead. This company of Israelite exiles who are in Canaan will possess the land as far as Zarephath; the exiles from Jerusalem who are in Sepharad will possess the towns of the Negev." (Obadiah :19-20). The land of the ungodly will be turned over to those who recognise and rely upon the Lord. If we do not wish the same fate to befall us, it is time that we started to learn from the past.

Result.

The consequences of opposition to God and reliance on earthly rather than spiritual things will be diminution, degradation and impoverishment, leading ultimately to complete destruction:

Diminution: "See, I will make you small among the nations; you will be utterly despised." (Obadiah :2).

Degradation: "Though you soar like the eagle and make your nest among the stars, from there I will bring you down" (Obadiah :4).

Impoverishment: "If thieves came to you, if robbers in the night – Oh, what a disaster awaits you – would they not steal only as much as they wanted? If grape pickers came to you, would they not leave a few grapes? But how Esau will be ransacked, his hidden treasures pillaged!" (Obadiah :6).

Destruction: "Because of the violence against your brother Jacob, you will be covered with shame; you will be destroyed for ever... the house of Esau will be stubble, and they will set it on fire and consume it. There will be no survivors from the house of Esau." (Obadiah :10 and 18).

We are told that: "The day of the LORD is near for all nations. As you have done, it will be done to you; your deeds will return upon your own head. Just as you drank on my holy hill, so all the nations will drink continually; they will drink and drink and be as if they had never been." (Obadiah :15-16). These are uncomfortable words for us to hear. They remind us that "with the measure [we] use, it will be measured to [us]." (Matthew 7:2). As well as words of judgment, however, there are also phrases of hope and a message of salvation: "But on Mount Zion will be deliverance; it will be holy, and the house of Jacob will possess its inheritance. The house of Jacob will be a fire and the house of Joseph a flame ... Deliverers will go up on Mount Zion to govern the mountains of Esau. And the kingdom will be the LORD's." (Obadiah :17-18 and 21). The picture is of the wicked subordinated to the godly in a land that ultimately is under the sovereign rule of the High King of Heaven. To persist in our pride will take us down one path. Repenting of our sinfulness and turning back to God will take us down another.

Conclusion.

The *Titanic* stands as a monument to human pride and folly. In *Mere Christianity*, C. S. Lewis describes pride as the worst of all the sins, since it is the sin that caused Lucifer to fall. It is a sin of which we are currently guilty in high degree, for there is no greater example of it than seeking to deny, demean or displace God. We are guilty, too, of the other sins of the Edomites, which caused the Lord to bring upon them a judgment so complete that his prophet warned: "There will be no survivors from the house of Esau." (Obadiah :18). If we were ever in doubt as to the seriousness of our current predicament, these words should dispel any uncertainty. We are not just riding for a fall, but for something far worse. The wisdom of Solomon is as apposite today as it has always been, for it is indeed the case that "Pride goes before destruction and a haughty spirit before a fall." (Proverbs 16:18).

We face a choice: the way of destruction or the way of salvation. At present, everything about this nation is conspiring to take us down the path of ruin. The message from God is clear, but somehow it is not getting through. We need envoys to take this message to our people: to explain again the consequences of our continued apostasy, to point out the judgment that is upon us by reason of our pride and our denial of God and to illumine the way back to the Lord. For God's call is never solely one of condemnation. Always he reminds us of the forgiveness and rebirth that he longs to bestow: "Deliverers will go up on Mount Zion to govern the mountains of Esau. And the kingdom will be the LORD's." (Obadiah 1:21).

The prophet Isaiah asked: "Who has believed our message and to whom has the arm of the LORD been revealed?" (Isaiah 53:1). Thankfully, there remain those in England who have believed the message and to whom the arm of the Lord has been revealed. Even now it is not too late. We need to raise our voices afresh.

44. Hard times

2 Chronicles 7:11-22

Key word: response.

Amidst the turmoil of great events, life for most people has always been tough. Throughout the nineteenth century and well into the twentieth, the lot of the poor in England's cities was often grim in the extreme. Many lived on or below the poverty line. For those lucky enough to have a regular job, work was usually hard, hours long, pay minimal and conditions primitive. At the start of the Great War there were five millions in domestic service and a million working down the mines.

One little lad born during that first conflict with Germany suffered more than most. His mother fled a drunken, violent husband and it was many years before she saw her son again. The deserted father gave scant attention to the children left in his care. Neglected and forced to fend for himself, the youngster was soon going to school barefoot, forever hungry, stealing and scavenging to survive. He quit education at the earliest possible moment, with no qualifications. A series of odd jobs followed – as delivery boy, waiter, pageboy and cabin boy – but after his return from sea the desperate circumstances of nineteen thirties Britain meant he was unable to secure another post. Destitution and starvation beckoned, for in those days there was almost nothing in the way of social security. He went to see his father, who by then had remarried, only to find himself disowned and thrown out onto the streets.

With no job and no home, the urchin lived rough in London for a month, lying down to sleep on the warm air vents around the Savoy Hotel and then on stone steps in front of the Marshal Foch statue by Victoria Station. Somehow he kept alive, sneaking into cinemas to keep warm and to doze, washing in public lavatories. He was then fourteen years old. The army saved him. Despite his youth and total lack of musical knowledge, he persuaded a military band to let him enlist. With his regiment he travelled to India, learnt to ride a horse, played rugby, grew accomplished on many instruments and became army flyweight boxing champion. During these years he would often clown around for the amusement of comrades, developing skills and routines that he put to good use later. For after leaving the forces he went on to become a star of stage and screen, the most successful British comedian since Charlie Chaplin. Indeed he was considered by many, including Chaplin himself, to be the inheritor of that great man's mantle. His name was Norman Wisdom.

Attentiveness.

Norman Wisdom's life is an astonishing story of triumph against the odds. From the most unpromising start, his guts and determination, his steadfast refusal to wallow in misfortune or to feel sorry for himself helped fashion a successful career in one of the most demanding and unforgiving of arenas. Were we ever in doubt about it, his experience and those of countless others shows that it is our response to circumstances that matter most. We will all face hardship, pain, loss, unfairness and worse. This is an inevitable consequence of living in a world broken and marred by sin. We can allow ourselves to be overcome by these things or we can try to do something about them. Now, the reality is that there is little we can do on our own to fix the fundamental brokenness that is at the heart of so much deprivation and unhappiness. Human beings simply do not have the remedy, but God does. If we want to change our lives, therefore, the best start we can make is by responding to our Maker.

We see the interplay of response and counter-response that comes from relationship with God as "the LORD appeared to [King Solomon] at night" (2 Chronicles 7:12). The visitation is in response to the king coming before God in prayer, for the Lord says: "I have heard your prayer" (2 Chronicles 7:12). It is the second time that Scripture records God appearing to this king: see also 2 Chronicles 1:7-12 and 1 Kings 3:5-15. On this subsequent occasion, the Lord's appearance takes place "When Solomon had finished the temple of the LORD and the royal palace, and had succeeded in carrying out all he had in mind to do in the temple of the LORD and in his own palace" (2 Chronicles 7:11). We may infer from God's response that Solomon's prayer was a request for the Almighty to bless the temple and to come by his Spirit to reside there, for the king is told: "I ... have chosen this place for myself as a temple for sacrifices." (2 Chronicles 7:12). Intriguingly, this divine confirmation came only after the temple had already been built and dedicated. The sequence of events emphasises the degree of faith that was necessary on Solomon's part. For although the king's father David had told his son of God's plan that Solomon should be the one to build the temple (see 1 Chronicles 22:6-10), the task was still daunting. New to the throne, acknowledging that "I am only a little child and do not know how to carry out my duties" (1 Kings 3:7), Solomon nevertheless needed to strike out in faith to implement a hugely ambitious building project. It is ever thus: whether what is required of us be great or small, the step of faith needs first to be made.

When faith is present, God is attentive to us and to our needs. He hears and responds to Solomon's prayer and promises similar responsiveness in future: "I will hear from heaven ... my eyes will be open and my ears attentive to the prayers offered in this place." (2 Chronicles 7:14-15). However, this responsiveness is conditional, for God does not automatically act on each childish whim of man, nor does he say that he will respond when we ignore the reciprocal nature of our relationship with him. Thus he says: "When I shut up the heavens so that there is no rain, or command locusts to devour the land or send a plague among my people, if my people, who are called by my name, will humble themselves and pray and seek my face and turn from their wicked ways, then I will hear from heaven and forgive their sin and will heal their land." (2 Chronicles 7:13-14). The pivot of this sentence is the word "if."

This reminds us that our relationship with God is not one-sided. We also have to be attentive. The Lord's promise to respond is premised on a response on our part:

Humility: "... if my people ... will humble themselves ..." (2 Chronicles 7:14). Instead of relying on ourselves, we must rely on God.

Prayer: "... and pray ..." (2 Chronicles 7:14). Prayer is a two-way street. It involves listening to God as well as asking him for things.

Seeking: "... and seek my face ..." (2 Chronicles 7:14). Through prayer and reading of the Bible we should aim to understand the will of God, and what part he has for us to play.

Repentance: "... and turn from their wicked ways ..." (2 Chronicles 7:14). The best evidence of a change of heart is a change in the way we act.

Use of the word "and" shows that these four things are not alternatives. Nor can we pick and choose the ones that are convenient for us. They must all happen if we are to fulfil the conditions that trigger God's promise to "hear ... and ... forgive [our] sin and ... heal [our] land." (2 Chronicles 7:14).

Choices.

Our destiny, in other words, hinges on choice. As with attentiveness, choices are inter-connected. God makes choices: "I have chosen this place for myself as a temple for sacrifices ... I have chosen and consecrated this temple so that my Name may be there for ever. My eyes and my heart will always be there." (2 Chronicles 7:12 and 16). The Lord's choices influence ours and vice versa.

At the point in Israel's history where Solomon undertakes the building of a temple in Jerusalem, her choices have resulted in divine favour: hence God's decision to choose and consecrate this temple and to make it a place for himself.

However, there have been and will in future be times when choices lead in the opposite direction. This is "When I [God] shut up the heavens so that there is no rain, or command locusts to devour the land or send a plague among my people" (2 Chronicles 7:13). When such events occur, the nation must get back on track again through repentance, prayer and action so that the Lord's blessing will be renewed. The cycle is no less true for us than it was for the Israelites of old.

Consequences.

Our choices bring consequences, both personal and collective. God makes clear to Solomon not only the consequences of his own personal choices but also the consequences for the nation of the collective choices made either by it or by its king on its behalf:

Personal: "As for you, if you walk before me as David your father did, and do all I command, and observe my decrees and laws, I will establish your royal throne, as I covenanted with David your father when I said, 'You shall never fail to have a man on the throne of Israel.'" (2 Chronicles 7:17-18).

Collective: "But if you turn away and forsake the decrees and commands I have given you and go off to serve other gods and worship them, then I will uproot Israel from my land, which I have given them, and will reject this temple which I have consecrated for my Name. I will make it a byword and an object of ridicule among all peoples." (2 Chronicles 7:19-20).

There is no secret in this. Neither can we claim to be taken in any way by surprise. Through the Bible, God spells out for us equally clearly what the personal and collective consequences of our actions are. These consequences are not unjust, random or perverse. They are fair and logical and are built into the system that God had designed. Human beings are made to operate in accordance with God's laws, under his guidance and in relationship with him. When this proper order is disrupted, things go awry in the lives of individuals, nations and the world as a whole. The effects extend beyond the realm of man into the entire created order: "We know that the whole creation has been groaning as in the pains of childbirth right up to the present time." (Romans 8:22).

A series of opposites is set before us:

To "walk before me" (2 Chronicles 7:17) or to "turn away" (2 Chronicles 7:19).

To "do all I command" (2 Chronicles 7:17) or to "forsake the decrees and commands I have given you" (2 Chronicles 7:19).

To "observe my decrees and laws" or to "go off to serve other gods and worship them" (2 Chronicles 7:19).

We cannot escape the collective consequences of bad choices by pleading that we have personally been beyond reproach. A nation that acquiesces in a wrong course chosen for it by its rulers is complicit and will suffer accordingly.

Both implicit and explicit consequences are set before Solomon. By implication: that God will not "establish your royal throne" (2 Chronicles 7:18) and that there will come a time when "you shall ... fail to have a man on the throne of Israel." (2 Chronicles 7:18). Explicitly: "[God] will uproot Israel from

[his] land ... will reject this temple ... [and] will make it a byword and an object of ridicule among all peoples." (2 Chronicles 7:19-20). The picture is of severe disruption and malaise in the political, social, economic and religious life of the country. Such are the consequences with which we are living at present.

Conclusion.

Norman Wisdom's films are seldom shown nowadays and are perhaps too quaint for modern taste. They are about the little man, the ordinary, unprepossessing, put-upon Everyman who somehow manages to get the girl and put one over on those who think themselves above him. In our pride we perhaps identify less readily than previous generations with the underdog. Too often we tend to think ourselves a cut above the rest. We look with satisfaction upon careers, possessions, achievements and what-have-you, with thought only for our own needs and wants.

We are far from being attentive to God. Our attention wanders, too often in directions that are wholly unworthy of it, and God is ignored. We look at the temples that we have built for ourselves, in brick and stone, in the mind and in the arts, and we feel pleased with what we have done. We need to remind ourselves of what the Lord says about such things. There will come a time when they are broken and forgotten, for the Almighty "will bring disaster upon" (2 Chronicles 7:22) those who treat him this way: "And though this temple is now so imposing, all who pass by will be appalled and say, 'Why has the LORD done such a thing to this land and to this temple?'" (2 Chronicles 7:21).

The reply appears in the very next verse: "People will answer: 'Because they have forsaken the LORD, the God of their fathers, who brought them out of Egypt, and have embraced other gods, worshipping and serving them – that is why he brought all this disaster on them.'" (2 Chronicles 7:22). It takes little imagination to see how readily this description fits us. We have turned our backs on the Lord and we have substituted his worship with all the idols of modern life. It is a scandal and a tragedy. All about us are strewn the broken ruins that are its result.

We desperately need our heavenly Father to "hear ... forgive [our] sin and ... heal [our] land." (2 Chronicles 7:14). We have not even begun to fulfil the conditions that will trigger his promise to do so. We need to reflect with the utmost seriousness and urgency on how we can do so: by humbling ourselves, by praying, by seeking God's face and by turning from our wicked ways. Whilst we love to make things complicated, what is required is in fact quite simple. We do not need fine words, high-flown phrases or fancy formulations. The Lord will not reject us if our hearts are right.

45. So near

3 John 1.

Key word: friendship.

Until the early years of the twentieth century, no man had set foot at the South Pole. In the short polar summer of 1911-12 both British and Norwegians set out with this end in mind: the former under Captain Robert Falcon Scott of the Royal Navy (who had blazed the trail through his successful Antarctic expedition of 1901-04) and the latter under veteran arctic explorer Roald Amundsen. Up to the last moment, Amundsen deliberately gave the false impression that the expedition he was preparing would again be heading to the Arctic, and studiously avoided attempts by Scott to speak or meet with him beforehand. The Norwegian's secrecy greatly increased his prospects of success by ensuring that his adversary's planning was founded on a false premise – that he had the field to himself, when in fact he was up against some of the most experienced skiers and dog drivers in the world.[104] For good measure, Amundsen also tried to buy up all available Greenland Huskies so as to deny Scott access to the best dogs. Only during a stop-over at New Zealand on his way to Antarctica, when it was too late to change anything, did Scott learn that he would be taking part in a race.

Amundsen landed sixty miles closer to the Pole than Scott's party by taking the risk of setting up base on an ice sheet. Reliance on dogs alone allowed his men to set out on 19 October 1911, twelve days before the British, who used less hardy ponies (alongside motorised tractors and some dogs) to supplement manpower in the early stages and thereafter relied exclusively on hauling their sledges themselves.[105] As Scott knew from the outset, only a mishap amongst the Norwegians could prevent their being first. In the event, the hapless British were bedevilled by bad luck whilst good fortune smiled on their competitors. To their dismay, the five Britons who made the final push to the Pole found that Amundsen had arrived some weeks beforehand. On the weary trek homewards,

---

[104] Amundsen's conduct was considered by many to be underhand. The erstwhile hero was regarded with shame in Norway when news of what he had done first broke.

[105] Scott's eventual decision not to use dogs all the way to the Pole did not reflect prejudice or ignorance on his part as to their usefulness, but he had been sickened by the appalling cruelty and suffering that it was necessary to inflict on them. Experience also suggested that dogs were unsuited to certain terrain, particularly heavily crevassed areas of the kind his expedition not unreasonably expected to encounter.

they encountered freak weather, with temperatures regularly some 10°C or more below normal. Winds blew from the north instead of from the south, full in their faces rather than helping them on their way. At length, shut in by a blizzard of fierce intensity and many days' duration, the three surviving team members died a lonely death from cold, exhaustion and hunger, just eleven miles short of the depot whose supplies could have saved their lives.

The names of all five men of the Polar party are rightly remembered with pride and honour: Scott, Bowers, Evans, Oates and Wilson. Their last days were recorded in Scott's diaries, carried back by their comrades from base camp, who came eight months later to bury the dead and to find out how they had met their end. As it transpired, the conduct of these men in defeat turned out to be more splendid than any triumph. The diaries showed a group noble amidst the wreckage of their plans, plucky in adversity and selfless in regard for their fellows. In one of his last letters Scott wrote: "We are weak, writing is difficult, but for my own sake I do not regret this journey, which has shown that Englishmen can endure hardships, help one another and meet death with as great a fortitude as ever in the past. We took risks, we knew we took them; things have come out against us, and therefore we have no cause for complaint, but bow to the will of Providence, determined still to do our best to the last ... Had we lived, I should have had a tale to tell of the hardihood, endurance and courage of my companions which should have stirred the heart of every Englishman. These rough notes and our dead bodies must tell the tale."

It was no perversity for the nation to make of this the stuff of legend.

Competitiveness.

Both Scott and Amundsen were strenuously competitive men. It could hardly have been otherwise amongst those called to lead and inspire others across the most forbidding of landscapes and in the most extreme of climates. There is nothing intrinsically wrong with being competitive, as long as this urge is directed in the right way and kept within proper bounds. If not, it is a trait that can be highly damaging. It can be corrosive of friendship, blind us to God and assure us that the end justifies the means. Jesus tells us to put others' needs before our own. Competitiveness that is not harnessed and channelled into godly activity leads to the exact opposite. The apostle John tells of just such a case: "I wrote to the church, but Diotrephes, who loves to be first, will have nothing to do with us." (3 John 1:9).

Misdirected competitiveness breeds acts of enmity, not friendship: "So if I come, I will call attention to what he is doing, gossiping maliciously about us. Not satisfied with that, he refuses to welcome the brothers. He also stops those who want to do so and puts them out of the church." (3 John 1:10). The result is division, distance and hatred rather than togetherness, closeness and love.

By contrast, John emphasises the values of true friendship, repeating the phrase "dear friend" four times (3 John 1:1, 2, 5 and 11). Where there is friendship, we will:

Wish the best for others, both materially and spiritually: "Dear friend, I pray that you may enjoy good health and that all may go well with you, even as your soul is getting along well." (3 John 1:2).

Rejoice in our friends' progress and achievements: "It gave me great joy to have some brothers come and tell me about your faithfulness to the truth and how you continue to walk in the truth. I have no greater joy than to hear that my children are walking in the truth." (3 John 1:3-4).

Encourage others by acknowledging the good things they do: "Dear friend, you are faithful in what you are doing for the brothers, even though they are strangers to you." (3 John 1:5).

Let others know our regard for them: "They have told the church about your love." (3 John 1:6).

Be prepared to give wise and helpful advice: "You will do well to send them on their way in a manner worthy of God. It was for the sake of the Name that they went out, receiving no help from the pagans. We ought therefore to show hospitality to such men so that we may work together for the truth." (3 John 1:6-8).

Robert Scott had the gift of friendship. His concern for his men and their dependants was ceaseless. His last diary entry pleads: "For God's sake look after our people." Wilson, who was to die alongside him, said: "He is thoughtful for each individual and does little kindnesses that show it."

Faithfulness.

Friendship requires faithfulness. To be faithless is to be no true friend at all. The men who made the journey back from the Pole stuck to each other through thick and thin, not for self-interest of self-preservation but because they were comrades. They struggled on with Evans even when he became incapacitated and slowed their progress alarmingly. They did the same with Oates, though his hands and feet were so appallingly frostbitten that it took him hours to get dressed each day. One night he walked out of the tent, saying: "I am just going outside and may be some time." He knew he was walking to certain death, but did it for the sake of his friends. It was the last they saw of him.

These five were faithful to each other and they were faithful to God. Around 22 March 1912, with food and fuel already exhausted, Bowers wrote to his mother: "I am still strong and hope to reach [the depot eleven miles away] with Dr Wilson and get the food and fuel necessary for our lives. God alone knows what will be the outcome ... but my trust is still in Him and in the abounding grace of my Lord and Saviour whom you brought me up to trust and who has been my stay through life ..." At more or less the same time Wilson wrote to his wife: "Birdie [Bowers] and I are going to try and reach the depot eleven miles north of us and return to this tent where Captain Scott is lying with a frozen foot ... [If we do not succeed] I shall simply fall asleep in the snow ... All is for the best to those that love God, and oh, my Ory, we have both loved Him with all our lives ..." In the event, the blizzard continued and they had no choice but to stay confined in their tent. By the time the wind eased a little on 29 March, they were too weak to set out. Scott's last diary entry was made either that day or the day following.

Faithfulness figures large alongside friendship in what John writes. There is faithfulness in thought: "your faithfulness to the truth" (3 John 1:3). There is faithfulness in action: "you are faithful in what you are doing" (3 John 1:5). We need both. Having the right ideas is no good unless we put them into practice. Ultimately, going through the right motions is no good unless these are inspired by proper motives.

Imitation.

To help us get it right, we can harness the power of example: "Dear friend, do not imitate what is evil but what is good. Anyone who does what is good is from God. Anyone who does what is evil has not seen God." (3 John 1:11).

We can follow the good example of others and we can ourselves set a good example. This is the real way to honour and glory. Vain seeking after being first may deliver brief moments in the spotlight, but those will fade and we shall eventually find their trophies tarnished. Amundsen died a bitter and aloof man, who fell out even with his own brother and pursued a law suit against him. By contrast, a good name, a good report and real friendship will last for all time: "Demetrius is well spoken of by everyone – and even by the truth itself. We also speak well of him, and you know that our testimony is true." (3 John 1:12).

If ever there were a fine example to follow, it is that of Scott and his men. During his last days of life, Scott wrote: "We have done the greatest march ever made and come very near to great success ... We are in a desperate state, feet frozen etc. No fuel and a long way from food, but it would do your heart good to be in our tent, to hear our songs and the cheery conversation ... We are very near the end, but have not and will not lose our good cheer."

To Wilson's wife Scott addressed this message: "If this letter reaches you, Bill and I will have gone out together. We are very near it now and I should like you to know how splendid he was at the end – everlastingly cheerful ... I can do no more to comfort you than to tell you that he died as he lived, a brave, true man – the best of comrades and the staunchest of friends." To Bowers' mother he wrote that her son "had come to be one of my closest and soundest friends ... As the troubles have thickened his dauntless spirit ever shone brighter and he has remained cheerful, hopeful and indomitable to the end."

Conclusion.

Scott, Bowers and Wilson covered 1,450 miles in the worst conditions imaginable, hauling heavy loads and suffering the agonies of frostbite. Had they managed just 350 yards more each day after leaving the Pole they would have reached the depot that could have saved them. They failed to do so in large part because they would not leave their weaker companions, first Evans and then Oates. Jesus said: "Greater love has no-one than this, that he lay down his life for his friends" (John 15:13). That was what these three did. Their friendship and their faithfulness should inspire us all.

When it was all over, one of the men who had been with Amundsen, Helmer Hanssen, said: "It is no disparagement of Amundsen and the rest of us when I say that Scott's achievement far exceeded ours ... Just imagine what it meant for Scott and the others to drag their sleds themselves, with all their equipment and provisions to the Pole and back again. We started with 52 dogs and came back with eleven, and many of these wore themselves out on the journey. What shall we say of Scott and his comrades, who were their own dogs? Anyone with experience will take off his hat to Scott's achievement. I do not believe men have shown such endurance at any time, nor do I believe there ever will be men to equal it."

Tryggve Gran, a Norwegian who accompanied Scott's expedition as ski instructor, wrote on the journey back from finding the dead men's bodies: "I think of Scott, I think of Amundsen. I have learned that something called friendship exists. I have come to know men willing to sacrifice themselves for their country and for their convictions." In fulfilment of a promise made to Oates, Gran subsequently fought for England in the First World War as a pilot in the Royal Flying Corps.

It is time for hard questions and hard searching. We do not lack the finest of examples. We know what true friendship looks like. Jesus says, "I no longer call you servants, because a servant does not know his master's business. Instead I have called you friends, for everything that I learned from my Father I have made known to you." (John 15:15). If he offers us his friendship, it behoves us to reciprocate. That means deeds as well as thoughts and words. It means following the example of others and setting an example for others to follow in their turn. We have not been setting much of an example in recent years, but it is never too late to start.

46. So far

Ezra 4.

Key word: obstacles.

In 1914 Ernest Shackleton[106] set sail for the Antarctic in a vessel called *Endurance*. In view of what later transpired, she was aptly named. Her commander was already a veteran polar explorer, having accompanied Scott's expedition of 1901-04 and himself come within 100 miles of the South Pole in 1908. This time, his aim was to cross the Antarctic continent from the Weddell to the Ross Sea. He was experienced, well prepared and well equipped, but the *Endurance* became trapped in pack ice: Shackleton and his men could only watch helplessly as it was gradually crushed to matchwood. They spent months drifting on ice floes, facing the prospect of slowly starving or freezing to death.

The men had rescued the ship's lifeboats before *Endurance* sank and eventually took refuge on Elephant Island barely two hundred miles outside the Antarctic Circle, using the boats for shelter. Leaving most of his companions there under the command of Frank Wild, Shackleton and five others set out in the most seaworthy of the skiffs to row nearly over eight hundred miles to South Georgia and fetch help. With a combination of luck and skill, they made it, only to beach their wrecked vessel on the south side of the island, where nobody lived. Nothing daunted, they set out to climb the high mountains that ringed their landing-place. They climbed the first one, but could find no way down. So they climbed another, and another and another. Seven times they climbed, until at last they could make their way into the valley beyond. Finally, Shackleton and his weary, half-starved men stumbled into a whalers' hut, raised the alarm and oversaw an expedition to rescue their remaining shipmates.

It was Shackleton's proud boast that he did not lose a single man throughout the entire period of this expedition. By the time they returned to Britain, they had been away for two years.

False friends.

Like Shackleton, Ezra had to combat adverse circumstances. The obstacles that he faced threatened to sidetrack him from his God-given assignment. He

---

[106] Shackleton was born in Ireland but came to England at the age of ten and served in the Merchant Navy and the Royal Naval Volunteer Reserve before embarking with Scott's Antarctic expedition of 1901-04.

had to deal with attempts to undermine the project from within, with misrepresentation of his objectives and motivations, and with hostility from those in power. Handling this took a man of extraordinary qualities. More to the point, it took a man of great godliness, a man with the wisdom that only comes from having a close relationship with the Almighty, knowing the word of the Lord and putting this into practice. His God-centred approach enabled Ezra to deal with circumstances that would have broken lesser men. It enabled him and his co-workers to see through false protestations of friendship and to ride out the storm of official hostility and opposition.

The first attack was subtle. It came in the guise of godliness, brotherhood and proffered assistance: "When the enemies of Judah and Benjamin heard that the exiles were building a temple for the LORD, the God of Israel, they came to Zerubbabel and said, 'Let us help you build because, like you, we seek your God and have been sacrificing to him since the time of Esarhaddon king of Assyria, who brought us here.'" (Ezra 4:1-2). On its face, this seems reasonable, worthy even. Set alongside it, the response appears harsh, intolerant, ungrateful and bigoted: "But Zerubbabel, Jeshua and the rest of the heads of the families of Israel answered, 'You have no part with us in building a temple to our God. We alone will build it for the LORD, the God of Israel, as King Cyrus, the king of Persia, commanded us.'" (Ezra 4:3).

The implications of this interchange for us are profound, for they go to the heart of the way in which we should deal with other religions. Since this is an area where misunderstanding so easily arises, it is worth emphasising that there is no ground on which to discriminate against anyone merely because they come from a different race or culture. Nor should we fall into the trap of thinking that the religious labels that human beings attach to each other cut any ice with God, for "everyone who calls on the name of the LORD will be saved" (Joel 2:32). Time and again Jesus made clear that what God is interested in is the reality of what is in our hearts, not the outward show: and hence, by and large, he did not discuss theological niceties with the ordinary people he met during the course of his earthly ministry. From this concentration on substance rather than form it flows inevitably that there will be some who profess belief in Jesus to whom he will say, "I never knew you. Away from me, you evildoers!" (Matthew 7:23). Correspondingly, there will be others who will be surprised when he acknowledges them as one of his own (see Matthew 25:37-39). All this, however, is a long way from saying that any religious viewpoint can be adopted and it will be all right with God as long as we are sincere in what we believe.

Regrettably, our thinking has become confused. We should by all means recognise that there are many of good faith who espouse other religions and the mere fact of their adherence to another creed does not make them bad people: in many cases, quite the contrary. At the same time we need to be realistic and clear-sighted about what other religions stand for and the direction in which they tend to lead. The simple fact is that a significant minority of Christians does not go around trying to blow up their fellow citizens, even though the persecution suffered by Christians in many parts of the world is grievous, deeply rooted and ongoing. Forbearance does not come about because Christians have less cause to take affront than do those of other faiths, for daily the name of Jesus is traduced, vilified and spat upon. The reason that these outrages do not spill into violence is simple: the Bible leaves no room for doubt that such a response would be contrary to the will of God.

People are not daft. Some will always do right and some will always do wrong, but the vast majority act according to prevailing circumstances and the information at their disposal. By uncritically sharing a platform with other religions, by failing to confront their errors and by giving the impression that they have more in common with Christianity than is in fact the case, by promoting and subsidising them, the message that we are giving is this: that all religions stand for much the same thing and consequently it does not matter which we believe. Indeed, people would be entitled to draw a further conclusion: that the excesses of one religion could just as easily be the product of another and since each is as bad as the next they should all be avoided at every cost. Our lack of courage and insight thus places an unnecessary obstacle in the way of those who are searching for the right path. Ezra and his companions did not lack those qualities. They were prepared to say no, even at the risk of provoking a hostile reaction.

False deeds.

The proof of the pudding is in the eating. When the reply from the Israelites was made known, those who had earlier professed friendship and insisted that they wished to make common cause showed their true colours. They used propaganda, the threat of violence and appeals to the government: "Then the peoples around them set out to discourage the people of Judah and make them afraid to go on building. They hired counsellors to work against them and frustrate their plans during the entire reign of Cyrus king of Persia and down to the reign of Darius king of Persia. At the beginning of the reign of Xerxes, they lodged an accusation against the people of Judah and Jerusalem." (Ezra 4:4-6). The grudge was kept going for decades and through the reigns of several kings. When one ruler proved deaf to entreaty, the attack was simply renewed under the next. The scene is all too familiar in the present day, with lobbyists and propagandists manipulating and misusing legal and political systems for their own ends. The techniques were the same then as now:

A body of the great and the good was gathered to present the case: "the commanding officer ... the secretary ... the judges and officials" (Ezra 4:9).

Flattery was combined with readiness to massage facts to produce the desired outcome: "the great and honourable Ashurbanipal deported and settled in the city of Samaria and elsewhere in Trans-Euphrates [people from various other regions]" (Ezra 4:10) – a statement that appears to be at odds with the earlier assertion that "Esarhaddon king of Assyria ... brought us here." (Ezra 4:2).

Events and motives were misrepresented expressly or by implication: "the Jews who came up to us from you have gone to Jerusalem and are rebuilding that rebellious and wicked city. They are restoring the walls and repairing the foundations." (Ezra 4:12).

Political and budgetary implications were said to be dire: "if this city is built and its walls are restored, no more taxes, tribute or duty will be paid, and the royal revenues will suffer." (Ezra 4:13).

Good faith and honest intent were proclaimed: "Now, since we are under obligation to the palace and it is not proper for us to see the king dishonoured, we are sending this message to inform the king, so that a search may be made in the archives of your predecessors." (Ezra 4:14).

History and precedent were prayed in aid: "In these records you will find that this city is a rebellious city, troublesome to kings and provinces, a place of rebellion from ancient times. That is why this city was destroyed." (Ezra 4:15).

Imagined consequences were exaggerated: "We inform the king that if this city is built and its walls are restored, you will be left with nothing in Trans-Euphrates." (Ezra 4:16).

Precisely the same can be expected in modern Britain by any who go about the business of "building the temple of the LORD" (Ezra 4:1). We should not let appearances deceive us. As Shakespeare had King Duncan remark in *Macbeth*, "There's no art to find the mind's construction in the face." This is why we need to look at what men do as well as what they say, at results as well as pious platitudes.

False thinking.

Just as in the time of Ezra, we face a situation where law and the establishment are nowadays almost as likely to come down on the side of wrong as of right. The reasons are many, from muddle-headed attempts at pursuing an agenda of fairness and equality to slavish adherence to rules badly conceived or implemented to barefaced political calculation. King Artaxerxes drew incorrect conclusions from the evidence and hence reached a poor decision: "The king sent this reply ... The letter you sent us has been read and translated in my presence. I issued an order and a search was made, and it was found that this city has a long history of revolt against kings and has been a place of rebellion and sedition. Jerusalem has had powerful kings ruling over the whole of Trans-Euphrates, and taxes, and tribute and duty were paid to them." (Ezra 4:17-20). No opportunity was given for the Israelites to put their side of the story and no proper investigation seems to have been carried out as to the true nature of the facts, nor as to the motives behind the complaint that was made.

Similarly, the intellectual climate in our land is one in which proper investigation and debate seems more and more to be curtailed and constrained. Increasingly, we fall back on the totems of political correctness rather than looking squarely at the issues before us. The self-censorship that results is no less a form of compulsion than the edicts of a tyrant, no more logical and no more likely to promote good outcomes. The result in Ezra's case was perverse: "Now issue an order to these men to stop work, so that this city will not be rebuilt until I so order. Be careful not to neglect this matter. Why let this threat grow, to the detriment of the royal interests?" (Ezra 4:21-22). We have perversity aplenty in our land, where systems often conspire to promote the bad and hobble the good.

When the power of the state is brought to bear against those who seek to do God's work, the condition of a nation is dire indeed. This was the situation that confronted Ezra: "As soon as the copy of the letter of King Artaxerxes was read to Rehum and Shimshal the secretary and their associates, they went immediately to the Jews in Jerusalem and compelled them by force to stop. Thus the work on the house of God in Jerusalem came to a standstill until the second year of the reign of Darius king of Persia." (Ezra 4:23-24). It takes only a cursory examination of the daily papers to find examples of precisely the same in our country today.

Conclusion.

Shackleton faced enormous challenges. Some were external: cold, lack of shelter, shortage of supplies, shipwreck, impassable mountains and sheets of pack ice. Some were internal: the tendency to defeatism, faction or pursuit of self-interest instead of the common good. His experience was extreme, but every individual and each generation faces challenges both within and without. There are obstacles enough without our creating them for ourselves. Hence we should "watch out for those who cause divisions and put obstacles in your way that are contrary to the teaching you have learned. Keep away from them." (Romans 16:17).

There are obstacles that are placed in our way and obstacles that we place in the way of others. Each needs to be addressed and overcome after its own fashion. As regards those that are placed in our way, we need the same courage, insight and unwillingness to compromise the truth that Ezra and his companions brought to bear. As regards our tendency to create obstacles for others, we should take to heart the advice of St Paul: "Instead make up your mind not to put any stumbling-block or obstacle in your brother's way." (Romans 14:13).

Above all, the Lord has a job for us to do: "Build up, build up, prepare the road! Remove the obstacles out of the way of my people." (Isaiah 57:14).

47. Lost

Philippians 3:7-11.

Key word: suffering.

Even today, after decades of logging, the Brazilian rainforest remains mind-boggling in its extent and largely unexplored. As recently as the nineteen twenties it was almost wholly unmapped. No aircraft had then crossed its widest expanses. Numerous Indian tribes had never been contacted by white men. It was a region of possibility, opportunity and fantasy. Although the legend of El Dorado had been consigned to the realms of mere fable, tales of ancient cities in the jungle seemed plausible: there was much to suggest that both the population and level of civilisation in the Amazon basin had once been greater than in the present day.[107]

Into this inhospitable region stepped a British officer of engineers: Lieutenant-Colonel P.H. Fawcett. From 1906 to 1925 he criss-crossed the wildest reaches of a hostile landscape, convinced that ruins of age-old splendours were within his grasp. His log books survive, and they give some flavour of the privations he suffered during these explorations. On one occasion rations were gone, no game had been sighted for days and his small party was at the end of its resources. Fawcett describes it thus:

"It was a miracle that saved us – at least, for me it was then, and always will be, the nearest thing to what we like to call a miracle. On October 13, feeling that we had come to our last gasp, I did what I had never known to fail when the need was sufficiently pronounced, and that is to pray audibly for food. Not kneeling, but turning east and west, I called for assistance – forcing myself to *know* that assistance would be forthcoming. In this way did I pray, and within fifteen minutes a deer showed itself in a clearing three hundred yards away. The others saw it at the same time, and a breathless silence fell as I unslung my rifle. It was almost hopeless range for a violently kicking Winchester carbine; and at the end of one's tether from hunger or thirst the sight is not reliable, nor is it easy to hold the rifle steady. 'For God's sake don't miss, Fawcett!' The hoarse whisper came from close behind me. Miss! As I sighted along the shaking barrel I knew the bullet would find its mark. The power that answered my prayer

---

[107] Modern scholarship tends to support this view.

would see that it did. Never have I made a cleaner kill – the animal dropped with severed spine where it stood!"

The men made it to safety. After a brief respite, Fawcett returned to the jungle again. In due course, it became his prison.

Profit and loss.

St Paul's letter to the church at Philippi is written from prison. It is nevertheless full of hope and cheerfulness. He says: "Now I want you to know, brothers, that what has happened to me has really served to advance the gospel. As a result, it has become clear throughout the whole palace guard and to everyone else that I am in chains for Christ. Because of my chains, most of the brothers in the Lord have been encouraged to speak the word of God more courageously and fearlessly." (Philippians 1:12-14). As well as reporting his own circumstances and thanking the Philippians for sending him a gift, St Paul used his letter to encourage these believers to stand firm in the face of suffering and to rejoice regardless of circumstances. It is an approach that might at first sight seem to fly in the face of all logic.

The explanation lies in how we assess and value what takes place in our lives and the lives of those around us. The apostle says: "But whatever was to my profit I now consider loss for the sake of Christ. What is more, I consider everything a loss compared to the surpassing greatness of knowing Christ Jesus my Lord, for whose sake I have lost all things. I consider them rubbish" (Philippians 3:7-8). This is something that each generation needs to re-learn. In every age the lure of monetary reward and material things looms large. For each of us, the anguish of privation and suffering can threaten to outweigh and obscure the wider picture of God's love and care. The issue of suffering remains for many the single most important factor in an inability or unwillingness to believe in the God who is described in the Bible. It is thus worthwhile reminding ourselves that suffering only presents such a problem within Christian theology. Other religions deal with it in quite different ways. Islam treats everything that happens as part of the immutable will of an unknowable and unchallengeable God, in the face of whom man has to submit without question. The primary response which this engenders to suffering is fatalism. Hinduism holds that those who suffer deserve it, for they must have done something wrong in this or previous lives to bring such bad 'karma' on themselves. The primary response which this engenders is indifference. Buddhism treats suffering as illusory, like all the things of *Samsara* (the world of the senses). The primary response which this engenders is denial. Other religious viewpoints posit equal and opposite forces of good and evil, ascribing all suffering to a malign force that the good cannot control. Yet others imagine a Creator who takes no further interest in his creation, in effect making suffering the product of divine inattention.

All these concepts are alien to Christianity, with its belief in a God who is defined by his loving nature, who is actively involved in human affairs, is all-mighty, all-powerful and all-knowing. Such a God is outraged by suffering, which is a scar on the beautiful world which he created and on all that he desires for mankind. This is a God who permits suffering, but in no way desires it. He permits it because choices must have consequences if they are to be real choices, and bad choices bring wretched consequences. Suffering, in other words, is an inevitable result of the exercise of our free will, and we must have free will for without it we would be mere automatons. To blame God for what we have brought upon ourselves by our stupidity and sinfulness is inaccurate, craven and blasphemous. We need to lay these reactions aside and see things as they really are.

Along with St Paul, we should "put no confidence in the flesh" (Philippians 3:3), whether in its power (by relying on what we can bring about in our own strength) or in its lack of power (as our weakness is exposed by suffering). As always, the real issues are spiritual. So is the dimension in which our battles are to be fought and won.

Knowing Christ.

The fact that he puts "no confidence in the flesh" (Philippians 3:3) leads St Paul away from relying on his own achievements and prowess, and in a quite different direction. His dearest wish is that "I may gain Christ and be found in him, not having a righteousness of my own that comes from the law, but that which is through faith in Christ – the righteousness that comes from God and is by faith. I want to know Christ and the power of his resurrection" (Philippians 3:8-10).

Here St Paul goes to the heart of Christianity: relationship. God is not distant and unknowable. He is not indifferent to our suffering, but grieves with us and feels for us. His mercy and the consistency of his character and behaviour are demonstrated by the fact that he continues to show his love and goodness in our suffering even when we deserve what has come upon us. He weeps with us when we suffer through the malice or negligence of others. Jesus himself is hardly a stranger to hardship, being "despised and rejected by men, a man of sorrows, and familiar with suffering." (Isaiah 53:3). Yet he nevertheless invites us to adopt a different perspective on our pain and promises good things to those who suffer on account of him: "Blessed are you when people insult you, persecute you and falsely say all kinds of evil against you because of me. Rejoice and be glad, because great is your reward in heaven, for in the same way they persecuted the prophets who were before you." (Matthew 5:11-12).

The remarkable thing is this: through God, our suffering can be turned to good account. St Paul's experiences are a case in point. These bear out the apostle's positive viewpoint, as the results of his suffering are seen in their effect upon individual believers and non-believers and, through them, in the wider context of an expanding gospel. The concentric circles of influence and effect eventually spread to all corners of the earth:

To believers: "Because of my chains, most of the brothers in the Lord have been encouraged to speak the word of God more courageously and fearlessly." (Philippians 1:14).

To non-believers: "it has become clear throughout the whole palace guard and to everyone else that I am in chains for Christ." (Philippians 1:13).

Worldwide: "Now I want you to know, brothers, that what has happened to me has really served to advance the gospel." (Philippians 1:12).

So great is St Paul's desire "to know Christ and the power of his resurrection" (Philippians 3:10) that he also wishes to experience "the fellowship of sharing in his sufferings, becoming like him in his death" (Philippians 3:10). This is neither foolishness nor masochism. All people experience suffering. The issue is whether we experience it on our own and for no good purpose, or with God alongside us and in the knowledge that something worthwhile will come of it.

Suffering and death.

Suffering has great power. We are all too familiar with its negative side: the capacity to maim and mar, to twist, frustrate, dampen, snatch away, pervert and deny. We reflect less often on its positive side: its impetus to self-sacrifice and courage, its ability to force reflection and growth, the achievements that are possible through it and the example that can be given in it. Both the greatest example in the face of suffering and the greatest achievement through it belong to the crucifixion and resurrection of Jesus. It is for precisely this reason that St Paul says: "I want to know Christ and the power of his resurrection and the fellowship of sharing in his sufferings, becoming like him in death, and so, somehow, to attain to the resurrection from the dead." (Philippians 3:10-11).

This is not the expression of a death wish and nor is it evidence of suicidal tendencies. Earlier in the same letter the apostle says: "For to me, to live is Christ and to die is gain. If I am to go on living in the body, this will mean fruitful labour for me. Yet what shall I choose? I do not know! I am torn between the two: I desire to depart and be with Christ, which is better by far; but it is more necessary for you that I remain in the body. Convinced of this, I know that I will remain, and I will continue with all of you for your progress and joy in the faith, so that through my being with you again your joy in Christ Jesus will overflow on account of me." (Philippians 1:21-26). It is, then, simply an honest recognition that "the power of [Christ's] resurrection" (Philippians 3:10) was only possible because of the suffering and death that preceded it. This power is replicated in humanity and in nature: "I tell you the truth, unless a grain of wheat falls to the ground and dies, it remains only a single seed. But if it dies, it produces many seeds." (John 12:24).

Conclusion.

Fawcett and his eldest son, who by that stage was accompanying him, went missing in 1925. A younger son several times led search parties into the jungle, but no reliable trace of father or brother was ever found. Intense media interest slowly gave way to apathy and then forgetfulness on the part of all but the closest family and friends. Today, few have even heard of Fawcett. The cities that he searched for so intently have never been found.[108]

The story of Colonel Fawcett contains a surfeit of suffering: of men in extreme conditions, of a family bereft of loved ones and uncertain whether they live or die, of those perhaps held against their will in some remote encampment or done to death in the most barbaric of ways. On the face of it, it has no happy ending. Yet St Paul would not see it that way, and neither should we. The apostle wrote: "we also rejoice in our sufferings, because we know that suffering produces perseverance; perseverance, character; and character, hope. And hope does not disappoint us, because God has poured out his love into our hearts by the Holy Spirit, whom he has given us." (Romans 5:3-5).

We are right to be outraged by suffering. It is good for us to do all we can to prevent it and to lessen its impact. Yet there is a danger in taking this too far. If we are repelled by suffering to the extent that we are unable to face it, if we are afraid to look upon it in any form and turn away from those whose suffering discomforts us, we deny the positive power of suffering, we detract from the work of Jesus on the cross and we fail to put into practice what he taught. We will seek to cocoon ourselves in material comfort to the exclusion of venturing into those difficult regions where there are spiritual battles to be fought. We will become flabby and inactive, marooned on an island of plenty whilst all around God's work waits undone. We will look to precisely those things that St Paul told the Christians in Philippi they should disregard. Squeamishness about death and suffering is not just a denial of reality. It is a denial of the will to fight for what we believe. It is a denial of growth in favour of stagnation.

We have become slaves, devotees of a new religion that promises escape from all hardship and an end to suffering if only we will indulge ourselves to the utmost and always seek our own self-interest. It is all lies and illusion. Through these no good can come.

---

[108] Recent satellite images have begun to suggest possible locations.

48. Praying for our lives

Nehemiah 12:27-47.

Key word: service.

The Great War produced the first widespread experience in Europe of three battlefield phenomena which daily compounded the terrors and discomforts of that conflict: gas poisoning, shell shock and trench foot. Few front-line troops escaped the latter. It was the result of soldiers standing day after day with their feet in the muddy water that collected at the bottom of trenches, never taking off their boots. When the water froze, their feet froze with it, and soon the flesh began to rot. Often, boot leather and flesh moulded together so that men quite literally had to have their boots cut off when they were finally moved back to a rest area. When we survey the attrition of four years of trench warfare, when we read stories of gas attacks and men drowning in mud, it is difficult to take in the sheer ghastliness of what soldiers lived through day by day. It is humbling to think that for the first two years of conflict Britain, alone of the combatant nations, fought with an army composed entirely of volunteers. Only as the dreadful losses from the Somme began to mount was conscription finally introduced.

The First World War has seared itself into our consciousness because of its many horrors. Not for nothing is it called the Great War. To all other outrages of this most brutal of conflicts is added the poignancy of a generation that for a brief while dared to believe that they had fought a 'war to end all wars', but who just over two decades later were fated to send their own sons off to fight again. After that have come wars and more wars. In the whole of the twentieth century, there was only one year when a British serviceman did not die in action: 1968, the year before the army was sent to Northern Ireland. At the eleventh hour of the eleventh month each year we honour those who served and remember those who died in all our wars, great and small. We turn with compassion to those who survived but were scarred physically or emotionally by what they experienced. We acknowledge our debt to each one of them. We thank them for their sacrifice and we recognise that, without them, our way of life might be very different.

On Remembrance Day, marking the Armistice that ended the Great War, we do all this through ceremony. We gather at war memorials and we go to church. In this way we give meaning and dignity to what we do. This chapter will reflect on what exactly is involved in this process by looking at words that were written a very long time ago. The book of Nehemiah in the Old Testament records events that took place 2,400 years ago (440BC or thereabouts). It may seem incredible that something so old can have anything to say to us today, but the writers of the Bible were inspired by the Holy Spirit (in 2 Timothy 3:16 St

Paul calls the words of Scripture "God-breathed") to create a text through which God still speaks to those who have ears to hear.

Memorials.

At the time Nehemiah wrote, Babylon was the regional superpower. It ruled a vast empire, roughly corresponding to modern Iraq, Syria, Lebanon and Israel. The Babylonians had a brutally effective way of dealing with conquered peoples: mass deportation. The leading citizens of the Israelite kingdom of Judah were deported by the Babylonians and kept in captivity for 70 years. At the end of that period, they were allowed to go home, which they did in dribs and drabs over succeeding decades. Nehemiah was amongst the later returnees. He found Jerusalem in a sorry state: its walls were in ruins, the people had got into bad ways and enemies were all around. Nehemiah galvanised rebuilding of the walls of the city, but much more importantly he oversaw a rebuilding of the nation – physically, morally, spiritually. He records their trials and triumphs in the first 11 chapters of his book. Then, with his work almost done, in chapter 12 he tells us about the dedication of the rebuilt walls.

The opening 26 verses of Nehemiah 12 comprise just a list of names. Or, more correctly, they are not 'just' a list, because something very important is going on as Nehemiah records the people who worked with him to bring the rebuilding of the nation to fruition. He is building a memorial: not a memorial of stone like the ones we gather round on Remembrance Day, but a memorial of words. He does not want those who come after him to forget what has been done.

God does not want what he has done to be forgotten, either. Time and again throughout the pages of the Bible, we find God telling his people to remember. He provides symbols to help them do so. At Passover the Jews are to eat unleavened bread flavoured with bitter herbs to recall the bitterness of their captivity in Egypt (Exodus 12:8). We take bread and wine at communion in recollection of the Last Supper of Jesus and his disciples before the crucifixion (Luke 22:19). Yet we forget so easily. To overlook the contributions that individual men and women have made to the life of our nation is one thing. To fail to notice what God has done and continues to do for us, to ignore the way that he wants us to live as a nation and as individuals is without excuse. We need to find again what the people of Israel had to rediscover in the time of Nehemiah.

Service and integrity.

Amongst other things, we need to rediscover the virtues of service and integrity. These are things that mark out the best of what our forces stand for. Not for nothing do we refer to them as 'armed services', because service and high principle are such strong parts of their ethos, putting nation and comrades before self.

The people of Nehemiah's day offered themselves to serve for the common good. Priests and their helpers (the Levites), gatekeepers, singers and those in charge of storerooms all came forward. They were joined by those who worked to rebuild the walls and to provide watchmen. Everybody had a role to play, no matter how small. They gave their labour free of charge to help in the great task of rebuilding the nation. All this was well, but there was something even more important. The nation needed to turn again to God, to walk in his ways and to observe his commandments. It had to re-learn what was known to previous generations but had been forgotten. Thus they "performed the service of their God and the service of purification" (Nehemiah 12:45).

There is so much that is good and so much that is right in our land, but it is difficult to avoid thinking that (like the Israelites of Nehemiah's day) we have lost our way somewhat. We need to take the forms of proper conduct and make them alive and real. With that in mind, it is instructive to compare their actions with ours on Remembrance Day:

They had a procession (Nehemiah 12:31 and 38), just as we do.

They took their place in the house of God (Nehemiah 12:40) just like us, for a church is a house of God.

They sang, gave praise and thanks to God and celebrated joyfully (Nehemiah 12:27-28, 31, 38 and 40), exactly as we do through our hymns and worship.

They ritually purified themselves (Nehemiah 12:30), which is what we do when we confess our sins honestly to God and sincerely ask for his forgiveness.

They offered sacrifices and made contributions towards the religious life of the nation (Nehemiah 12:43 and 47), precisely as we have the opportunity do through our giving and by our service.

For the Israelites, this was not a matter of empty ritual. Their hearts were in what they did. Their ritual purity was intended to teach and to reflect God's holiness and moral purity: Leviticus 16:30. They encircled the walls to mark out Jerusalem symbolically as a place set apart for God and his people. They acknowledged that God had his hand upon their nation.

The Lord at work.

We, too, should remember that God has had his hand upon our nation. The last time we held National Days of Prayer in this land was during the Second World War. They were all attended by spectacular results, but two in particular stand out. The first took place just prior to the Dunkirk evacuation (Operation

Dynamo). By early 1940 Poland, Denmark, Belgium, the Netherlands, Luxembourg and Norway had fallen in swift succession to German Blitzkrieg. A demoralised France surrendered only six weeks after the start of the Wehrmacht's western offensive. Despite giving the invaders a modest check at Arras, the British Expeditionary Force (BEF) was outfought, out-manoeuvred and forced to retreat. Nigh on half a million British and French troops crowded into shrinking pockets around Dunkirk and Calais as their enemy closed for the kill.

Nobody thought the BEF stood a chance. General Sir Edmund Ironside, chief of the Imperial General Staff, murmured, "This is the end of the British Empire." King Leopold III of Belgium agreed that "The cause of the Allies is lost." Against a backdrop of despair Archbishop of Canterbury William Temple, supported by King George VI, Prime Minister Winston Churchill and other leading politicians called a National Day of Prayer for 26 May 1940. The response was overwhelming as people begged God for deliverance. Just twenty-four hours later, for reasons that have never been fully explained, Hitler ordered his armies to halt. His generals were dumbfounded, for although the British rearguard fought stubbornly (even to the death) at both Dunkirk and Calais, it is doubtful that a determined German assault could have been long held off.

For six days following the National Day of Prayer the normally choppy waters of the English Channel were almost dead calm. Allied soldiers scrambled aboard warships and the flotilla of "little ships" that had answered the call to rescue the beleaguered men, whilst the RAF flew round the clock. Planners initially hoped to lift a few thousands from the beaches, but results massively exceeded expectations, with 338,226[109] being brought back to England. When the evacuation was finally over, General Ironside wrote of it: "I still cannot understand how it is that [the Germans] have allowed us to get [our troops] off in this way. It is almost fantastic that we have been able to do it in the face of all the bombing and gunning." Alexander Cadogan, Permanent Undersecretary at the Foreign Office, called it quite simply "a miracle."

Even then, the country was not out of the woods by any stretch of the imagination. As the Battle of Britain raged, a youth day of prayer was called on 11 August 1940. Within a month the focus of the campaign changed. Airfields, which had been mercilessly pummelled to the point when the RAF was almost on its knees, were unaccountably spared as the Luftwaffe suddenly switched its attention to terror bombing of cities, London first being attacked on 7 September. The Chief of Fighter Command Air Chief Marshall Sir Hugh Dowding stated afterwards: "I can say with absolute conviction that I can trace

---

[109] Of these, about 100,000 were French. The vast majority of these chose to return home rather than carry on the fight.

the intervention of God, not only in the battle itself, but in the events that led up to it; and that if it had not been for this intervention the battle would have been joined in conditions which, humanly speaking, would have rendered victory impossible." [110]

Conclusion.

On Remembrance Day we remember our dead – the "glorious dead" it says on many a war memorial. We need to ask whether we also sufficiently remember the living: the ever-living God. The Israelites under Nehemiah acted with gladness and with hearts on fire for God: Nehemiah tells us that the people "… offered great sacrifices, rejoicing because God had given them great joy … the sound of rejoicing in Jerusalem could be heard far away." (Nehemiah 12:43). We should reflect on whether we really put God first in our lives, whether there is substance in what we do, or whether it is just empty ritual. We must question whether we sincerely wish to serve others, or only seek to look after ourselves. We have to ask whether we truly remember what God has done for us and genuinely give him credit for it.

Things do not just happen in life. It was God's will that Jerusalem should be restored in the time of Nehemiah, but it took that man's courage and visionary leadership, along with active participation by the whole nation, to bring it about. God gave the Israelites the land of Canaan to be their home, a "land flowing with milk and honey" (Exodus 3:8), but they had to fight for it. God wishes to bless our nation, to bring us back to him and to restore us in the same way that Israel was restored under Nehemiah, but he will not wave a magic wand to make this happen. He will bring it about through us, every single one of us, and if we do not actively take a hand in the process, it will not come to pass. Our armed forces epitomise service and integrity. We need to bring those same

---

[110] National days of prayer also took place on (1) 8 September 1940: exactly one week later came the greatest air battle, with 185 German aeroplanes shot down, whilst barges intended for the invasion of Britain were sunk in a storm (2) 23 March 1941: storms further disrupted German invasion plans, continued resistance by Yugoslavia fatally delayed Operation Barbarossa (the German attack on Russia) and Ethiopia was liberated (3) September 1942: victory at El Alamein the following month is an acknowledged turning point in the war (4) 3 September 1943: the Italian mainland was invaded, leading to Italy's surrender on 7 September 1943 (5) Spring 1944: Group-Captain Stagg (in charge of weather forecasting for the D-Day invasion) predicted with astonishing accuracy the three-day window of relative good weather that allowed landings to take place on 6 June 1944. Hardly were troops and supplies ashore than severe storms blew up, which would have made invasion impossible until the following year had this opportunity been missed.

qualities to bear in the service of our nation and of our God. Revival and restoration require that we each resolve to make a reality of God's words to us, so that we are "for [him] a kingdom of priests and a holy nation." (Exodus 19:6).

49. Seeing a way through

Galatians1:11-24

Key word: calling.

In 1890 a British schoolboy attested to the tremendous sense of calling that he felt on his life. He spoke these words to a friend:

"I can see vast changes coming over a now peaceful world; great upheavals, terrible struggles; wars such as one cannot imagine; and I tell you London will be in danger – London will be attacked and I shall be very prominent in the defence of London … I see further ahead than you do. I see into the future. The country will be subjected somehow to a tremendous invasion … but I tell you I shall be in command of the defences of London and I shall save London and the Empire from disaster."

The youngster was sixteen years old. His name was Winston Spencer Churchill.

There is no need to look in Christian literature to find this story: it appears in mainstream history books, related not just by Churchill himself, but confirmed by the friend to whom he spoke, a man called Murland Evans. It is not a wild tale from a distant past, but almost within spitting distance of us: there are people still alive who knew Churchill, who died as recently as 1965. Yet we fail to reflect properly on what the future war leader did on this occasion. He prophesied. Here in our own recent history is an example of a man who foresaw and foretold what was to come. Not a particularly godly man, so far as history records, but a man touched by God for great things.

A large proportion of the Bible is taken up with prophecy. Of the thirty-nine books of the Old Testament, no less than seventeen comprise works of prophecy and there are examples of prophecy scattered throughout most of the remainder. In the New Testament the book of Revelation is the major work of prophecy, but there are elements of prophecy in other books, too. Jesus himself prophesied.[111] Now, there are people who say that the prophesies in the Bible cannot be what they appear on their face – they cannot be written by those who say they wrote them, nor at the time when they say they were written – because if they were this would involve telling in advance what will come to pass, and such things cannot happen. Whether that view represents ignorance or wilful

---

[111] See for example Matthew 24:1-35.

blindness each must judge. The rational and open-minded, however, should recognise that there are good grounds for confidence in biblical prophecy. This confidence is based not on blind unreason but on our ability to test and confirm that prophecy is real, that God does empower people to tell forth his Word and on occasion to foretell the future.

Again and again Churchill showed that he possessed an unshakeable sense of purpose. In *My Early Life*, he wrote that: "I felt as if I were walking with destiny, and that all my past life had been but a preparation for this hour and this trial ..." This conviction sustained him through a career that was littered with spectacular failures: he was the architect of the disastrous landings at Gallipoli in the Dardanelles during the First World War and by the mid nineteen thirties was firmly consigned to the political wilderness, derided as a madcap and a maverick. Yet in her time of greatest trial the nation turned to him, who had warned so long and so loud about the threat posed by Nazi Germany.

The Damascus road.

Just as there are good grounds for confidence in biblical prophecy, so too there are good grounds to rely on the truth of the miraculous events recorded in the Bible. In the New Testament, these are explicitly said to be based on eyewitness testimony. The apostle John, for example, talks about that "which we have heard, which we have seen with our eyes, which we have looked at and our hands have touched" (1 John 1:1). Luke bases his gospel on an account "handed down to us by those who from the first were eye-witnesses" (Luke 1:2). The apostle Peter likewise says: "We did not follow cleverly invented stories when we told you about the power and coming of our Lord Jesus Christ, but we were eye-witnesses of his majesty." (2 Peter 1:16) and describes himself as "a witness of Christ's sufferings" (1 Peter 5:1).

In his letter to the early church in Galatia, St Paul also speaks from first-hand experience. He tells of his life before and after he saw a blinding light on the road to Damascus and the risen Jesus spoke to him there: see Acts 9:1-30. He tells his readers: "I want you to know, brothers, that the gospel I preached is not something that man made up. I did not receive it from any man, nor was I taught it; rather, I received it by revelation from Jesus Christ ... I assure you before God that what I am writing to you is no lie." (Galatians 1:11-12 and 20).

We are able to test the reliability of what St Paul says because Christianity contains within itself a fail-safe check of a kind that is completely absent from other religions: he independently received a message which conformed completely with that which had already been given to the other apostles (see Galatians 2:1-2 and 6-10).

The road apart.

St Paul's behaviour after his life-changing encounter with Jesus is likewise powerful circumstantial evidence of the truth of Christianity. Here was a man who writes of "how intensely I persecuted the church of God and tried to destroy it." (Galatians 1:13). He tells of how "I was advancing in Judaism beyond many Jews of my own age and was extremely zealous for the traditions of my fathers." (Galatians 1:14). Yet this same man spent something like the next thirty years going from place to place to preach "Jesus Christ, and him crucified." (1 Corinthians 2:2). He gave up home, family, country, security, wealth and honour to do so.

Nor did St Paul merely forego comforts. He endured trials that most can scarcely imagine: "I have worked much harder, been in prison more frequently, been flogged more severely, and have been exposed to death again and again. Five times I received from the Jews the forty lashes minus one. Three times I was beaten with rods, once I was stoned, three times I was shipwrecked, I spent a night and a day in the open sea, I have been constantly on the move. I have been in danger from bandits, in danger from my own countrymen, in danger from Gentiles; in danger in the city, in danger in the country, in danger at sea; and in danger from false brothers. I have laboured and toiled and have often gone without sleep; I have known hunger and thirst and have often gone without food; I have been cold and naked." (2 Corinthians 11:23-27).

Throughout the ages, many have believed preposterous and even evil things, giving up comfort and enduring hardship for them. It is rare, however, to find someone who persists so long in error in the face of such obstacles. Sober reflection suggests that the claims made by St Paul deserve the most serious examination.

The great apostle to the Gentiles was called from his "previous way of life in Judaism" (Galatians 1:13) by God for a work that had been prepared for him: "God, who set me apart from birth and called me by his grace, was pleased to reveal his Son in me so that I might preach him among the Gentiles" (Galatians 1:15). In the same way, God calls and sets apart all those he will use. The calling may be dramatic, like St Paul's and the sense of purpose strong, like Churchill's, but they may not. They are no less real for being revealed in "a still small voice." (I Kings 19:12).

The road to glory.

Under divine guidance, St Paul took an unexpected road following his conversion: "I did not consult any man, nor did I go up to Jerusalem to see those who were apostles before I was, but I went immediately into Arabia and later returned to Damascus. Then after three years, I went up to Jerusalem to get acquainted with Peter and stayed with him fifteen days. I saw none of the other apostles – only James, the Lord's brother ... Later I went to Syria and Cilicia." (Galatians 1:16-19 and 21).

The result was that "I was personally unknown to the churches of Judea that are in Christ. They only heard the report: 'The man who formerly persecuted us is now preaching the faith he once tried to destroy.' And they praised God because of me." (Galatians 1:22-24).

St Paul did not rely on human instruction, but instead was taught by God. He "received [the gospel] by revelation from Jesus Christ." (Galatians 1:12). Jesus told Ananias: "This man is my chosen instrument to carry my name before the Gentiles and their kings and before the people of Israel. I will show him how much he must suffer for my name." (Acts 9:15-16). God took a man whose talents had until then been wrongly used and caused them to flow in a different channel. The work that was to come needed a man who was "extremely zealous" (Galatians 1:14). It needed someone committed and single-minded, qualities that St Paul had shown in "how intensely I persecuted the church of God and tried to destroy it." (Galatians 1:13). What God did was to turn this fire from "the traditions of my fathers" (Galatians 1:14) and towards the truth of the gospel.

In the same way God will take our qualities and use them, if we allow him to do so. The very things that we may consider useless, the very things that may be the cause of shame or embarrassment, the very trials and sufferings that have brought us low can be things that the Lord employs most mightily. Churchill considered that: "all my past life had been but a preparation for this hour and this trial ..." It can be the same for us. There can come a day when we will be able to say of others that "they praised God because of me." (Galatians 1:24).

This does not mean that we will instantly be turned into paragons of Christian virtue. We will retain human frailties and weaknesses, although over time we will increasingly "be conformed to the likeness of [Christ]" (Romans 8:29). Though he was called to so momentous a task, human foibles were certainly a large part of Churchill's makeup. Throughout his life he was a prey to depression, which he called his "black dog." He frequently did not get up until midday and then worked all through the night, fuelled by an alarming consumption of alcohol. So exasperating was the Prime Minister and so given to calamitous meddling in military affairs that Lord Alanbrooke commented: "We cannot win with him and we cannot win without him."

Conclusion.

Churchill's powerful sense of calling gave him confidence in victory even when all seemed lost. At a cabinet meeting shortly after the Dunkirk evacuation and the capitulation of France, when several ministers argued (not without reason) that negotiation with Hitler was the only sensible course, the Prime Minister said: "If this island story of ours is to end, let it only do so when each one of us is lying here choking in his own blood." The same indomitable spirit governed all his days. Towards the end of his life, he had words of advice for pupils at his former school: "Never give up: never, never, never."

Sometimes the problems of the world can seem insurmountable, but we do not have to be a man on the scale of Winston Churchill to make a difference for God. It is in the small things, the unseen things, the un-remarked acts of kindness and gentleness and love that God is so often revealed. He told St Paul that: "My power is made perfect in weakness." (2 Corinthians 12:9). In fact, one of the tricks of the enemy is to make us so overwhelmed by what we think needs to be done that we become paralysed by it, or to make us so guilty that we take on more than we should and become crippled by it. The antidote is to start small and build up to something bigger as and when we feel able.

What, then, should we do? This is the question that people asked of John the Baptist when they heard his preaching and of Peter when he preached at Pentecost: see Luke 3:10, 12 and 14; Acts 2:37. The answer will be different for each of us, but the basic areas for all to consider are the same:

Are we praying enough? Much prayer brings much power, little prayer little power and no prayer no power.

Are we listening enough? Like the young Samuel we need to hearken to God's voice and respond to it: see 1 Samuel 3:2-10.

Are we doing enough? We need to consider what we can do to give expression to our faith and to show the love of Jesus to others. There is no lack of opportunity, either in the private or the public sphere.

Are we giving enough? This is not just, or even primarily, a question of money, but also of time: wherever we spend most of our time, there will our heart be. We cannot fool ourselves that we are too busy if we spend hours every week watching television.

Through our prayers, words and actions, we can echo to our nation the call that God places on us and on our lives. Above all, we should not give up. We should not give up on God, we should not give up on ourselves, we should not give up on others and we should not give up on our country. Each of us has a calling. Each of us can help to advance the kingdom of God. Each of us has a part to play in turning around the situation in this land. Rare is the man who has a sense of destiny as strong as Winston Churchill and rare is the man who has a calling like St Paul. If we wait for that kind of certainty we will never achieve anything. The one thing that can be guaranteed is that we will not make a difference unless we make a start. Let today be the day.

50. Tin legs

1 Thessalonians 1.

Key word: conviction.

During the inter-war years a young RAF pilot had a catastrophic crash. Both legs were amputated and his life hung by a thread. In excruciating pain, he lay week after week in a hospital bed: first better, then worse until at length his spirit began to ebb away. As his grip on this world loosened, pain left him and he felt a great sense of peace. Then outside his room he heard one nurse upbraid another: "Be quiet! Don't you know there's a dying man in there?" Suddenly his old combativeness asserted itself and he determined that he would not die. He roused himself, the agony returned and he lived.

Douglas Bader proceeded to astound all who met him. He was told that he would never walk again without a stick, but he did. He was told that he would never drive a car again, but he did. He was told that he would never fly an aeroplane again, but he did. So desperate was the need for pilots during the Battle of Britain that Bader managed to wangle a return to combat duty. Given command of a badly demoralised Canadian squadron, he made it one of the best in Fighter Command. Promoted to Wing Commander, he revolutionised RAF fighter tactics. He became one of the most successful aces of the day.

Eventually, he was shot down over St Mâlo in France.[112] To escape from his damaged aircraft, he had to tear one of his false legs loose and leave it behind in the blazing cockpit. The Germans sportingly arranged for the RAF to deliver a spare. As a prisoner of war, Bader then made himself such a nuisance that at one point his captors took away his false legs again. He was sent to the 'escape-proof' Colditz castle, reserved for serial escapees and troublemakers, where he remained until liberation by American troops in 1945. After the war he devoted himself to helping and inspiring disabled ex-servicemen.

Being inspired.

Douglas Bader was in the prime of life on the day of his aircraft crash. A man who lived for flying and delighted in his sporting ability was suddenly made a cripple. He was told that he would never more be able to take part in things that up till then had been his all in all. Yet "in spite of severe suffering" (1 Thessalonians 1:6) he did not quietly let go of life when he had the chance, but

---

[112] Recent research suggests that he may have been a victim of friendly fire.

287

chose quite deliberately to return to a world of pain and uncertainty. He did so because he was inspired. He was inspired to beat the odds, to prove doubters wrong and to fight on when the cause seemed lost.

St Paul talks of the Christians in Thessalonica as being people who are "inspired" (1 Thessalonians 1:3). Their inspiration comes from "hope in our Lord Jesus Christ." (1 Thessalonians 1:3). Indeed, in these early believers as in any Christian, inspiration was quite literal: the word conveys the idea of breathing into someone or something. In a theological sense inspiration connotes supernatural influence, especially that exerted by the Holy Spirit to impart a divine element to what we think and say and do. Inspiration of this kind is seen when "the LORD God formed the [first] man from the dust of the ground and breathed into his nostrils the breath of life, and the man became a living being." (Genesis 2:7). It is also evident following the resurrection, when Jesus appeared to his disciples and "breathed on them and said, 'Receive the Holy Spirit'" (John 20:22).

St Paul knew that the Thessalonians were inspired "because our gospel came to you not simply with words, but also with power, with the Holy Spirit and with deep conviction." (1 Thessalonians 1:4-5). This same conviction was at work in Jesus' disciples following the coming of the Holy Spirit at the first Pentecost. Men who hitherto had been afraid and demoralised suddenly began to speak and act fearlessly. Peter, who not long before had been so scared and so determined to save himself that he thrice denied Christ,[113] stood up in front of the crowds in the temple and told them plainly that "God has made this Jesus, whom you crucified, both Lord and Christ." (Acts 2:36).[114] His inspiration and conviction communicated themselves to his hearers, who "were cut to the heart" (Acts 2:37).

Inspiration and conviction inevitably bring about action and reaction. They did so in Peter, they did so in Douglas Bader and they will do so in us. When the gospel comes to us "not simply with words, but also with power, with the Holy Spirit and with deep conviction" (1 Thessalonians 1:4-5), that is evidence that we are "brothers loved by God, [and] that he has chosen [us]" (1 Thessalonians 1:4-5). Where there is an absence of inspiration and conviction, we have to question the spiritual depth of what the lips proclaim.

---

[113] See Matthew 26:70, 72 and 74; Mark 14:68, 70 and 71; Luke 22:57, 58 and 60; and John 18:17, 25 and 27.

[114] Shortly afterwards, Peter repeated claims about Jesus that the Jewish authorities would have considered blasphemous, saying that he is "the Holy and Righteous One" (Acts 3:14) and "the author of life" (Acts 3:15). The penalty for blasphemy was death.

Being productive.

In what is probably the earliest of his canonical letters, St Paul focuses on three essentials that later form the subject of an expanded discourse in 1 Corinthians 13: faith, hope and love (charity, *caritas*). These things are not mere abstract concepts, worthless playthings of the mind, but are real and produce effects in the world around us: the effects are manifest in work, labour and endurance.

Salvation is by grace through faith alone, but this faith is no dull intellectual thing. It is nothing if it does not make us act and cause us to be productive for God. St Paul commends his readers for "your work produced by faith, your labour prompted by love, and your endurance inspired by hope" (1 Thessalonians 1:3). These people did not just listen to what they were taught, they took it to heart. They did not just give intellectual assent to high-minded ideals, they acted upon them. They did not give up at the first sign of trouble, but stuck it out through thick and thin. James encourages us to respond in the same way when he says: "What good is it, my brothers, if a man claims to have faith but has no deeds? ... In the same way, faith by itself, if it is not accompanied by action, is dead." (James 2:14 and 17).

If our work and labour are to be productive and our endurance worthwhile, we need God in our lives – Father, Son and Holy Spirit. In writing to the congregation at Thessalonica, St Paul is conscious of the activity of all three members of the Trinity. The church is said to be "in God the Father and the Lord Jesus Christ" (1 Thessalonians 1:1), whilst "our gospel came ... with the Holy Spirit" (1 Thessalonians 1:5). In the same way, we need to access the power of God in all its fullness. We need to "be filled with the Spirit" (Ephesians 5:18) and to "keep in step with the Spirit" (Galatians 5:25). If we do not, we will cease to be productive, as Jesus makes clear: "Remain in me and I will remain in you. No branch can bear fruit by itself; it must remain in the vine. Neither can you bear fruit unless you remain in me. I am the vine; you are the branches. If a man remains in me and I in him, he will bear much fruit; apart from me you can do nothing. If anyone does not remain in me, he is like a branch that is thrown away and withers; such branches are picked up, thrown into the fire and burned." (John 15:4-6). This should hardly surprise us: someone who loses the source of their inspiration ends up just going through the motions, living the opposite of "life in all its fullness" (John 10:10). Someone who speaks and acts without conviction achieves nothing lasting or worthwhile, and will have no enduring influence on others.

Being a model.

God wants us to be inspired in every sense of the word, and if we are inspired we can scarcely help being inspirational. The best way of learning is by doing. If we show by our lives what Christianity in action looks like, others will watch and take note. Some might ignore the lesson, but those who pay attention will themselves become an inspiration to others. So it has always been:

In Thessalonica St Paul provided the first example: "You know how we lived among you for your sake." (1 Thessalonians 1:5).

Christian converts watched and learnt from him: "You became imitators of us and of the Lord; in spite of severe suffering, you welcomed the message with the joy given by the Holy Spirit." (1 Thessalonians 1:6).

They in turn inspired others: "And so you became a model to all the believers in Macedonia and Achaia." (1 Thessalonians 1:7).

The effects were felt far and wide: "The Lord's message rang out from you not only in Macedonia and Achaia – your faith in God has become known everywhere." (1 Thessalonians 1:8).

Tales of what had happened returned to the apostle to encourage and strengthen him: "Therefore we do not need to say anything about it, for they themselves report what kind of reception you gave us. They tell how you turned to God from idols to serve the living and true God, and to wait for his Son from heaven, whom he raised from the dead – Jesus, who rescues us from the coming wrath." (1 Thessalonians 1:8-10).

There were three components to the way in which the Christians in Thessalonica became a model to others: becoming "imitators of us and of the Lord", persevering "in spite of severe suffering" and "[welcoming] the message with the joy given by the Holy Spirit." (1 Thessalonians 1:6). Being a model and learning from others involves hard work: "We do not want you to become lazy, but to imitate those who through faith and patience inherit what has been promised." (Hebrews 6:12). Douglas Bader certainly needed all his patience and courage as he learned to walk again. It was only possible after long hours of practice, frequent falls and severe discomfort as metal chafed against the stumps where once his legs had been.

Bader was and remains an inspiration and a model just as the early Christians in Thessalonica were "a model to all the believers in Macedonia and Achaia ... [and] everywhere." (1 Thessalonians 1:7). Every single one of us is called to be a model to those around us, to inspire and influence, to teach, encourage and strengthen. We will never be able to do this unless we come close enough for people to know us, to see what we do and to understand why we do it. We cannot remain in a holy huddle, barricading ourselves against the world outside. We must go out and at the same time we must welcome people in. We must inspire and enable people to belong, so that through belonging their beliefs and behaviour might follow on behind.

In the process of modelling belonging, belief and behaviour for others, we must never lose sight of the fact that all that we do and say is only possible through the work of God in our lives. Doing this should spark thanksgiving, prayer and remembrance as it did for St Paul:

Thanksgiving: "We always thank God for all of you" (1 Thessalonians 1:2).

Prayer: "We [are] always ... mentioning you in our prayers." (1 Thessalonians 1:2).

Remembrance: "We continually remember before our God and Father your work produced by faith, your labour prompted by love, and your endurance inspired by hope in our Lord Jesus Christ." (1 Thessalonians 1:3).

Thereby we will help ensure that we remain "in God the Father and the Lord Jesus Christ" (1 Thessalonians 1:1).

Conclusion.

Douglas Bader was a larger-than-life character and a war hero in classic mould. Perhaps his most lasting legacy, however, is in attitudes towards and treatment of the disabled. He showed that even those who had suffered the most severe injuries need not be consigned to a life of uselessness and dependency, but could aspire to great achievement. The pilot's determination not to die caused him to rouse himself from his death-bed. His conviction that he could and would do again things that everyone told him could not be done caused him to confound all experts. He has left a tremendous example of how indomitable can be the human spirit.

Many imagined that that all Bader had to look forward to following his crash was a lifetime of hobbling around on crutches, forever looking to others to provide for him, but it turned out that he had not been consigned to the scrap-heap after all. Like the early Christians in Thessalonica there was "work ... [and] labour" (1 Thessalonians 1:3) aplenty for him, for which he would need all his "endurance" (1 Thessalonians 1:3). The same is true for each of us, no matter how scarred and beaten up we are by life, no matter how much we have been disfigured or crippled by what we have experienced. Nobody is consigned to the scrap-heap by the Lord, whatever other people may say and think. There are important things for every one of us to do and worthwhile contributions that we each have to make. They may not always feel significant and valuable to us, but that is because we tend to reckon in the way that the world does, not like God. Faith, hope and love can work the same wonders in our lives as they have worked in the lives of countless others. It all comes down to inspiration and conviction.

Instead of denying the inspiration within, we should give it free rein so that its breath becomes the mighty wind that God intends. We need to start speaking and acting with conviction instead of cowering in the corner as though we had a shameful secret. We must stop denying Christ and start to proclaim him.

51. Bearing the unbearable

Psalm 27.

Key word: forgiveness.

Allied troops captured by the Japanese during the Second World War suffered appalling brutality and privation. Years afterwards, one former POW told of his experience of working on the notorious Death Railway between Bangkok and Rangoon. It is said that a man died for every sleeper that was laid for its track.[115] Since this particular soldier was the senior officer in the prison camp to which he was sent, the Japanese would regularly beat him: for infractions of rules by his men, for failure to meet work quotas, or just because they enjoyed it. He described the awful, daily anticipation of yet another thrashing, of how time and again he felt that he could not stand it, but he knew it was his duty to suffer in order to prevent his men experiencing even worse treatment from their captors. Somehow he found the ability to carry on.

Few are likely to experience trials of this kind, but it is rare indeed to find someone whose life is completely free of fear. Sometimes the fear is physical, but it need not be. Mental anguish can be just as dreadful. We all go through patches when it feels as though life is beating us up on a daily basis, and doing it just for the fun of it. In such times of testing, pain and stress, we need to find the resources to go on. Even better, we need to access the spiritual strength that King David had, so that he was able to write: "Though an army besiege me, my heart will not fear; though war break out against me, even then will I be confident" (Psalm 27:3). It seems a tall order, but Psalm 27 helps us to understand how the shepherd boy turned king was able to do this.

David's experience.

Lest we imagine that David was able to write in such an uplifting way because he had things easy, it is worth recalling some of the major events of his life:

Adult burdens were placed on his shoulders from the earliest age, as he was charged with caring for his father's flocks and protecting them from wild animals: 1 Samuel 17:34-36.

---

[115] The British surveyed the route of the railway before the Second World War, but abandoned the project since they thought the cost in human life would be too high.

He was misunderstood, insulted and belittled: 1 Samuel 17:28.

Whilst "only a boy" (1 Samuel 17:42) he was caught up in war between the Israelites and the Philistines, taking responsibility when every adult was afraid to do so and killing the formidable enemy champion, Goliath: 1 Samuel 17:40-50.

Still just a young man, he was driven into exile and subsequently hunted down by the Israelite king Saul, who wanted to kill him: 1 Samuel 19-21 and 26.

During this time, when he was almost constantly on the run and knew little security, his wife Michal was forcibly taken from him by her father Saul and given to another man, with David powerless to do anything about it: 1 Samuel 25:44.

He suffered severe illness (Psalm 38:3-10), had a child who died soon after birth (2 Samuel 12:13-19), a daughter who was raped (2 Samuel 13:1-21), a son who was murdered (2 Samuel 13:23-33) and another who rebelled against him and was killed (2 Samuel 15 and 18).

He committed adultery and murder, leading to appalling guilt: 2 Samuel 11 and Psalm 51.

He experienced the disappointment of not being allowed by God to build a temple to the Lord in Jerusalem: 1 Chronicles 22:7-8.

Perhaps our collective memory of war is now receding, but David's other experiences remain all too commonplace. We may not be exiled in the sense of having to seek refuge in a foreign land, but many know an internal exile that consists in estrangement from friends, family or colleagues. As for the rest – burdens beyond our years, misunderstandings, insults, sickness, family strife, disappointed ambitions, terrible hurts done to and by beloved children, the consciousness of our own sinfulness and its consequences each retain their grip on humankind. Whatever else, we can hardly say that David had an easy life. It was a life brim full of insecurity and fear, anger, pain, upset and regret. It is therefore important to understand how he could write as he did.

The Lord is my salvation.

The answer appears in verses 1-2 of Psalm 27, where he asserts: "The LORD is my light and my salvation ... the stronghold of my life ..." Both at the beginning and at the end of the Psalm he states his confidence in God: verse 3 says "I will be confident" and verse 13 repeats, "I am still confident ..."

In short, David's strength is founded on putting God at the centre of his life and trusting in him, no matter what may be happening in the world around. It is his confidence, or faith, that is the key. Verses 13-14 of the Psalm encourage us to wait patiently for something that will surely come ("I *will* see the goodness of the Lord in the land of the living"), even though we do not see it yet. Verse 14 tells us: "Wait for the LORD, be strong and take heart and wait for the LORD."

The repetition of the phrase "wait for the LORD" is no accident and nor is it poetic licence on the part of an accomplished wordsmith. There are times when we do have to wait. We have to wait even though we are suffering in mind or in body or in spirit. Abraham had to wait beyond all reasonable expectation before God fulfilled the promise to give him a son by his wife Sarah: "after waiting patiently, Abraham received what was promised." (Hebrews 6:15). It is during times of waiting that we most need to hold fast to faith. David looked beyond the troubles of the moment. Instead, in verse 4 he says that he seeks to "dwell in the house of the LORD all the days of my life, to gaze upon the beauty of the LORD and to seek him in his temple ..." This is the "one thing" that David asks of God (verse 4) because he knows that it is through this that he will:

"be exalted above the enemies who surround me" (verse 6);

"sacrifice [at the Lord's tabernacle] with shouts of joy" (verse 6);

"sing and make music to the LORD" (verse 6); and that

"the LORD will receive me" (verse 10).

He understands that the fundamental thing is his relationship with God and that everything else flows from this. He therefore looks beyond the earthly realm to the heavenly kingdom. Psalm 27 is a resounding statement of faith in the face of adversity. The misfortune that David confronts is no less real than the troubles we face day by day, for enemies surround him (verse 6), there is a real chance that even his parents may forsake him (verse 10), he faces oppressors (verse 11) and false witnesses rise up against him (verse 12).

Psalm 27 makes it clear that the fact that the Lord is our salvation does *not* mean that we will be saved from all trials and tribulations. In fact, Christians might expect to suffer more than others, not less. The Bible reminds us that "our struggle is not against flesh and blood, but against ... the spiritual forces of evil in the heavenly realms" (Ephesians 6:12) and those powers certainly have an interest in attacking us, to weaken our faith and to divert us from fighting what St Paul calls "the good fight of the faith" (1 Timothy 6:12). So if it does not mean taking away all earthly trials and tribulations, salvation must mean something else. David explores this in the middle verses of the Psalm. Verses 7-10 picture the world of salvation as one where God will:

"hear my voice when I call"

"[be] merciful to me and answer me"

"not hide [his] face from me"

"not turn [me] away in anger"

"not reject or forsake me"

"receive me"

The image is the very opposite of being godforsaken, of being abandoned by God in the way that is described in Psalm 22. The emphasis is on relationship with God. David does not allow calamity to turn him away from the Lord. He does not rail against the Almighty or blame him for what is happening. He does not reject him or try to work things out apart from him. Instead, he seeks greater closeness to the one who is his "light and salvation" (Psalm 27:1).

Although salvation comes by grace through faith alone, David knows that we still have our part to play. It is for this reason that he says: "Teach me your way, O LORD; lead me in a straight path because of my oppressors." (Psalm 27:11). The word ' because' in that sentence is a useful reminder for us: it is precisely when we are oppressed, by people or circumstances, that we have such need of being led by God, for in our sorrow and suffering it is so easy for us to take a wrong turning – away from God rather than closer to him.

Psalm 27 explores David's experience and reactions, but it speaks also of the experience of Jesus, who even in the agony of his crucifixion never lost sight of God as his salvation. This goes to the heart of the Christian message: that we can achieve forgiveness through Christ's atonement on the cross and we can achieve salvation as a result of faith. Jesus said: "I am the Way, the Truth and the Life" (John 14:6). He was, and is, God made man for our salvation. Jesus died in order to free us from guilt, addiction, fear and death. He made forgiveness possible, bringing us friendship with God, the experience of his love and the power to change. Consequently, he liberates us to love, forgive and serve others and to become more like himself. These things are at the heart of the biblical understanding of salvation.[116] This salvation, love and forgiveness are not things that we could ever achieve ourselves. They are free gifts from God.

Conclusion.

Those taken prisoner by Nippon returned with harrowing tales of what they suffered in captivity. The health of many was broken by years of brutal

---

[116] There is an intimate connection between forgiveness and salvation. At the Last Supper, Jesus told his disciples: "This is my blood of the covenant, which is poured out for many for the forgiveness of sins." (Matthew 26:28). Speaking of the infant John the Baptist, his father Zechariah prophesied that he would "give his people the knowledge of salvation through the forgiveness of their sins" (Luke 1:77).

treatment, malnutrition, disease and overwork. Many found it difficult to forgive the Japanese for what they had done. That is hardly surprising: they had seen friends beaten to death, bound with barbed wire and used for bayonet practice, pumped full of water and jumped on, or slowly starved to death. Each day they lived with what they called 'rice balls': the skin of the scrotum and inner thigh made painful and raw through lack of nutrients contained in the worthless shavings from rice, which their captors refused to give them. Forgiveness on one side has been in short supply and genuine regret on the other seldom evident.

This makes all the more remarkable another story from those times, also true, but this time with a happy ending. John Baxter, a corporal in the Royal Engineers, was captured in Java in 1942. His final two years in captivity were spent labouring in mines in the southern Japanese island of Kyushu. There he and his comrades also suffered starvation, beatings and inhumane treatment, but found one guard was unlike all others. Hyato Hirano smuggled extra food rations made by his wife to the starving prisoners and excused sick men from work. Years after the end of the war the two met again. The former guard begged forgiveness from the former prisoner. Gradually, painfully, a relationship developed and, over the course of many meetings, they became friends. We can only imagine the hurt, anger and guilt they had to overcome as they journeyed together along the road of forgiveness, but eventually their relationship developed to a point where the former prison camp guard was able to confide what he had until then kept secret: the Japanese was a Christian.

If these two could find forgiveness and friendship, so can each of us. If they could endure pain and hurt and at the end of it triumphantly proclaim through their lives a part of the forgiveness that God makes available to all, so can we. Forgiveness is one of the central planks of the Christian life. It is through forgiveness that we can help set ourselves free and unlock the full measure of God's blessing in our lives and in our nation. We live in a land that groans under a welter of hurts and amongst a people who nurse untold grievances and sorrows. We will never truly salve these wounds and bring healing without love and forgiveness. The need for us to love and to forgive if we are to be made whole is one of the central insights that Jesus taught: "Love your enemies and pray for those who persecute you." (Matthew 5:44). "Forgive, and you will be forgiven." (Luke 11:37).

Life is full of fear and difficulties, hurts and upsets. David faced trials that would have crushed most, but was able to rise above them. The key was his relationship with and trust in God. It is not easy, but we need to keep our eyes on the real prize, the "one thing" that David talks about in verse 4 of Psalm 27. We need to do what verse 14 of this Psalm encourages us to do: "be strong and take heart and wait for the LORD."

52. Living with evil

Esther 3.

Key word: constancy.

One day a young Englishwoman named Christabel Bielenberg summoned the family doctor to her eldest son, who lay stricken with a fever. A little to her surprise, he spent the night helping look after the child, whose temperature had by morning subsided. As the man turned to leave, he asked if she still wanted him to be their physician. She had vaguely noticed that of late he seemed less busy than formerly but, tired as she was, did not at first grasp his meaning. Then he explained: he was a Jew, they were living in Hamburg in the nineteen thirties and the Nazis were in power. The paediatrician, dedicated and respected, had been warned of dire consequences if he did not cease contact with Aryan children and hand over his business to a non-Jew.

Though married to a German and for some years resident in the Third Reich, this was Bielenberg's first personal experience of the Nazis' racial policies. It was by no means her last. In wartime a young couple came to call, nervously seeking shelter. They also were Jews, and were on the run. With her husband away, the young housewife sought advice from a trusted friend and neighbour, whom she knew to be against the New Order. The man warned vehemently against her taking in Jews: the family were already in danger enough by reason of her husband's opposition to the regime, and liable to discovery if they drew attention to themselves. She agonised, but found she could not refuse. "Very well," she said, "but only for two nights." At the end of that time she woke to find the couple gone, their bedding neatly stowed. She discovered later that they were arrested trying to board a train and sent to Auschwitz concentration camp. Bitterly she recalled: "That was when I knew that Hitler had turned me into a murderer."

Action replay.

Like Christabel Bielenberg, the beautiful young Jewess Esther and her uncle Mordecai had to live with evil. The book of Esther recounts their trials and eventual triumph. To this day, each year during the feast of Purim[117] Jews celebrate this story and their deliverance "during the time of Xerxes." (Esther

---

[117] The name derives from *Pur*, meaning lot, a reference to the lots that Haman cast to decide on which day he should destroy the Jews: see Esther 3:7.

1:1). On one level, the book is a straightforward struggle by two outsiders, Haman and Mordecai, to gain influence with Xerxes. At a deeper level it is part of an ongoing battle between good and evil, the former represented by followers of the one true God and the latter by the Amalekites. This tribe fought the Israelites during their journey from Egypt to the Promised Land (see Exodus 17:8-16 and Deuteronomy 25:17-19) and are described as people who "had no fear of God." (Deuteronomy 25:18).

The protagonists are explicitly linked with this earlier conflict. Haman is "son of Hammedatha, the Agagite" (Esther 3:1) – a descendant of Agag, the Amalekite king whom King Saul of Israel failed to kill: see 1 Samuel 15:9. Mordecai is "son of Jair, the son of Shimei, the son of Kish" (Esther 2:5) – a descendant of Kish, the father of King Saul: see 1 Samuel 9:1-2. Through Esther and Mordecai, God's promise that he "will completely blot out the memory of Amalek from under heaven" (Exodus 17:14) is fulfilled. Timing also reflects previous events in redemption history. Haman begins plotting "to destroy all Mordecai's people, the Jews, throughout the whole kingdom of Xerxes" (Esther 3:6) in the very month in which Jews celebrate their Passover deliverance from Egypt.

Plots and plans.

At first, evil seems to prosper: "Xerxes honoured Haman son of Hammedatha the Agagite, elevating him and giving him a seat of honour higher than that of all the other nobles. All the royal officials at the king's gate knelt down and paid honour to Haman, for the king had commanded this concerning him." (Esther 3:1-2). Having got its foot in the door, evil does what it always does. It grows, spreads, corrupts, infects and undermines before finally overreaching itself. We should study and learn from this, since the methods that evil uses are the same in every age and in every place:

Human beings demand the homage that belongs to God: Mordecai is required to "kneel down or pay him [Haman] honour." (Esther 3:2).

The coercive power of the state is brought to bear in matters that are properly the concern of individual conscience: "Then the royal officials at the king's gate asked Mordecai, 'Why do you disobey the king's command?'" (Esther 3:3).

Attempts are made to override all moral scruple: "Day after day they spoke to him but he refused to comply." (Esther 3:4).

Hatred is in men's hearts and grudges are borne: "Therefore they told Haman about it to see whether Mordecai's behaviour would be tolerated, for he had told them he was a Jew." (Esther 3:4). The implication is that the royal officials thought

Mordecai's behaviour would not be tolerated, presumably because Haman's dislike of Jews was well known.

Reaction to any transgression is disproportionate: "Haman looked for a way to destroy all Mordecai's people, the Jews, throughout the whole kingdom of Xerxes." (Esther 3:6).

Free rein is given to evil elements of all kinds: "they [Haman's accomplices, probably the astrologers who assist him later in the story: see Esther 5:10 and 14, 6:12-13] cast the *pur* (that is, the lot) in the presence of Haman" (Esther 3:7).

Individuals or groups are singled out and made victims because they are in some way distinctive: "Then Haman said to King Xerxes, 'There is a certain people dispersed and scattered among the peoples in all the provinces of your kingdom whose customs are different from those of all other peoples'" (Esther 3:8).

The weak are particularly vulnerable: the Jews are easy victims because they are "dispersed and scattered" (Esther 3:8).

Self-interest and fear of those who are different are manipulated: "a certain people ... do not obey the king's laws; it is not in the king's best interest to tolerate them." (Esther 3:8).

Bribery is used: "If it pleases the king, let a decree be issued to destroy them, and I will put ten thousand talents of silver into the royal treasury for the men who carry out this business." (Esther 3:9).

Power is devolved to those who are not fit to exercise it and those in authority abrogate responsibility: "So the king took off his signet ring from his finger and gave it to Haman son of Hammedatha, the Agagite, the enemy of the Jews." (Esther 3:10).

Pride undermines judgment: "'Keep the money,' the king said to Haman, 'and do with the people as you please.'" (Esther 3:11).

Things are done in haste without proper investigation and without due process of law: Haman and his accomplices cast lots "in the first month, the month of Nisan" (Esther 3:7) and he then has to engineer an interview with Xerxes, but even so "on the thirteenth day of the first month the royal secretaries were summoned." (Esther 3:12).

Legitimate power and authority is subverted and misused: "Haman's orders ... were written in the name of King Xerxes himself and sealed with his own ring." (Esther 3:12).

Promise of gain and personal enrichment are held out: when the Jews are killed there will be "plunder" (Esther 3:13).

Laws are promulgated that have no regard to morality: "A copy of the text of the edict was to be issued as law in every province and made known to the people of every nationality so that they would be ready for that day." (Esther 3:14).

Victims are given no opportunity to defend themselves: "Spurred on by the king's command, the couriers went out, and the edict was issued in the citadel of Susa." (Esther 3:15).

A compact is made between evil and those in authority: "The king and Haman sat down to drink" (Esther 3:15).

The reactions of evil are irrational, uncontrolled and characterised by extremes of emotionally negative behaviour. Haman is "enraged" (Esther 3:5) and "having learned who Mordecai's people were, he scorned ... killing only Mordecai" (Esther 3:6). The delight of evil is "to destroy, kill and annihilate ... and to plunder" (Esther 3:13). "Haman's orders to the king's satraps, the governors of the various provinces and the nobles of the various peoples" (Esther 3:12) are an early version of the Germans' notorious *Vernichtungsbefehl* (annihilation order). Evil is pitiless and merciless. Those to be killed include "young and old, women and little children" (Esther 3:13).

Staying true.

Mordecai and Esther show us how to deal with evil. Their response is secured by three anchors:

They are true to what they believe in, despite all dangers and threats: "Mordecai would not kneel down or pay [Haman] honour." (Esther 3:2) and "he [Mordecai] refused to comply." (Esther 3:4).

They do not despair: They do not give up even though the order to kill all Jews has actually been promulgated: "the edict was issued in the citadel of Susa" (Esther 3:15).

They do not react violently, but instead make use of the influence that is available to them: Esther bravely petitions the king to "grant me my life ... and spare my people" (Esther 7:3). The request is granted and Haman is hung "on the gallows he had prepared for Mordecai." (Esther 7:10). Chapters 8-10 record the king's subsequent edict on behalf of the Jews, the triumph of the Jews and the honour heaped on Mordecai.

These things come down to constancy: constancy of belief, constancy of hope and constancy of action. Esther and Mordecai do not slacken in the homage they give to the Lord, nor give in to temptation to divert that homage elsewhere. Through constancy to God and his ways Esther and Mordecai survive, prevail and prosper. Through them their people are also blessed. In Nazi Germany, and in particular in its concentration camps, some see the ultimate absence of God: proof of the fact that he does not exist or, if he does, that he is indifferent. The message of Esther, however, is very different. It is not only the princess and her uncle who are constant, but God, too.

Intriguingly, the book of Esther is the only one in the Bible that does not specifically refer to the Almighty. Neither does it mention worship, prayer or sacrifice. Fasting is the single explicit religious observance. Yet this does not mean that the Lord is forgotten or absent. His sovereign rule is assumed throughout. The every thought and action of the book's hero and heroine, Mordecai and Esther, is based on the assumption that God exists, hears prayer, works justice and protects his people. The fact that the Jews are in the end lifted up and Haman, who sought to do them ill, suffers the fate that he had prepared for others vindicates this viewpoint.

Conclusion.

We each live with evil every day. Thankfully, we do not live under a regime where evil has taken over all the levers of power in the way that it did under Haman and under the Nazis. Yet we must nevertheless be alert to its tendency to undermine and work through legitimate channels. It is present in the small things of life no less than in the large. We must have no tolerance for it, in whatever grand or petty ways it may be manifest around us. We must root out our own tendencies to the attitudes and behaviour that allow it to thrive. Above all, we should not fool ourselves: the same strategies and effects that existed when Xerxes allowed free rein to Haman or Adolf Hitler bestrode the world stage are alive in our land, too.

God deserves our homage. If it is not given to him, it will be given elsewhere and when that which is due to our Creator is given elsewhere it is necessarily deployed on the side of evil. We cannot and must not be indifferent to the first signs of evil at work, for if it is unchecked it will surely grow. Christabel Bielenberg had no reason to castigate herself. She and her family did more than most to confront evil at a time when and in a place where it was rampant. Suspected of involvement in the plot to kill Hitler of 20 July 1944, her husband was arrested and sent to Ravensbrück concentration camp. To save him she voluntarily agreed to undergo interrogation by the Gestapo and, as a direct result, he was released. Many years later she wrote in her autobiography of the "simple Christian upbringing [that] had provided me with a sturdy conviction as to the ultimate triumph of good over evil." This faith enabled her to remain constant through great hardship. We must be constant, too. If our "faith small as a mustard seed" (Matthew 17:20) does not lead us to bestir ourselves, it is a poor tale. If we cannot find it in us to raise our voices now, when the threats against us are so minor in comparison with what she and countless others have lived through and continue to endure, our inconstancy will merit whatever then befalls.

53. Sticking it out

Romans 12:1-16.

Key word: sacrifice.

Words of courage and defiance echo down the years and still have power to make the spine tingle:

"I say to the House as I said to ministers who have joined this government, I have nothing to offer but blood, toil, tears and sweat. We have before us an ordeal of the most grievous kind. We have before us many, many months of struggle and suffering.

"We shall go on to the end ... We shall defend our island, whatever the cost may be. We shall fight on the beaches, we shall fight on the landing grounds, we shall fight in the fields and in the streets, we shall fight in the hills; we shall never surrender."

These quotations are probably familiar to most Englishmen. Both come from speeches that Winston Churchill made to the House of Commons, just over three weeks apart. The first was given on 13 May 1940, being part of Churchill's first address to the House of Commons after his appointment as Prime Minister. The second was made on 4 June 1940, the day that the Dunkirk evacuation ended. Twenty-one days later, France capitulated and Britain stood alone against the Axis powers, facing imminent invasion. It is difficult to hear Churchill's words, even today, without something stirring in the blood and thrilling at all that is contained in the proud boast: we shall never surrender. It plays to our concept of what our nation stands for, of what it means to be free rather than a slave, to be a man rather than something less than human.

The wartime years and their aftermath certainly brought sacrifice aplenty. There was no shortage of blood, toil, tears and sweat. When it was over and the dust had settled, it came to be seen that although Britain was on the winning side, she was greatly diminished: vanished was her maritime and commercial supremacy, liquidated were her overseas investments and gone to all intents and purposes was her freedom of action, for the nation was deeply in debt. In due course her Empire and her former position of pre-eminence in the world were fled, too. Her great cities were cratered by bomb sites. Millions were homeless or living in jerry-built prefabs. Great sacrifices for freedom had denuded her strength. Whilst the United States enjoyed unprecedented prosperity, the people of these islands lived cramped and crabbed lives. Conditions for the majority were spartan. National service continued. Industry was kept turning at full pelt with increasingly worn and antiquated equipment. Rationing was not finally abolished on all items until the early 1960s. Yet through all the years of austerity, almost nobody doubted that the sacrifice was worth it.

Worship.

St Paul writes about a sacrifice worth making. It is a sacrifice that we are called to make voluntarily, not forced by circumstances: "Therefore I urge you, brothers, in view of God's mercy, to offer your bodies as living sacrifices, holy and pleasing to God – this is your spiritual act of worship." (Romans 12:1). Here are concepts that were revolutionary by the standards of the pagan religions of the Roman Empire:

Sacrifice is to be offered "in view of God's mercy" (Romans 12:1). In other words, it is to be given out of gratitude and love in response to what God has already done and continues to do for us, not as an attempt to bribe or propitiate an angry and unpredictable deity.

Sacrifice does not consist in goods or slaughtered animals, but instead comprises "[our] bodies" (Romans 12:1). This is a human sacrifice like no other. It involves not death, but its opposite: we are to be "living sacrifices" (Romans 12:1), available to serve God each and every day.

We are to offer ourselves as people who are "holy and pleasing to God" (Romans 12:1). The words emphasise that what God is most interested in is our inner disposition, not the outward forms of worship that we employ or the magnificence of the material possessions that we lay on an altar.

Through offering ourselves in this way we perform a "spiritual act of worship" (Romans 12:1). This is something of which we need to remind ourselves continually: to worship God in spirit and truth is not a matter of ritual. Neither does it rely on prescribed incantations, nor even on the presence of things of beauty. All these may be an aid to our worship, but they are not its heart. Only the free giving of ourselves, without let or hindrance, can be that.

Worshipping the Almighty in the way that St Paul describes is not something that can be confined to an hour or so in church once a week. It is something that must permeate and inform our every moment. It involves the sacrifice of our daily lives, so that we are alive to and actively seek opportunities throughout each day to do something for our Lord. What we are able to do may be so small that we think it of no worth. At such times, we need to remind ourselves how Jesus reacted to the giving of the widow's mite: "this poor widow has put in more than all the others. All these people gave their gifts out of their wealth; but she out of her poverty put in all she had to live on." (Luke 21:3-4).

We should never look down on anything done for God when it is proportionate to what we are able to give and when the motive behind the giving is a right one.

Surrender.

Surrender is a necessary part of the kind of worship that is most pleasing to our heavenly Father. This should not be confused with abandon. To surrender ourselves in the way that the Lord wants does not necessarily mean that we have to give way to wild displays of emotion. It does not mean giving up or giving in, for it is not about capitulation in the face of an enemy. It instead involves surrender in its oldest and deepest sense: a giving of the self (from the French *se rendre*). It can be hard for us to let go in this way. It flies in the face of every proud shout of 'no surrender' that human beings have ever uttered. It leads us to imagine that we will somehow be taken prisoner and lose our individuality, that we will be swamped or taken over by God. The experience of everyone who has allowed themselves to surrender in this way, however, is that this is not how God works. Indeed, through surrender to God our personality is if anything heightened, for we are thereby freed to become the people we were always intended to be.

If true worship involves giving ourselves, it follows that it must primarily be about service. For us to serve effectively, we must recognise and accept where we stand in relation to God and our fellow man. This requires a proper appreciation of our place in the scheme of things, and an understanding not only of our worth in the sight of God but also of the fact that others have equal worth. St Paul makes clear that there is no room for conceit : "For by the grace given to me I say to every one of you: Do not think of yourself more highly than you ought, but rather think of yourself with sober judgment, in accordance with the measure of faith that God has given to you." (Romans 12:3). Later he emphasises the point: "Live in harmony with one another. Do not be proud, but be willing to associate with people of lowly position. Do not be conceited." (Romans 12:16).

Not everyone is called to serve in the same way. There are reasons for the differences between us. These should not be the occasion for point-scoring or competition, but should rather cause us to wonder at the wisdom of the one who made us: "Just as each of us has one body with many members, and these members do not all have the same function, so in Christ we who are many form one body and each member belongs to all the others. We have different gifts, according to the grace given us." (Romans 12:4-6).

The important thing is that the gifts we have been given should be used, and used properly. They should be deployed for the purpose that God intended and they should be exercised in a way that brings glory to his name: "If a man's gift is prophesying, let him use it in proportion to his faith. If it is serving, let him serve; if it is teaching, let him teach; if it is encouraging, let him encourage; if it is contributing to the needs of others, let him give generously; if it is leadership, let him govern diligently; if it is showing mercy, let him do it cheerfully." (Romans 12:6-8).

Transformation.

True worship and selfless service will lead inevitably to transformation. We are called to be revolutionaries, not conformists. This involves an act of will on our part and an act of grace on the part of God. Once we choose no longer to conform to what is bad, then God will cause us to be renewed: "Do not conform any longer to the pattern of this world, but be transformed by the renewing of your mind." (Romans 12:2). The transformation and renewal will be mental and spiritual in nature, with the result that: "Then [we] will be able to test and approve what God's will is – his good, pleasing and perfect will." (Romans 12:2).

This bears investigation. St Paul is saying that conformity to the ways of thinking of the world around us affects our minds so that we are no longer able to reason clearly. It removes us so far from God's way of thinking and acting that we cannot begin to comprehend what he is doing, still less how and why he acts as he does. Only when we take our blinkers off can we then test God's will, see that it is "good, pleasing and perfect" (Romans 12:20) and therefore approve it. Hence we must break the link to "the pattern of this world" (Romans 12:2) that holds us in thrall. To do this, we have to be far more critical in judging the things that belong to our culture which are not in accordance with God's laws. It is perhaps unrealistic to imagine that we can blot these out altogether but we can choose what to watch on television, we can choose whether to go along with certain kinds of behaviour and we can decide to reject ideas that are inconsistent with our beliefs. Above all, we can choose to ask for God's help in renewing our minds.

St Paul describes things that are at one and the same time evidence of what transformed thinking and a transformed life look like and the means by which these comes about:

"Love must be sincere." (Romans 12:9).

"Hate what is evil, cling to what is good." (Romans 12:9).

"Be devoted to one another in brotherly love." (Romans 12:10).

"Honour one another above yourselves." (Romans 12:10).

"Never be lacking in zeal, but keep your spiritual fervour, serving the Lord." (Romans 12:11).

"Be joyful in hope, patient in affliction, faithful in prayer." (Romans 12:12).

"Share with God's people who are in need. Practice hospitality." (Romans 12:13).

Some of these are easier than others. To "Rejoice with those who rejoice; mourn with those who mourn" (Romans 12:15) demands empathy with and concern for others, but many will find that this injunction does not tax them too greatly. It is another thing entirely to be told: "Bless those who persecute you; bless and do not curse." (Romans 12:14). More often we are apt to react as did Winston Churchill, who in 1941 said of the Germans: "We will mete out to them the measure, and more than the measure, that they have meted out to us." Yet although it does not come naturally, we must do all we can to staunch our propensity to revenge, self-righteousness and self-justification. These things merely stoke conflict and tie us to the ways of the world.

Conclusion.

With each year that passes our society draws further from the attitude of mind and heart that is needful if we are to worship God and serve as he wishes. Our relentless self-promotion and self-indulgence are amongst the symptoms of a culture that gives in to the self at every point, but finds it almost impossible to give of the self. Our own desires are increasingly the object of our worship and the one who made us is forgotten. All thought of self-sacrifice falls by the wayside. It is an ugly spectacle and one that is set only to grow worse unless urgent steps are taken.

Change cannot come about unless we alter what is in our hearts. Through the prophet Isaiah the Lord has told us what to do: "Stop bringing your meaningless offerings! ... wash and make yourselves clean. Take your evil deeds out of my sight! Stop doing wrong, learn to do right! Seek justice, encourage the oppressed. Defend the cause of the fatherless, plead the case of the widow." (Isaiah 1:13 and 16-17).

What we believe affects how we behave. The practical outworking of the Christian faith involves surrender and service: service of God and service of our fellow men. For every act of service that is required of us, there is a corresponding enabling gift from God. The trick is to identify our gifts and then to make sure that we use them for godly purposes. We must sit on our hands no longer. For sure, life can be a slog. Everyone experiences times of pain, hardship, discouragement and despair, but we must stick it out and see it through as did previous generations. It will involve sacrifice on our part, but there is not a shadow of a doubt that, of all the sacrifices that might be asked of us, this is the one most worth making.

54. A New Jerusalem

Amos 5:21-27.

Key word: justice.

Britain was still at war with Germany when a report by the Committee on Social Insurance and Allied Services was published in 1942. It is known from the name of the Committee's chairman as the Beveridge Report and became the basis of the post-war Welfare State. Ambitious in its scope and breathtaking in its vision for a country with a long slog to victory still ahead, its aim was no less than to banish forever what it called the Five Giants: of Illness, Ignorance, Disease, Squalor and Want. The language was almost messianic. Now the nation was fighting not merely to defeat Nazism but to usher in a new era of justice. The hope engendered gave echo to Blake's words and spawned a conviction that there might after all be a new "Jerusalem builded here, amongst these dark, satanic mills."

A start was made almost straightaway through the Education Act of 1944, which for the first time compelled local authorities to provide free schooling for all children, and threatened imprisonment for recalcitrant parents. After the landslide victory by the Labour Party in the post-war election of 1945, further steps were implemented, leading to creation of the National Health Service and nationalisation of large sectors of the economy. In the course of time, a wide degree of consensus was reached across the political spectrum as to the role of the state in making a new society. It was to be more equal than before, with the hard edges of capitalism smoothed by unemployment pay, a state pension, free health care and free education for all.

Arguments continue to this day about whether, in its pursuit of this dream, Britain missed the chance to re-tool and re-equip her industry and thereby forfeited greater long-term prosperity. Certainly, there were some in America who looked askance at what they saw as the misuse of Marshall Aid. On this view, Britain was featherbedding her workers rather than doing what was really needed for post-war reconstruction.

At home, too, there were concerns about whether the country could afford generosity on this scale. Right from the start, national insurance contributions proved inadequate – the initial assumption was that use of the National Health Service would decline as the nation's health improved: the elasticity of demand was not foreseen. Neither was the tendency for some foreigners to come to England for free medical treatment. As Britain slid into the turmoil of the nineteen seventies, the utopia seemed to be turning distinctly sour.

God's politics.

Attempts to create just societies abound. They have been inspired by all manner of creeds and credos, covered the entire gamut of political views and been both religious and secular in their inspiration. Lollards, Diggers and Levellers all provide examples from English history of groups whose egalitarianism was self-consciously grounded in Scripture. Elements in modern-day socialism, too, have Christian roots. Others, most notably Marxism and its offshoots, deny the very existence of God. Yet progressive policies have by no means been a purely left-wing phenomenon: the world's first social insurance programme was implemented not in democratic Britain but in autocratic Germany, not by a socialist regime but by the decidedly reactionary Otto von Bismarck. Whatever the inspiration and its expression, though, our longing for justice is a constant.

We know that God yearns for justice, too. His desire is that we should "let justice roll on like a river, righteousness like a never-failing stream!" (Amos 5:24). Time and again we are told to "defend the cause of the fatherless, plead the case of the widow" (Isaiah 1:17, also forming a prayer to God in Psalm 82:3). The Lord instructs his people to "follow justice and justice alone" (Deuteronomy 16:20). The devil, however, is in the detail. Each society needs to work out for itself how to translate this into the circumstances of its own time and place. God provides the template of ideas and the desire in our hearts, but Scripture does not prescribe a detailed programme. In this Christianity differs markedly from Islam, for example, where the Koran contains rules and regulations for all aspects of daily life that many Muslims claim apply to every age, regardless of changing circumstances.

We face a different situation and a tougher challenge. At various stages Christianity has tended to be identified with particular political standpoints. Modern instances include the so-called Religious Right in America or the Christian Democracy movement in continental Europe. Yet when we look dispassionately at what the Almighty says in the Bible, we are driven to the conclusion that, much as we may wish it to be otherwise, God's approach cannot be shoehorned into any human philosophy or the manifesto of any political party. The Lord's vision for humanity is simply above and beyond anything that we can conceive. It straddles and surpasses the narrow confines of our imagination. It goes far beyond all slogans and electioneering. Elements of it surface from time to time in most mainstream parties, but none are able to realise its fullness. We would do well to remember this in our political discourse: no man and no party have a monopoly on wisdom.

Christianity is intensely political in the sense that God's concern for the world and its people demands engagement with the issues of the day. It is distinctly apolitical in the sense that it should not be identified solely with any one standpoint, nor constrained within the bounds of any organisation but the church. We are called to give effect to the whole of God's Word in all its richness and variety, not to pick and choose those parts that conform to our own prejudices and pet schemes.

What God is concerned about is not form but substance, not outward show but inward disposition, not whether we wear a particular badge of allegiance but whether we have hearts that seek the things which he esteems.

God's religion.

This emphasis applies equally to religious affairs. In the days of Amos, the Israelites continued to perform the rituals prescribed in the laws of Moses. They would therefore have been astonished to be told: "I hate, I despise your religious feasts; I cannot stand your assemblies. Even though you bring me burnt offerings and grain offerings, I will not accept them. Though you bring choice fellowship offerings, I will have no regard for them. Away with the noise of your songs! I will not listen to the music of your harps." (Amos 5:21-23).

There are echoes in this of God's differing reactions to the sacrifices made to him by Cain and Abel: "Now Abel kept flocks, and Cain worked the soil. In the course of time Cain brought some of the fruits of the soil as an offering to the LORD. But Abel brought fat portions from some of the firstborn of his flock. The LORD looked with favour on Abel and his offering, but on Cain and his offering he did not look with favour." (Genesis 4:2-5). The book of Hebrews clarifies the reason why this was so: "By faith Abel offered God a better sacrifice than Cain did." (Hebrews 11:4). It was not that one type of sacrifice was intrinsically better than another, merely that Abel's heart was right with God and Cain's was not. Our motivation is of the utmost importance.

The Israelites of Amos' time probably thought that they had avoided one of the traps into which Cain fell. Their sacrifices involve "choice fellowship offerings" (Amos 5:22), whereas Cain did not bring the best of his produce, only "some of the fruits of the soil" (Genesis 4:3). This bringing of the firstborn, the choice offering and the "lamb without spot or blemish" (Leviticus 22:21) is important only to the extent that it evidences a state of mind, however. The real issue is that "if you do not do what is right, sin is crouching at your door; it desires to have you, but you must master it." (Genesis 4:7).

The fact that the attitude of the heart is what matters, not the form of the sacrifice, is emphasised again when God says: "Did you bring me sacrifices and offerings for forty years in the desert, O house of Israel?" (Amos 5:25). They did not. Israel's right relationship with God was never founded primarily on sacrifices. It was based instead on obedience.

Far from having the right attitude towards God, the Israelites have become idolaters: "You have lifted up the shrine of your king, the pedestal of your idols, the star of your god – which you made for yourselves." (Amos 5:26). Whilst keeping all the outward forms of religion, they have therefore infringed the most basic of God's laws in the Ten Commandments: to "have no other gods before me ... [and] not make for yourself an idol" (Exodus 20:3-4).

We have also become idolaters. We have become a society that elevates form over substance. Political correctness has taken the place of a search for truth. Slavish adherence to a welfare system put in place over sixty years ago has taken the place of proper engagement with the real social justice issues of the present. An ideology of equality regardless of merit replaces relationships based on love for God and for our neighbours. This is far from what God means when he asks for "justice [to] roll on like a river, righteousness like a never-failing stream!" (Amos 5:24).

God's rewards.

The fact that God concentrates on substance rather than form should cause us daily to examine our hearts and to reconsider whether what we do and say is really honouring to God and in conformity with his laws. God is not religious in the sense that we often tend to use the word. Jesus had no time for the organised religion of his day: "do not pray like the hypocrites, for they love to pray standing in the synagogues and on the street corners to be seen by men. I tell you the truth, they have received their reward in full. But when you pray, go into your room, close the door and pray to your Father, who is unseen. Then your Father, who sees what is done in secret, will reward you." (Matthew 6:5-6).

The only reward that the hypocrites receive is such pleasure as they derive from being seen by men and judged by them to be religious – they will receive nothing from God. Whilst men may account them righteous, God does not. He sees things differently: "The LORD does not look at the things man looks at. Man looks at the outward appearance, but the LORD looks at the heart." (1 Samuel 16:7). Reward from God comes for those whose hearts are in the right place.

Correspondingly, those who do not do right will be repaid for their wrongdoing. The Israelites are told that their continued apostasy has a price: "'Therefore I will send you into exile beyond Damascus,' says the LORD, whose name is God Almighty." (Amos 5:27). As for religion, so for justice, truth, mercy, forgiveness and all the other things commanded by God. There is a price to be paid by people and by societies which do not seek these things. We are paying that price at this very moment.

Conclusion.

We need to ask ourselves: in what ways do our individual conduct and the behaviour of our nation fall short of the justice and righteousness for which God longs? An honest evaluation will not assume that we must be achieving the desired result just because we have a Welfare State, nor because we have laws against discrimination, nor any of the other things that form the panoply of modern life. These are but forms and outward show. If the inner disposition of our hearts is wrong, they will never bring about justice and righteousness. Neither should ways of doing things be accepted uncritically merely because they conform to the prejudices of the day. We must heed the warning that God gave his people when he brought them out of Egypt: "Do not pervert justice by siding with the crowd" (Exodus 23:2).

We have to be much clearer in our thinking. There are those who say that only things that can be scientifically evaluated are real. This viewpoint has been widely espoused in the West for well over a century. It contains a contradiction, however, for there are many things that are a central part of human experience that cannot be quantified in this way. Love, justice and truth are abstract concepts, but no less real for that. We may not be able to measure love scientifically, but we know when it is present and we feel its absence keenly. We may argue about the mechanisms for bringing about justice, but we demand it. We readily recognise injustice and are affronted by it. Indeed, children usually have a concept of fairness that puts many an adult to shame. We acknowledge that truth is better than falsehood.

Anyone who has a desire to understand mankind and the world in which we live must come to terms with this. Some may wish to ignore these inconveniences, but that will not do. A scientific theory that does not fit the facts should by rights be discarded in favour of one that does a better job. It does us no favours to hold to a discredited approach in spite of every observation.

Christians believe that concepts like love, truth and justice have been placed in our hearts by God: "'This is the covenant that I will make with the house of Israel after that time,' declares the LORD. 'I will put my law in their minds and write it on their hearts. I will be their God, and they will be my people.'" (Jeremiah 31:33). The Lord told the prophet Ezekiel that he would transform those who believe in him: "I will give them an undivided heart and put a new spirit in them; I will remove from them their heart of stone and give them a heart of flesh." (Ezekiel 11:19, repeated with substitution of "you" for "them" in Ezekiel 36:26). The same transformation, of ourselves and of our land, will come about if we turn again to our loving heavenly Father.

A wholesale re-evaluation of our society is called for. Those who count Jesus Christ their Lord must take the lead: "Hear me, you who know what is right, you people who have my law in your hearts: do not fear the reproach of men or be terrified of their insults." (Isaiah 51:7).

55. Letting go

2 Timothy 2:14-26.

Key word: opposition.

Two hundred and ninety years of British presence in India[118] appeared to have reached a new high water mark at the Delhi Durbar of 1903, which was staged to mark the accession of Edward VII. Its glittering array of maharajahs presented a magnificent facade, but behind this splendid frontage the mansion was starting to look decidedly rickety. Although Indians fought under British colours in large numbers during the First World War, by 1919 its educated elite were chafing against their continued exclusion from real power and influence. One man above all others, an English-trained barrister by the name of Mohandas Karamchand Gandhi, gave discontent a new popular impetus and focus. Drawing not only on Hindu scriptures but also on the New Testament and Tolstoy's principles of non-violence and the abandonment of materialism, he called on Indians to harness *satyagraha*[119] in a campaign of passive resistance to British rule.[120]

Civil disobedience and the armed power of the state collided most infamously at Amritsar on 13 April 1919. Following violence at Delhi railway station on 30 March and the savage beating of a British woman called Manuella Sherwood by a mob on 11 April, Brigadier-General Rex Dyer issued proclamations prohibiting all meetings and processions, stating unambiguously that "all gatherings will be fired on." These orders were ignored and a crowd of some 20,000 collected in defiance. General Dyer was as good as his word. Two armoured cars and fifty native troops were despatched. By the time their guns fell silent 379 were dead and more than 1,500 wounded.

There was uproar, not just amongst Indians but also amongst the British. In India, General Dyer was summoned before an enquiry. In Britain, his actions

---

[118] In 1613 the English East India Company first established itself in the subcontinent with a trading post at Surat on the north-west coast.

[119] *Satyagraha* is derived from *Sat* (meaning truth) and *Agraha* (meaning firmness). It is usually rendered into English as "soul force." Of Christianity, Gandhi said: "If all Christians acted like Christ, the whole world would be Christian."

[120] Gandhi had hitherto been a loyal servant of the Crown. During the Boer War he helped recruit and lead an Indian medical corps and was awarded the war medal as a result. He offered his services again during the First World War and encouraged others to do likewise, even taking part in a recruiting campaign in India.

were heavily criticised in Parliament. Even the arch imperialist Winston Churchill denounced the "monstrous event" and said that firing on unarmed civilians was "not the British way of doing things." The future war leader called the Amritsar Massacre "the most frightful of all spectacles, the strength of civilisation without its mercy." In the event, although General Dyer was never prosecuted he was swiftly invalided out of the army, his career finished. British rule in India stuttered on, but the occupiers had no real stomach for the repression that would have been necessary to maintain their position. By 1947 they were almost indecent in their haste to be gone. Amid the horrors of Partition, the new states of India and Pakistan were born at the stroke of midnight on 14 August that year.

Approval.

For much of the post-war period the British Empire and all it entailed have often seemed more a cause of shame than of pride. Yet in our readiness to dredge up all that is unseemly about the Empire (and admittedly, there is much), we are in danger of ignoring the good. Alongside Britons who acted from base motives, there were many whose intent was high-minded: "In a large house there are articles not only of gold and silver, but also of wood and clay; some are for noble purposes and some for ignoble. If a man cleanses himself from the latter, he will be an instrument for noble purposes, made holy, useful to the Master and prepared to do any good work." (2 Timothy 2:20-21). In India the British stamped out suttee and thuggee,[121] not primarily for reasons of public order or so as to project their own power, but because these things were wrong. In doing so they immeasurably improved the lot of women and the safety of wayfarers. There are countless other examples of good being done, often in the face of determined local opposition, not because it was of personal benefit to the rulers, but because it was the right thing to do.

Of course, our sinfulness and the fact that we live in a fallen world mean that our good deeds sit alongside our imperfections and wrongdoing, but the times that we fall short or take a wrong turning should not discourage us or stop us trying again. St Paul encourages Timothy to: "Do your best to present yourself to God as one approved, a workman who does not need to be ashamed and who correctly handles the word of truth." (2 Timothy 2:15). This has four elements:

---

[121] Suttee (abolished in 1829) was the practice of a widow immolating herself on the funeral pyre of her dead husband. Today India has 40 million widows, the largest number of any nation. Thuggee (suppressed 1828-35) was a fraternity of religious assassins. Also suppressed were infanticide and licentious orgies.

"Do your best" (2 Timothy 2:15). We are only called on to do the best we can with what God gives us, not to be supermen without the least frailty or weakness: "the LORD ... knows how we are formed, he remembers that we are dust." (Psalm 103:13-14).

"[Present] yourself to God as one approved" (2 Timothy 2:15). We do not need to be without any blot on our record in order to gain God's approval. Were it so, we would have no hope of salvation. Despite everything, we can come before God with confidence because of what Jesus did for us by dying on the cross.

"[Be] a workman who does not need to be ashamed" (2 Timothy 2:15). A workman will not be ashamed if he has done a good job, worked hard and provided value for money. It follows that in everything we do, whether it is directly for God or otherwise, we must avoid idleness, malingering, overcharging, cutting corners, skimping and shoddy workmanship.

"[Be someone] who correctly handles the word of truth." (2 Timothy 2:15). God's Word is precious. It is not to be diluted, belittled, trashed or ignored. It is instead to be treasured, spoken and acted upon.

If we follow this advice and cleanse ourselves from ignoble purposes, then we will "be an instrument for noble purposes, made holy, useful to the Master and prepared to do any good work." (2 Timothy 2:21). Through God's Spirit working within us, this is within the reach of every single human being. It does not require us to have the right pedigree. Nor does it demand exceptional education, intelligence or good looks. Still less does it need huge material wealth. All it takes is openness and effort. As in any endeavour, the more we practice, the better we will get. Our application will be rewarded, for in this way we will place ourselves and our society on the surest of foundations.

Foundation.

British imperial rule, in India as elsewhere, proved eventually to rest on insecure foundations. The contrast between the transitory nature of earthly things and the permanence of the kingdom of heaven is a constant theme of Scripture. St Paul emphasises the same point: "Nevertheless, God's solid foundation stands firm, sealed with this inscription: 'The Lord knows those who are his,' and 'Everyone who confesses the way of the Lord must turn away from wickedness.'" (2 Timothy 2:19).

We help to place ourselves on "God's solid foundation" (2 Timothy 2:19) not just through faith but also by putting our faith into practice. This involves obeying God's commands. St Paul gives Timothy practical advice about how to do this:

"Avoid godless chatter, because those who indulge in it will become more and more ungodly." (2 Timothy 2:16).

"Flee the evil desires of youth, and pursue righteousness, faith, love and peace, along with those who call on the Lord out of a pure heart." (2 Timothy 2:22).

"Don't have anything to do with foolish and stupid arguments, because you know they produce quarrels. And the Lord's servant must not quarrel; instead he must be kind to everyone, able to teach, not resentful." (2 Timothy 2:23-24).

"Warn them before God against quarrelling about words; it is of no value, and only ruins those who listen." (2 Timothy 2:14).

These examples illustrate the same theme: that we are affected by and tend to become like the things we desire, hear and practice. We should therefore turn our backs on what is wrong and reach for things that are good. Above all, we should "Love the LORD [our] God with all [our] heart and with all [our] soul and with all [our] strength." (Deuteronomy 6:5; see also Matthew 22:37-38).

Opposition.

Time and again in the affairs of men we see the power that love has to dissolve opposition, whilst force does the reverse: "A gentle answer turns away wrath, but a harsh word stirs up anger." (Proverbs 15:1). This was evidently lost on General Dyer. He resolved to meet Gandhi's "soul force" with "fist force." His response could not have been further from the one which St Paul advises Timothy to adopt when faced with opposition: "Those who oppose him [the pastor] must gently instruct, in the hope that God will grant them repentance leading them to a knowledge of the truth, and that they will come to their senses and escape from the trap of the devil, who has taken them captive to do his will." (2 Timothy 2:25-26). To be fair to the general, we have to recognise that there are differing degrees and sources of opposition, calling for varying responses:

Those who evidence goodwill, but who are mistaken or misled: these we should "gently instruct" (2 Timothy 2:25).

Those who are brutish and impervious to all things spiritual, on whom we should waste no time once their attitude is clear: "Do not give dogs what is sacred; do not throw your pearls to pigs. If you do, they may trample them under their feet, and then turn and tear you to pieces." (Matthew 7:6).

Those who undermine the church from within, who must be stopped: "Their teaching [that of people who indulge in godless chatter] will spread like gangrene. Among them are Hymenaeus and Philetus, who have wandered away from the truth. They say that the resurrection has already taken place, and they destroy the faith of some." (2 Timothy 2:17-18).

Those who are on the side of evil, with whom we should have no truck and whom we must do our utmost to resist: "Resist the devil and he will flee from you" (James 4:7).

Needless to say, these categories are not always clear-cut. When in doubt, we should err on the side of the gentle instruction that St Paul recommends, remembering that Jesus tells us "Love [our] enemies" (Matthew 5:44, Luke 6:27) and to "love [our] neighbour as [ourselves]." (Matthew 19:19).

Conclusion.

The achievement of Mahatma ("great soul") Gandhi was immense and his campaign of civil disobedience a model for the oppressed everywhere. A proper appreciation of these events, however, requires that we also weigh the other side of the equation. It takes two to tango. The brutal reality is that, in another era or under another ruling power, Gandhi would not long have survived. There was no shortage of great souls in Nazi Germany. Many were sent to concentration camps. Others were killed outright: those involved in the plot to kill Hitler on 20 July 1944 were hung on meat-hooks to die, whilst the SS filmed their final agonies. The terrible truth is that, wherever one nation has had dominion over another, this has led to oppression and often to massacre. The remarkable thing about such events in the British Empire is how rare they were, that they did not reflect central government policy and that, when they did occur, they were heavily criticised by the British themselves.

This is not to say that General Dyer was justified, neither that British rule in India and elsewhere was wholly benign, but it does suggest that there was something unique about the British Empire and its Christian underpinnings. The logic of Christianity was that, when faced with widespread opposition to their rule during the middle years of the twentieth century, the British usually chose to let go with as good grace as they could muster rather than continue to impose their rule by force. Likewise, Jesus tells us that we need to let go of our enmities if we are to achieve wholeness: "Do not judge, and you will not be judged. Do not condemn, and you will not be condemned. Forgive and you will be forgiven." (Luke 6:37).

One of the few things in life of which we can be sure is that we will face opposition. Indeed, if we do not we should begin to question whether we really are being effective in our Christian witness. An ineffective believer can safely be ignored by Satan but the devil will do his utmost to derail one who is active. If we keep quiet about our faith, no-one will challenge us, but as soon as we begin to speak out, voices will be raised against us. The best witness we can bear is through our own lives. Gandhi flirted with Christianity and for a time attended church, but concluded: "I like your Christ. I do not like your Christians. Your Christians are so unlike your Christ." Sadly, this remains a state of affairs that still describes us all too well. Things will not change and opposition will not be disarmed until we learn to let go of worldly things and truly put into practice St Paul's advice: "Flee the evil desires of youth ... pursue righteousness, faith, love and peace ... [avoid] foolish and stupid arguments ... [do] not quarrel ... be kind to everyone, able to teach, not resentful." (2 Timothy 2:22-24).

56. Against all odds

Jude 1:1-25.

Key word: glory.

The Korean War of 1950-1953 is a largely neglected conflict, though it claimed some four million lives. It pitted United Nations troops against North Koreans and Chinese. The fighting was heavy, the landscape harsh. The Korean peninsula, mountainous and cut by deep ravines, is prone to extremes of temperature. In winter, men left too long outside on guard duty could literally freeze to death. The cold was both literal and metaphorical: divided into a communist north and pro-western south following defeat of its former colonial power Japan in 1945, Korea was a microcosm of the Cold War. Early hopes of unification were dashed and the two halves of the country became increasingly hostile one to another.

Backed by the Soviet Union, the North Koreans carried out a surprise attack on their southern neighbour in June 1950. At first they swept all before them until General Douglas Macarthur engineered a brilliant seaborne landing at Inchon behind enemy lines. United Nations forces, largely American, then pushed the Communists back whence they came. Scenting victory, careless of Chinese reaction and disdainful of politicians' caution Macarthur continued to push north in an attempt to wrest the entire peninsula from Red control. This Chairman Mao could not stomach. Chinese troops crossed the Yalu River in force, taking their over-extended enemy by surprise and forcing them to retreat.

During the resulting withdrawal, the Gloucester Regiment played a major part at the battle of the Imjin River. Due to a misunderstanding, they were left unsupported as massively superior forces of the Chinese 63rd Shock Army launched human wave attacks against defences on Hill 235 (Gloster Hill). Outnumbered at least seven to one the British held out for three days, inflicting appalling casualties, until running out of ammunition, food and water. They were then ordered to break out. Sixty three managed to slip through the opposing lines to safety, but the remainder were taken into captivity. They did not see home again for two years. For their courage, endurance and self-sacrifice these Glorious Glosters became one of only two British regiments to receive the U.S. Presidential Distinguished Unit Citation.

Thereafter the war settled into stalemate, though it took two more years to broker a truce. The ceasefire eventually agreed in July 1953 fixed the border between North and South along the 38th Parallel, where it remains to the present. The peace reflected the priorities of the combatants: to end a bloody and costly war, to prevent a wider conflict and to stabilise the Korean peninsula along pre-existing borders. Similarly, we must set priorities.

Priorities.

The writer of Jude (Hebrew Judah, Greek Judas) was probably one of the brothers of Jesus. No doubt out of modesty, he identifies himself as "a brother of James" (Jude 1:1), by whom he almost certainly means another of Jesus' siblings who was prominent in the early church in Jerusalem. The message is as pertinent to modern Britain as to the time in which and people to whom it was originally written. Jude says that "although I was very eager to write to you about the salvation we share, I felt I had to write and urge you to contend for the faith that was once for all entrusted to the saints." (Jude 1:3). He adjusts his priorities because there is a pressing need amongst his readers.

The need is one that we share. We, too, need "to contend for the faith" (Jude 1:3). Of late, we seem to have forgotten how to do this. We have sunk into apathy and are mired in defeatism. We find it difficult to bestir ourselves, either when our faith is threatened at home or when our Christian brothers and sisters are under attack overseas. This is to our shame and disgrace. We must reclaim whole areas of our nation and its people for God and this can only happen if we are prepared to stand up and be counted. To contend means to exert oneself in defence or support of anything; to strive to obtain or keep; to compete; to dispute; to maintain by argument; to strive in opposition. The definition neatly sums up the actions that are required. These should be our priorities.

What Jude next says is instructive: "Though you already know all this, I want to remind you that the Lord delivered his people out of Egypt, but later destroyed those who did not believe." (Jude 1:5). Like his readers, we already know the facts behind God's work of redemption and the consequences for those who reject the Almighty, but we need to be reminded. We need to be reminded about the spiritual significance of these things, about their impact on individual lives and about our need to take action as a result.

We have to adjust our priorities. It is wholesome and good to reflect upon "the salvation we share" (Jude 1:3), but if this is all we do, we will miss the bigger picture.

Panorama.

The wider canvas comprises the spiritual conflict of which our lives form part. It is played out on a personal, national and international level. We cannot and should not be indifferent to its impact:

Personal. The ungodly lifestyles that are pursued and promoted in our land and further afield are not simply an issue of personal choice with no wider significance. They lead directly to the degradation and ultimately the damnation of individuals. They involve rebellion against God and are akin to speaking maliciously against what is good, for they discredit and undermine those who stand for righteousness: "In the very same way, these dreamers pollute their own bodies, reject authority and slander celestial beings." (Jude 1:8).

National. The effect of large numbers thinking, choosing and acting in ungodly ways is that their personal degradation is mirrored countrywide. When such people are allowed to set the agenda for the nation and to dominate debate, they project their own misdeeds and misconceptions onto the land as a whole: "these men speak abusively against whatever they do not understand; and what things they do understand by instinct, like unreasoning animals – these are the very things that destroy them." (Jude 1:10). If we do not provide a counterweight through our voices and example, we will leave our nation "like sheep without a shepherd" (Numbers 27:17, I Kings 22:17 and Matthew 9:36).

International. Across the globe we see the consequences: "Woe to them! They have taken the way of Cain; they have rushed for profit into Balaam's error; they have been destroyed in Korah's rebellion." (Jude 1:11). The ills of the world are not random events. They have a cause. They are subject to the same laws of action and reaction as govern the rest of the universe. Where there is selfishness, unrestrained appetite, hatred and murder (the way of Cain), greed and a desire for personal gain (Balaam's error) or rebellion against rightful leadership and godly laws (Korah's rebellion), human suffering results.

If we allow these things to persist without raising our voices against them, we are complicit in what is being said and done. We need a good shaking. When "Sodom and Gomorrah and the surrounding towns gave themselves up to sexual immorality and perversion ... [they suffered] the punishment of eternal fire." (Jude 1:7). These towns were doubtless full of people who abhorred the conduct around them, but did nothing about it. They therefore shared the fate of those who were directly involved in sinful behaviour. In the same way, the decent majority in this land will share in the degradation of a sinful minority unless action is taken.

Programme.

Lest we give way to feelings of helplessness and hopelessness, we need at this point to remind ourselves of something else. We worship a God "who is able to keep you from falling and to present you before his glorious presence without fault and with great joy – to the only God our Saviour be glory, majesty, power and authority, through Jesus Christ our Lord, before all ages, now and for evermore. Amen." (Jude 1:24-25).

Twice mentioned in these lines is glory: "his glorious presence" (Jude :24) and "to the only God our Saviour be glory" (Jude 1:25). This reminds us that glory when applied to God has two meanings. It describes the superlative honour that should be given to God by everything in the universe and this is the sense in which Jude says, "to the only God our Saviour be glory" (Jude 1:25). However, it also describes one of God's attributes, something which belongs to him alone and which is an outward expression of his excellence. This glory is the bright light that surrounds God's presence and his revelation of himself: "You are clothed with honour and majesty, you who cover yourself with light as with a garment" (Psalm 104:1).

God's glory is reflected, albeit imperfectly, by the activities of believers in every field of endeavour. Although our good deeds are often tainted by sinful motives, they can nevertheless mirror the excellence of our Creator and thereby bring glory to him. To reflect God's glory and to bring him glory should be our aims in life. Jude has seven pieces of advice to help us in this. It is a programme which we can readily put into effect in our daily lives:

"Build yourselves up in your most holy faith" (Jude 1:20).

"Pray in the Holy Spirit" (Jude 1:20).

"Keep yourselves in God's love as you wait for the mercy of our Lord Jesus Christ to bring you to eternal life." (Jude :21).

"Be merciful to those who doubt" (Jude 1:22).

"Snatch others from the fire and save them" (Jude 1:23).

"To others show mercy, mixed with fear – hating even the clothing stained by corrupted flesh." (Jude 1:23). In other words, to quote St Augustine of Hippo: "hate the sin and love the sinner."

We were made by God to reflect his glory. St Paul speaks of our being "changed into his likeness from one degree of glory to another" (2 Corinthians 3:18). This should embolden us and give us confidence. In following each of the pieces of advice that Jude gives, we have the security of knowing that the Lord himself will "keep [us] from falling" (Jude 1:24) and that he will "present [us] before his glorious presence without fault and with great joy" (Jude 1:24).

Conclusion.

General Douglas Macarthur was Supreme Allied Commander in the Pacific during the Second World War. It was he who masterminded the island-hopping campaign that chipped away at Japanese conquests in that theatre and made possible their ultimate defeat. On Japan's surrender, he became for several years America's viceroy in its defeated foe, ruling as de facto Emperor. Undoubtedly, it was his masterstroke at Inchon which saved the whole of South Korea from being overrun by the North. Unfortunately, he was a man whose genius was matched only by cantankerous self-regard. In the end this brought him low. He was relieved of command by President Truman in 1951, deemed a danger and a menace in a world where every conflict was liable to draw in opposing power blocs and threaten nuclear war. It was an inglorious end to a glorious career. Macarthur died in 1964, the blot on his record never wholly erased.

In following his own whims and disregarding the orders of his commander-in-chief, the President of the United States, General Macarthur overstepped the mark. Glory became vainglory, and hence the high renown he had won earlier was tarnished. By contrast (and with the exception of a lucky few), rather than dreams of glory those men of the Gloucester Regiment who fought on the Imjin River faced the ignominy of captivity. As they trudged weary and defeated into long, hard months as prisoners of a ruthless enemy, they were not to know that their conduct had won them lasting honour. They battled on even though victory seemed impossible and surrender might have appeared the sensible option.

So it is with us. What seems great and glorious to man is not always so. Neither should we take at face value the things that others deem unworthy and despised, for outcomes are often hidden from us. Our aim is the pursuit of true glory: the glory of God and our ultimate presentation "before his glorious presence" (Jude 1:24). The road that leads thither does not lie through an easy country, nor does it wend by way of things that the world esteems. These are fool's gold, trinkets and trifles that are undeserving of serious consideration or concern. Our path involves "[contending] for the faith that was once for all entrusted to the saints" (Jude 1:3). There will assuredly be times when victory looks impossible for us, too, when surrender to the enemy seems the advisable course and when our courage fails us. Jude exhorts us then to "remember what the apostles of our Lord Jesus Christ foretold. They said to you, 'In the last times there will be scoffers who will follow their own ungodly desires.' These are the men who will divide you, who follow mere natural instincts and do not have the Spirit." (Jude 1:17-19). We must follow a different course and not break rank. Whatever might be happening around us, we should obey our commander-in-chief, "the only God our Saviour" (Jude 1:25).

We should not let appearances deceive us and neither should we slacken, for ahead lies something glorious.

57. Crisis

Malachi 3:6-15.

Key word: blessing.

Anthony Eden was Britain's youngest foreign secretary when he was appointed in 1935, but had to wait twenty years to become Prime Minister. By that time he was 58 years old and youthful promise had been blunted by age and ill health. Scarred by memories of the appeasement of Hitler's Germany in the nineteen thirties, for him the nationalisation of the Suez Canal by Egyptian President Gamal Abdel Nasser in 1956 was the act of another dangerous dictator in the making. In concert with France, Eden therefore secretly encouraged Israel to attack Egypt on the understanding that an Anglo-French force would intervene on the pretext of stopping the fighting. The resulting campaign was a military success but a political disaster. The United States under President Eisenhower made clear its displeasure. Such was Britain's economic dependence on her wartime ally that she had no option but to withdraw, leaving the Suez Canal blocked by sunken ships, but under Egyptian control. The humiliation was enormous and Eden resigned in 1957.[122]

With the threadbare nature of British power laid bare, Eden's successor Harold Macmillan fondly imagined that the country could still play Athens to the United States' Rome. So, as the nation struggled to come to terms with its diminished status it strove nevertheless to outdo America in art, music and sport. The pale shadow of Americana that resulted only served to emphasise the gulf, for in reality there was no contest: Elvis Presley or Cliff Richard, Marilyn Monroe or Diana Dors, Hollywood or the Rank Charm School, Muhammad Ali or Henry Cooper. In business, the story was the same: the car giants of Detroit or strike-ridden British Leyland, the power and innovation of American finance or the stuffy, clubby Old Boys' network of the City, the all-conquering greenback or rickety sterling.

The harsh truth was that the country was in hock to the United States: for war loans, Marshall Aid and defence against the Soviet threat. She seemed in perpetual economic crisis, her industry bedevilled by labour disputes, her confidence dented not just by Suez but by devaluation in 1967, her public

---

[122] The war had been far from universally popular at home. At a demonstration in Trafalgar Square on 4 November 1956, for example, Labour politician Aneurin Bevan (1897-1960) said: "It is not possible to create peace in the Middle East by jeopardising the peace of the world."

finances wrecked by profligate government and the burdens of Empire, her innovation stifled by ruinous taxes. A miners' strike brought about a three-day week and in due course a loan from the International Monetary Fund. Even then, the madness continued. During the Winter of Discontent from 1978 to 1979 there were heaps of rotting rubbish in the streets and corpses lay unburied. Civil servants talked unashamedly of their job being to "manage decline" whilst Macmillan spoke of the "wind of change" in terms that suggested that the country had no choice but to drift rudderless before it. Within the political classes, there seemed little hope or expectation of anything but a long slide towards being a second- or even a third-rate power.

Changing and unchangeable.

Britain had once been ruler of the greatest Empire the world has ever known, encompassing a quarter of the earth's land mass and a similar proportion of her population. As recently as 1900 her power had seemed unassailable and set only to grow. Yet sixty years later she was bereft, unsure and hesitant. If a nation can be gauged by those it honours, the change in outlook was as dramatic as those in circumstance: musicians and media stars took the place occupied not so long before by engineers, soldiers and statesmen. Well might some have said, "It is futile to serve God. What did we gain by carrying out his requirements and going about like mourners before the LORD Almighty? But now we call the arrogant blessed. Certainly the evildoers prosper, and even those who challenge God escape." (Malachi 3:14-15).

Yet whilst our outward circumstances change, God does not: "I the LORD do not change. So you, O descendants of Jacob, are not destroyed." (Malachi 3:6).[123] This is something that we need to hold on to at times of crisis, both national and personal. The same faithfulness that the Lord displayed to our forefathers is what he continues to show to us, despite all that we have said and done against him. It is for this reason that "we are not destroyed." (Malachi 3:6). God longs to go beyond merely keeping us from destruction, however. His greatest desire is to bless. It is in his nature to do so, for he "is compassionate and gracious, slow to anger, abiding in love. He will not always accuse, nor will he harbour his anger for ever; he does not treat us as our sins deserve or repay us according to our iniquities ... as a father has compassion on his children, so the LORD has compassion on those who fear him" (Psalm 103:8-10 and 13). The fullness of blessing that once was ours in this land can be ours again if we will only turn back to our heavenly Father in repentance and faith.

---

[123] The unchanging nature of God does not mean that he is inactive. On the contrary, he performs "great and awesome deeds" (Deuteronomy 4:34).

Honouring God, robbing God.

Seldom, if ever, do we reflect at the deepest level on how and why Britain gained an Empire "acquired in a fit of absence of mind"[124] and then so suddenly lost it. We tend to examine the issue in terms of mechanics, but not in terms of the spiritual. The lack of introspection is not merely curious, but almost negligent. If we are to understand properly the way in which God has worked in the life of this nation, to learn from what we have done right and what we have done wrong, we need to consider the past. We need to ask: for what purpose was such dominion given to a small offshore island, whose resources were not the greatest, whose population was not the largest, whose enemies were frequently confounded as to how she was able to defeat them? For what reason was this same dominion then taken away?

The answer comes down to this: honouring God and robbing God. Our nation has in years gone by honoured God and thus was used by him. We were elevated to one end: "But I have raised you up for this very purpose, that I might show you my power, and that my name might be proclaimed in all the earth." (Exodus 9:16). This does not mean that we were the brightest or the best, still less that we were in any way superior to other peoples. It means simply this: that the Lord worked through us. As time passed, we forgot this basic truth. We began to imagine that dominion was the result of our own genius and our own innate abilities. We began to see ourselves as above others. One of the most depressing results of Empire is that it persuaded us that we were racially superior. That concept is not just morally repugnant. It is wholly unscriptural.

By thinking and acting in this way, we robbed God. We robbed him of the glory that belongs to his name and of the credit for what he has done through us. God was justified in telling us: "you rob me" (Malachi 3:8) and "You have said harsh things about me" (Malachi 3:13). The result for us was the same as it was for the Israelites in the days of Malachi: "You are under a curse – the whole nation of you – because you are robbing me." (Malachi 3:9). We are an illustration of the fact that those who neglect or squander what is given them will become doubly impoverished. We are like the servant in the parable told by Jesus, to whom his master said: "to everyone who has, more will be given, but as for the one who has nothing, even what he has will be taken away." (Luke 19:26). Jesus made the same point elsewhere: "Whoever has will be given more, and he will have an abundance. Whoever does not have, even what he has will be taken from him." (Matthew 13:12).

---

[124] In *The Expansion of England* (1883) historian Sir John Seeley wrote: "We seem, as it were, to have conquered and peopled half the world in a fit of absence of mind."

We cannot say that we deserved the Empire God gave us, but we certainly deserved to have it taken away. It ceased to be for his glory and became for ours, and in doing so it became worthless in the eyes of the Almighty. The curse that we experienced by robbing God is one under which we still labour today. For all our worldly possessions, great buildings and material comforts we have very little that is of spiritual value, and much of what we have has not been used wisely. We have done the equivalent of digging a hole in the ground and putting our gifts from God in it, instead of using them to do his work. We stand under his judgment and under his curse as a result.

Returning to God.

The prescription for lifting the curse is the same as in Malachi's day: "'Ever since the time of your forefathers you have turned away from my decrees and have not kept them. Return to me and I will return to you,' says the LORD Almighty." (Malachi 3:7). If we are to return to God, we need to regain a godly perspective. Malachi describes a number of common misconceptions that are prevalent in our day, as of old:

"It is futile to serve God" (Malachi 3:14). To ascribe futility to service of the very person who gives meaning to all life and to every human endeavour, who is indeed the source of life itself, shows a pitiful grasp of reality. It demonstrates a confusion of truth and falsehood that is a particular bane of our present condition. Life is futile without God. With him there is purpose, fulfilment and meaning. To say otherwise turns everything upside down and inside out.

"[We gained nothing] by carrying out [God's] requirements and going about like mourners before the LORD Almighty" (Malachi 3:14). Here several misconceptions are rolled into one: that serving God is about our material gain, that proper service of God requires our "going about like mourners" and that carrying out God's requirements brings no benefit. The truth is that serving God brings blessing, that material gain and godliness do not necessarily go hand in hand and that we should "consider it pure joy whenever [we] face trials of many kinds." (James 1:2).

"[Now] we call the arrogant blessed" (Malachi 3:15). Inversion of truth and falsehood, coupled with perversion of proper values and rewarding of those who do not deserve it, typifies much of the moral corrosion of this nation in the post-war period. We need to turn things back the right way round.

"Certainly the evildoers prosper" (Malachi 3:15). A sense of helplessness in the face of evil is the very last thing that we should feel. The Lord has given us "divine power to demolish strongholds" (2 Corinthians 10:4).

"[Those] who challenge God escape" (Malachi 3:15). A delay in punishment is not the same as a lack of retribution. St Paul counsels: "Do not be deceived: God cannot be mocked." (Galatians 6:7).

God characterises each of these misconceptions as "harsh things" (Malachi 3:13) said against him. Through them, we find excuses for not honouring God, for not obeying his laws, for failing to confront evil and for permitting blasphemy. The slightest reflection will show these up for what they are: excuses, nothing more or less, devoid of intellectual coherence, lacking moral content, without any underpinning of empirical evidence – an abdication of free will in favour of apathy. Little wonder that the servant who takes his one talent and buries it in the ground is so roundly criticised and harshly punished: "You wicked, lazy servant! ... you should have put my money on deposit with the bankers, so that when I returned I would have received it back with interest ... throw that worthless servant outside, into the darkness, where there will be weeping and gnashing of teeth." (Matthew 25:26-27 and 30).

Conclusion.

The fact that Britain pulled out of her downward spiral was not a foregone conclusion. In 1916 Argentina was the sixth biggest economy in the world. A prolonged period of misgovernment and civil strife turned her by the 1970s into the archetype of the Latin American banana republic and military dictatorship. There is nothing to say that the same could not have happened in Britain. The Lord placed his saving hand upon us and ensured that we "[were] not destroyed." (Malachi 3:6). We should remember this with wonder and gratitude. "Jesus Christ is the same yesterday, today and forever." (Hebrews 13:8). He is the one who says to his faithful ones, "I will never leave you or forsake you." (Joshua 1:5). We are told that "the LORD will not reject his people, he will never forsake his inheritance."(Psalm 94:14). At the same time, we are warned that "The LORD is with you when you are with him. If you seek him, he will be found by you, but if you forsake him, he will forsake you." (2 Chronicles 15:2).

Once we were a people who aspired to serve God and our nation. Now it seems that we aspire only to serve ourselves. The cult of the self and of the individual that we thus embrace does not set us free, but enslaves us. In seeking to serve ourselves, we in fact serve false gods and are prey to all the degradation that results. Meanwhile, we turn our backs on the true God, who offers us genuine freedom and the manifold blessings of his love. Rather than rejecting our Lord, we should instead renounce what is wrong: "Let the wicked forsake his way and the evil man his thoughts. Let him turn to the LORD, and he will have mercy on him, and to our God, for he will freely pardon." (Isaiah 55:7).

To release the fullness of God's blessing, we need to: "'Bring the whole tithe into the storehouse, that there may be food in my house. Test me in this,' says the LORD Almighty, 'and see if I will not throw open the floodgates of heaven and pour out so much blessing that you will not have room enough for it. I will prevent pests from devouring your crops, and the vines in your fields will not cast their fruit,' says the LORD Almighty. 'Then all the nations will call you blessed, for yours will be a delightful land,' says the LORD Almighty." (Malachi 3:10-12). God's blessing awaits.

58. Down to the sea

2 Samuel 22:1-25.

Key word: deliverance.

Born in 1901, Sir Francis Chichester was both aviator and yachtsman. In 1929 he became only the second person to fly solo between England and Australia. Shortly afterwards he was the first to fly solo east to west across the Tasman Sea from New Zealand to Australia (a journey equal to three quarters of the crossing from England to the United States). In 1931 he made the world's first solo long-distance seaplane flight from New Zealand to Japan, surviving a horrific crash shortly after alighting on the Japanese mainland. He devised new methods of aerial navigation, and during the Second World War was Chief Instructor at the Empire Central Flying School. After the war he started his own map publishing business.

In the nineteen fifties this driven man sought a new challenge by taking up ocean racing, naming a succession of yachts 'Gypsy Moth' in memory of the biplane in which he had made many of his most famous flights. Despite being a latecomer to single-handed sailing, Chichester won his first solo transatlantic race in 1960, the first yacht race of any kind east to west across the Atlantic. It was a tremendous achievement for someone pushing sixty, the more so since not long before he had almost died of lung cancer. At the height of his sickness his weight fell to 40lbs. Medical experts were unanimous in saying that an operation on his lung was the only thing that could save him, his wife equally adamant that he was so weakened that this would kill him. Her view prevailed. After months when his life hung by a thread, he strengthened enough to move from a hospital bed.

Still an invalid, he was unaccountably struck by a sudden desire to go to the south of France. In his autobiography he says simply: "It seemed an irresistible urge." No sooner had he arrived in St Paul de Vence than he took a turn for the worse. Breathing was so difficult that a doctor was summoned. Chichester described what then transpired: "What I regarded as a miraculous chain of events had started in London when I felt the urge to go to the south of France. There I reached a doctor who had been considered one of the cleverest lung physicians in Paris before he settled in Vence; also I had fetched up in a town which had been considered a health resort, with a magic quality of air for lungs, since the time of the Romans. How did this come about?"

He wrote of this time: "When I was at my worst, [my wife] rallied many people to pray for me, my friends and others ... I feel shy about my troubles being imposed on others, but the power of prayer is miraculous. Hardly anyone would doubt its power for evil – for example the way the Australian aborigines can will a member of their tribe to death; so why should its power for good be doubted? ... I regard it as miraculous that within thirty-two months of being first taken ill, and within fifteen months of my appealing to Dr. Mattei for oxygen in Vence, I was able to cross the starting line for the toughest yacht race that has ever taken place, and able to finish it in forty and a half days."

As a cancer case no less than as aviator and yachtsman, Chichester might have echoed the words that King David used to describe a time of trial and his deliverance from it: "The waves of death swirled about me; the torrents of destruction overwhelmed me. The cords of the grave coiled about me; the snares of death confronted me ... He [God] reached down from on high and took hold of me; he drew me out of deep waters." (2 Samuel 22:5-6 and 17).

Expectation.

The Israelites were not a seafaring nation. For them, the sea was a place of such dread that it became a symbol of all that was spiritually dark, threatening and inconstant. Wickedness, doubt and ungodliness are all described in the Bible using images of the sea: "The wicked are like the tossing sea." (Isaiah 57:20); "he ... who doubts is like a wave of the sea, blown and tossed by the wind" (James 1:6); "They [the ungodly] are wild waves of the sea, foaming up their shame" (Jude :13). Correspondingly, the perfect re-creation brought about by God at the end of time is characterised by the absence of such things: "Then I saw a new heaven and a new earth, for the first heaven and the first earth had passed away, and there was no longer any sea." (Revelation 21:1).

This background gives added resonance to the maritime images used in the song of praise that "David sang to the LORD ... when the LORD delivered him from the hand of all his enemies and from the hand of Saul" (2 Samuel 22:1). The same song is also preserved, with some minor variations, as Psalm 18. God is depicted as:

A place of strength and safety: "The LORD is my rock, my fortress and my deliverer; my God is my rock, in whom I take refuge, my shield and the horn of my salvation. He is my stronghold, my refuge and my saviour – from violent men you save me." (2 Samuel 22:2-4).

One who hears and responds to prayer: "In my distress I called to the LORD; I called out to my God. From his temple he heard my voice; my cry came to his ears." (2 Samuel 22:7).

Sovereign over all Creation: "The valleys of the sea were exposed and the foundations of the earth laid bare at the rebuke of the LORD, at the blast of breath from his nostrils." (2 Samuel 22:16).

One who intervenes in his Creation and in human history: "He parted the heavens and came down; dark clouds were under his feet ... He reached down from on high and took hold of me; he drew me out of deep waters." (2 Samuel 22:10 and 17).

A rescuer: "my deliverer ... my saviour ... He brought me out into a spacious place; he rescued me because he delighted in me." (2 Samuel 22:2, 3 and 20).

The repository of all power and majesty: "The earth trembled and quaked, the foundations of the heavens shook; they trembled because he was angry. Smoke rose from his nostrils; consuming fire came from his mouth, burning coals blazed out of it ... He mounted the cherubim and flew; he soared on the wings of the wind. He made darkness his canopy around him – the dark rain clouds of the sky. Out of the brightness of his presence bolts of lightning blazed forth." (2 Samuel 22:8-9 and 11-13).

David had every expectation that his Lord would intervene in the world around him. Despite what we claim to believe, too often we act as if there were no prospect of deliverance for us. We imagine that we have to struggle on alone, forgotten and overwhelmed by adverse circumstances. The truth is that God longs for the chance to help, and only awaits our invitation. Like David, we need to cry out to him: "I call to the LORD, who is worthy of praise, and I am saved from my enemies." (2 Samuel 22:4).

Confrontation.

When things are beyond us (2 Samuel 22:18-19), the Almighty does the fighting for us: "He shot arrows and scattered the enemies, bolts of lightning and routed them." (2 Samuel 22:15). Evil people and wretched circumstances may surround us. There is no promise to make them disappear in a puff of smoke, but they need not be things that define and constrain us. If we ask God to intervene, he will sustain us so that we can make our way to calmer waters: "They confronted me in the day of my disaster, but the LORD was my support ... He brought me out into a spacious place" (2 Samuel 22:19-20).

We pay lip service to the idea of God as the Almighty but tend to tiptoe timidly through life as though this were merely a polite fiction. David had no such reservations. His song shows the Lord surrounded by the images and indicators of his presence and power:

Earthquake: "The earth trembled and quaked, the foundations of the heavens shook; they trembled" (2 Samuel 22:8);

Thunder: "The LORD thundered from heaven; the voice of the Most High resounded." (2 Samuel 22:14);

Lightning: "bolts of lightning blazed forth ... He shot ... bolts of lightning" (2 Samuel 22:13 and 15).

Fire: "Smoke rose from his nostrils; consuming fire came from his mouth, burning coals blazed out of it." (2 Samuel 22:9).

Glory: "Out of the brightness of his presence" (2 Samuel 22:13).

When we experience these natural phenomena, we catch a glimpse of the might and magnificence of the one who made and commands them, whose reach extends across all the earth and whose power knows no limit: "The valleys of the sea were exposed and the foundations of the earth laid bare at the rebuke of the LORD, at the blast of breath from his nostrils." (2 Samuel 22:16).[125] This is the one who confronts evil and all its works. He it is who saves and redeems, who delivers us from our enemies and even from death itself.

In the log he kept during his single-handed race across the Atlantic in 1960, Chichester wrote, "I shall put my trust in the Almighty who I am convinced has it all arranged anyhow." It was a sentiment that King David would have endorsed wholeheartedly.

Navigation.

Finding our way across land or sea requires that we have something to steer by and something to aim for, since otherwise we will wander aimlessly. The Lord is "the bright Morning Star" (Revelation 22:16) to guide us on the journey and to be its goal, but that is not to say that it will be beer and skittles all the way. Storms are to be expected and there will be moments when we are becalmed, for each human being comes across things that block the path ahead, which form shackles and traps or are the cause of anguish: "cords of the grave ... snares of death ...distress" (2 Samuel 22:6-7). Yet with God, these can be unravelled, disarmed and sidestepped so that we can make headway, freed from fear and restraint to experience life as he meant it to be lived: "He brought me out into a spacious place; he rescued me because he delighted in me." (2 Samuel 22:20).[126]

To steer properly we need to keep a clear head. We need to keep our eyes skinned and our minds on the task in hand. Nobody can expect to come out

---

[125] It is intriguing that David speaks of "the valleys of the sea." He could not conceivably have known from personal experience that the sea does indeed have valleys – a fact that until relatively recently some scientists disputed.

[126] God helps us and delivers us "because he delighted in [us]" (2 Samuel 22:20). He is under no compulsion to do so, but acts out of his goodness and mercy since each human being is precious to him.

right if their attention is forever wandering and their brain befuddled. The same holds true in spiritual matters just as much as in any map-reading exercise. David had this clarity of mind and purpose. He says: "The LORD has dealt with me according to my righteousness; according to the cleanness of my hands he has rewarded me ... The LORD has rewarded me according to my righteousness, according to my cleanness in his sight." (2 Samuel 22:21 and 25). This is not self-righteous boasting. Nor does it convey the idea that we can bargain with God or produce an automatic reaction from him in the same way that we might by putting a coin in a slot machine. Rather, it recognises that God rewards those who serve him and it expresses a desire to please God. This should be our motivation in all that we do.

It is likewise a claim of moral integrity, not sinless perfection, when David says: "For I have kept the ways of the LORD; I have not done evil by turning from my God. All his laws are before me; I have not turned away from his decrees. I have been blameless before him and have kept myself from sin." (2 Samuel 22:22-24). No human being is perfect. We all make mistakes. Yet if we stick sincerely to our course, deliverance will be ours. The important thing is to keep going and not to allow ourselves to be sidetracked. Sir Francis Drake, greatest of the Elizabethan sea dogs, made precisely this point in one of his prayers: "O Lord God, when thou givest to thy servants to endeavour any great matter, grant us also to know that it is not the beginning but the continuing of the same until it be thoroughly finished, which yieldeth the true glory; through him that for the finishing of thy work laid down his life, our Redeemer Jesus Christ. Amen." We could do worse than to make this prayer our own.[127]

Conclusion.

Even after his transatlantic exploits, Chichester still was not finished. From 1966 to 1967 he sailed around the world single-handed in his boat Gypsy Moth IV. Like many men of action, he seems to have been given more to doing rather than to reflection, but the power of wind and waves inevitably stirs thoughts of our own weakness and our corresponding need for deliverance. As the Psalmist said: "They that go down to the sea in ships, that do business in great waters; these see the works of the LORD, and his wonders in the deep." (Psalm 107:23-24, KJV).

Most of us are now so cosseted from nature that we have lost this daily reminder of our need. Often only the failing of our bodies brings it home to us.

---

[127] Drake was a devout Protestant and was punctilious about conducting regular divine services on his ships. Chichester quotes this prayer in *Alone against the Atlantic*, the story of his 1960 transatlantic race.

There is a message that our pleasure-seeking land desperately needs to hear: "Remember your Creator in the days of your youth, before the days of trouble come and the years approach when you will say, 'I find no pleasure in them'" (Ecclesiastes 12:1).

59. Turning the tide

2 Kings 6:8-23.

Key word: insight.

During the Falklands War of 1982[128] a battalion of the Parachute Regiment was striking across country to the capital Port Stanley when they met Argentine forces dug in at Goose Green. At once Colonel H. Jones ordered an attack. It was hard going. The British were outnumbered and fighting uphill across ground that gave little cover. When the assault bogged down, Colonel Jones grabbed a machine gun and charged the enemy lines. He was killed as he did so, and for his bravery was awarded a posthumous Victoria Cross.

As night fell, the British found themselves back almost where they had started. Their attack had failed, their commander and many comrades were dead, the enemy was still firmly entrenched and conventional wisdom said that the Argentine position could not be taken with the forces at their disposal. At that point, the battalion's second-in-command Major Chris Keble says that he prayed, and as he did so it suddenly became clear to him what he should do. The next morning, under cover of a white flag, he walked up the hill to the Argentine trenches and asked them to surrender. Incredibly, they did – and the way to Port Stanley was clear.

Odds against.

It does not take too much human sympathy to imagine what might have been going through the mind of Major Keble on the night before the Argentine surrender. There would have been grief at the loss of friends and colleagues, fear of what the next day held, a longing for guidance and direction, the heavy burden of responsibility, doubt as to his ability to follow in the footsteps of an inspirational leader, loneliness, sorrow and perhaps despair. From every rational point of view, the odds were heavily stacked against him and his men.

From time to time we are all prey to emotions of this kind. Our nation faces difficult times and we do not know what tomorrow will bring. We want

---

[128] Like many before him, Argentine leader General Leopoldo Galtieri fatally underestimated the character and resolve of his opponents when he ordered an invasion of "las Malvinas." Speaking to U.S. Secretary of State Alexander Haig during frantic diplomatic efforts to avoid war, he said: "Why are you telling me this? The British won't fight."

someone to reassure us and show us the way. We want to know that we are still cared for and supported. We want to know that we are in safe hands. We tremble at the forces that are ranged in opposition to us, in the face of which our own resources seem so inadequate.

The second book of Kings describes a time when "the king of Aram was at war with Israel" (2 Kings 6:8). The preponderance of force was on the side of the Arameans. When their king learnt that the prophet Elisha was in Dothan, he "sent horses and chariots and a strong force there. They went by night and surrounded the city." (2 Kings 6:14). Since Dothan was far inside Israelite territory[129] and the Arameans were apparently able to deploy without interference from Israelite troops, their military superiority must have been considerable. The odds seemed to be stacked against Israel just as they appeared to be stacked against the British at Goose Green.

Eyes wide shut.

This, however, was only part of the story. From the start God, through Elisha, had repeatedly "warned the king [of Israel about Aramean troop movements], so that he was on his guard in such places [where the Arameans had set up camp]." (2 Kings 6:10). The Lord was active and present even though the results of his intervention were not seen for what they were. When the Aramean king's plans were repeatedly forestalled, he assumed that a spy must be at work: "This enraged the king of Aram. He summoned his officers and demanded of them, 'Will you not tell me which of us is on the side of the king of Israel?'" (2 Kings 6:11).

Exactly the same thing happens all around us, every day of the week. God is at work in this land no less than in days gone by, but people do not recognise him for who he is, nor do they ascribe to him the results of his activity. We need to have our eyes opened and to gain spiritual insight, for without this we will never be able to see beyond human agency to what is really going on. Insight involves the power of observation or discernment of the real character of things. It means the ability to penetrate appearances and see depths that may be hidden to others. It is an inevitable result of shining the light of God's truth into dark corners.

The story shows that neither spiritual blindness nor spiritual insight is the monopoly of one nation. Amongst the Arameans was a man who realised the truth: "'None of us [is a spy], my lord the king,' said one of his officers, 'but Elisha, the prophet who is in Israel, tells the king of Israel the very words you

---

[129] It lies on a hill about halfway between Jezreel and Samaria, both of which had royal residences.

speak in your bedroom.'" (2 Kings 6:12). Correspondingly, an Israelite lacked discernment: "When the servant of the man of God [that is, Elisha] got up and went out early the next morning, an army with horses and chariots had surrounded the city. 'Oh, my lord, what shall we do?' the servant asked." (2 Kings 6:15). Just as we are apt to do, Elisha's servant saw clearly enough when it came to identifying the difficulties and obstacles of life, but was unable to look beyond them. Elisha's servant focussed on the problem, not on God's provision. He saw only a mighty host of Aramean soldiers. His master Elisha had a different perspective. "'Don't be afraid,' the prophet answered. 'Those who are with us are more than those who are with them.' And Elisha prayed, 'O LORD, open his eyes so that he may see.' Then the LORD opened the servant's eyes, and he looked and saw the hills full of horses and chariots of fire all round Elisha." (2 Kings 6:16-17).

Shortly after the eyes of the servant were opened, those of Israel's enemies were closed: "As the enemy came down towards him, Elisha prayed to the LORD, 'Strike these people with blindness.' So he struck them with blindness, as Elisha had asked." (2 Kings 6:18). In order to come to a realisation of the truth, these enemies first had to be blinded to their immediate, sinful objective. With this done, Elijah was able to lead them from the path of wrongdoing into the path of righteousness: "Elisha told them, 'This is not the road and this is not the city. Follow me, and I will lead you to the man you are looking for.' And he led them to Samaria." (2 Kings 6:19).

Once the Arameans had been led away from the wrong path and objective, they were then in a position to have their eyes opened, too: "After they had entered the city, Elisha said, 'LORD, open the eyes of these men so that they can see.' Then the LORD opened their eyes and they looked, and there they were, inside Samaria." (2 Kings 6:20). In just the same way, we must become blind to sin. Only when our eyes are taken off what is wrong and our focus is shifted from problem to provision will we be able to look about us and see the reality that lies behind appearance. We may feel that we are outnumbered, surrounded and abandoned to our fate, but it is not so.

Counterpunch.

As well as gaining insight to see things as they really are, we need to know how to react to the circumstances that confront us. A range of lessons and responses appears from Elisha's encounter with the Arameans. These form the basis for our counterattack:

Godly intervention is no excuse for human inactivity or carelessness. Elisha warned the king of Israel what the Arameans were up to, but the king still "checked on the place indicated by the man of God ... [and] was on his guard in such places." (2

Kings 6:10). As Elisha advised, we need to "Beware" (2 Kings 6:9) when the forces of darkness are on the march.

Sometimes we need to stand our ground in the face of danger. Elisha was able to tell "the very words you [the king of Aram] speak in your bedroom" (2 Kings 6:12) and thus presumably knew that troops would be sent to surround Dothan. Yet instead of running away, he stayed put in order to bring God's plans to fruition.

The advice of godly people should be sought, weighed and when appropriate acted upon. The king of Israel asked Elisha: "Shall I kill them [the Arameans], my father? Shall I kill them?" (2 Kings 6:21). He did as Elisha said: "'Do not kill them,' [Elisha] answered, 'Would you kill men you have captured with your own sword or bow? Set food and water before them so that they may eat and drink and then go back to their master.'" (2 Kings 6:22).

We are called to be merciful even to the ungodly. In the same way that Elisha told the king of Israel to "set food and water before [the Arameans] so that they may eat and drink" (2 Kings 6:22), we are told that "when your enemy hungers, give him food and when he thirsts, give him drink" (Proverbs 25:21). By our treatment of our opponents, we will win many for Christ.

Our prayers should focus on God's provision for us rather than on the problems we face: "'Don't be afraid,' the prophet answered. 'Those who are with us are more than those who are with them.'" (2 Kings 6:16). We should seek insight for others as well as for ourselves and actively call for God's intervention in the world: "O LORD, open his eyes so that he may see." (2 Kings 6:17).

We should always be ready to show people the way, to tell them that "This is not the road and this is not the city. Follow me and I will lead you to the man you are looking for." (2 Kings 6:19). The person to whom we should lead them, of course, is "our Lord Jesus, that great Shepherd of the sheep" (Hebrews 13:20).

Our nation is hardly awash with godliness and insight is in short supply. This does not mean that God has given up on us. On the contrary, he has great things in store for us and for our nation: "'For I alone know the plans I have for you,' declares the LORD, 'plans to prosper you and not to harm you, plans to give you hope and a future. Then you will call upon me and come and pray to me, and I will listen to you.'" (Jeremiah 29:11-12). His army of angels awaits only the right response from us to enter the fray on our side. The king of Aram sought to take over Israelite territory but God frustrated his designs so that in the end "the bands from Aram stopped raiding Israel's territory." (2 Kings 6:23). If we will only do as the Lord asks, he will deliver us in the same way.

Conclusion.

We face a time of uncertainty, a time when our nation seems to be on a downward spiral, when large numbers suffer grievously and many feel like saying: "Oh, my lord, what shall we do?" (2 Kings 6:15). Yet we can take comfort, find assurance and obtain guidance from what happened in the days of Elisha.

We need to take up the mantle of our forebears. Just as Major Keble had to take over command from Colonel Jones on the latter's death, we must step into the breach of those who fought and died in years gone by to make this a Christian land. We have before us their example, as well as that of the great men of God whose stories are told in the Bible. Elisha was spiritual heir to Elijah and quite literally inherited his mantle: see 2 Kings 2:13. The "hills full of horses and chariots of fire" (2 Kings 6:17) that surrounded Dothan are part of the same army that accompanied Elijah, in whose presence "suddenly a chariot of fire and horses of fire appeared" (2 Kings 2:11). This godly army has not disappeared. Nor has it been defeated. It is still all around us.

With this in mind, we should remind ourselves whom it is that we worship and serve. He is the Creator of the universe, a God who is not distant but who is engaged with his world and with each one of us. We have seen him at work in our nation, in our church and in our own lives. We know him to be faithful, not just because the Bible tells us but because he has shown us himself that this is his nature. He will not abandon or fail us and we know that "nothing is impossible with God." (Luke 1:37). His message to us remains as it has always been: "Be strong and courageous. Do not be afraid or terrified ... for the LORD your God goes with you; he will never leave you nor forsake you." (Deuteronomy 31:6).

This does not mean that we will be free from hardship, neither that we will never be subject to attack, nor that doubt and fear will be absent from our hearts. We will be tested and we must expect every one of these things. God never promised that the Christian life would be easy, but he has repeatedly promised that: "I will never leave you or forsake you." (Joshua 1:5).[130] Whatever assaults we may face, however mighty and unremitting the forces ranged against us may appear to be, we should never lose sight of the fact that "Those who are with us are more than those who are with them" (2 Kings 6:16) and that for all their seeming power our enemies can be "struck with blindness" (2 Kings 6:18). God has done this time and again. In just this way, the Argentine forces at Goose Green were blinded to the strength of their position and to the difficulties faced by their opponents.

---

[130] See also Psalm 94:14 and Hebrews 13:5

For our part, we must open our eyes so that we may truly see. Insight is an essential weapon in our fight: insight to see God at work, insight into things that otherwise are hidden from men, insight into the enemy's plans and how to confound them, insight into the real strength of our position and our opponents' weakness, insight into the power of prayer and how to use it wisely, insight into when to ask for advice and when to follow it, insight into how to treat our enemies. St Paul acknowledged the power of godly insight when he said: "Reflect on what I am saying, for the Lord will give you insight into all this." (2 Timothy 2:7).

With Elisha, we need to pray: "O LORD, open [our] eyes so that [we] may see." (2 Kings 6:17).

60. Standing firm

1 Kings 19:1-18

Key word: perseverance.

Being in a minority of one is usually a very uncomfortable place to be. Margaret Thatcher famously relished taking on other heads of state during European summits and opponents of all stripes at home. This uncompromising approach led to her becoming known as Tina, an acronym derived from her oft-repeated mantra: "There is no alternative." In practice, few have such a taste for conflict and confrontation. Most prefer the comfort of being one of a crowd, basking in the warmth and approval of others. We have all sorts of phrases for it: we talk of not sticking our heads above the parapet, of not rocking the boat, of being a team player. The awkward reality, though, is that there are times when the majority are wrong and the minority are right. When that time comes, we need to line up on the side of truth, however difficult this may be. As American anti-slavery lawyer Wendell Phillips (1811-84) put it: "One on God's side is a majority."

Elijah was a man who took God's side. His ministry shows what the Lord can do through the life of someone who is prepared to stand up for what is right, even when that means standing alone. The prophet was an outspoken declarer of God's righteousness, yet he was also all too human, with weaknesses and insecurities like anyone else. He was not above feeling sorry for himself and was on occasion guilty of wallowing in his predicament. Perhaps most surprising of all for such a great man of God, he could sometimes completely fail to understand what the Lord was saying and how he was working. The events in 1 Kings 19 have much to teach us through Elijah's experience, both where he got it right and where he got it wrong.

A great prophet.

Elijah's name means the Lord (Yahweh, Jehovah) is God, which neatly sums up the message and focus of his ministry: to proclaim the lordship and sovereignty of the one true God, to condemn and destroy the worship of idols. Of all the prophets who came after Moses, Jews consider Elijah the greatest. The claim to greatness rests on his fearless proclamation of God's word; the events of his life; the fact that he was taken up into heaven rather than dying a normal death (2 Kings 2:3-12); and the prediction of his return before "the day of the LORD" (Malachi 4:5). Indeed, to this day Jews keep a place for Elijah at every Passover meal. They believe that he will return and that when he does he will resolve every point on which rabbis have been unable to agree down the years and that he will also usher in the coming of the Messiah.

Now, Christians will take issue with that last point, but the evidence of Elijah's ministry is powerful. He certainly did not fight shy of confrontation, either with the civil power, the religious authorities or even with the Almighty himself: in 1 Kings 17 Elijah stood alone to confront King Ahab, a notoriously dangerous and unpredictable man, by predicting three years of drought; in 1 Kings 18 Elijah again stood alone, this time by confronting four hundred and fifty prophets of Baal on Mount Carmel; and in 1 Kings 19 Elijah stood alone once more to confront God on Mount Horeb. The prophet was hardly a shrinking violet. So great was his legacy that Jesus deliberately paralleled some of the events of Elijah's life (fasting in the desert for forty days and nights,[131] exercising command over nature,[132] providing food where there was none,[133] raising a widow's son[134]), showing himself greater than Elijah, both a fulfilment and a greater fullness of what had gone before.

Reaching breaking point.

Yet despite this greatness Elijah reached breaking point. Terrified when he learnt that Queen Jezebel wanted him dead, he "ran for his life." (1 Kings 19:3). He fled all the way to Beersheba, in the very south of Israelite territory, more than a hundred miles from Ahab's kingdom. There he left his servant and "went a day's journey into the desert." (1 Kings 19:4).

Elijah was at the end of his tether. He was so despondent and downhearted that he "prayed that he might die." (1 Kings 19:4). He said words that most have felt like saying at one time or another: "I have had enough, LORD." (1 Kings 19:4). I am sick to death of it. I cannot take any more. I cannot stand it. There can be few human beings who have never felt the same. It should give us tremendous encouragement that one of the greatest men of God there has ever been experienced such despair. As James tells us, Elijah "was a man just like us" (James 5:17-18).

God answered Elijah's prayer by giving him the exact opposite of what he had asked for. Again, the experience is a common one. Elijah prayed: "Take my life" (1 Kings 19:4) and God responded by twice providing food to keep him

---

[131] See 1 Kings 19:8 and Matthew 4:1-2.

[132] See 1 Kings 17:1, 1 Kings 18:1, 2 Kings 2:8 and Luke 8:22-25.

[133] See 1 Kings 17:12-16 and Luke 9:10-17.

[134] See 1 Kings 17:17-23 and Luke 7:11-17.

alive (1 Kings 19:6 and 1 Kings 19:7). The point, of course, is that the Lord lovingly gives us what we need, not what we want.

Listening to God.

This ushered in a period of listening to God: "Strengthened by [the food the Almighty had provided, Elijah] travelled for forty days and forty nights until he reached Horeb, the mountain of God. There he went into a cave and spent the night." (1 Kings 19:8-9). In the cave God spoke to Elijah. He asked a question: "What are you doing here, Elijah?" (1 Kings 19:9). Elijah's answer totally missed the point. What God put his finger on was that the prophet had come to this place by following his own devices, not because God had told him to. Just like Jonah, he had run about as far as he could get from where God wanted him to be, and all he could focus on was what was important to him. His reply was full of self-pity and exaggerated his condition: "I am the only one left and now they are trying to kill me" (1 Kings 19:10). The first part of this statement was simply not true. There were many other men of God active at this time, as the succeeding events recounted in 1 Kings make clear. Yet humanity in all its weakness, childishness and petulance was here displayed in one of the mightiest prophets of them all. So often, we feel like we are the only ones who are doing something or going through a particular experience. In our heart of hearts we often know that it is not true, but that does not stop us from bleating.

In response, God told Elijah: "Go out and stand on the mountain in the presence of the LORD, for the LORD is about to pass by." (1 Kings 19:11). So Elijah went to stand on Mount Horeb. This mountain (usually identified as Mount Sinai) was a tremendously significant place for the remaining events of 1 Kings 19 to unfold. It was the place where Moses and the people of Israel received the Ten Commandments. These were given in a dramatic revelation accompanied by "thunder and lightning, with a thick cloud over the mountain and a very loud trumpet blast ... Mount Sinai was covered with smoke, because the LORD descended on it in fire. The smoke billowed up from it like smoke from a furnace, the whole mountain trembled violently, and the sound of the trumpet grew louder and louder." (Exodus 19:16 and 19:18-19).

The revelation from God in the time of Moses included earthquake ("the whole mountain trembled violently"), wind ("the smoke billowed") and fire ("the LORD descended ... in fire"), which no doubt coloured Elijah's expectations about what he would experience as he stood on the mountain. Indeed Elijah did experience each of these things, but God was not in any of them. Only later, presumably after Elijah had returned to his cave, did he experience his own mighty revelation. It came in "a gentle whisper" (1 Kings 19:12) or, as other translations put it, "a still, small voice" (KJV) or "a sound of sheer silence" (NRSV). Perhaps the last of those translations most accurately conveys what happened, because at all events it does not seem as though anything distinctly audible or completely intelligible was said.

It is worth reflecting on where Elijah was at this point. He prayed to God to die and got the exact opposite. He cried out to God in despair and fear but was given no direct reply. Instead he was told to stand on a mountain to see the Lord pass by, yet experienced nothing but emptiness. He did as God said but heard only the sound of sheer silence. This mighty prophet, whose prayers God had so often answered in dramatic fashion, must have felt abandoned and literally godforsaken, as though he were praying into a void. Nevertheless, Elijah remained a man of steadfast faith. When he felt the first faint footfalls of God's presence "he pulled his cloak over his face and went out and stood at the mouth of the cave." (1 Kings 19:13). That is just what we need to do at difficult points in our lives: to stand at the mouth of the cave, listening and waiting on God. We need calm and we need quiet to appreciate fully who God is, how is he is working and what he wants to say to us. Especially when surrounded by all the frenetic activity of modern life, we must create space to: "Be still and know that I am God" (Psalm 46:10).

God spoke. The interchange between him and Elijah was poignant and almost comic, because God gave him another chance to get the right answer and for the second time Elijah misunderstood. Again God asked: "What are you doing here, Elijah" (1 Kings 19:13) but Elijah had no greater insight than before and merely repeated his previous response (1 Kings 19:14). What Elijah wanted and expected was a God of vengeance, justice and retribution, a God of undisguised power, a God to smite the evildoer and scatter his foes. Instead he got a God of gentleness, love and compassion, the God of the still, small voice. This is the one who says: "Not by strength nor by power but by my Spirit" (Zechariah 4:6), who encourages us to "Take my yoke upon you and learn from me, for I am gentle and humble in heart, and you will find rest for your souls." (Matthew 11:29). Quite simply, Elijah misunderstood how the Almighty was moving at this point. In his own mind he had emphasised one aspect of God at the expense of another. There is a time for earthquake, wind and fire – indeed, they were present at other points in Elijah's ministry[135] – but this was not it.

Prayer and action.

When God next spoke, he said: "Go back the way you came" (1 Kings 19:15). These words are just as important for us to hear. When we have taken a wrong track, the only thing to do is to turn round and get back to where we were

---

[135] Fire fell on the altar that Elijah prepared on Mount Carmel (1 Kings 18:38) and a whirlwind took him up to heaven (2 Kings 2:11).

last going the right way. Or, to put it another way: when we are in a hole, we should stop digging. So often we blunder on, making things worse and worse. To his credit, Elijah did as he was told. His ministry was not yet over. The Lord's work continued. God used the prophet to ensure the succession to a new generation of religious and political leaders. Hence Elijah was told to "anoint Hazael king over Aram. Also, anoint Jehu ... king over Israel and anoint Elisha ... to succeed you as prophet." (1 Kings 19:15-16). Furthermore, Elijah recovered his courage to declare God's righteousness again by confronting Ahab over his theft of Naboth's vineyard and murder of Naboth and his sons: 1 Kings 21.

In response to prayer, Elijah took action: strong, determined, vigorous and courageous action. The kinds of prayers he prayed were important, too, because the prophet was never afraid to pray for inconvenient things. He prayed for three years of drought, with the result that his own source of water dried up and he did not know how he would eat.[136] He prayed for fire from heaven, knowing that it would make him a marked man in the eyes of Ahab and Jezebel.[137] He was always ready to put himself in the line of attack and to be an instrument for God to use. We need to do the same. This does not have to mean that we undertake life-threatening or impossible missions, but we should be prepared to become the answers to our own prayers. So, instead of praying "God, comfort that heartbroken family", we might pray "God, use me to bring comfort to that family". Instead of praying "Lord, bring my neighbour to faith", we might pray "Lord, use me to help lead my neighbour to you."

Conclusion.

The lessons from Elijah's experience boil down to this: we need to stick it out in times of discouragement and despair; we should not be surprised if sometimes we seem to get the opposite of what we ask for; when we are at breaking point, God will be there if we seek him; we have to accept that God does not act according to our expectations; we must go back to basics and reflect on whether we are in the place where God wants us to be, and whether we are acting at his prompting or following the devices and desires of our own hearts; we need to create space to "Be still and know that I am God" (Psalm 46:10); when we are in a hole, we should stop digging; and we should challenge each other to pray inconvenient prayers, offering ourselves to be the means of our prayers' fulfilment.

---

[136] 1 Kings 17:7

[137] 1 Kings 18:16-38

Nobody claims this is easy. Elijah did not find it easy at one crisis point in his life, but it can be done. If we are serious about making a difference in the life of our country and in the world, it must be done. We need to "[pull our] cloak over [our] face and [go] out and [stand] at the mouth of the cave." (1 Kings 19:13). Above all, as a nation we must "go back the way [we] came" (1 Kings 19:15), leave off going down the wrong road and hasten back to where we were last on track. Then will we be able to pick up the threads again and do as the Lord wishes.

61. Turning aside

Jonah 1.

Key word: flight.

In the early 1960s Mary Whitehouse founded the National Viewers' and Listeners' Association to lobby against what she saw as the increasingly dubious moral content of radio and television programmes. In 1965 she said this: "The enemies of the West saw that Britain was the kingpin of western civilisation: she had proved herself unbeatable on the field of battle because of her faith and her character. If Britain was to be destroyed, those things must be undercut."

For her courage in speaking out, Mary Whitehouse was constantly derided, mocked and belittled. The media treated her as a national laughing stock and whipping boy. Yet she was right. She was right about the role played by this country in western civilisation. She was right about the sustained attack on the values that had made the country amongst the greatest of all nations. She was right about the moral and social corruption that lay around the corner.

Many times Britain has been instrumental in saving Europe from dictatorship and oppression: Louis XIV, Napoleon Bonaparte, Kaiser Wilhelm II and Adolf Hitler might all have achieved greater and more durable dominion but for this nation's opposition. It was of the utmost importance, not only to these islands but to the world, that our forefathers stood firm during these trials and did not flee from the task in hand.

Summons.

The prophet Jonah was also required to stand firm in the face of difficulty. He ministered during the period 800-750 BC and was called by God to a task of international importance. Although he was an Israelite, God told him: "Go to the great city of Nineveh and preach against it, because its wickedness has come up before me." (Jonah 1:2). Nineveh was one of the largest cities in the world at this time. It was capital of Assyria, the nation which a mere thirty years or so later (in 722-721 BC) was responsible for the destruction of the northern Israelite kingdom of Israel. This conquest brought in its wake killing, enslavement and mass deportation.

The summons that the Lord issued to Jonah was unexpected, unwelcome and extraordinary in every degree. It required a prophet of Israel to preach to a Gentile nation, with the prospect that the nation concerned might hear the word of God, repent and be saved. Nor did the people to whom Jonah was told to preach seem in any way worthy of divine favour: Assyria was a byword for wickedness and cruelty, where captives were routinely skinned alive and had

349

hands or feet cut off. Moreover, even in Jonah's day the Assyrian Empire was a direct threat to the Israelite kingdoms of Israel and Judah.

It is thus scarce surprising that Jonah did not relish the job and ducked the responsibility: "But Jonah ran away from the Lord and headed for Tarshish. He went down to Joppa, where he found a ship bound for that port. After paying the fare, he went aboard and sailed for Tarshish to flee from the LORD." (Jonah 1:3). The location of Tarshish is not completely certain, but it may have been the Phoenician trading post at Tartessus in south-west Spain – at the opposite end of the Mediterranean from Israel and Judah. At all events, the picture is of a man going as far as he can physically travel within the then known world.

Although he was called to be a prophet, at this point Jonah clearly had an uncertain grasp of exactly who God is and how he works. The Lord is constrained neither by time nor space, as the earlier writings of King David clearly recognised: "Where can I go from your Spirit? Where can I flee from your presence? If I go up to the heavens, you are there; if I make my bed in the depths, you are there. If I rise on the wings of the dawn, if I settle on the far side of the sea, even there your hand will guide me, your right hand will hold me fast. If I say, 'Surely the darkness will hide me and the light become night around me,' even the darkness will not be dark to you; the night will shine like the day, for darkness is as light to you." (Psalm 139:7-12).

Jonah thought he was doing one thing (fleeing God), but the Lord was doing another (teaching Jonah and preparing him for his eventual journey to Nineveh). God's control over events and his ability to turn even the most unpromising of circumstances to good account are clearly demonstrated. This echoes Joseph's experience at the hands of his brothers: "You intended to harm me, but God intended it for good to accomplish what is now being done, the saving of many lives." (Genesis 50:20). In just the same way, Jonah saved many lives by preaching repentance to the people of Nineveh.

Disobedience.

Ironically, this life-saving mission began with lives being threatened: "Then the LORD sent a great wind on the sea, and such a violent storm arose that the ship threatened to break up. All the sailors were afraid and each cried out to his own god. And they threw the cargo into the sea to lighten the ship. But Jonah had gone below deck, where he lay down and fell into a deep sleep." (Jonah 1:4-5). For the second time in the story, Jonah is spiritually inactive (asleep this time instead of running away) when he should be alert to what is going on.

Whilst the prophet slept, even a pagan could see what needed to be done: "The captain went to him and said. 'How can you sleep? Get up and call on your god! Maybe he will take notice of us, and we will not perish.'" (Jonah 1:6). In our own nation, presently sleepwalking to disaster, these words should ring out like a clarion call. We, too, need to awake, to "get up and call on [the LORD]" (Jonah 1:6).

When identified by the casting of lots as author of the misfortune, Jonah replied to the sailors' questions about who he was and where he came from by saying: "I am a Hebrew and I worship the LORD, the God of heaven, who made the sea and the land." (Jonah 1:9). The statement is orthodox, but that very orthodoxy shows how far Jonah had yet to travel in spiritual terms. For, although he mouthed the correct formula, he denied its truth through his failure to obey God. The same indictment can be laid against us.

That said, Jonah recognised that his disobedience had consequences, just as ours does: "Pick me up and throw me into the sea ... and it will become calm. I know that it is my fault that this great storm has come upon you." (Jonah 1:12). The sailors at first tried to save themselves by their own efforts, but when this was unavailing "they took Jonah and threw him overboard, and the raging sea grew calm. At this the men greatly feared the LORD, and they offered a sacrifice to the LORD and made vows to him." (Jonah 1:15). Even the pagan seamen gained a glimmer of spiritual insight through what happened to the recalcitrant prophet.

Reliability.

When Jonah should by rights have been a dead man, God stepped in: "But the LORD provided a great fish to swallow Jonah, and Jonah was inside the fish three days and three nights." (Jonah 1:17). Some consider this improbable and hence treat the story, or at least this part of it, as allegory. However, Jesus clearly took a different view, using Jonah's experiences as an analogy for his own death and resurrection: see Matthew 12:39-41. As so often with challenging parts of Scripture, difficulty begins to recede and new possibilities emerge on investigation and reflection. Extraordinary as it may at first seem, this story is about a real person and real events:

Jonah is not a character invented just for this tale. He appears elsewhere in Scripture. The military success of King Jeroboam II of Israel against Aramea was foretold "in accordance with the word of the LORD, the God of Israel, spoken through his servant Jonah son of Amittai, the prophet from Gath Hepher." (2 Kings 14:25).

The most likely candidate for the "great fish" described in Jonah 1:17 is either a sperm whale or a Great White shark. Both are found in the Mediterranean. At the time of the events recorded in the book of Jonah there was even a Phoenician whaling industry based on Joppa (Jaffa).

There are several recorded instances of men being swallowed by sperm whales and Great White sharks. In 1863 an American called Peleg Nye fell from a boat whilst trying to harpoon a whale and was taken into the creature's mouth as it dived. He survived. Within two hours the animal that had swallowed him died, its body floated to the surface and his crewmates recovered it. Inside the carcass was the man who was known until his death at the age of 79 as "the Jonah of Cape Cod."[138]

In the third century BC Berosus, a Babylonian priest and historian with access to earlier Babylonian sources, wrote of a mythical creature called Oannes which emerged from the sea to bring divine wisdom to men. Since Berosus lived during the Hellenistic period, he wrote in Greek. Oannes is one of two ways used in the Old Testament to render the name Jonah in Greek.

In Phoenicia the fish-god (Dagon) was a favourite object of worship. The centre of worship for this god was Nineveh. Indeed, in Assyrian mythology Semiramis, daughter of a fish-goddess and the god of wisdom, was said to have been the wife of Ninus, the founder of Nineveh.[139]

Nineveh herself was eventually destroyed by the Babylonians under Nabipolassar in 612 BC. The city was obliterated so completely that some denied its very existence until the remains were excavated by Austen Henry Layard from 1845-47. The ruins lay under two mounds (or tells) called *Kuyunjik* and *Nabi Yunus*. The latter means 'the prophet Jonah' in Arabic.

These facts are not conclusive. They are, however, highly suggestive that Jonah really lived and that his memory was preserved in association with both the sea and with Nineveh. They show that it is perfectly possible for a man to be swallowed by a whale or other large sea creature and survive. The subsequently disproved assertion that there was no such city as Nineveh (or at any rate that a conurbation as large as that described in the Bible[140] could not have existed at the time in question) should chasten the sceptic.

What we see in truth is the remarkable sureness and foresight of God's provision. He contrived for his prophet to be "vomited ... onto dry land" (Jonah 2:10)[141] by a large sea creature in an area where fish-gods were especially venerated. We may infer that the impact of this extraordinary apparition was

---

[138] In 1891 James Bartley, lost overboard from the *Star of the East,* is said to have survived even longer inside a whale.

[139] Semiramis is said to have ruled alone after the death of Ninus and then to have founded Babylon.

[140] Jonah 3:3 says that "Nineveh was a very important city – a visit required three days."

[141] Emptying of the stomach in this way is common amongst dying whales and sharks.

increased by Jonah's own appearance, since his hair and skin would presumably have been bleached white by the gastric juices of the great fish. Not surprisingly, when he eventually went to Nineveh and preached "they [the inhabitants of the city] turned from their evil ways" (Jonah 3:10).

God is reliable and his Word is reliable. Like Jonah, we are by rights dead men. We should pray that the Lord will nevertheless step into our lives and the life of our nation.

Conclusion.

The creation of a multi-racial, multi-faith Britain has led to colossal confusion on the part of officialdom, and hence on the part of people as a whole. We have rightly shown no tolerance towards discrimination on racial or ethnic grounds: to treat someone as being of lesser worth by reason of their race or country of origin is odious in the extreme, and is directly contrary to biblical teaching. The Bible affirms that we are all descendants of Adam and Eve, and that there is no distinction between "Greek or Jew, circumcised or uncircumcised, barbarian, Scythian, slave or free, but Christ is all, and is in all." (Colossians 3:11).

However, in doing this we have increasingly overlooked the fact that there is a positive kind of discrimination: the ability to distinguish between good and evil, right and wrong, true and false. In opposing so strongly discrimination in the negative sense, we are increasingly proving incapable of exercising it in the positive. We flee the responsibility of decision. We flee from where God wants us to be. We are spiritually inactive by reason of our running away or our sleepwalking through life. We are too lazy even to investigate God's Word and to decide whether there is really any basis for the supposition that what is recounted there is nothing but a set of fairy tales with no application to the present day. We need to heed Jesus' warning: "The men of Nineveh will stand up at the judgment with this generation and condemn it; for they repented at the preaching of Jonah, and now one greater than Jonah is here." (Matthew 12:41).

We need to get away from the kind of things that Mary Whitehouse described and against which she fought, for these are undercutting the very foundations of our nation. Fleeing from God is not the answer. The Lord wants us to take flight, but in a wholly different sense. His desire is for us to be amongst "those who hope in the LORD [and] will renew their strength. They will soar on wings like eagles; they will run and not grow weary, they will walk and not be faint." (Isaiah 40:31). Through the power of God working in us we can do something extraordinary. We can take wing.

62. Sirens

Titus 3.

Key word: devotion.

Bertrand Russell's *History of Western Philosophy* runs to over 780 pages in paperback, a magisterial survey of European thought from the ancient Greeks to the present day. Yet this towering edifice is but an incomplete snapshot of all the ideas that mankind has had about God, the world in which we live and our own nature. By definition it excludes those generated over the greater part of the earth's surface and by the greater part of its population. Understandably, it deals with the main strands of thought rather than exploring all their highways and byways. It gives a flavour, and a good one at that, but cannot render the whole. Even this imperfect and incomplete glimpse, however, is enough to give an inkling of how many and various have been man's speculations on life's most fundamental questions.

Those who have been accounted great thinkers have included men of genius, but also a fair smattering of charlatans, the deranged and the deluded. With the benefit of hindsight, it is difficult not to be struck by how few ways of looking at the world have stood the test of time and how inadequate all our ideas seem when confronted with the vastness of the universe.[142] Shakespeare's Hamlet hit the nail on the head when he said: "There are more things in heaven and earth, Horatio, than are dreamt of in your philosophy."

Nor can we fail to be saddened by things done in the name of misguided ideals, be they religious or secular. One of the most successful revolutionaries of any age spoke these words on his deathbed: "I have made a great mistake. Our main purpose was to give freedom to multitudes of oppressed people. But our method of action has created worse evil and horrible massacres. You know that my deadly nightmare is to feel that I am lost in an ocean of blood coming from innumerable victims. It is too late to turn now, but in order to save our country ... we should have had ten men like Francis of Assisi. With ten such men, we would have saved Russia." His name was Vladimir Ilyich Ulyanov (Lenin).

---

[142] Of the logical positivism espoused by Bertrand Russell, A. J. Ayer, whose book *Language, Truth and Logic* (1936) did much to promote it, later said: "Nearly all of it was false." Professor of Philosophy Ronald Nash commented: "Today it is quite difficult to find any philosopher who is willing to claim publicly the label of logical positivism. The movement is dead, and quite properly so."

The idea in the name of which Lenin, his accomplices and successors perpetrated their crimes was the dialectical materialism of Karl Marx. Its demonstrable failings of logic[143] did not prevent many from taking up the cause, in this country as elsewhere. Bolsheviks, Mensheviks, Trotskyists, Leninists, Stalinists, Maoists and a dozen shades in between worked for the overthrow of the state and the building of a workers' paradise. It was all illusion. The collapse of the Soviet Union showed the reality: environmental degradation and human misery on a massive scale.

The descent of dream into nightmare has been the story of every utopian vision that man has conjured up to supplant God. Yet still the siren voices call.

Revolution.

Christianity involves revolution, but not in the way that Lenin would have understood. This is made clear in the advice which St Paul gives to Titus, a convert whom he left on Crete to "straighten out what was left unfinished and appoint elders in every town, as I directed you." (Titus 1:5). St Paul tells him to "Remind the people to be subject to rulers and authorities, to be obedient" (Titus 3:1). The phrase "rulers and authorities" encompasses all forms and levels of human government. Instead of direct confrontation with the powers that be, even when they are ungodly, Christianity involves living and working in such a way as will change society from within. The gospel involves a radical challenge to all human assumptions and all existing ways of doing things, yet whilst this inevitably involves engagement with the political process it is not primarily through political action that Christian revolution comes about. Rather, real and lasting change is underscored by and grounded on the revolution in our hearts and minds.

The book of Titus explains how God brings revolution about: through those chosen by God to do his work (Titus 1), through Christian teaching (Titus 2) and through God's own activity (Titus 3). The series of opposites that St Paul lists in chapter three shows how great is this revolution: "At one time we too were foolish, disobedient, deceived and enslaved by all kinds of passion and pleasure. We lived in malice and envy, being hated and hating one another." (Titus 3:3). To these qualities and ways of behaviour belong "foolish controversies and genealogies and arguments and quarrels about the law ... [which] are unprofitable

---

[143] Dialectical materialism purports to be based on logical inference from what we see around us, without the need for pre-existing ideas. However, tenets such as the inevitability of the dictatorship of the proletariat, the withering away of law and the reaching of a state of abundance cannot be derived in this way.

and useless." (Titus 3:9). The kind of person who indulges in such things is "divisive ...warped and sinful; he is self-condemned." (Titus 3:10-11).

Thanks to God's activity and the effect of the gospel, all this is supplanted by: "the kindness and love of God our Saviour ... [and] his mercy" (Titus 3:4-5). Kindness replaces enslavement, love replaces malice and envy, mercy replaces hatred. Instead of what is "unprofitable and useless" (Titus 3:9), there are "things [that] are excellent and profitable for everyone." (Titus 3:8). Those who previously were "foolish, disobedient, deceived and enslaved by all kinds of passion and pleasure" (Titus 3:3) are now to "to slander no-one, to be peaceable and considerate, and to show true humility towards all men." (Titus 3:2). In short, they are to "be careful to devote themselves to doing what is good." (Titus 3:8). This gospel is revolution indeed. Were it find widespread application, the effect would be electrifying. This is an ideal that really is worthy of our devotion.

Ideals.

The ideals and the essential basis of the Christian revolution are summarised by St Paul in just two sentences: "But when the kindness and love of God our Saviour appeared, he saved us, not because of righteous things we had done, but because of his mercy. He saved us through the washing of rebirth and renewal by the Holy Spirit, whom he poured out on us generously through Jesus Christ our Saviour, so that, having been justified by his grace, we might become heirs having the hope of eternal life." (Titus 3:4-7). The whole of redemption history is packed into a few short phrases:

The one true God is Trinitarian, as seen by the activity of God (the Father), Jesus Christ our Saviour (the Son) and the Holy Spirit.

This God took the initiative in rescuing man from the consequences of rebellion and sin, appearing to and amongst men, as Saviour and as an embodiment of "kindness and love" (Titus 3:4).

Salvation cannot be earned. It comes by virtue of God's mercy rather than "because of righteous things we had done" (Titus 3:5).

The consequence of salvation is that we are cleansed from sin by the "washing of rebirth and renewal by the Holy Spirit ... poured out on us generously through Jesus Christ our Saviour" (Titus 3:5-6).

We are "justified [vindicated, exonerated] by God's grace" (Titus 3:7) and thereby saved from the penalty that would otherwise attend our sin.

We are adopted into God's family and "become heirs having the hope of eternal life." (Titus 3:7).

Appropriately, this masterly summary ends with the words: "This is a trustworthy saying." (Titus 3:8).

Productivity.

It is all very well to have a revolution and to pursue an ideal, but what is thereby built needs to be administered and cared for properly. This involves good governance, allied with hard work, careful planning and sound administration. In Titus, St Paul leaves matters in capable and willing hands. Titus was a believer from a Gentile background and was probably relatively young at the time this letter was written, but he did not lack experience. As well as working alongside St Paul on Crete, he had already accompanied the apostle on the journey to Jerusalem that is described in Galatians 2:1-3 and been with him in Corinth, as well as travelling on his own: see 2 Corinthians 2:12-13, 7:5-6, 8:6 and 8:23. It is likely that Titus was also with St Paul in Ephesus and later went independently on a mission to Dalmatia: see 2 Timothy 4:10.

Titus is advised to concentrate on essentials and not to be taken down blind alleys. There is a warning for us, too, when St Paul tells him to "avoid foolish controversies and genealogies and arguments and quarrels about the law ... [which] are unprofitable and useless." (Titus 3:9). We need to be constantly alert lest we become sidetracked in this way. Certainly, we need to have proper regard for the Word of God, but to stick to the central truths of the faith rather than waste time disputing matters about which Christians can in good faith disagree. A huge amount of effort and energy has been and still is being expended on what are essentially sideshows, blunting and undermining the work of the worldwide church. One of the characteristics of extremist groups is their tendency to split and splinter. Such scattering is typical of the work of Satan and the very opposite of the gathering that God wishes to bring about. It is to our shame if we allow such things to characterise our discourse and activity.

The aim is that revolution will result in godly action: "Do everything you can to help Zenas the lawyer and Apollos on their way and see that they have everything they need. Our people must learn to devote themselves to doing what is good, in order that they may provide for daily necessities and not live unproductive lives." (Titus 3:13-14). Unlike revolutionaries of the stamp of Lenin or modern-day Islamists, for the Christian the end does not justify the means. We must continue to "devote [ourselves] to doing what is good" (Titus 3:14), come what may. Neither belief in God's providence nor certainty about the sufficiency of his provision entitle us to sit back and wait for the Almighty to wave a magic wand over whatever ills or troubles surround us. Certainly, God works through us and at times intervenes in ways that are very obviously miraculous, but usually we are the agency by which others are helped and through which "the necessities of daily life" (Titus 3:13) are provided. Christianity values hard work, personal effort and individual achievement, so long as these are channelled in ways that honour God and do not usurp his place in our hearts.

Conclusion.

It is in the nature of men to devote themselves to people or to things. Some are devoted to hobbies, some to the pursuit of pleasure, some to ideals. The things to which we devote ourselves have an impact on our own lives and on the lives of those around us. It is thus of prime importance that we choose the objects of our devotion wisely. The merest glimpse at a long line of twentieth century demagogues who gained the devotion of entire nations should be enough to convince us of this. We must exercise discretion in our choices, taking time to weigh the options and to assess where they are likely to lead. There are many things which are harmless in moderation, perhaps even beneficial, but which will corrode if pursued to excess. There are other things that should not be countenanced at any price. Jesus told us how to weigh the competing choices: "Watch out for false prophets. They come to you in sheep's clothing, but inwardly they are ferocious wolves. By their fruit you will recognise them. Do people pick grapes from thornbushes, or figs from thistles? Likewise every good tree bears good fruit, but a bad tree bears bad fruit. A good tree cannot bear bad fruit, and a bad tree cannot bear good fruit." (Matthew 7:16). We can expect good results from things that are of God and conversely we can expect ultimately harmful results from things that are not. The proof of the pudding is in the eating.

Rarely has there been a time with such an abundance of false prophets, of gurus and fakirs both religious and secular. Most are shooting stars that flash and flicker in the firmament for a brief while and then are gone. For the greater part they are distinguished not only by harmful results whilst they are in the ascendant but also by their impermanence. As Cardinal John Henry Newman (1801-1890) observed, "True religion is slow in growth and, when once planted, is difficult of dislodgement; but its intellectual counterfeit has no root in itself; it springs up suddenly, it suddenly withers." The English have traditionally been noted for their lack of aptitude for and their distrust of abstract philosophy. At various times in our past this has stood us in good stead, inoculating us to some extent from the wilder excesses of human invention. Regrettably, we are not currently showing immunity to the plagues of materialism, consumerism and all the fashionable ideas that have grown up to help persuade us that our selfishness and self-indulgence are not merely acceptable, but right and proper.

The contrast between such things and the gospel of Jesus Christ could not be greater. The Christian is instructed to show the reality of his faith by "being careful to maintain good works" (Titus 3:8). We are to do so "... while we wait for the blessed hope – the glorious appearing of our great God and Saviour, Jesus Christ, who gave himself for us to redeem us from all wickedness and to purify for himself a people that are his very own, eager to do what is good." (Titus 2:13-14). We must devote ourselves to this end and to our Lord, who makes all things possible, with renewed vigour and commitment.

63. Drift

Song of Songs 3.

Key word: seeking.

Trainspotting by Irvine Welsh tells the story of Edinburgh drug addicts, but could be set in any town in the land. The tale is fictionalised, though based on personal experience. In the *Sunday Times* column, *The best of times, the worst of times*, the author commented that, if you have nothing to believe in, drugs will always get the better of you.

We live in a society that is awash with drugs. Not only the illicit potions with which we dose ourselves in frightening quantities, nor licit chemicals such as alcohol, tobacco and Prozac. They include other narcotics that we call fame, wealth, achievement, beauty and personal fulfilment. They encompass all the stresses and strivings of a nation that no longer seems to believe in anything. We wander aimlessly in search of a palliative for the emptiness in our hearts. We seem to be forever seeking, but never finding, always on the move, but never arriving. We are lost souls, adrift in scenery without feature or landmark, where everything is said to be just as 'valid' as everything else and consequently nothing has real value.

American novelist F. Scott Fitzgerald called the hedonistic lifestyles of his own Jazz Age "despair turned inside out." Drugs, hedonism and consumerism are all symptoms of our despair. We long for happiness, togetherness and meaning. Instead we find only indulgence, excess and oblivion. We have not yet learnt to recognise that words written almost sixteen centuries ago by St Augustine of Hippo are true: "You [God] have created us for yourself, and our hearts are restless till they find their rest in you."

Search.

In the Song of Songs King Solomon describes an anguished search for an object of great desire: "All night long on my bed I looked for the one my heart loves; I looked for him but did not find him." (Song of Songs 3:1). Freed from the distractions of the day, often it is as we try to get to sleep that our minds begin to wander and our real concerns force themselves upon us. With nothing to divert us, fears and imaginings have free rein. The longing in this case is so powerful and the ache in the heart so agonising that the seeker is driven to rise in the middle of the night to roam hither and thither: "I will get up now and go about the city, through its streets and squares; I will search for the one my heart loves. So I looked for him but did not find him." (Song of Songs 3:2).

The picture is of a desperate seeking in the small hours, careless of rest, safety and reputation: "The watchmen found me as they made their rounds in the city. 'Have you seen the one my heart loves?'" (Song of Songs 3:3). Even those keeping a look-out on the walls and ramparts, whose duty is to tell what is going on and warn of impending danger, have not seen "the one my heart loves" (Song of Songs 3:1). The fact that the watchmen cannot help is hardly encouraging about the environment that surrounds the seeker, for the prophets were supposed to be God's spiritual watchmen: "Son of man, I have made you a watchman for the house of Israel; so hear the word I speak and give them warning from me." (Ezekiel 3:17). With no proper direction from those who should be providing it, the seeker starts by looking in the wrong places, in the wrong way, at the wrong time and asking the wrong questions of the wrong people. There are thousands upon thousands doing the same in this nation today.

Nevertheless, after repeated trial and error the search at last ends successfully because the goal and attitude of heart are the right ones: "Scarcely had I passed them when I found the one my heart loves. I held him and would not let him go till I had brought him to my mother's house, to the room of the one who conceived me." (Song of Songs 3:4). When finally the object of desire is attained, the seeker recognises its value, holds fast to it and brings it to a place of safety. The Bible consistently tells us that if we genuinely look for God, our search will not be in vain, no matter how spiritually desolate may be our starting point, nor how inept our seeking:

Moses says it: "But if from there you seek the LORD your God, you will find him if you look for him with all your heart and with all your soul." (Deuteronomy 4:29).

King David says it: "If you seek him, he will be found by you" (1 Chronicles 28:9).

King Solomon says it: "those who seek me find me." (Proverbs 8:17).

The prophets say it: "You will seek me and find me when you seek me with all your heart." (Jeremiah 29:13).

Jesus says it: "Ask and it will be given to you; seek and you will find; knock and the door will be opened to you. For everyone who asks receives; he who seeks finds; and to him who knocks, the door will be opened." (Matthew 7:7-8).

The issue, then, is first and foremost whether we are seeking the right object with the right attitude, although obviously our search will be the quicker if we seek in the right way, in the right place, at the right time and by asking the right questions of the right people.

Goal.

Clearly, we will never find something if we do not look for it. Our society invests tremendous time and energy in seeking what is entirely illusory and even detrimental. Rampant addiction is merely one symptom of the desolation that follows. By contrast, the Song of Songs adjures us to avoid artificial stimulation, whether sexual or otherwise: "Daughters of Jerusalem, I charge you by the gazelles and by the does of the field: do not arouse or awaken love until it so desires." (Song of Songs 3:5).

To find that for which all human beings really long in the deepest reaches of their hearts we need to lay aside all artificiality and illusion and to ensure that the aim of our desire is worthwhile. The goal of the seeker in the Song of Songs is described as "coming up from the desert like a column of smoke" (Song of Songs 3:6). The phrasing is reminiscent of the Israelites' flight from Egypt, when "By day the LORD went ahead of them in a pillar of cloud to guide them on their way and by night in a pillar of fire to give them light" (Exodus 13:21). In each case, the pillar of cloud or column of smoke is a visible symbol of God's presence with his people, also symbolised by the things that were brought as gifts to Jesus at his birth by the wise men (see Matthew 2:11):

Gold (together with purple and a crown) as a symbol of royalty: "King Solomon made for himself the carriage; he made it of wood from Lebanon. Its posts he made of silver, its base of gold. Its seat was embroidered with purple, its interior lovingly inlaid by the daughters of Jerusalem. Come out, you daughters of Zion, and look at King Solomon wearing his crown, the crown with which his mother crowned him on the day of his wedding, the day his heart rejoiced." (Song of Songs 3:9-11).

Frankincense as a symbol of worship, sacrifice and the priesthood: "incense made from all the spices of the merchant" (Song of Songs 3:6).

Myrrh as a symbol of crucifixion and death: "perfumed with myrrh" (Song of Songs 3:6). As Jesus hung on the cross "they offered him wine mixed with myrrh [to relieve pain], but he did not take it." (Mark 15:23). Myrrh was also applied to Jesus' body after his death (see John 19:39-40).

The object of the seeker's desire can thus be seen as a prototype of Jesus Christ "the desired of all nations" (Haggai 2:7). This same Jesus should be the goal of our search, for he is "the way and the truth and the life. No-one comes to the Father except through [him]." (John 14:6). There is no object more worthy of our search, no end more estimable, no person more perfect or beautiful.

Attainment.

When finally the object of desire is found, he brings with him the means to quiet the restless imaginings of the small hours: "sixty warriors, the noblest of Israel, all of them wearing the sword, all experienced in battle, each with his sword at his side, prepared for the terrors of the night." (Song of Songs 3:7-8). In the same way, the Lord will enable us to resist the "terrors of the night" (Song of Songs 3:8), for "God did not give us a spirit of timidity, but a spirit of power, of love and of self-discipline." (2 Timothy 1:7). Instead of things artificial or illusory, the Lord gives us "the fruit of the Spirit [which] is love, joy, peace, patience, kindness, goodness, faithfulness, gentleness, and self-control." (Galatians 5:22). Of all gifts, these are amongst those most worth having. Indeed, God offers much more than this. He says: "Seek me and live" (Amos 5:4), for his greatest gift is our salvation and, consequent on that, eternal life.

Salvation and the gifts of the Spirit are the very opposite of the results that come from our misplaced striving, as St Paul cautions his readers in Galatia: "The acts of the sinful nature are obvious: sexual immorality, impurity and debauchery, idolatry and witchcraft; hatred, discord, jealousy, fits of rage, selfish ambition, dissensions, factions and envy; drunkenness, orgies, and the like. I warn you, as I did before, that those who live like this will not inherit the kingdom of God." (Galatians 5:21). We pay a terrible price for our indulgence, excess and seeking after oblivion.

One of the tricks of the forces of darkness is to claim to offer good things. Satan never shows us the end result, but only a pleasurable beginning. Drug-taking is but one example. Nobody starts off with the aim of becoming a helpless addict. Nobody wants to live out their days in squalor and end them in misery. Nobody would take drugs if the experience were not at first enjoyable. Only over time does gratification wear thin and the physical and moral toll become apparent. Any man who imagines he can be a heavy long-term drug user without becoming a thief and any woman that she can doing so without prostituting herself is dreaming, but sadly many prefer fancies to confronting reality. As St Paul warned: "For the time will come when men will not put up with sound doctrine. Instead, to suit their own desires, they will gather round them a great number of teachers to say what their itching ears want to hear. They will turn their ears away from the truth and turn aside to myths." (2 Timothy 4:3-4). We see in our own land the skewed set of values that results. We esteem things that are worthless and fail to treasure what is priceless. Unless and until we start to address this, we will continue to make disastrous choices.

Jesus told two parables to help us gain a proper sense of perspective. They teach that the kingdom of heaven is of such worth that people should be willing to give up all they have to gain it: "The kingdom of heaven is like treasure hidden in a field. When a man found it, he hid it again, and then in his joy went and sold all he had and bought that field. Again, the kingdom of heaven is like a merchant looking for fine pearls. When he found one of great value, he went away and sold everything he had and bought it." (Matthew 13:44-46). People regularly sell all they have, even their very bodies and souls, to gain their next fix. It is infinitely rarer to find those who sell their all to gain the kingdom of heaven. That is an appalling commentary on modern Britain. It is above all a stinging indictment of generations of Christians (ours most of all), who have succeeded in making the radical message of the gospel and the excitement of a life with Jesus appear boring, who have made being a Christian synonymous in many eyes with being a hypocrite and who have so trimmed and temporised that for many Christianity appears to be devoid of power and capable of being fitted into whatever mould we choose for it.

When it comes to seeking, we have much to do. We need to seek God's forgiveness for what we have done with his church and with his gospel. We need to "Seek the LORD while he may be found [and] call on him while he is near." (Isaiah 55:6).

Conclusion.

The band *The Verve* sang: "the drugs don't work." Neither do any of the other foolish things that our nation currently chases after as though they be worthy of desire. It is time for us to be bolder in proclaiming that there is only one worthwhile object of human striving and only one person whom we should seek. His name is Jesus Christ, Son of the living God.

King Solomon "spoke three thousand proverbs and his songs numbered a thousand and five" (1 Kings 4:32), but what he calls the "song of songs" (Song of Songs 1:1) is the one that surpasses all others. It is beautiful poetry, but much more besides. On one level it is a straightforward love story, involving a king who "loved many foreign women besides Pharoah's daughter – Moabites, Ammonites, Edomites, Sidonians and Hittites ... [who] had seven hundred wives of royal birth and three hundred concubines ..." (1 Kings 11:1 and 3). On another level it is something quite different, sacred rather than profane: an allegory of God's love for his chosen people, Israel; of Christ's love for his bride, the church (see Ephesians 5:22-23); and of Christ's love for the soul of each and every human being.

This nation is drifting and our people are aimless, "like sheep oppressed for lack of a shepherd" (Zechariah 10:2). Many feel themselves without direction or hope. It need not be so. We need only seek and we will find. Over and over again the Lord has said it: "You will seek me and find me when you seek me with all your heart." (Jeremiah 29:13). There is no cause to hang back through shame or misplaced pride. There is nothing wrong in acknowledging our need by turning our hearts to God and seeking his healing for our land and its people.

64. New landscape

Haggai 1.

Key word: rebuilding.

Recent years have seen the transformation of London with a series of iconic buildings by world-renowned British architects. The Lloyds Building, the Swiss Re building (the so-called Gherkin) and others use new materials and new design technologies in ways that were previously unimaginable. These eye-catching edifices have been mirrored across the country, not only in major public works and the headquarters of large corporations, but in modest homes and everyday shops and offices. The drab, drear offerings of the immediate post-war reconstruction boom, with its prefabs and ugly tower blocks, seem far removed from a style of architecture altogether more sympathetic to the human spirit, but which at the same time speaks of ambition and confidence.

In parallel with its celebration of the new, the nation has learnt to appreciate better the value of its old buildings and to fight for their upkeep. Of course, uninspired starter homes and shoddy estates still proliferate too widely, but there is a renewed appreciation that beauty and aesthetic appeal in our physical surroundings matter in ways that cannot be expressed simply in terms of monetary value.

We have seen a time of rebuilding.

Time.

The prophet Haggai, writing in about 520 BC, speaks God's word at a time when there needs to be rebuilding in Israel. Eighteen years beforehand, after long years of waiting and expectation, Cyrus, king of Persia and conqueror of Babylon, had decreed that Jewish exiles should be allowed to return to their homeland. About 50,000 Jews made the journey. With rejoicing and enthusiasm they started to build a new temple in Jerusalem to replace the one destroyed during the Babylonian conquest. Soon, however, objections from Samaritans and other neighbouring peoples who feared the social, religious and political implications led to work being halted.

It remained stalled until Darius the Great came to the throne of Persia in 522 BC. Then God took a hand by means of his prophet "Haggai the LORD's messenger" (Haggai 1:13). The words that Haggai speaks are addressed to God's appointed leaders and through them to the people at large: "In the second year of King Darius, on the first day of the sixth month, the word of the LORD came through the prophet Haggai to Zerubbabel son of Shealtiel, governor of Judah, and to Joshua son of Jehozadak, the high priest" (Haggai 1:1).

Through Haggai, God says that the time has come to restart work. Excuses for further delay are brushed aside: "This is what the LORD Almighty says, 'These people say, 'The time has not yet come for the LORD's house to be built'' Then the word of the LORD came through the prophet Haggai: 'Is it a time for you yourselves to be living in your panelled houses, while this house remains a ruin?'" (Haggai 1:2-4). The clear implication is that it is not. There must be no more prevarication. Work must restart straightaway.

Things happen at the right moment and in the fullness of God's timing. The Lord says that "At the appointed time I will return" (Romans 9:9, based on Genesis 18:10 and 14). In human affairs, too: "There is a time for everything, and a season for every activity under heaven ... a time to tear down and a time to build" (Ecclesiastes 3:1) and a "wise heart will know the proper time" (Ecclesiastes 8:5).

Location.

The Israel to which Haggai speaks is a place of outward prosperity. Indeed, there is such luxury that people are "living in ... panelled houses" (Haggai 1:4). Formerly, interior panelling was the preserve of royalty, whose dwellings were lined with cedar (see 1 Kings 7:3 and 7 and Jeremiah 22:14), but now it is widespread. Possessions do not bring real benefit, however. Just as in our nation, the very material wellbeing of the Israelites was a cause of sloth, slackness and spiritual laxity.

In words that could have been crafted with modern Britain in mind, the Lord urges people to reflect and consider: "Give careful thought to your ways. You have planted much but harvested little. You eat, but never have enough. You drink, but never have your fill. You put on clothes, but are not warm. You earn wages, only to put them in a purse with holes in it ... You expected much, but see, it turned out to be little." (Haggai 1:5-6 and 9). There is consumption aplenty, but it does no good. Wealth runs through their fingers without lasting benefit. Momentary pleasures bring no fulfilment. They have little to show for their efforts.

This does not come about by chance, nor is it undeserved. It is a consequence of God's just and righteous response to man's actions: "'What you brought home, I blew away. Why?' declares the LORD Almighty. 'Because of my house, which remains a ruin, while each of you is busy with his own house. Therefore, because of you the heavens have withheld their dew and the earth its crops. I called for a drought on the fields and the mountains, on the grain, the new wine, the oil and whatever the ground produces, on men and cattle, and on the labour of your hands.'" (Haggai 1:9-11). Our neglect of God and concentration on things material rather than spiritual bring the opposite of what we desire. They bring scarcity instead of abundance, alienation instead of possession and want instead of plenty. Our selfishness is bad for us.

This should give us pause. The description that we read in Haggai is not of a faraway place and a distant time. It is our own face in the mirror, right here and now.

Resources.

As always, God is good. He provides what is needful, if we will only look about us and apply ourselves properly to the task in hand: "'Give careful thought to your ways. Go up into the mountains and bring down timber and build the house, so that I may take pleasure in it and be honoured,' says the LORD." (Haggai 1:7-8).

The issue is seldom a lack of resources. It certainly was not at this particular time and place. It was rather a question of priorities, desire and application:

Priorities. The building materials that were needed were readily available. The Israelites had only to "go up into the mountains" (Haggai 1:8) to find timber. Indeed, they had timber in abundance but had used it for their own "panelled houses" (Haggai 1:4). They had simply set the wrong priorities.

Desire. To get our priorities right, our desires need to be for the right things. Up till then, the Israelites had desired their own ease and comfort, preferring to build their houses rather than God's. Now they are told to desire something different – that the Lord may "take pleasure in [his house] and be honoured." (Haggai 1:8).

Application. All that was needed on the part of the Israelites was hard work. They needed to "go up into the mountains and bring down timber and build" (Haggai 1:8). There are three elements to this: accessing resources ("go up into the mountains"), bringing resources to where they are needed ("bring down timber") and using resources for the task God wants us to accomplish ("build").

The same holds good for us. We need to set the right priorities, desire the things that God wants and apply ourselves to his work. For this we need to access the resources that he supplies, bring those resources to where they are needed and use them to do the Lord's work.

People.

There is an appointed time and place for our labour, and God will provide the resources we need for the tasks in hand. The last piece in the jigsaw concerns our own selves. We need to hear what God is saying and then to act accordingly: "Then Zerubbabel son of Shealtiel, Joshua son of Jehozadak, the high priest, and the whole remnant of the people obeyed the voice of the LORD their God and the message of the prophet Haggai, because the LORD their God had sent him. And the people feared the LORD." (Haggai 1:12). The Israelites' response shows what is needed:

There must be wholesale engagement, as reflected in the words of Haggai 1:12 – engagement by the civil authorities ("Zerubbabel son of Shealtiel"), by religious leaders ("Joshua son of Jehozadak, the high priest") and by the population as a whole ("the whole remnant of the people").

God's word must be heard, listened to and acted on: "[they] obeyed the voice of the LORD their God" (Haggai 1:12).

Proper authority must be recognised: "[they] obeyed ... the message of the prophet Haggai, because the LORD their God had sent him" (Haggai 1:12).

Priorities should be reordered so that God and his ways are put first: "And the people feared the LORD." (Haggai 1:15).

When this is done, the Lord will be with his people, will bless them and will strengthen them: "Then Haggai, the LORD's messenger, gave this message of the Lord to the people: 'I am with you,' declares the LORD. So the LORD stirred up the spirit of Zerubbabel son of Shealtiel, and the spirit of Joshua son of Jehozadak, the high priest, and the spirit of the whole remnant of the people. They came and began work on the house of the LORD Almighty, their God, on the twenty-fourth day of the sixth month in the second year of Darius." (Haggai 1:13-15). Through "[stirring] up the spirit" (Haggai 1:14) God will give us the ability to accomplish those things that we are to undertake for him and on his behalf.

Conclusion.

Just as the Israelites had no excuse for further delay in the days of Haggai, we have no cause to put off action. A time has come for us to rebuild our nation, not in bricks and mortar, but morally and spiritually: "I tell you, now is the time of God's favour, now is the day of salvation." (2 Corinthians 6:2). We are "living in [our] panelled houses while [the LORD's] house remains a ruin" (Haggai 1:4). This is an utter disgrace. It must not be allowed to continue.

To their credit, once God's wishes became known the Israelites did not waste time. The prophet's first message was delivered "In the second year of King Darius, on the first day of the sixth month" (Haggai 1:1). By "the twenty-fourth day of the sixth month in the second year of King Darius" (Haggai 1:15) work on the temple restarted: "They came and began work on the house of the LORD Almighty, their God" (Haggai 1:14). A mere three weeks to start work is pretty good going. If we were able to do as much it would be reason for encouragement indeed.

Regrettably, we have a long road to travel before we get to this point. We have yet to undertake the kind of reflection that God calls us to when he says: "Give careful thought to your ways." (Haggai 1:5 and 7). A starting point will be for us to consider why we have so signally failed to build anything of lasting worth on the foundation of our material prosperity and our technological achievement. We have been busy "[storing] up for [ourselves] treasures on earth, where moth and rust destroy and thieves break in and steal." (Matthew 6:19). We need to ask: why do so many fall between the cracks of our Welfare State? Why do our institutions so often seem to promote perverse results? Why does the good so often seem to be hobbled and the bad to be promoted? This is just the beginning: the questions are legion.

Recent events have given us a nasty shock and brought us up short. The foundations of our prosperity no longer seem quite so secure. Things of this kind happen to gain our attention. This is our "time to seek the LORD until he comes and showers righteousness on [us]" (Hosea 10:12). If we will turn aside from wrongdoing and instead "store up for [ourselves] treasures in heaven, where moth and rust do not destroy and thieves do not break in and steal" (Matthew 6:20) then we will assure ourselves of salvation, "For where your treasure is, there your heart will be also." (Matthew 6:21).

God has a great deal to say about rebuilding and renewal. He is "the LORD [who] will rebuild Zion and appear in his glory." (Psalm 102:16). At the very end of the Bible, Jesus reminds us that "I am making everything new!" (Revelation 21:5). The Almighty wants to rebuild and renew us, as a nation and as individuals. His is a new architecture in which we become living stones, the very building blocks of a new temple: "Him who overcomes I will make a pillar in the temple of my God. Never again will he leave it. I will write on him the name of my God and the name of the city of my God, the new Jerusalem, which is coming down out of heaven from my God; and I will also write on him a new name." (Revelation 3:12). We need to put our shoulder to the wheel and to rebuild in a manner worthy of our heavenly Father, no longer being "busy with [our] own house" (Haggai 1:9), but determined that the Lord's house should no more remain a ruin in this land.

65. New citizens

Job 19:23-27.

Key word: renewal.

Until surprisingly recently the inhabitants of this country were described not as citizens but as subjects, defined in legal terms by connection to the monarchy. The relationship was one with obligations on both sides, but the role of subject was essentially subservient. Being citizens is felt to reflect more accurately the modern position and our status in a democratic society.[144]

With that in mind, it is humbling to reflect that God does not describe us as his subjects. He has authority and power beyond the wildest dreams of any earthly ruler, "but our citizenship is in heaven." (Philippians 3:20). Our status before God is not that of subjects. It is of those having "the full rights of sons" (Galatians 4:5), being "heirs of God and co-heirs with Christ" (Romans 8:17), God's "fellow workers" (1 Corinthians 3:9) and "friends" (John 15:15).

God renews us and transforms us despite all we have been and all we have suffered. He lifts us up beyond anything we can conceivably deserve. Through the phrases that describe our legal status before him we gain the merest glimpse of how wonderful will be the coming glory. Fine words; but fine words do not put food on the table, nor take away pain nor deal with the many ills of our daily lives. The ability to face such things and overcome them without losing sight of the renewal to come is something with which we need to grapple constantly. The experience of Job shows how.

Undeserved misfortune.

Job was a righteous and God-fearing man, wealthy and respected, but Satan said that Job only honoured God because of what the Almighty had done for him. Satan challenged God to "stretch out your hand and strike everything [Job] has and he will surely curse you to your face." (Job 1:11). Yet God had confidence in Job's integrity and replied to Satan: "Very well, then, everything he has is in your hands, but on the man himself do not lay a finger." (Job 1:12). From that moment, Job suffered calamity upon calamity. His children and his servants were killed; his wealth and his health were taken from him. Even his wife said that the only thing for him to do was to "curse God and die."(Job 2:9).

---

[144] The change to citizenship was effected by the British Nationality Act 1981, which came into force on 1 January 1983.

The context of Job 19:23-27 is that the afflicted man is in discussion with friends about the reason that sudden misfortune has come upon him. In accordance with the received wisdom of the day, the friends say that Job must have brought this on himself through his own sin, but Job protests his innocence. In the course of responding to his friends' arguments, Job says something insightful and, in the context, unexpected: "I know that my Redeemer lives, and that in the end he will stand upon the earth. And after my skin has been destroyed, yet in my flesh I will see God." (Job 19:25-26)

This is one of the most profound statements in the Bible: it shows Job's faith growing in the face of adversity, not diminishing, and it shows a penetrating discernment of the spiritual reality that lies behind the passing moment. A man who has lost everything is not crushed by the experience, even though he is weighed down and sore afflicted. His spirit soars to a new level of understanding as everything that might previously have been a source of pride and perceived strength is stripped away.

Unquenched faith.

We need to learn the perspective that Job had. We live in circumstances that cloud our vision: disconnected from nature, we imagine that we can tame its power; well clothed and shod, we do not see our spiritual nakedness; with our bellies full and our houses stuffed with possessions, we do not recognise their emptiness and our own need to be filled by God. When these material things are stripped away, as they surely will be, we will be nothing without our Redeemer.

We need to go through the same process that Job went through. As the discussions with his friends continue, his faith in a heavenly solution to his earthly sufferings becomes more and more assured. As so often when times are difficult, it is a case of two steps forward and one step back:

He starts by bemoaning the fact that there is nobody to intercede between him and God. "If only there were someone to arbitrate between us …" (Job 9:33).

He next recognises that he does have someone to plead his case, although at this point he regards this person as still being somewhat remote from him: "my witness is in heaven, my advocate is on high." (Job 16:19).

Then he comes to the painful realisation that the people he counted on for help and support in his distress cannot or will not provide these things: "He has alienated my brothers from me; my acquaintances are completely estranged from me. My kinsmen have gone away; my friends have forgotten me. My guests and my maidservants count me a stranger … all my intimate friends detest me; those I love have turned against me." (Job 19:13-15 and 19).

From that low point, when all earthly help and hope is exhausted, he comes to the triumphant recognition that "my Redeemer lives." (Job 19:25).

That Job's trust in God is well placed is shown by the book's epilogue: "After Job had prayed for his friends, the LORD made him prosperous again and gave him twice as much as he had before ... The LORD blessed the latter part of Job's life more than the first. He had fourteen thousand sheep, six thousand camels, a thousand yoke of oxen and a thousand donkeys. And he also had seven sons and three daughters ... After this Job lived a hundred and forty years; he saw his children and their children to the fourth generation. And so he died, old and full of years." (Job 42:10, 42:12-13 and 42:16-17).[145]   It is noteworthy that Job's first thought is for his friends, not for the restoration of his former health and prosperity. These things are presumably given to him as well for the same reason that they were given to Solomon after he prayed for wisdom: "The LORD was pleased ... So God said, 'Since you have asked for this and not for long life or wealth for yourself, nor have you asked for the death of your enemies ... I will give you what you have not asked for – both riches and honour'" (1 Kings 3:10-13). In the same way, Jesus reminds us to "seek first [God's] kingdom and righteousness, and all these things [food, drink, clothing and other material needs] will be given to you as well." (Matthew 6:33).

Uncertainty disarmed.

In just the same way, we can confidently place our trust in God and in his Word, the Bible. We can work through areas of doubt as Job did, growing in faith as we do so and disarming the uncertainty that so often makes us less effective than we can and should be. The harmony of the message and teaching contained in Scripture should greatly reassure and encourage us. This collection of sixty-six separate books, written at different times and places by authors from every walk of life, using different languages and literary forms, with no way of knowing that their work would be gathered one with the other yet forms a cohesive whole that is entirely congruent in doctrine, teaching and prophecy.

The book of Job is a case in point. It is commonly reckoned to be the oldest in the Bible, dating at least from the patriarchal period – the time of Abraham, over 4,000 years ago. Some even speculate that it records an oral tradition dating back to the end of the last Ice Age, based on its numerous references to extremes of cold weather. For example, when God appears to

---

[145] Job is given double his previous possessions but only the same number of sons and daughters. The inference is that the sons and daughters who died are waiting for him in heaven.

confront Job at the end of the book, he says: "From whose womb comes the ice? Who gives birth to the frost from the heavens when the waters become hard as stone, when the surface of the deep is frozen?" (Job 38:29-30).[146] Given this, the consistency of what Job says with what Jesus taught and demonstrated through his life on earth is striking, the surest of antidotes to the frequently expressed (but never proven) claim that the Bible is full of contradictions. Consider the statements in Job 19:25-26:

"[My] Redeemer lives …" Job does not say that a Messiah will come at some indeterminate point in the future. He says that right here and now he has a living Saviour.

"[In] the end he [the Redeemer] will stand upon the earth …" The Redeemer will actually come amongst us here on earth.

"[After] my skin has been destroyed, yet in my flesh I will see God." This statement must have seemed nonsense to Job's friends: how can a man's skin be destroyed and yet the man in his flesh be able to see God? From a Christian perspective, of course, it sounds like a straightforward affirmation of belief in physical resurrection.

"I will see God." Even in the time of Jesus, the Pharisees and the Sadducees could not agree on whether there was resurrection of the dead, yet here Job says it as clear as day.

Well over 4,000 years ago was made a statement that is completely compatible with Christian belief, which stands as a glorious affirmation of faith in the most trying of circumstances and a forms timely reminder for those suffering adversity: our Redeemer lives.

Uncommon power.

Job's statement of faith does not exist in isolation. It is not there so that we may give it mere intellectual assent and then forget about it. It does not float in ether, divorced from the real world. It is part of God's Word and as such it has power. The Lord says: "As the rain and the snow come down from heaven and do not return to it without watering the earth and making it bud and flourish, so

---

[146] See also Job 37:6-10: "[God] says to the snow, 'Fall on the earth,' and to the rain shower, 'Be a mighty downpour.'… The tempest comes out from its chamber, the cold from the driving winds. The breath of God produces ice, and the broad waters become frozen." and Job 38:22: "Have you entered the storehouses of the snow or seen the storehouses of the hail?"

that it yields seed for the sower and bread for the eater, so is my word that goes out from my mouth: it will not return to me empty, but will accomplish what I desire and achieve the purpose for which I sent it." (Isaiah 55:11).

Job tells us how we should treat this Word: "Oh, that my words were recorded, that they were written on a scroll, that they were inscribed with an iron tool on lead, or engraved in rock for ever!" (Job 19:23-24). This prayer is answered, for what Job says is recorded for posterity. What is written does not just comprise artfully crafted phrases. The words affirm a central and overarching truth: that there is a heavenly solution to earthly sufferings and that God will renew his people. The renewal takes a number of forms:

It affects our legal status and our spiritual wellbeing: as "Redeemer" (Job 19:25), the Lord will buy back his people from slavery and set them free.

It sets at nought the effects of age, disease, decay and death: "after my skin has been destroyed, yet ..." (Job 19:26).

It gives rise to new birth in a glorious resurrection body: "in my flesh I will see God, I myself will see him with my own eyes – I and not another." (Job 19:26-27).

It brings us into the presence of God for an eternity of close fellowship with him: "I will see God" (Job 19:26).

Job tested these words and found them to be true. He relied upon God in the most appalling circumstances and discovered that it was possible to come through the tunnel of suffering and into a place of blessing on the other side. God brought renewal.

Conclusion.

Our nation desperately needs renewal. With Job we might say, "How my heart yearns within me!"(Job 19:27). We should plead with our Redeemer to bring this renewal about, to free our society from the things that bind it and to set it on a new course involving close relationship with him and obedience to his Word.

At the same time, we need to reflect on the means by which God might bring renewal about and the consequences of renewal for our everyday lives. We need to translate our citizenship of heaven into a new concept of how our earthly citizenship should be played out, both to enable renewal and to allow God to give effect to it through us. Modern England has again become a nation of subjects, of people who are slaves to every passing whim, blown hither and thither by the blandishments of advertising and the tittle-tattle of media without the firm anchor of faith to stay their course. This land desperately needs to hear, believe and act upon the words spoken by Job: "my Redeemer lives" (Job 19:25). We must tell forth this word so that our people once more have the chance to be citizens of the heavenly kingdom. Only then will renewal come.

66. New resolve

Luke 2:41-52

Key word: determination.

Each January brings the season of New Year's resolutions. Whether we make them or not, whether we keep them or not, they are hard to avoid. Perhaps they bore us, perhaps they excite us, perhaps they offer new possibilities or perhaps they only make us feel guilty. Sometimes the resolutions we come across are frivolous. Sometimes they are worthy. Sometimes they are just this year's fashion. If we are serious about making the best of resolutions for the year ahead, however, we need to consider what the Bible has to say about them.

A resolution is a resolve or settled purpose. It involves being determined, firm and bold in sticking to the goals we have set. In terms of the Christian life, there are both negative and positive resolutions that we need to make. That is to say, there are things that we must resolve *not* to do and things we must resolve *to* do. We need to turn away from what is bad. We need to make a deliberate effort to turn our backs on thoughts and words that are wrong. Thus King David says: "I have resolved that my mouth will not sin" (Psalm 17:3). We need to free our deeds from things that are displeasing to God, even when that means going against what society considers normal or acceptable. So the young Daniel, a slave in Babylon and subject to his captors' whims, risked punishment and perhaps even death for his defiance when "he resolved not to defile himself" (Daniel 1:8).

Those are the negative resolutions. The positive ones involve turning towards and seeking out what is good. St Paul says: "I resolved to know nothing while I was with you but Jesus Christ, and him crucified" (1 Corinthians 2:2). Turning away from the bad and to the good is part of the process of growing in faith and reaching spiritual maturity. If we are to achieve this, we need to open ourselves to the work of the Holy Spirit in our lives and thereby allow God to help us become the people he created us to be. This is about maximising our potential, not in the way peddled by countless self-help books as something for our own selfish use, but so that we can do the things that Jesus identified as being the foundation for everything else of real value – loving God and loving our fellow men: see Mark 12:28-31 and Luke 10:27-28.

Growth.

The story of the young Jesus at the temple provides a template. We read that "Jesus grew in wisdom and stature, and in favour with God and men." (Luke 2:52). This short phrase contains an important concept (growth) and four equally important descriptions of the areas in our lives in which growth needs to take place: in wisdom, in stature, in favour with God and in favour with men. The starting point is that we all need to grow. Even Jesus had to grow. Though he was God made man, there is no indication that he had all knowledge and wisdom from birth. The human part of him seems to have matured like any other youngster. We read of his being a "baby" (Luke 2:16), a "child" (Luke 2:40) and a "boy" (Luke 2:43). He had to grow physically and he had to grow in other ways, too. In this, he was exactly like us.

There is physical growth, but there is also moral and spiritual growth. We have a lot less control over our physical growth than we might like, although advertising tells us different and tries to sell us products to make us better looking or to reverse the effects of ageing. At the same time, we have more control over our moral and spiritual growth than we often care to admit, although advertising denies this and says we should give in to our every desire. Notice the irony: advertising tells us we can control what in truth we cannot and asserts that we cannot control what in truth we can.

We make sure that we grow in the right way by making right choices, by exercising our free will in a godly way. The best way to ensure we choose correctly is by following the advice that the Bible gives. To do things through ritual, without real thought or engagement, is not the answer. We are told that: "Every year [Jesus'] parents went to Jerusalem for the Feast of the Passover. When he was twelve years old, they went up to the Feast, according to the custom." (Luke 2:41-42). Both Mary and Joseph experienced God breaking into their lives in extraordinary ways and there is no reason to suppose that they went to Jerusalem just because it was something they did "every year" and was the "custom." Yet then, as now, there would have been those who did precisely that. We cannot expect to grow if this is our attitude.

Wisdom.

Many rightly bemoan the materialism of our culture, and indeed the Bible exhorts us to keep the things of this world in perspective: "Wisdom is the principal thing, therefore get wisdom; and with all thy getting, get understanding" (Proverbs 4:7, KJV). In his letter to the early church, James (the brother of Jesus) tells us what this wisdom is that we should be seeking: "The wisdom that comes down from heaven is first of all pure; then peace-loving, considerate, submissive, full of mercy and good fruit, impartial and sincere." (James 3:17).[147] This is something quite different from what mankind means by intelligence and

---

[147] Godly wisdom is not the same as worldly wisdom. Eve confused the two when she "saw that the fruit of the tree [of the knowledge of good and evil] was ... also desirable for gaining wisdom." (Genesis 3:6).

knowledge, which often mistakenly double for our idea of wisdom. It involves looking at things God's way rather than judging by human standards. It means seeking God's timeless truths rather than relying on passing fashions in human thought, which we set such store by and yet which are so frequently built on the flimsiest of foundations. Over and over again we have seen today's science or philosophy become tomorrow's childish fancy. That should not surprise us, for the Lord says: "I will destroy the wisdom of the wise, the intelligence of the intelligent I will frustrate." (Isaiah 29:14 and 1 Corinthians 1:19). We will do well to remember that "the foolishness of God is wiser than man's wisdom, and the weakness of God is stronger than man's strength." (1 Corinthians 1:25).

We may not be clever, but we can still be wise. All we have to do is to ask God: "If any of you lacks wisdom, he should ask God, who gives generously to all without finding fault, and it will be given to him." (James 1:5).[148] When we ask, we should remember that: "The fear of the LORD is the beginning of knowledge, but fools despise wisdom and discipline." (Proverbs 1:7). We should remember, too, that gaining in wisdom means spending time with God and making the effort to learn, just as Jesus did: "After three days they found him in the temple courts, sitting among the teachers, listening to them and asking them questions." (Luke 2:46). Our application will be richly rewarded. We cannot expect to achieve the measure of wisdom that Jesus had, for "Everyone who heard him was amazed at his understanding and his answers." (Luke 2:47). Yet if we apply ourselves properly we will gain a portion of it all the same. This being so, we should ask ourselves: why put off asking God for wisdom?

Stature.

We all know that physical size and moral or spiritual stature are not the same. When God told the prophet Samuel to anoint a new king of Israel to replace Saul, he led him to the house of Jesse, a man with seven sons. The eldest, Eliab, was physically impressive and "... Samuel ... thought, 'Surely the LORD's anointed stands here before the LORD.' But the LORD said to Samuel, 'Do not consider his appearance or his height, for I have rejected him. The LORD does not look at the things man looks at. Man looks at the outward appearance, but the LORD looks at the heart.'" (1 Samuel 16:6-7). In the event, God instructed Samuel to anoint Jesse's youngest son, David, someone the Bible describes as "a man after God's own heart" (1 Samuel 13:14).

David's first public appearance before Israel emphasises the difference between inner and outer stature: "A champion named Goliath ... came out of the

---

[148] See also Proverbs 2:6: "... for the Lord gives wisdom."

Philistine camp. He was over nine feet tall" (1 Samuel 17:4),[149] but little David, who was "only a boy" (1 Samuel 17:42), cut him down with a slingshot. Whilst he did so, King Saul cowered behind his own lines, even though by rights he should have been the one to confront the Philistine giant, for Saul was "an impressive young man without equal among the Israelites – a head taller than any of the others." (1 Samuel 8:1-2).

Most of us do not feel like people of power, influence or wealth. Most of us do not turn heads when we enter a room or have others craving our attention. Yet that does not mean that we cannot grow great in moral and spiritual stature if we invite Jesus into our lives. This is what God wants for us and will work in us if we let him. We should ask ourselves: how can I stand tall with God, for God and through God?

Favour with God.

Favour is not the same as favouritism. The Bible frequently asserts that God does not show favouritism: "Then Peter began to speak: 'I now realise how true it is that God does not show favouritism, but accepts men from every nation who fear him and do what is right.'" (Acts 10:34-5). St Paul makes the same point: "For God does not show favouritism" (Romans 2:11) and "there is no favouritism with him." (Ephesians 6:9). Moreover, "Anyone who does wrong will be repaid for his wrong, and there is no favouritism." (Colossians 3:25).

The Lord does not favour an individual because of his station in life, his nationality or his material possessions, though he does respect our characters and judge our work. Hence "Noah found favour in the eyes of the LORD ... [because he was] a righteous man, blameless among the people of his time, and he walked with God." (Genesis 6:8-9). There is a reward for obedience: the Lord tells us that "If you follow my decrees and are careful to obey my commands ... I will look on you with favour and make you fruitful and increase your numbers, and I will keep my covenant with you." (Leviticus 26:3 and 9). Solomon makes the same point: "Let love and faithfulness never leave you; bind them around your neck, write them on the tablet of your heart. Then you will win favour in the sight of God and man." (Proverbs 3:3-4). These things bring God's blessing and favour: when we align our will with his, seek the things that he seeks and put into practice the things that Jesus taught. In these ways we show our love for our Saviour and our thankfulness for all that he has done for us. In these ways, too,

---

[149] Goliath's height is considered by some to be exaggerated and the whole story fanciful yet Henry Cooper (1853-99), the so-called Yorkshire Giant, stood eight feet six inches high.

we gladden his heart. We should ask ourselves: how can I bring joy to God today?

Favour with men.

We must avoid all temptation to curry favour with men at the expense of the things that God holds dear. Jesus tells us that this is a trap into which we must be wary of falling: "... woe to you when all men speak well of you ..." (Luke 6:26). He earned admonishment, not approval, for staying behind in Jerusalem: "When his parents saw him, they were astonished. His mother said to him, 'Son, why have you treated us like this? Your father and I have been anxiously searching for you.'" (Luke 2:48). His explanation cut no ice: "'Why were you searching for me?' he asked. 'Didn't you know that I had to be in my Father's house?' But they did not understand what he was saying to them." (Luke 2:49-50). In the same way, we must expect to be misunderstood when we put God first.

Our duty is to hold to the truth even when it makes us unpopular. Yet if we really practice Jesus' teaching to "love your neighbour as yourself" (Matthew 22:39) and to "Do to others as you would have them do to you" (Luke 6:31), we will find favour with men. When it does not run counter to the will of God, we should submit to others and do our best to help them, as Jesus did: "Then he went down to Nazareth with them and was obedient to them." (Luke 2:51). We should ask ourselves: how can I bless other people today?

Conclusion.

In the famous Gettysburg address of 19 November 1863, delivered on one of the great and bloody battlefields of the American Civil War, Abraham Lincoln challenged his fellow countrymen to make a resolution: "... We here should highly resolve that the dead shall not have died in vain, that this nation, under God, shall have a new birth of freedom; and that government of the people, by the people, and for the people, shall not perish from the earth ..." The call to resolutions of the highest and noblest kind was taken up by another famous American President almost exactly one hundred years later. In his Inaugural Address on 20 January 1961 John F. Kennedy said: "My fellow Americans, ask not what your country can do for you; ask what you can do for your country. My fellow citizens of the world, ask not what America will do for you, but what together we can do for the freedom of man." In a culture that tends to emphasise rights over the corresponding duties and individualism over collective identity, sympathy and effort, we need to regain a sense of duty to our country, to each other and to the world. If we wish to give the fullest possible expression to such duty, we need God's help to do so.

The Christian life is a call to be the best that we can be, not for our own sake, but for God, our nation and our fellow men. It is a call to reach beyond the everyday, beyond the glib slogans of advertising, beyond apathy and low expectations to the fulfilment of a life with Jesus. It is a call to reach for the stars. Of course we will often fall short. Of course we will often be afraid, discouraged or driven off track – perhaps each of those things. Yet through it all God will teach, lead, guide and shape us if only we will allow him to do so. Our challenge is to make a resolution. Not a half-hearted one based on what we can do, but a lofty one based on what God can do in us and through us. We must not put it off for another year. Now – this hour, this minute and this second – is the time when God wants to meet with us and to come into our lives. Now is the time when he wants to redeem us and the great nation of which we are part. Please do not turn him away.

Epilogue

In the long and sorry litany of man's inhumanity to man England has her share, and more. Yet in the space of almost sixteen hundred years something else has been at work in the life of this nation. To our enduring shame, we participated enthusiastically in the slave trade, but we were the ones who led its abolition. We built an Empire, and then gave it away. For the most part it was not wrested from us. Rather, it was rendered back without compulsion and subject peoples granted freedom with good grace.[150] These things are without precedent. It behoves us to ask why they should have been so.

Freedom and its offspring, representative government, are constant threads in the warp and weft of English history. They alone are not the answer, however. Ancient Athens had both (at least at certain times and for certain sections of society), but saw no contradiction in maintaining human bondage and an empire based expressly on exploitation of the downtrodden. She did not relinquish either dominion voluntarily.

So we must look elsewhere. The circumstances recounted in this book set before us a striking possibility: that England became what she was because of Christianity and this more than any other reason was the source of her distinctiveness. They suggest that God has been actively involved in the daily life of this nation, guiding its people, sustaining and protecting us at key points, moulding, shaping, leading and inspiring. That this should so often have been done through people with such manifest flaws and weaknesses as (amongst others) Sir Francis Drake, Oliver Cromwell, Robert Clive, James Wolfe, Horatio Nelson, Florence Nightingale, Charles Gordon and Winston Churchill is all the more remarkable.

To consider whether the results of these endeavours are now compatible with other cultures and religions is to miss the point. The fact is that, but for the sincere application of Christian principles by large numbers of English men and women, much of what is best in the world simply would not be. That being so, it is a measure of what we stand to lose if the Christian foundations of this nation are undermined further or, heaven forbid, removed entirely. It is a measure of the duty that we each bear to cause this land to turn once again in true worship, thanksgiving and service to our Lord.

---

[150] The United States and Ireland being the major exceptions.

The reader must judge whether this hypothesis is compelling or not. For each who counts it so, a question arises that was asked at other times and in other places: "What, then, should we do?" (Luke 3:10, 12 and 14; Acts 2:37). What should we do to serve our God and what should we do to serve our nation? How can we raise our voice? Edgar Vincent, Viscount d'Abernon, once said that "an Englishman's mind works best when it is almost too late." Let us pray that we have not gone past the point of no return and that our heavenly Father will guide and save us, just as he guided and saved those who went before.

The clock is ticking louder than ever, but our Lord is a great and mighty God. He longs to redeem and to bless, so that "The desert and the parched land will be glad; the wilderness will rejoice and blossom. Like the crocus it will burst into bloom; it will rejoice greatly and shout for joy." (Isaiah 35:1-2).

Appendix 1

Murders per 100,000 people.

The figures set out in the table below were compiled by criminologist Manuel Eisner. They are taken from *Freakonomics* by Steven D. Levitt and Stephen J. Dubner.

Date	England	Netherlands and Belgium	Scandinavia	Germany and Switzerland	Italy
C13th - 14th	23.0	47.0	n.a.	37.0	56.0
C15th	n.a.	45.0	46.0	16.0	73.0
C16th	7.0	25.0	21.0	11.0	47.0
C17th	5.0	7.5	18.0	7.0	32.0
C18th	1.5	5.5	1.9	7.5	10.5
C19th	1.7	1.6	1.1	2.8	12.6
1900-1949	0.8	1.5	0.7	1.7	3.2
1950-1994	0.9	0.9	0.9	1.0	1.5

Bibliography

Green, John Richard, *A short history of the English people*, Macmillan & Co 1902.

Fisher, D. J. V. *The Anglo-Saxon Age*, Longman Group Limited 1973.

Lacey, Robert and Danziger, Danny, *The year 1000*, Little, Brown and Company 1999.

Roesdahl, Else, *The Vikings*, Penguin Books Ltd 1991.

Barrow, G.W. S. *Feudal Britain*, Edward Arnold (Publishers) Ltd 1976.

Green, V, H. H. *The Later Plantagenets*, Edward Arnold (Publishers) Ltd 1962.

Webber, Ronald, *The Peasants' Revolt*, Terence Dalton Limited 1980.

Creasy, Sir Edward, *The Fifteen Decisive Battles of the World from Marathon to Waterloo*, Sisley's Ltd 1886.

Moynahan, Brian, *If God spare my life*, Abacus 2003.

Sugden, John, *Sir Francis Drake*, Pimlico 2006.

Falkus, Christopher, *The Life and Times of Charles II*, Weidenfeld and Nicolson 1992.

Fraser, Antonia, *Cromwell, our chief of men*, Orion Books Ltd 2002.

Kitson, Frank, *Old Ironsides*, Phoenix Press 2007.

Wanklyn, Malcolm and Jones, Frank, *A Military History of the English Civil War*, Pearson Longman 2005.

Cook, Faith, *Fearless Pilgrim: the life and times of John Bunyan*, Evangelical Press 2008.

Davies, Norman, *Europe, a History*, Pimlico 1997.

Garrett, Richard, *General Wolfe*, Arthur Barker Limited 1975.

Hough, Richard, *Captain James Cook*, Hodder & Stoughton1994.

Richards, Denis and Quick, Anthony, *Britain 1714-1851*, Longman 1974.

Sugden, John, *Nelson: a dream of glory*, Pimlico 2005.

Southey, Robert, *The Life of Nelson*, Constable & Co Ltd 1916.

Rolt, L. T. C. *Brunel*, Penguin Books 1986.

Pelling, Henry, *A History of British Trade Unionism*, Penguin Book Ltd 1963.

Wilson, A. N. *Eminent Victorians*, BBC Books 1989.

Hopkirk, Peter, *The Great Game*, Oxford University Press 2001.

Regan, Geoffrey, *Great Military Blunders*, Channel Four Books 2000.

Nutting, Anthony, *Gordon: martyr and misfit*, The Reprint Society 1967.

Ferguson, Niall, *Empire: how Britain made the modern world*, Penguin Books Ltd 2003.

Kee, Robert, *The Green Flag, volumes I-III* Penguin Books Ltd 1972.

Wisdom, Norman, *My Turn*, Arrow Books Ltd 2003.

Fiennes, Ranulph, *Captain Scott*, Hodder & Stoughton 2003.

Preston, Diana, *A First Rate Tragedy*, Constable and Company Limited 1997.

Kendall, R.T. *Thanking God*, Zondervan Publishing 2006.

Fawcett, Lt.-Col P.H., *Operation Fawcett*, The Companion Book Club (Odhams Press Ltd) 1954.

Smith, Colin, *England's last war against France*, Phoenix (Orion Books Ltd) 2010.

Braddon, Russell, *The Naked Island*, Pan Books Ltd 1973.

Baxter, John, *Missing, Believed Killed*, Aurum Press Ltd 2010.

Bielenberg, Christabel, *The past is myself*, Corgi Books (Chatto & Windus Ltd) 1984.

Gandhi, Mohandas Karamchand, *The story of my experiments with truth*, Penguin Books Ltd 2007.

Chichester, Francis, *Alone across the Atlantic*, George Allen & Unwin Ltd 1961.

Chichester, Francis, *The lonely sea and the sky*, Hodder & Stoughton 1964.

Keyword Index

Index of Scripture References

Subject Index

Redeeming a Nation